TRAV
IN
CHINA,

CONTAINING
DESCRIPTIONS,
OBSERVATIONS, AND
COMPARISONS, MADE AND
COLLECTED IN
THE COURSE OF A SHORT
RESIDENCE AT THE IMPERIAL
PALACE OF
YUEN-MIN-YUEN, AND ON A
SUBSEQUENT JOURNEY
THROUGH
THE COUNTRY FROM
PEKIN TO CANTON

By **JOHN BARROW**

CHAP. I.
PRELIMINARY MATTER.

Introduction.—General View of what Travellers are likely to meet with in China.—Mistaken Notions entertained with regard to the British Embassy—corrected by the Reception and Treatment of the subsequent Dutch Embassy.—Supposed Points of Failure in the former, as stated by a French Missionary from Pekin, refuted.—Kien Long's Letter to the King of Holland.—Difference of Treatment experienced by the two Embassies explained.—Intrigues of Missionaries in foreign Countries.—Pride and Self-Importance of the Chinese Court.—List of European Embassies, and the Time of their Abode in Pekin.—Conclusion of Preliminary Subject.

IT is hardly necessary to observe that, after the able and interesting account of the proceedings and result of the British Embassy to the court of China, by the late Sir George Staunton (who was no less amiable for liberality of sentiment, than remarkable for vigour of intellect) it would be an idle, and, indeed, a superfluous undertaking, in any other person who accompanied the embassy, to dwell on those subjects which have been treated by him in so masterly a manner; or to recapitulate those incidents and transactions, which he has detailed with equal elegance and accuracy.

But, as it will readily occur to every one, there are still many interesting subjects, on which Sir George, from the nature of his work, could only barely touch, and others that did not come within his plan, one great object of which was to unfold the views of the embassy, and to shew that every thing, which could be done, was done, for promoting the interests of the British nation, and supporting the dignity of the British character; the Author of the present work has ventured, though with extreme diffidence, and with the consciousness of the disadvantage under which he must appear after that "Account of the Embassy," to lay before the public the point of view in which *he* saw the Chinese empire, and the Chinese character. In doing this, the same facts will sometimes necessarily occur, that have already been published, for reasons that it would be needless to mention; but whenever that happens to be the case, they will briefly be repeated, for the purpose of illustrating some position, or for deducing some general inference. Thus, for instance, the document given to the Embassador of the population of China will be noticed, not however under the colour of its being an unquestionably accurate statement, but, on the contrary, to shew that it neither is, nor can be, correct; yet at the same time to endeavour to prove, by facts and analogy, that, contrary to the received opinion, the country is capable of supporting not only three hundred and thirty-three millions of people, but that it might actually afford the means of subsistence to twice that number. The confirmation, indeed, of new and important facts, though very different conclusions be drawn from them, cannot be entirely unacceptable to the reader; for as different persons will generally see the same things in different points of view, so, perhaps, by combining and comparing the different descriptions and colouring that may be given of the same objects, the public is enabled to obtain the most correct notions of such matters as can be learned only from the report of travellers.

With regard to China, if we except the work of Sir George Staunton, and the limited account of Mr. Bell of Antermony, which was not written by himself, it may be considered as unbeaten ground by Britons. We have heard a great deal of Chinese knavery practised at Canton, but, except in the two works abovementioned, we have not yet heard the sentiments of an Englishman at all acquainted with the manners, customs, and character of the Chinese nation. The voluminous communications of the missionaries are by no means satisfactory; and some of their defects will be noticed and accounted for in the course of this work; the chief aim of which will be to shew this extraordinary people in their proper colours, not as their own moral maxims would represent them, but as they really are—to divest the court of the tinsel and the tawdry varnish with which, like the palaces of the Emperor, the missionaries have found it expedient to cover it in their writings; and to endeavour to draw such a sketch of the manners, the state of society, the language, literature and fine arts, the sciences and civil institutions, the religious worship and opinions, the population and progress of agriculture, the civil and moral character of the people, as may enable the reader to settle, in his own mind, *the point of rank which China may be considered to hold in the scale of civilized nations.*

The stability of the Chinese government; the few changes that have been made in its civil institutions for such a number of ages; the vast extent of empire and immense population, forming one society, guided by the same laws, and governed by the will of a single individual, offer, as Sir George Staunton has observed, "the grandest collective object that can be presented for human contemplation or research." The customs, habits and manners, the wants and resources, the language, sentiments and religious notions, of "the most ancient society and the most populous empire existing amongst men," are, without doubt most interesting subjects for the investigation of the philosopher, and not unworthy the attention of the statesman. But the expectations of the man of science, the artist, or the naturalist, might perhaps be rather disappointed, than their curiosity be gratified, in travelling through this extensive country. It can boast of few works of art, few remains of ancient grandeur. The great wall, that for a time defended its peaceable inhabitants against the attacks of the roving Tartars, the walls of its numerous cities, with their square towers and lofty gates, and here and there an old pagoda, are its only architectural antiquities; and, when these are excepted, there is not perhaps a single building in the whole extent of China that has withstood the action of three centuries. There are no ancient palaces nor other public edifices, no paintings nor pieces of[5] sculpture, to arrest the attention of the traveller, unless it might be from the novelty of their appearance. In travelling over the continent of Europe, and more especially on the classic ground of Italy and Greece, every city, mountain, river, and ruin, are rendered interesting by something on record which concerns them; the theme of some poet, the feat of some philosopher or lawgiver, the scene of some memorable action, they all inspire us with the liveliest sensations, by reviving in the mind those pleasures which the study of their history afforded in early life. To Europeans the history of China has hitherto furnished no materials for such recurrence, and the country itself is therefore incapable of communicating such impressions. In vain should we here look for the massy and stupendous fabrics that appear in the pyramids and the pillars of the ancient Egyptians; the beautiful and symmetrical works of art displayed in the temples of the Greeks; the grand and magnificent remains of Roman architecture; or that combination of convenience and elegance of design which characterize the modern buildings of Europe. In China every city is nearly the same: a quadrangular space of ground is enclosed with walls of stone, of brick, or of earth, all built upon the same plan; the houses within them of the same construction; and the streets, except the principal ones that run from gate to gate, invariably narrow. The temples are, nearly, all alike, of the same awkward design as the dwelling-houses, but on a larger scale; and the objects that are known in Europe by the name of pagodas, are of the same inelegant kind of architecture, from one extremity of the empire to the other, differing only in the number of rounds or stories, and in the materials of which they are constructed. The manners, the dress, the amusements of the people, are nearly the same. Even the surface of the[6] country, as far as regards the fifteen ancient provinces, is subject to little variation, and especially those parts over which the grand inland navigation is carried; the only parts, in fact, that foreigners travelling in China have any chance of visiting.

In this route no very great variety nor number of subjects occur in the department of natural history. Few native plants, and still fewer wild animals, are to be expected in those parts of a country that are populous and well cultivated. Indeed the rapid manner in which the present journey was made, was ill suited for collecting and examining specimens even of those few that did occur.

On these considerations it is hoped that the indulgence of the reader will not be withheld, where information on such points may appear to be defective. A French critic[1] (perhaps without doing him injustice he may be called a hypercritic) who happened to visit Canton for a few months, some fifty years ago, has, with that happy confidence peculiar to his nation, not only pointed out the errors and defects of the information communicated to the world by the English and the Dutch embassies, but has laid down a syllabus of the subjects they ought to have made themselves completely acquainted with, which, instead of seven months, would seem to require a residence of seven years in the country. But the author of the present work rests his confidence in the English critics being less unreasonable in their demands; and that their indulgences will be proportioned to the difficulties that occurred in collecting accurate information. [7]With this reliance, the descriptions,

2

observations, and comparisons, such as they are, he presents to the public, candidly acknowledging that he is actuated rather by the hope of meeting its forbearance, than by the confidence of deserving its approbation.

Perhaps it may not be thought amiss, before he enters on the more immediate subject of the work, to correct, in this place, a very mistaken notion that prevailed on the return of the embassy, which was, that an unconditional compliance of Lord Macartney with all the humiliating ceremonies which the Chinese might have thought proper to exact from him, would have been productive of results more favourable to the views of the embassy. Assertions of such a general nature are more easily made than refuted, and indeed unworthy of attention; but a letter of a French missionary at Pekin to the chief of the Dutch factory at Canton is deserving of some notice, because it specifies the reasons to which, according to the writer's opinion, was owing the supposed failure of the British embassy. In speaking of this subject he observes, "Never was an embassy deserving of better success! whether it be considered on account of the experience, the wisdom, and the amiable qualities of Lord Macartney and Sir George Staunton; or of the talents, the knowledge, and the circumspect behaviour of the gentlemen who composed their Suite; or of the valuable and curious presents intended for the Emperor—and yet, strange to tell, never was there an embassy that succeeded so ill!

"You may be curious, perhaps, to know the reason of an event so unfavourable and so extraordinary. I will tell you in a few words. These gentlemen, like all strangers, who know China only from books, were ignorant of the manner of proceeding, of the customs and the etiquette of this court; and, to add to their misfortune, they brought with them a Chinese interpreter still less informed than themselves. The consequence of all which was that, in the first place, they came without any presents for the Minister of State, or for the sons of the Emperor. Secondly, they refused to go through the usual ceremony of saluting the Emperor, without offering any satisfactory reason for such refusal. Thirdly, They presented themselves in clothes that were too plain, and too common. Fourthly, They did not use the precaution to fee (graisser la patte) the several persons appointed to the superintendance of their affairs. Fifthly, Their demands were not made in the tone and style of the country. Another reason of their bad success, and, in my mind, the principal one, was owing to the intrigues of a certain missionary, who, imagining that this embassy might be injurious to the interests of his own country, did not fail to excite unfavourable impressions against the English nation."

The points of failure enumerated in this letter of Monsieur Grammont, were so many spurs to the Dutch factory to try their success at the court of Pekin the following year. No sooner did Mr. Van Braam receive this dispatch, by the return of the English embassy to Canton, than he prepared a letter for the Commissaries General at Batavia, in which he informed them, that as it was the intention of the different nations who had factories established in Canton, to send embassadors to the Capital, for the purpose of congratulating the Emperor on his attaining the age of eighty-four years, which would be in the sixtieth year of his reign, he had resolved to proceed on such a mission on the part of the Batavian Republic, and requested that he might be furnished, without delay, with suitable credentials. To this application the Commissaries General, who had been sent out the same year to retrench the expences of the Company in their Indian settlements, and to reform abuses, returned for answer, That, "however low and inadequate their finances might be to admit of extraordinary expences, yet they deemed it expedient not to shew any backwardness in adopting similar measures to those pursued by other Europeans trading to China; and that they had, accordingly, nominated Mr. Titsingh as chief, and himself (Mr. Van Braam) as second Embassador to the Court of China."

Mr. Titsingh lost no time in repairing to Canton, and these two Embassadors, determining to avail themselves of the hints thrown out in Monsieur Grammont's letter, and thereby to avoid splitting on the same rock which, they took for granted, the British Embassador had done, cheerfully submitted to every humiliating ceremony required from them by the Chinese, who, in return, treated them in the most contemptuous and indignant manner. At Canton they were ordered to assist in a solemn procession of Mandarines to a temple in the neighbourhood, and there, before the Emperor's name, painted on cloth, and suspended above the altar, to bow their heads nine times to the ground, in token of gratitude for his great condescension in permitting them to proceed to his presence, in order to offer[10] him tribute. They submitted even to the demands of the state-officers of Canton, that the letter, written by the Commissaries General at Batavia to the Emperor of China, and translated there into the Chinese language, should be broke open, and the contents read by them; and that they should further be allowed to make therein such alterations and additions as they might think proper. The Embassador, resolving not to be wanting in any point of civility, requested to know when he might have the honour of paying his respects to the Viceroy; and received for answer, that the customs of the country did not allow a person in his situation to come within the walls of the Viceroy's palace, but that one of his officers should receive his visit at the gate; which visit *to the gate* was literally made. Mr. Van Braam, in relating this circumstance in his journal, observes, that the Viceroy "assured his Excellency, he ought not to take his refusal amiss, as the same terms had been prescribed to Lord Macartney the preceding year." Mr. Van Braam knew very well that Lord Macartney never subjected himself to any such refusal; and he knew too, that the same Viceroy accompanied his Lordship in a great part of his journey from the Capital: that he partook of a repast, on the invitation of Lord Macartney, at the British factory; when, for the first time, both Mr. Van Braam and the supercargoes of all the European nations had been permitted to sit down in the presence of one of his rank.

At Pekin they were required to humiliate themselves at least thirty different times, at each of which they were obliged, on their knees, to knock their heads nine times against the ground,[11] which Mr. Van Braam, in his journal, very coolly calls, performing the salute of honour, "*faire le salut d'honneur.*" And they were finally dismissed, with a few paltry pieces of silk, without having once been allowed to open their lips on any kind of business; and without being permitted to see either their friend Grammont, or any other European missionary, except one, who had special leave to make them a visit of half an hour, the day before their departure, in presence of ten or twelve officers of government. On their arrival in this Capital they were lodged, literally, in a stable; under the same cover, and in the same apartment, with a parcel of cart-horses. Mr. Van Braam's own words are, "*Nous voilà donc à notre arrivée dans la célèbre residence impériale, logés dans une espèce d'écurie. Nous serions nous attendus à une pareille avanture!*"

After such a vile reception and degrading treatment of the Dutch Embassy, what advantages can reasonably be expected to accrue from a servile and unconditional compliance with the submissions required by this haughty government? It would rather seem that their exactions are proportioned to the complying temper of the persons with whom they have to treat. For it appears, not only from Mr. Van Braam's own account of the Embassy, but also from two manuscript journals in the Author's possession, one kept by a Dutch gentleman in the suite, and the other by a native Chinese, that the Embassadors from the Batavian Republic were fully prepared to obviate every difficulty that might arise from the supposed points of failure in the British Embassy, as directed to their notice by M. Grammont. In the first place, they not only carried[12] presents for the Ministers of State, but they calmly suffered these gentlemen to trick them out of the only curious and valuable articles among the presents intended for the Emperor, and to substitute others, of a mean and common nature, in their place. Secondly, they not only complied with going through the usual ceremony of saluting the Emperor, but also of saluting the Emperor's name, painted on a piece of silk, at least fifty times, on their journey to and from the Capital: which degrading ceremony they even condescended to perform before the person of the Prime Minister. With regard to the third point, it certainly appears that no expence had been spared in providing themselves with splendid robes for the occasion; but, unfortunately, they had but few opportunities of making use of them, their baggage not arriving at the Capital till many days after they had been there. Nor does it seem that the dress of a foreign Embassador is considered of much consequence in the eyes of the Chinese; for, when these gentlemen wished to excuse themselves from going to court, on account of their dusty and tattered clothes, in which they had performed a most painful journey, the Master of the Ceremonies observed, that it was not their *dress*, but their *persons*, which the Emperor, his master, was desirous to see. And, it can hardly be supposed, they would omit observing the fourth article, which, Mr. Grammont is of opinion, was neglected by Lord Macartney. And, in the last place, they stand fully acquitted of any want of *humility* in the tone and style of their communications, after having allowed their credentials to be new modelled by the officers of Government at Canton; from which city they had also an interpreter, a very proper one, no doubt, appointed to attend them.[13]

Their mission, it is true, was not well calculated for making terms or rejecting proposals. The Chinese were not unacquainted with the declining finances of the Dutch; they knew very well that the embassy had originated in Canton, and that it was accredited only from their superiors in Batavia. In their journey they were harassed beyond measure; sometimes they were lodged in wretched hovels, without furniture and without cover; sometimes they were obliged to pass the night in the open air, when the temperature was below the freezing point; frequently for four and twenty hours they had nothing to eat. Van Braam observes that, owing to the fatigues of the journey, the badness of the victuals, their early rising and exposure to the cold, he lost about five inches in the circumference of his body. Being rather corpulent, and not very expert in performing the Chinese ceremony at their public introduction, his hat happened to fall on the ground, upon which the old Emperor began to laugh. "Thus," says he, "I received a mark of distinction and predilection, such as never Embassador was honoured with before. I confess," continues he, "that the recollection of my sufferings from the cold in waiting so long in the morning, was very much softened by this incident." No man will certainly envy this gentleman's happy turn of mind, in receiving so much satisfaction in being laughed at.

The tone of the Emperor's letter, with which they were dismissed, while it speaks the vain and arrogant sentiments of this haughty government, shews at the same time how well acquainted they were with the circumstances that gave rise to the mission, and the degree of estimation in which they held it. It[14] was written in the Tartar, Chinese, and Latin languages, from the last of which, as rendered by the missionaries, the following is a literal translation. The contents were addressed to the Council of India, but on the outside wrapper, "*To the King of Holland.*" It may serve at the same time as a specimen of Chinese composition.

"I have received from heaven the sceptre of this vast empire. I have reigned for sixty years with glory and happiness; and have established the most profound peace upon the four seas[2] of the said empire, to the benefit of the nations bordering upon them. The fame of my majesty and proofs of my magnificence have found their way into every part of the world, and they constitute the pride and the pleasure of my vast domains.

"I consider my own happy empire, and other kingdoms, as one and the same family; the princes and the people are, in my eye, the same men. I condescend to shed my blessings over all, strangers as well as natives; and there is no country, however distant, that has not received instances of my benevolence. Thus, all nations send to do me homage, and to congratulate me incessantly. New and successive Embassadors arrive, some drawn in chariots over land, and others traverse, in their ships, the immensity of the seas. In fact, I attend [15] to nothing but the good administration of my empire. I feel a lively joy in observing the anxiety with which they flock together from every quarter to contemplate and admire the wise administration of my government. I experience the most agreeable satisfaction in participating my happiness with foreign states. I applaud therefore your government, which, although separated from mine by an immense ocean, has not failed to send me congratulatory letters, accompanied with tributary offerings.

"Having perused your letters, I observe that they contain nothing but what I consider as authentic testimonies of your great veneration for me, from whence I conclude that you admire my mode of governing. In fact, you have great reason to applaud me. Since you have carried on your trade at Canton, (and it is now many years,) strangers have always been well treated in my empire; and they have individually been the objects of my love and affection. I might call to witness the Portuguese, the Italians, the English, and others of the same sort of nations, who are all equally esteemed by me, and have all presented me with precious gifts. All have been treated, on my part, after the same manner, and without any partiality. I give abundantly even when those things I received from them are of no value. My manner of doing these things is undoubtedly known in your country.

"Concerning your Embassador, he is not, properly speaking, sent by his King; but you, who are a company of merchants,[16] have supposed yourselves authorized to pay me this respect. Your Sovereign, however, having directed you to chuse a favourable moment of my reign, you have now sent to felicitate me accordingly in the name of your said Sovereign. The sixtieth year of my reign was about to be completed. You, a company, too distant from your Sovereign, could not announce it to him. Interpreting this to be his pleasure, you have undertaken to send, in his name, to do me homage; and I have no doubt this prince is inspired towards me with the same sentiments which I have experienced in you. I have, therefore, received your Embassador as if he had been sent immediately by his King. And I am desirous you should be made acquainted that I have remarked nothing in the person of your Embassador, but what bore testimony of his respect for me, and of his own good conduct.

"I commanded my great officers to introduce him to my presence. I gave him several entertainments, and permitted him to see the grounds and the palaces that are within my vast and magnificent gardens of *Yuen-min-yuen.* I have so acted that he might feel the effects of my attention, dividing with him the pleasures which the profound peace of my empire allows me to enjoy. I have, moreover, made valuable presents, not only to him, but also to the officers, interpreters, soldiers, and servants of his suite, giving them, besides what is customary, many other articles, as may be seen by the catalogue.[17]

"Your Embassador being about to return to the presence of his sovereign, I have directed him to present to this Prince pieces of silk and other valuable articles to which I have added some antique vases.

"May your King receive my present. May he govern his people with wisdom; and give his sole attention to this grand object, acting always with an upright and sincere heart: and, lastly, may he always cherish the recollection of my beneficence! May this King attentively watch over the affairs of his kingdom. I recommend it to him strongly and earnestly.

"The twenty-fourth day of the first moon of the sixtieth year of the reign of Kien Long."

The very different treatment which the English embassy received at the court of Pekin is easily explained. The Chinese are well informed of the superiority of the English over all other nations by sea; of the great extent of their commerce; of their vast possessions in India which they have long regarded with a jealous eye; and of the character and independent spirit of the nation. They perceived, in the manly and open conduct of Lord Macartney, the representative of a sovereign in no way inferior to the Emperor of China, and they felt the propriety, though they were unwilling to avow it, of exacting only the same token of respect from him towards their sovereign, that one of their own countrymen, of equal rank, should pay to the portrait of his Britannic majesty. It must, however, have been a[18] hard struggle between personal pride, and national importance, before they resolved to reject so fair a proposal, and consent to wave a ceremony which had never, on any former occasion, been dispensed with. It is easy to conceive how strong an impression the refusal of an individual to comply with the ceremonies of the country was likely to make on the minds of the Emperor and his court; how much they must have suffered in their own opinion, and how greatly must their pride have been mortified, to find that by no trick, nor artifice, nor stretch of power, could they prevail on an English Embassador to forego the dignity and respect due to the situation he held at their court, whither they were now convinced he had not come, as was signified in painted letters on the colours of the ships that transported the embassy up the *Pei-ho,* "*to offer tribute to the Emperor of China.*"

With regard to the intrigues of the Portugueze missionary, mentioned in Mr. Grammont's letter, Lord Macartney was sufficiently aware of them long before his arrival in the capital, and took such measures, in consequence of the information, as were most likely to be effectual in counteracting any influence that he might secretly exert, injurious to the interests of the British nation. But the intrigues of churchmen are not always easily obviated, especially where they are suspicious of their errors being exposed or their ignorance detected. It is a painful truth (and is noticed here with reluctance, on account of the many worthy members of the society) that the ministers of a certain branch of a religion whose distinguishing feature is meekness and forbearance, should have so far perverted the intention of its benevo[19]lent author, as to have produced more intrigues, cabals, and persecutions, than even the relentless Mahomedans, whose first article of faith inculcates merit in destroying those of a different persuasion. Their political intrigues and interference in state affairs, have done material injury to the cause of Christianity in almost every country into which their missions have extended.

The malignant spirit of this same Portugueze missionary was not confined to the framing of falsehoods and misrepresentations with regard to the views of the British embassy, but has continued to exert its influence at the court of Pekin, in the same secret and dishonourable way, whenever an opportunity occurred that seemed favourable for raising unwarrantable suspicions in the minds of the Chinese against the English nation. Towards the close of the last war, when it was found expedient to take possession of some of the Portugueze colonies, and an expedition for this purpose was actually sent out to secure the peninsula of Macao, this missionary lost no time in suggesting to the Chinese court, that the designs of the English in getting possession of Macao might be of the same nature as those they had already practised in India; and that if they were once suffered to get footing in the country, China might experience the same fate as Hindostan. Fortunately for the concerns of the British East India Company this officious interference and the malevolent insinuations of *Bernardo Almeyda* took a very different turn to what he had expected. The intelligence of a hostile force so near the coast of China coming first from an European missionary, implied a neglect in the Viceroy of Canton, and an angry letter was addressed to him from court,[20] ordering him to give immediate and accurate information on the subject. The Viceroy, nettled at the officious zeal of the Portugueze, positively denied the fact of any hostile intention of the English, "who, being a brave people, and terrible in arms, had intimidated the Portugueze at Macao, though without reason, as their ships of war, as usual, came only to protect their ships of commerce against their enemies." When this dispatch of the Viceroy reached Pekin, the Emperor was so exasperated to think that the Court had suffered itself to be misled by an European missionary, that he ordered Almeyda to appear before the master of the household, and on his knees to ask forgiveness of a crime, which, he was told, deserved to be punished with death; and he was dismissed with a caution never more to interfere in the state affairs of China. The whole of this curious transaction is published in the Pekin Gazette of last year; so that the English have gained a considerable degree of reputation by it, so much, indeed, that the Chinese at Canton (and a great deal depends upon their representations) would have no objection to see the English in possession of Macao; for they cordially hate, I believe it is not too much to say they despise, the Portugueze, and they speak with horror of the French. What a moment then is this for England to turn to its advantage!

Independent, however, of the machinations of missionaries, such is the pride and the haughty insolence of the Chinese government, that, in no instance on record, but that of the British embassy, has it ever relaxed from its long established customs, nor acquiesced in any demands of foreign embassadors,[21] whether the tone in which they were made was supplicating or authoritative. The forms of the court they contend to be as immutable as were the laws of the Medes and Persians. Every thing must be conducted by prescriptive usage, and no deviation allowed from the rules which for ages have been established by law, and registered by the council of ordinances; much less the remission of any duty that might derogate from the reverence and respect which are considered to be due to the person of the Emperor.

It may be imagined, then, that an event so new as a refusal to submit to the degrading ceremony required from an embassador, at his public introduction, could not fail of making a very strong impression on the minds of those about the person of his Imperial Majesty; who, as Mr. Van Braam says, were (and without doubt they were) much better satisfied with the complying temper of the Dutch, than with the inflexible pertinacity of the English. Yet, they did not venture to lodge the latter in a stable, nor think proper to persevere in demanding unreasonable homage. Neither was any pique or ill-nature apparent in any single instance, after the departure of the embassy from the capital, but very much the contrary. The officers appointed to conduct it to Canton testified the most earnest desire to please, by a ready attention to every minute circumstance that might add to the comforts of the travellers, or alleviate, if not entirely remove, any little inconvenience. It was a flattering circumstance to the embassador to observe their anxiety for the favourable opinion of a nation they had now begun to think more highly of, and of whom, in measuring[22] with themselves, it was not difficult to perceive, they felt, though too cautious to avow, the superiority.

The British embassy was a measure which it was absolutely necessary to adopt, for reasons that are stated at full length in the first chapter of Sir George Staunton's valuable work, and the foundation it has laid for future advantages more than counterbalances the trifling expence it occasioned to the East India Company, which did not exceed two per cent. on the annual amount of their trade from England to Canton. Those who had formed immoderate expectations must have little understood the laws and customs of China, which admit not the system of mutual intercourse between distant nations, by means of embassadors or resident ministers at the respective courts. Their custom is to receive embassadors with respect and hospitality; to consider them as visitors to the Emperor, and to entertain them accordingly as his particular guests, from the moment they enter the country till they return to the boundaries of his empire. This being necessarily attended with an enormous expence[3], the court of ceremonies has prescribed forty days for the residence of foreign embassadors, either in the capital, or wherever the court may happen to be; though on particular occasions, or by accident, the term may sometimes be extended to double that time.

Thus by consulting the accounts of the different European embassies that have been sent to China in the two last centu[23]ries, it will be found that the residence of none of them was extended to thrice the term fixed by the court of ceremonies, and two of them did not remain the period allowed.

The first embassy sent by the Dutch arrived in Pekin the 17th July 1656, and departed the 16th October following, having remained ninety-one days.

The second Dutch embassy arrived in Pekin the 20th June 1667, and departed the 5th August, having resided forty-six days.

The first Russian embassy arrived at the capital on the 5th November 1692, and left it on the 17th February 1693, having remained there one hundred and six days.

The second Russian embassy arrived at Pekin on the 18th November 1720, and did not leave it till the 2d March 1721, being one hundred and fourteen days.

These two embassies were immediately connected with the commercial concerns of the two nations, which were then transacted in the capital of China, but now confined to the adjoining frontiers.

The Pope's embassy arrived in Pekin on the 15th December 1720, and departed the 24th March 1721, being ninety-nine days.[24]

The Portugueze embassy entered Pekin the 1st May 1753, and left it the 8th June following, being only thirty-nine days.

The British embassy arrived in Pekin the 21st August 1793, and departed the 7th October, being forty-seven days.

The third Dutch embassy entered the capital the 10th January 1795, and left it the 15th February, being thirty-six days.

On the whole, then, it may be concluded, that neither Monsieur Grammont, nor they who conceived that an unconditional and servile compliance, on the part of the British Embassador, would have been productive of more favourable results, were right in their conjectures. On the contrary, it may, perhaps, be rather laid down as a certain consequence, that a tone of submission, and a tame and passive obedience to the degrading demands of this haughty court, serve only to feed its pride, and add to the absurd notions of its own vast importance.

CHAP. II.
Occurrences and Observations in the Navigation of the Yellow Sea, and the Passage up the Pei-ho, or White River.

Different Testimonies that have been given of the Chinese Character.—Comparison of China with Europe in the sixteenth Century.—Motives of the Missionaries in their Writings.—British Embassy passes the Streights of Formosa.—Appearance of a Ta-fung.—*Chu-san Islands.—Instance of Chinese Amplification.—Various Chinese Vessels.—System of their Navigation—their Compass, probably of Scythian Origin—foreign Voyages of.—Traces of Chinese in America—in an Island of the Tartarian Sea—in the Persian Gulph—traded probably as far as Madagascar.—Commerce of the Tyrians.— Reasons for conjecturing that the Hottentots may have derived their Origin from China.—Portrait of a Chinese compared with that of a Hottentot.—Malays of the same descent as the Chinese.—Curious coincidences in the Customs of these and the Sumatrans.—Cingalese of Chinese Origin.—One of the Brigs dispatched to* Chu-san *for Pilots.—Rapid Currents among the Islands.—Visit to the Governor.— Difficulties in procuring Pilots.—Arbitrary Proceeding of the Governor.—Pilots puzzled with our Compass—Ignorance of—Arrive in the Gulph of* Pe-tche-lee.—*Visit of two Officers from Court, and their Present—enter the* Pei-ho, *and embark in convenient Yachts.—Accommodating Conduct of the two Officers.—Profusion of Provisions.—Appearance of the Country—of the People.—Dress of the Women.— Remarks on their small Feet.—Chinese an uncleanly and frowzy People.—Immense Crowds of People and River Craft at* Tien-sing.—*Decent and prepossessing Conduct of the Multitude.—Musical Air sung by the Rowers of the Yachts.—Favourable Traits in the Chinese Character.—Face and Products of the Country.—Multitudes of People Inhabitants of the Water.—Another Instance of arbitrary Power.— Disembark at* Tong Tchoo, *and are lodged in a Temple.*

"IF any man should make a collection of all the inventions,[25] and all the productions, that every nation, which now is, or ever has been, upon the face of the globe, the whole would fall far short, either as to number or quality, of what is to be met with in China." These, or something similar,[26] are the words of the learned Isaac Vossius.

The testimony given by the celebrated authors of the *Encyclopédie des Connoissances humaines* is almost equally strong: "The Chinese who, by common consent, are superior to all the Asiatic nations, in antiquity, in genius, in the progress of the sciences, in wisdom, in government, and in true philosophy; may, moreover, in the opinion of some authors, enter the lists, on all these points, with the most enlightened nations of Europe."

How flattering, then, and gratifying must it have been to the feelings of those few favoured persons, who had the good fortune to be admitted into the suite of the British Embassador, then preparing to proceed to the court of that Sovereign who held the government of such an extraordinary nation; how greatly must they have enjoyed the prospect of experiencing, in their own persons, all that was virtuous, and powerful, and grand, and magnificent, concentrated in one point—in the city of Pekin!

And if any doubts might have arisen, on consideration that neither the learned Canon of Windsor, nor the celebrated Authors of the Encyclopédie, were ever in China; that the first was wonderfully given to the marvellous, and the latter had no other authorities, than those of the Jesuits, and other missionaries for[27] propagating the Christian faith, yet such doubts were more inclined to yield to the favourable side, as being supported by the almost unanimous concurrence of a multitude of testimonies, contained in the relations that have, at various times, been published not only by the missionaries, but also by some other travellers.

The late Sir William Jones, indeed, who deservedly took the lead in oriental literature, had observed, in speaking of the Chinese, that "By some they have been extolled as the oldest and wisest, as the most learned, and most ingenious, of nations; whilst others have derided their pretensions to antiquity, condemned their government as abominable, and arraigned their manners as inhuman; without allowing them an element of science, or a single art, for which they have not been indebted to some more ancient and more civilized race of men."

It is true, also, the researches of Mr. Pauw, the sagacious philosopher of Berlin, and the narrative of the elegant and impressive writer of Lord Anson's Voyage, convey to the reader's mind no very favourable ideas of the Chinese character; yet, as the enquiries of the one were entered upon in a spirit of controversy, and directed to one single point, and the author, as justly has been observed of him, delights sometimes to take a swim against the stream, many deductions were clearly to be made from the conclusions of Mr. Pauw. And with regard to the Narrative of Mr. Robins, it may be remarked that, to decide upon the general character of the Chinese, from the dealings Lord Anson had with them in the port of Canton,[28] would be as unfair, as it would be thought presumptuous in a foreigner to draw the character of our own nation from a casual visit to Falmouth, Killybeggs, or Aberdeen.

9

The same remark will apply to the accounts given of this nation by Toreen, Osbeck, Sonnerat, and some others, who have visited Canton in trading ships, none of whom were five hundred yards beyond the limits of the European factories.

It would also have been highly illiberal to suppose, that a body of men, remarkable, as the early Jesuit missionaries were thought to be, for probity, talent, and disinterestedness, should studiously sit down to compose fabrications for the mere purpose of deceiving the world. Even Voltaire, who had little partiality for the sacerdotal character, is willing to admit, that their relations ought to be considered as the productions of the most intelligent travellers that have extended and embellished the fields of Science and Philosophy. This remark, with proper allowances being made for the age in which they were written, may perhaps be applied to the narratives of the early missions to China, though not exactly to some others of a more modern date. All the praises bestowed by the former on this nation, the latter, it would seem, have, injudiciously, considered themselves bound to justify; without taking into account the progressive improvements of Europe within the last century and a half.

That China was civilized to a certain degree before most of the nations of Europe, not even Greece excepted, is a fact that will not admit of a doubt; but that it has continued to im[29]prove, so as still to vie with many of the present European states, as the missionaries would have it supposed, is not by any means so clear. From the middle to the end of the sixteenth century, compared with Europe in general, it had greatly the superiority, if not in science, at least in arts and manufactures, in the conveniences and the luxuries of life. The Chinese were, at that period, pretty much in the same state in which they still are; and in which they are likely to continue. When the first Europeans visited China, they were astonished to find an universal toleration of religious opinions; to observe *Lamas* and *Tao-tzes, Jews, Persees,* and *Mahomedans,* living quietly together, and each following his own creed without molestation; whilst most of the countries in Europe were, at that time, torn in pieces by religious schisms; and man was labouring with enthusiastic fury to destroy his fellow-creatures, in honour of his Creator, for a slight difference of opinion in matters of no real importance, or even for a different acceptation of a word. In China, every one was allowed to think as he pleased, and to chuse his own religion. The horrid massacre of the Protestants in Paris had terrified all Europe. China knew nothing of internal commotions, but such as were sometimes occasioned by a partial scarcity of grain. The art of improving vegetables by particular modes of culture, was just beginning to be known in Europe. All China, at that time, was comparatively a garden. When the King of France introduced the luxury of silk stockings, which, about eighteen years afterwards, was adopted by Elizabeth of England, the peasantry of the middle provinces of China were clothed in silks from head to foot. At this period, few or none of the little elegancies or conveniences of[30] life were known in Europe; the ladies' toilet had few essences to gratify the sense of smell, or to beautify, for a time, the complexion; the scissars, needles, pen-knives, and other little appendages, were then unknown; and rude and ill-polished skewers usurped the place of pins. In China, the ladies had their needlework, their paint-boxes, their trinkets of ivory, of silver in fillagree, of mother-pearl, and of tortoise-shell. Even the calendar, at this time so defective in Europe, that Pope Gregory was urged to the bold undertaking of leaping over, or annihilating, ten days, was found to be, in China, a national concern, and the particular care of government. Decimal arithmetic, a new and useful discovery of the seventeenth century in Europe, was the only system of arithmetic in use in China. In a word, when the nobility of England were sleeping on straw, a peasant of China had his mat and his pillow; and the man in office enjoyed his silken mattress. One cannot, therefore, be surprized if the impressions made upon these holy men were powerfully felt, or if their descriptions should seem to incline a little towards the marvellous. Nor may perhaps their relations be found to be much embellished, on a fair comparison of the state of China with that of Europe in general, from the year 1560 to the close of the same century.

These religious men, however, might have had their motives for setting this wonderful people in the fairest point of view. The more powerful and magnificent, the more learned and refined they represented this nation to be, the greater would be their triumph in the event of their effecting a change of the national faith. It may also have occurred to them, that com[31]mon prudence required they should speak favourably, at least, of a nation under whose power and protection they had voluntarily placed themselves for life. There is every reason to suppose, that in general they mean to tell the truth, but by suppressing some part of it, or by telling it in such a manner as if they expected it would one day get back to China in the language of that country, their accounts often appear to be contradictory in themselves. In the same breath that they extol the wonderful strength of filial piety, they speak of the common practices of exposing infants; the strict morality and ceremonious conduct of the people are followed by a list of the most gross debaucheries; the virtues and the philosophy of the learned are explained by their ignorance and their vices; if in one page they speak of the excessive fertility of the country, and the amazing extension of agriculture, in the next, thousands are seen perishing by want; and whilst they extol with admiration the progress they have made in the arts and sciences, they plainly inform us that without the aid of foreigners they can neither cast a cannon, nor calculate an eclipse.

Upon the whole, however, the British embassy left England under a favourable impression of the people it was about to visit. Whether the expectations of all those who composed it, independent of any political consideration, were realized, or ended in disappointment, may partly be collected from the following pages. The opinions they contain are drawn from such incidents and anecdotes as occurred in the course of an eight months' visit and from such as seemed best calculated to illustrate the condition of the people, the national character, and the nature[32] of the government. A short residence in the imperial palace of Yuen-min-yuen, a greater share of liberty than is usually permitted to strangers in this country, with the assistance of some little knowledge of the language, afforded me the means of collecting the facts and observations which I now lay before the public; and in the relation of which I have endeavoured to adhere to that excellent rule of our immortal poet,

——"Nothing extenuate,
Nor set down aught in malice."

And as the qualities of good and evil, excellence and mediocrity, in any nation, can only be fairly estimated by a comparison with those of the same kind in others, wherever a similitude or a contrast in the Chinese character or customs with those of any other people ancient or modern occurred to my recollection, I have considered it as not wholly uninteresting to note the relation or disagreement.

The dispatches from China, received by the British Embassador on his arrival at Batavia, communicated the agreeable intelligence that his Imperial Majesty had been pleased, by a public edict, not only to declare his entire satisfaction with the intended embassy, but that he had likewise issued strict orders to the commanding officers of the several ports along the coast of the Yellow Sea, to be particularly careful that Pilots should be ready, at a moment's notice, to conduct the English squadron to *Tien-sing*, the nearest port to the capital, or to any other which might be considered as more convenient and suitable for the British ships.[33]

By this communication a point of some difficulty was now considered to be removed. It was deemed a desirable circumstance to be furnished with the means of proceeding directly to Pekin through the Yellow Sea, and thus to avoid any intercourse with the port of Canton; as it was well known the principal officers of the government there were prepared to throw every obstacle in the way of the embassy, and if not effectually to prevent, at least to counteract, any representations that might be made at the imperial court, with regard to the abuses that exist in the administration of the public affairs at that place, and more especially to the exactions and impositions to which the commercial establishments are liable of the different nations whose subjects have established factories in this southern emporium of China. It could not be supposed, indeed, that their endeavours would be less exerted, in this particular instance, than on all former occasions of a similar nature.

The navigation of the Yellow Sea, as yet entirely unknown to any European nation, was considered as a subject of some importance, from the information it would afford the means of supplying, and which, on any future occasion, might not only lessen the dangers of an unknown passage, but prevent also much delay by superseding the necessity of running into different ports in search of Chinese Pilots, whom, by experience, we afterwards found to be more dangerous than useful.

We passed through the streight of Formosa without seeing any part of the main land of China, or of the island from whence the streight derives its name, except a high point[34] towards the northern extremity. The weather, indeed, during three successive days, the 25th, 26th, and 27th July was so dark and gloomy, that the eye could scarcely discern the largest objects at the distance of a mile, yet the thermometer was from 80° to 83° the greater part of these days. A heavy and almost incessant fall of rain was accompanied with violent squalls of wind, and frequent bursts of thunder and flashes of lightning; which, with the cross and confused swell in the sea, made the passage not only uncomfortably irksome, but also extremely dangerous, on account of the many islands interspersed in almost every part of the strait.

On the evening of the 25th the sun set in a bank of fog, which made the whole western side of the horizon look like a blaze of fire, and the barometer was observed to have fallen near one third of an inch, which, in these latitudes and at sea, is considered as a certain indication of a change of weather. There were on board some Chinese fishermen who had been driven out to sea in one of the East India company's ships, which we met with in the straits of Sunda. These men assured us that the appearance of the heavens prognosticated one of those tremendous gales of wind which are well known to Europeans by the name of *Ty-phoon* and which some ingenious and learned men have supposed to be the same as the Typhon of the Egyptians or τυφων of the Greeks. The Chinese, however have made use of no mythological allusion in naming this hurricane. They call it *Ta-fung* which literally signifies *a great wind*. The wind was certainly high the whole of the night and the following day, the thunder and lightning dread[35]ful, and the variable squalls and rain frequent and heavy; the depth of the sea from 25 to 30 fathoms.

The charts, however, of this passage into the Yellow Sea, constructed by Europeans when the Chinese permitted foreign nations to trade to *Chu-san*, are considered as sufficiently exact for skilful navigators to avoid the dangerous rocks and islands. By the help of these charts our squadron ventured to stand through the still more intricate and narrow passages of the Chu-san Archipelago, where, in the contracted space of about eight hundred square leagues, the surface of the sea is studded with a cluster, consisting, nearly, of four hundred distinct islands.

These islands appeared to us, in sailing among them, to be mostly uninhabited, extremely barren of trees or shrubs, and many of them destitute even of herbage, or verdure of any kind. In some of the creeks we perceived a number of boats and other small craft, at the upper ends of which were villages composed of mean looking huts, the dwellings most probably of fishermen, as there was no appearance of cultivated ground near them to furnish their inhabitants with the means of subsistence.

The squadron having dropped anchor, we landed on one of the largest of these islands; and walked a very considerable distance before we saw a human being. At length, in descending a valley, in the bottom of which was a small village, we fell in with a young peasant, whom with some difficulty, by means of an interpreter, we engaged in conversation. Embarrassed in thus suddenly meeting with strangers, so different from his own[36] countrymen, in dress, in features, and complexion, his timidity might almost be said to assume the appearance of terror. He soon, however, gained confidence, and became communicative. He assured us that the island on which we were, and of which he was a native, was the best in the whole groupe, and the most populous, except that of *Chu-san*; the number of its inhabitants being ten thousand souls. It was discovered, however, before we had been long in the country, that when a Chinese made use of the monosyllable *van*, which in his language signifies ten thousand, he was not to be understood as speaking of a determinate or precise number, but only as making use of a term that implied amplification. A state criminal, for example, is generally condemned to undergo the punishment of being cut into *ten thousand* pieces; the great wall of China is called the *van-lee-tchin*, or wall of *ten thousand lee*, or three thousand English miles, a length just double to that which the most authentic accounts have given of it. But when he means to inform any one that the emperor has *ten thousand* large vessels, for the purpose of collecting taxes paid in kind, on the grand canal, instead of the monosyllable *van* he invariably makes use of the expression nine thousand nine hundred and ninety-nine, as conveying a fixed and definite number, and, in this case, he will be understood to signify literally ten thousand. In this manner, I suppose, we were to understand the population of the island *Lo-ang*.

*W. Alexander del.*T. Medland sculp.*

A Foreign Trader.

*W. Alexander del.*T. Medland sculp.*
A Rice Mill.

Pub. May 2, 1804, by Messrs. Cadell, & Davies, Strand, London.

At the sight of our large ships, so different in their appearance from any of those belonging to the Chinese, a vast number of boats, issuing from every creek and cove, presently crowded together, in such a manner, and with so little manage[37]ment, as to render it difficult to pass through without danger of oversetting or sinking some of them; a danger, however, to which they seemed quite insensible. Vessels of a larger description, and various in the shape of their hulls and rigging, from twenty tons burden and upwards, to about two hundred tons, were observed in considerable numbers, sailing along the coast of the continent, laden generally with small timber, which was piled to such a height upon their decks, that no extraordinary force of wind would seem to be required to overturn them. Beams of wood, and other pieces that were too long to be received upon the deck of a single ship, were laid across the decks of two vessels lashed together. We saw at least a hundred couple thus laden in one fleet, keeping close in with the coast, in order to be ready, in case of bad weather, to put into the nearest port, being ill calculated to resist a storm at sea. The ships indeed that are destined for longer voyages appear, from their singular construction, to be very unfit to contend with the tempestuous seas of China. The general form of the hull, or body of the ship, above water, is that of the moon when about four days old. The bow, or forepart, is not rounded as in ships of Europe, but is a square flat surface, the same as the stern; without any projecting piece of wood, usually known by the name of cutwater, and without any keel. On each side of the bow a large circular eye is painted, in imitation, I suppose, of that of a fish. The two ends of the ship rise to a prodigious height above the deck. Some carry two, some three, and others four masts. Each of these consists of a single piece of wood, and consequently not capable of being occasionally reduced in length, as those of European ships.[38]The diameter of the mainmast of one of the larger kind of Chinese vessels, such as trade to Batavia, is not less than that of an English man of war of sixty-four guns. And it is fixed in a bed of massive timber laid across the deck. On each mast is a single sail of matting, made from the fibres of the bamboo, and stretched by means of poles of that reed, running across, at the distance of about two feet from each other. These sails are frequently made to furl and unfurl like a fan. When well hoisted up and braced almost fore and aft, or parallel with the sides of the ship, a Chinese vessel will sail within three and a half, or four points of the wind; but they lose all this advantage over ships of Europe by their drifting to leeward, in consequence of the round and clumsy shape of the bottom, and their want of keel. The rudder is so placed, in a large opening of the stern, that it can occasionally be taken up, which is generally done on approaching sands and shallows.

The Chinese, in fact, are equally unskilled in naval architecture, as in the art of navigation. They keep no reckoning at sea, nor possess the least idea of drawing imaginary lines upon the surface of the globe, by the help of which the position of any particular spot may be assigned; in other words, they have no means whatsoever of ascertaining the latitude or the longitude of any place, either by estimation from the distance sailed, or by observation of the heavenly bodies, with instruments for that purpose. Yet they pretend to say, that many of their early navigators made long voyages, in which they[39] were guided by charts of the route, sometimes drawn on paper, and sometimes on the convex surface of large gourds

13

or pumpkins. From this circumstance, some of the Jesuits have inferred, that such charts must have been more correct than those on flat surfaces. If, indeed, the portion of the convex surface, employed for the purpose, was the segment of a sphere, and occupied a space having a comparative relation to that part of the surface of the earth sailed over, the inference might be allowable; but this would be to suppose a degree of knowledge to which, it does not appear, the Chinese had at any time attained, it being among them, in every period of their history, an universally received opinion, that the earth is a square, and that the kingdom of China is placed in the very center of its flat surface.

The present system of Chinese navigation is to keep as near the shore as possible; and never to lose sight of land, unless in voyages that absolutely require it; such as to Japan, Batavia, and Cochin-China. Knowing the bearing, or direction of the port intended to be made, let the wind be fair or foul, they endeavour, as nearly as possible, to keep the head of the ship always pointing towards the port by means of the compass. This instrument, as used in China, has every appearance of originality. The natives know nothing, from history or tradition, of its first introduction or discovery; and the use of the magnet, for indicating the poles of the earth, can be traced, from their records, to a period of time when the greatest part of Europe was in a state of barbarism. It has been conjectured, indeed, that the use of the magnetic needle, in Europe, was first brought from China by the famous traveller Marco Polo the Venetian. Its appearance immediately after his death, or, according to some, while he was yet living, but at all events, in[40] his own country, renders such a conjecture extremely probable. The embassies in which he was employed by Kublai-Khan, and the long voyages he performed by sea, could scarcely have been practicable without the aid of the compass. Be this as it may, the Chinese were, without doubt, well acquainted with this instrument long before the thirteenth century. It is recorded in their best authenticated annals merely as a fact, and not as any extraordinary circumstance, that the Emperor *Chung-ko* presented an embassador of Cochin-China, who had lost his way in coming by sea, with a *Ting-nan-tchin* "a needle pointing out the south," the name which it still retains. Even this idea of the seat of magnetic influence, together with the construction of the compass-box, the division of the card into eight principal points, and each of these again subdivided into three, the manner of suspending the needle, and its diminutive size, seldom exceeding in length three quarters of an inch, are all of them strong presumptions of its being an original, and not a borrowed invention.

By some, indeed, it has been conjectured, that the Scythians, in the northern regions of Asia, were acquainted with the polarity of the magnet, in ages antecedent to all history, and that the virtue of this fossil was intended to be meant by the flying arrow, presented to Abaris by Apollo, with the help of which he could transport himself wherever he pleased. The abundance of iron ores, and perhaps of native iron, in every part of Tartary, and the very[41] early period of time in which the natives were acquainted with the process of smelting these ores, render the idea not improbable, of the northern nations of Europe, and Asia, (or the Scythians,) being first acquainted with the polarity of the magnet.

Yet even with the assistance of the compass, it is surprizing how the clumsy and ill-constructed vessels of the Chinese can perform so long and dangerous a voyage as that to Batavia. For, besides being thrown out of their course by every contrary wind, their whole construction, and particularly the vast height of their upper works above the water, seems little adapted to oppose those violent tempests that prevail on the China seas, known, as we have already observed, by the name of *Ta-fung*. These hurricanes sometimes blow with such strength that, according to the assertion of an experienced and intelligent commander of one of the East India Company's ships, "Were it possible to blow ten thousand trumpets, and beat as many drums, on the forecastle of an Indiaman, in the height of a *Ta-fung*, neither the sound of the one nor the other would be heard by a person on the quarter-deck of the same ship." In fact, vast numbers of Chinese vessels are lost in these heavy gales of wind; and ten or twelve thousand subjects from the port of Canton alone are reckoned to perish annually by shipwreck.

When a ship leaves this port on a foreign voyage, it is considered as an equal chance that she will never return; and when the event proves favourable, a general rejoicing takes place among the friends of all those who had embarked in the[42] hazardous enterprize. Some of these ships are not less than a thousand tons burden, and contain half that number of souls, besides the passengers that leave their country, in the hope of making their fortunes in Batavia and Manilla. A ship is seldom the concern of one man. Sometimes forty or fifty, or even a hundred different merchants purchase a vessel, and divide her into as many compartments as there are partners, so that each knows his own particular place in the ship, which he is at liberty to fit up and to secure as he pleases. He ships his goods, and accompanies them in person, or sends his son, or a near relation, for it rarely happens that they will trust each other with property, where no family connexion exists. Each sleeping place is just the length and breadth of a man, and contains only a small mat, spread on the floor, and a pillow. Behind the compass is generally placed a small temple, with an altar, on which is continually kept burning a spiral taper composed of wax, tallow and sandal-wood dust. This holy flame answers a double purpose; for while the burning of it fulfils an act of piety, its twelve equal divisions serve to measure the twelve portions of time, which make up a complete day. It should seem that the superstitious notions inculcated in the people have led them to suppose, that some particular influence resides in the compass; for, on every appearance of a change in the weather, they burn incense before the magnetic needle.

The losses occasioned among the ships that were employed to transport the taxes paid in kind from the ports of the southern and middle provinces to the northern capital, were so[13]great, at the time of the Tartar Conquest, in the thirteenth century, that the successors of Gengis-Khan were induced to open a direct communication between the two extremes of the empire, by means of the rivers and canals; an undertaking that reflects the highest credit on the Mongul Tartars, and which cannot fail to be regarded with admiration, as long as it shall continue to exist. The Chinese, however, say, that the Tartars only repaired the old works that were fallen into decay.

Six centuries previous to this period, or about the seventh century of the Christian æra, the Chinese merchants, according to the opinion of the learned and ingenious Mr. de Guignes, carried on a trade to the west coast of North America. That, at this time, the promontory of Kamskatka was known to them under the name of *Ta-Shan*, many of their books of travels sufficiently testify; but their journies thither were generally made by land. One of the missionaries assured me that, in a collection of travels to Kamskatka, by various Chinese, the names of the several Tartar tribes, their manners, customs, and characters, the geographical descriptions of lakes, rivers, and mountains, were too clearly and distinctly noted to be mistaken. It is, however, extremely probable that, as furs and peltry were always in great demand, they might also have some communication with the said promontory from the isles of Jesso, to which they were known to trade with their shipping; and which are only a very short distance from it. Mr. de Guignes, in support of his opinion, quotes the journal of a bonze, as the priests of Fo have usually been called, who[44] sailed eastward from Kamskatka to such a distance as, in his mind, puts it beyond a doubt that the country he arrived at was no other than the coast of California. The Spanish writers, indeed, of the early voyages to this country, make mention of various wrecks of Chinese vessels being found in different parts of the western coast of the New Continent; and they observe that the natives here were, invariably, more civilized than in the interior and eastern parts of America.

Even those on the eastern coast of South America have a very strong resemblance to the Chinese in their persons, though not in their temperament and manners. The Viceroy of the Brazils retains a dozen of these people in his service, as rowers of his barge, with the use of which he one day honoured us, to make the tour of the grand harbour of Rio de Janeiro. We observed the Tartar or Chinese features, particularly the eye, strongly marked in the countenances of these Indians; the copper tinge was rather deeper than the darkest of the Chinese; but their beards being mostly confined to the upper lip and the point of the chin, together with their strong black hair, bore a very near resemblance.

The island of Tcho-ka, or Saghalien, in the Tartarian sea, opposite the mouth of the Amour, has evidently been peopled by the Chinese. When Monsieur la Perouse visited this island, he found the inhabitants clothed in blue nankin, and "the form of their dress differed but little from that of the Chinese; their pipes were Chinese, and of Tootanague; they had long nails; and they saluted by kneeling and prostration,[15] like the Chinese. If," continues the navigator, "they have a common origin with the Tartars and Chinese their separation from these nations must be of very ancient date, for they have no resemblance to them in person, and little in manners." Yet from his own account it appears that both their manners and customs have a very close resemblance.

The Chinese at one period carried on a very considerable commerce with Bussora and other sea-ports in the Persian gulph, particularly *Siraff*, near which some small islands, as well as several remarkable points and headlands of the coast, still bear Chinese names. In some of the voyages it is observed that a Colony of Chinese had apparently settled in the kingdom of Soffala, the descendants of whom were, in the time of the writers, easily distinguished from the other natives, by the difference of their colour and their features. The early Portuguese navigators also observe that on the island St. Laurence or Madagascar they met with people that resembled the Chinese. That the celebrated traveller Marco Polo visited Madagascar in a Chinese vessel there can be little doubt, unless indeed, like his own countrymen, we chuse rather to reject the probable parts of his narrative as fabulous, and to believe the miracles performed by the Nestorian Christians in Armenia as the only truths in his book.

It is impossible not to consider the notices given by this early traveller as curious, interesting and valuable; and, as far as they regard the empire of China, they bear internal evidence of being generally correct. He sailed from China in a fleet con[46]sisting of fourteen ships, each carrying *four* masts, and having their holds partitioned into separate chambers, some containing *thirteen* distinct compartments. This is the exact number of divisions into which *all* the holds of those sea-faring vessels were partitioned that transported the presents and baggage from our own ships in the gulph of *Pe-tche-lee* into the river *Pei-ho*; and we observed many hundreds of a still larger description, that are employed in foreign voyages, all carrying *four* masts; such vessels, our sailors who are remarkable for metamorphosing foreign names, usually called *Junks*, from *Tchuan* which signifies a ship; the *Tsong-too* or viceroy of a province is called by them *John Tuck*.

Not only the form of the ships, but the circumstances of the voyage taken notice of by this ancient navigator stamp his relation with authenticity. The strong current between Madagascar and Zanzebar rendering it next to impossible for ships to get back to the northward; the black natives on that coast, the products of the country which he enumerates; the true description of the Giraffe or Camelopardalis, at that time considered in Europe as a fabulous animal, are so many and such strong evidences in favour of his narrative, as to leave little doubt that he either was himself upon the east coast of Africa, or that he had received very correct information from his Chinese shipmates concerning it. Yet Doctor Vincent has asserted, in his *Periplus of the Erythrean Sea*[4], that in the time of this Venetian traveller none but Arab or Malay vessels navigated the Indian Ocean. With all due deference to such high authority I cannot forbear observing that the [47]simple relation of Marco Polo bears internal and irresistible evidence that the fleet of ships in which he sailed were Chinese, of the same kind to all intents and purposes as they now are. Nor have we any reason for doubting the authority of the two Mahomedans who visited China in the ninth century, when they tell us that Chinese ships traded to the Persian gulph at that time. In a chart made under the direction of the Venetian traveller and still preserved in the church of St. Michael de Murano at Venice, the southern part of the continent of Africa is said to be distinctly marked down, though this indeed might have been inserted after the Cape of Good Hope had been doubled by the Portuguese.

Whether the Prince of Portugal had seen or heard of this chart, or consulted the Arabian Geographers, or had read of the circumnavigation of Africa in the first translation of Herodotus that made its appearance but a few years before the discovery of the southern promontory of this continent by Bartholomew Diaz; or whether the voyages were undertaken at that time on a general plan of discovery, authors seem not to have agreed, but the opinion, I understand, among the Portugueze is that Henry had good grounds for supposing that the circumnavigation of Africa was practicable.

And whether the Phœnicians did or did not, in the earliest periods of history, double the Cape of Good of Hope there is abundant reason for supposing they were well acquainted with the east coast of Africa as far as the *Cape of Currents*. Nor is it probable that the extent and flourishing condition of the trade[48] and commerce of *Tyrus* should have been limited to that part of the Indian ocean to the southward of the Red Sea, which is a more difficult navigation than to the northward. That this commerce was extensive we have the authority of the prophet Ezekiel, who, in glowing terms, has painted its final destruction, and who, it may be remarked, is supposed to have lived at the very time the Phœnicians sailed round Africa by order of Necho. "Thy riches and thy fairs, thy merchandise, thy mariners and thy pilots, thy caulkers, and the occupiers of thy merchandize, and all thy men of war that are in thee, and in all thy company which is in the midst of thee, shall fall into the midst of the seas in the day of thy ruin." It is probable therefore that the navigation of the Eastern Seas was known in the earliest periods of history, and there seems to be no reason for supposing that the Chinese should not have had their share in it.

Without, however, making any enquiry into the probability that an ancient intercourse might have subsisted between China and the East coast of Africa, either by convention for commercial purposes, or that Chinese sailors might have been thrown on that coast either in Phœnician, or Arabian, or their own vessels, I happened to observe in a former publication of "*Travels in Southern Africa*," as a matter of fact, "that the upper lid of the eye of a real Hottentot, as in that of a Chinese, was rounded into the lower on the side next the nose, and that it formed not an angle as in the eye of an European—that from this circumstance they were known in the colony of the Cape by the name of *Chinese Hottentots*." Further observations have confirmed me in the very striking degree of resemblance between them. Their physical characters agree in|19| almost every point. The form of their persons in the remarkable smallness of the joints and the extremities, their voices and manner of speaking, their temper, their colour and features, and particularly that singular shaped eye rounded in the corner next the nose like the end of an ellipsis, probably of Tartar or Scythian origin, are nearly alike. They also agree in the broad root of the nose; or great distance between the eyes: and in the oblique position of these, which, instead of being horizontal, as is generally the case in European subjects, are depressed towards the nose. A Hottentot who attended me in travelling over Southern Africa was so very like a Chinese servant I had in Canton, both in person, features, manners, and tone of voice, that almost always inadvertently I called him by the name of the latter. Their hair, it is true, and that only differs. This, in a Hottentot, is rather harsh and wiry, than woolly, neither long, nor short, but twisted in hard curling ringlets resembling fringe. I possess not a sufficient degree of skill in physiology to say what kind of hair the offspring would have of a Chinese man and Mozambique woman; much less can I pretend to account for the origin of the Hottentot tribes, insulated on the narrow extremity of a large continent, and differing so remarkably from all their neighbours, or where to look for their primitive stock unless among the Chinese.

I am aware it will appear rather singular to those, who may have attended to the accounts that generally have been given of these two people, to meet with a comparison between the most polished and the most barbarous, the wisest and the most ignorant of mankind; and I am therefore the less surprized at|50| at an observation made by the writers of the Critical Review "that the fœtus of the Hottentots may resemble the Chinese, as the entrails of a pig resemble those of a man; but on this topic our ingenious author seems to wander beyond the circle of his knowledge." I hope these gentlemen will not be offended at my taking this occasion to assure them that the comparison was not even then made on loose grounds, although no inference was drawn from it, and that on a closer examination, I am the more convinced of their near resemblance in mental as well as physical qualities. The aptitude of a Hottentot in acquiring and combining ideas is not less than of a Chinese, and their powers of imitation are equally great, allowance being made for the difference of education; the one being continually from his infancy brought up in a society where all the arts and conveniences of life are in common use; the other among a miserable race of beings in constant want even of the common necessaries of life.

But as assertions and opinions prove nothing, I have annexed the portrait of a real Hottentot, drawn from the life by Mr. S. Daniell, in order to compare it with one of a Chinese, taken also from the life by Mr. Alexander; and I have no doubt that a close comparison of these portraits will convince the reader, as well as the reviewer, that the resemblance I remarked to have found was not altogether fanciful.

17

A Chinese.A Hottentot

Indeed the people that have derived their origins from the same stock with the Chinese, are more widely scattered over the Asiatic continent and the oriental islands than is generally[51]imagined. All those numerous societies, known under the common name of Malays, are unquestionably descended from the ancient inhabitants of Scythia or Tartary; and it may perhaps be added, that their connection with the Arabs and their conversion to Islamism first inspired, and have now rendered habitual, that cruel and sanguinary disposition for which they are remarkable; for it has been observed that the natives of those islands, to which the baleful influence of this religion has not extended, have generally been found a mild and inoffensive people; as was the case with regard to the natives of the Pelew islands when discovered by Captain Wilson.

The perusal of Mr. Marsden's excellent history of Sumatra leaves little doubt on my mind that a Chinese colony at some early period has settled on that island. This author observes that the eyes of the Sumatrans are little, and of the same kind as those of the Chinese; that they suffer their nails to grow long; that they excel in working fillagree, making gunpowder, &c. that they register events by making knots on cords; that they count decimally, write with a style on bamboo; that they have little hair on their bodies and heads, which little, like the Chinese, they extract. In their language, many words, I perceive, are similar; and the corresponding words express the same idea in both languages; but on etymological comparisons I would be understood to lay little stress, for reasons which will be assigned in the sixth chapter. The similitude of a religious ceremony is much stronger ground to build upon; and the coincidence is sufficiently remarkable, that the manner practised by the Sumatrans in taking a solemn oath should exactly agree with the same ce[52]remony which is used in giving a solemn pledge among the common people of China, namely, by wringing off the head of a cock. Captain Mackintosh told me that having once occasion to place great confidence in the matter of a Chinese vessel, and doubting lest he might betray it, the man felt himself considerably hurt, and said he would give him sufficient proof that he was to be trusted. He immediately procured a cock, and, falling down on both knees, wrung off his head; then holding up his hands towards heaven, he made use of these words: "If I act otherwise than as I have said, do thou, *o tien*, (Heaven) deal with me as I have dealt with this cock!"

I have since been informed, from the best authority, that whenever, in the course of the concerns of the British East India Company with the merchants of China, it may be necessary to administer an oath to a Chinese, the same ceremony is gone through of wringing off the head of a cock, which is by them considered in a very serious light, a sort of incantation, whose effects upon their minds are not unlike those produced by supposed magic spells, once common in our own country, by which the vulgar were persuaded that the Devil was to be made to appear before them. In a Chinese court of justice an oath is never administered. In a late affair, where a Chinese was killed by a seaman of a British man of war, and the Captain was about to administer an oath to two of his people whom he produced as evidences in a Chinese court of justice, the chief judge was so shocked, that he ordered the court to be instantly cleared.[53]

The *Cingalese* are unquestionably of Chinese origin. Those who are acquainted with the Chinese manners and character, will immediately perceive the very close resemblance, on reading Mr. Boyd's relation of his embassy to the King of Candy. *Sin-quo*, kingdom of *Sin*, (from whence Sina, or China,) are Chinese words; the termination is European. So also is the name of the island Chinese, *See-lan*, *See-long*, or *See-lung*, the Western Dragon, in conformity to an invariable custom of assigning the name of some animal to every mountain.

Having no intention, however, to investigate minutely the extent of Chinese navigation and commerce in ancient times, but rather to confine my observations to their present state, I return from this digression, in order to proceed on our voyage.

One of the small brigs, attending the expedition, was dispatched without loss of time to the port of *Chu-san*, to take on board the pilots that, agreeable to the order contained in the Imperial edict, were expected to be found in readiness to embark. In some of the passages, formed by the numerous islands, the currents ran with amazing rapidity, appearing more like the impetuous torrents of rivers, swelled by rains, than branches of the great ocean. The depth too of these narrow passages was so great as to make it difficult, dangerous, and frequently impossible, for ships to anchor in the event of a calm; in which case they must necessarily drive at the mercy of the stream. As we approached, in the Clarence brig, the high rocky point of the continent called *Kee-too*,|51| which juts into the midst of the cluster of islands, the wind suddenly failed us; and the current hurried us with such velocity directly towards the point, that we expected momentarily to be dashed in pieces; but on coming within twice the length of the ship of the perpendicular precipice, which was some hundred feet high, the eddy swept her round three several times with great rapidity. The Captain would have dropped the anchor, but an old Chinese fisherman, whom we had taken on board to pilot us, made signs that it was too deep, and, at the same time, that there was no danger, except that of the bowsprit striking against the mountain. The Chinese vessels have no bowsprit. At this moment the lead was thrown, but we got no soundings at the depth of one hundred and twenty fathoms; yet the yellow mud was brought up from the bottom in such quantities, that the Nile, at the height of its inundations, or the great Yellow River of China, could not be more loaded with mud than the sea was in the whirlpool of *Kee-too* point. The current, in the Strait of Faro, setting directly upon the rocks of Scylla, and the whirlpool of Charybdis, those celebrated objects of dread to ancient navigators, could not possibly have been more awfully terrific, though perhaps more dangerous, than the currents and the eddies that boiled tumultuously round this promontory of the Chinese continent, where,

"When the tide rushes from her rumbling caves
The rough rock roars, tumultuous boil the waves;
They toss, they foam, a wild confusion raise,
Like waters bubbling o'er the fiery blaze."

The second whirl removed us to a considerable distance from the point, and, after the third, we were swept rapidly along|52| in a smooth uniform current. Our interpreter, a Chinese priest, who had been educated in the college *de propaganda fide* at Naples, was not quite so composed as his countryman the pilot. The poor fellow, indeed, had nearly been thrown overboard by the boom of the mainsail, in the first, which was the most rapid, whirl of the ship; the same blow striking a sailor tossed his hat overboard; and it afforded some amusement, in our supposed perilous situation, to hear the different ejaculations of these two persons on the same occasion. *Sanctissima Maria, est miraculum, est miraculum!* exclaimed the priest, with great eagerness; whilst the sailor, rubbing his head, and walking away, with much composure observed, *that the d—n'd boom had carried away his fore-top-gallant cap!*

The Chinese, it seemed, had already been apprized of our arrival, for we had not proceeded far before a large vessel bore down towards us, and, hailing the brig in their own language, desired we would bring her to anchor, and that they would conduct us early the following morning into the harbour of Chu-san. Some of the officers came on board, were extremely civil, and presented us with a basket of fruit; but they affected to know nothing of the occasion that had brought us thither. Our old fisherman took out of the sea, (among thousands that had floated round our vessel) one of those animal substances which, I believe, we vulgarly call *sea blubbers* (MOLLUSCA *medusa porpita*). If was at least a foot in diameter. Having dressed it for his supper, and seeing it wear the inviting appearance of a transparent colourless jelly, I was tempted to taste it; but the|56| effect produced by this, or the fruit, or both, was a severe sickness, which continued for several days.

We weighed anchor at day-break, and, with a pleasant breeze, sailed in company with the clumsy-looking *junk*, which, however, to the surprise of our seamen, sailed quite as well as the smart-looking Clarence.

Having anchored before the town, in a spacious bason formed by several islands, and paid the usual compliment of a salute, a few Mandarines (officers of government so named by the early Portugueze from *mandar*, to command) came on board. To every question that led to the main point of our visit, these people gave us evasive answers, affecting the most complete ignorance of every thing relating to the affairs of the embassy. They said the *Tsung-*

ping, or military governor of the island, was then absent, but that he would return in the course of the day, and would be happy to see us on shore the following morning. Chinese etiquette, I suppose, required that a day should elapse before our reception in form.

Accordingly, at an early hour in the morning the gentlemen of the embassy, who had been sent on this business, went on shore, and were received by the Governor with great politeness, and abundant ceremony, in his hall of public audience, which, as a building, had little to attract our notice. The usual minute enquiries being gone through, which, it seems, Chinese good-breeding cannot dispense with, such as the health of his visitors, of their parents and relations, and particularly[57] the name and age of each person, the object of our visit was explained to him; and at the same time a hope expressed that there would be no delay in getting the pilots on board. The old gentleman appeared to be much surprized at such violent haste, and talked of plays, feasts, and entertainments, that he meant to give us. Pilots, however, he said, were ready to take charge of the ships, and to carry them along the coast to the next province, where others would be found to conduct them still farther. On being told that such a mode of navigation was utterly impracticable for the large English ships, and that such pilots would be of no use to us, he begged to be allowed the remainder of the day to enquire for others. We little expected to have met with any difficulties with regard to pilots, in one of the best and most frequented ports in China, where, at that time several hundred vessels were lying at anchor. The remainder of the day was spent in a visit to the city of *Ting-hai;* but the crowd became so numerous, and the day was so excessively hot, that before we had passed the length of a street, we were glad to take refuge in a temple, where the priests very civilly entertained us with tea, fruit, and cakes. The officer who attended us advised us to return in sedan chairs, an offer which we accepted; but the bearers were stopped every moment by the crowd, in order that every one might satisfy his curiosity by thrusting his head in at the window, and exclaiming, with a grin, *Hung-mau! Englishman,* or, literally, *Redpate!* Rather disappointed than gratified, we were glad, after a fatiguing day, to throw ourselves into our cots on board the Clarence.[58]

When we went on shore the following morning, we found the military governor, attended by a civil magistrate, by whom, after the usual compliments, we were addressed, in a long oration, delivered apparently with a great deal of solemnity, the intention of which was to convince us that, as it had been the practice of the Chinese, for time immemorial, to navigate from port to port, experience had taught them it was the best. Finding, however, that his eloquence could not prevail on his hearers to relinquish their own opinions on the subject, the governor and he consulted together for some time, and at length resolved that a general muster should be made of all the persons in that place, who had at any time visited by sea the port of *Tien-sing.*

A number of soldiers were accordingly dispatched, and soon returned, with a set of the most miserable-looking wretches I ever beheld; who were thrust into the hall, and dropping on their knees, were examined in that attitude, as to their qualifications. Some, it appeared, had been at the port of *Tien-sing,* but were no seamen; others followed the profession, but had never been at that port; and several were hauled in, who had never set a foot on board a vessel of any description whatsoever. In short, the greater part of the day was consumed to no purpose; and we were about to conclude that we had a great chance of leaving the central and much frequented harbour of *Chu-san,* without being able to procure a single pilot, when two men were brought in, who seemed to answer the purpose better than any which had yet been examined. It appeared, however, that they had quitted the sea for many years, and[59] being comfortably settled in trade, had no desire to engage in the present service; on the contrary, they begged on their knees that they might be excused from such an undertaking. Their supplications were of no avail. The Emperor's orders must be obeyed. In vain did they plead the ruin of their business by their absence, and the distress it would occasion to their wives, their children, and their families. The Governor was inexorable; and they were ordered to be ready to embark in the course of an hour.

This arbitrary proceeding of the Governor conveyed no very exalted ideas of the justice or moderation of the government, or of the protection it afforded to the subject. To drag away from his family an honest and industrious citizen, settled in trade, and to force him into a service that must be ruinous to his concerns, was an act of injustice and violence that could not be tolerated in any other than a despotic government, where the subject knows no laws but the will of the tyrant. But we are yet on a distant island of the Great Empire, remote from the fountain of authority; and delegated power, in all countries, is but too liable to be abused. Besides, a Chinese might be impressed with sentiments equally unfavourable of our government, were he informed of the manner in which imperious necessity sometimes requires our navy to be manned.

One consideration, however, might with safety be drawn from the occurrences of this day, which was this, that long voyages are never undertaken where they can be avoided; but that the commerce of the Yellow Sea is carried on from[01] port to port; and that the articles of merchandize so transported must necessarily have many profits upon them, before they come to the distant consumer; which may, in some degree, account for the high prices many of the products of the country, as we afterwards found, bore in the capital. In like manner was the inland commerce of Asia conducted by caravans, proceeding from station to station, at each of which were merchants to buy or exchange commodities with each other, those at the limits of the journey having no connection nor communication whatsoever with one another; which will partly explain the ignorance of the Greeks with regard to the Eastern countries, from whence they derived their precious stones, perfumes, and other valuable articles.

The old Governor was evidently relieved from a load of anxiety at his success; and the tears and entreaties of the poor men served only to brighten up his countenance. From civility, or curiosity, or perhaps both, he returned our visit on board the brig, which had been crowded with the natives from morning till night, since her first arrival in the harbour. The want of curiosity, which has been supposed to form a part of the Chinese character, was not perceived in this instance; but it was that sort of curiosity, which appeared rather to be incited by the desire of looking narrowly at the persons of those who were to have the honour of being presented to their Great Emperor, than for the sake of gratifying the eye or the mind, by the acquirement of information or new ideas. The vessel, although so very different from their own, was an object of little notice; and although eager to get a transient glance at[01] the passengers, their curiosity was satisfied in a moment, and was generally accompanied with some vague exclamation, in which the words *Ta-whang-tee* occurred; and the main drift of which seemed to imply, "is this person to appear before our Great Emperor?" This was still more remarkable in the crowd of *Ting-hai*; nothing scarcely was there heard but the words *Ta-whang-tee* and *Hung-mau*, the Emperor and the Englishman.

The squadron had scarcely got under way, and cleared the narrow passages between the islands into the Yellow Sea, when it was perceived how very little advantage it was likely to derive from the Chinese pilots. One of them, in fact, had come on board without his compass, and it was in vain to attempt to make him comprehend ours. The moveable card was to him a paradox, as being contrary to the universal practice with them, of making the needle traverse the fixed points, and not the points described on the card to move (by the needle being attached to the card), as in those of Europe. The other was furnished with a compass, about the size of a common snuff-box, being an entire piece of wood, with a circular excavation in the centre, just large enough to admit the vibration of a very fine steel needle, not quite an inch in length, which, however, might be found sufficiently useful, in their short voyages, by means of a peculiar contrivance for preserving the center of gravity, in all positions of the ship, in coincidence nearly with the center of suspension. Nor is it necessary, in so short and fine a needle, to load one end more than the other, in order to counteract the dip, or tendency that the magnetic[62] needle is known to have, more or less, towards the horizon in different parts of the world. The Chinese, however, do not seem to have adopted their small needle from any knowledge either of the variation, or of the inclination of the magnetic needle. Although the needle be invariably small, yet it sometimes happens that the margin of the box is extended to such a size, as to contain from twenty to thirty concentric circles, containing various characters of the language, constituting a compendium of their astronomical (perhaps more properly speaking) astrological knowledge. As numbers of such compasses are in the museums of Europe, it may not perhaps be wholly unacceptable to give some notion of what these circles of characters contain.

1. Central circle, or the needle.

2. 8 mystical characters denoting the first principles of matter, said to be invented by *Fo-shee*, the founder of the monarchy.

3. The names of the 12 hours into which the day is divided.

4 and 5. Names of the circumpolar stars.

6. Characters of the 24 principal meridians or colures.

7. The 24 subdivisions or seasons of the year.

8. The characters of the cycle of 60 years.

9. Numerical characters relating to the above cycle.

10. Characters denoting the 28 signs of the Zodiac.

11. Certain astrological characters.

12. Eight sentences explanatory of the 8 mystical characters on the second circle.

13. A different arrangement of the Chinese cycle.

14. Characters of the five elements.

|63|

15. Repetition of the characters on the eighth circle.

16. Repetition of the eighth circle.

17, and 18. Characters of obscure mythology.

19. Names of 28 constellations and their places in the heavens.

20. Relates to the sixth and fifteenth circles.

21. The world divided according to the sidereal influences.

22. Corresponds with the eighth and fifteenth circles.

23. Contains the same as the above with the addition of the fourteenth circle.

24, and 35. Are inexplicable even by the Chinese.

26. An arrangement of certain characters and marks for calculating lucky, unlucky, and neutral days.

27, is the same as the nineteenth, and surrounds the whole[5].

The greatest depth of the Yellow Sea, in the track of the ships, did not exceed thirty-six fathoms, and it was frequently diminished to ten fathoms. The weather, as usually happens in shallow seas, was generally hazy. In doubling the projecting promontory of the province of Shan-tung, the land was hidden in thick fogs. And on these, fortunately, dissipating, it was perceived that the whole squadron was within four miles of the main land, and one of the ships close upon a rocky island. The pilots were as ignorant of our situa|64|tion as the meanest sailor in the squadron. Proceeding to the westward, a capacious bay was discovered. One of the pilots, after a minute examination of the land, which was now clear, asserted that he knew the place very well; that it was the bay of *Mee-a-taw*. The confidence with which he spoke, and the vast concourse of people, crowding down towards the shore, as if expecting our arrival, induced the Commander to steer directly into the bay: but the depth of water diminishing to five fathoms, and land appearing on every side, it was thought prudent to let go the anchor. Several boats from the shore were presently along-side; and we were soon convinced how little we had to trust to the knowledge of our pilots, even within sight of land. We were informed that the bay was called *Kee-san-seu*, and that *Mee-a-taw* was, at least, fifteen leagues farther to the westward.

The hills along this southern coast of the gulph of Pe-tche-lee have a very peculiar character. They are all of the same form and nearly of the same size, being regular cones with smooth sides as if fashioned by art, and entirely detached, each standing on its proper base, resembling in their shapes the summer caps worn by the officers of government; and having, as yet, no European names, they were noticed in the journals by the appellation of the first, second, third, &c., mandarin's bonnets.

Determining now to avail ourselves of the advice given by the magistrate of *Chu-san*, and to navigate from port to port, we here procured two new pilots to carry the ships to *Mee-a-taw*. They brought us indeed to this place, but, instead of a|65| harbour, we found only a narrow strait, with a rapid tide setting through it, and rocky anchoring ground. On the shore of the continent was a city of considerable extent, under the walls of which next the sea was a bason or dock, filled with vessels whose capacity might be from ten to one hundred tons.

22

The Governor of this city (the name of which we learned to be *Ten-tchoo-foo*) paid his respects to the embassador on board the Lion, and observed in the course of conversation that his orders from court were to render all the service in his power to the embassy, and to provide proper means of conveyance, either by land or by sea. He seemed to be about the age of five and thirty, a man of frank and easy manners, courteous, intelligent, and inquisitive. He stood higher in the opinion of all of us than any we had yet seen. The following morning he sent off what he was pleased to call a trifling refreshment, which consisted of four bullocks, eight sheep, eight goats, five sacks of fine white rice, five sacks of red rice, two hundred pounds of flour, and several baskets of fruit and vegetables.

We have always been taught to believe that the Chinese consider us as barbarians; but we have hitherto no reason to say that they treated us as such. At all events it was obvious that the expected arrival of the British embassy had made no slight impression on the court of Pekin.

Here we once more ventured on another pilot to carry the ships across the gulph of *Pe-tche-lee* to *Tien-sing*. He was an old man of 70 years, and seemed to possess a perfect knowledge[66] of all the bays and harbours in the gulph. He drew on paper the sketch of a port on the western coast to which he undertook to carry the ships. Fortunately, however, for us, it was considered more safe to send the small brigs a-head to sound, than to place any confidence in men who had already so often deceived us. They had scarcely departed before the signal of danger was made; a new course was steered for the night, and early the following morning, the same signal was repeated. No land was now in sight, yet the water had shallowed to six fathoms; it was therefore deemed prudent to come to an anchor. It was a very unusual situation for such large ships to ride thus at anchor in the middle of a strange sea, and out of sight of land, yet liable, in case of blowing weather, to strike against the bottom.

The commanders of the ships were exasperated against the pilots, and these on their part were almost petrified with fear. The poor creatures had done their best, but they possessed neither skill nor judgment, or, perhaps, it may be more charitable to suppose that they were confused by the novelty of their situation. It was in vain to endeavour to make them comprehend the difference in the draught of water between their own ships and ours, which, in the latter, was as many fathoms as feet in the former, although they were palpably shewn, by a piece of rope, the depth that was required.

As it was evidently impracticable to proceed farther with our own ships towards the land, which was now from twelve to fifteen miles distant, and so very low as not to be visible[67] the deck, one of the tenders was dispatched to the mouth of the *Pei-ho* or white river to report our arrival. Here two officers from the court had already embarked to wait on the Embassador, carrying with them a present of refreshments, consisting of bullocks, hogs, sheep, poultry, wine, fruit, and vegetables, in such quantities, as to be more than sufficient for a a week's consumption of the whole squadron, amounting nearly to six hundred men. It consisted in twenty small bullocks, one hundred hogs, one hundred sheep, one thousand fowls, three thousand pumpkins, as many melons, apples, pears, plumbs, apricots, and other fruits, with an abundance of culinary vegetables. The wine was contained in large earthen jars whose covers were closely luted. Numbers of the hogs and the fowls had been bruised to death on the passage, which were thrown overboard from the Lion with disdain, but the Chinese eagerly picked them up, washed them clean and laid them in salt.

The number of vessels they had dispatched to take on shore the presents and the baggage was between thirty and forty, the capacity of each not being less, and many of them more, than two hundred tons; so imperfect a judgment had these people formed of the quantity of articles to be transhipped. These were the vessels whose holds were divided into thirteen distinct compartments, separated by partitions of two inch plank, the seams of which were caulked with a preparation of fine lime made from shells, and fibres of bamboo, in order to render them water-tight. Their sails, cables, rigging and[68] cordage were all made of bamboo; and neither pitch nor tar was used on these or any part of the wood-work.

We detained about fifteen of these vessels to take on shore the Embassador's suite, the presents for the Emperor, and the baggage; after which the British ships returned to *Chu-*

*san*without the assistance of the Chinese pilots, whose skill in navigation was held very cheap, by the lowest seamen on board.

On entering the *Pei-ho* we observed a number of buildings erected on the right bank, with roofs of matting, but decorated in the most fantastical manner, with different coloured ribbands and variegated silks; and about three hundred soldiers in their uniforms (which appeared to our eye not much adapted to military purposes) were drawn out, with a band of music, near a temporary landing-place constructed of wood; all of which we understood had been hastily prepared for the reception of the Embassador; but as his Excellency was desirous of reaching the capital without delay, he declined going on shore, preferring to step into the accommodation yachts at once, that were ready to receive him, a little higher up the river, the moment that the presents should be transhipped into the river-craft. The officers who were deputed to conduct him to the capital observed, that so much haste was not at all necessary, as the Emperor's birth-day was yet distant; these people having no other idea of an embassy, as it seemed, than that of its being a mere compliment to their Sovereign. The yellow flags dis[69]played at the mast-heads of the river fleet, laden with the presents, and consisting of seventeen sail, gave, indeed, a more extended meaning of such a mission. These flags, in broad black characters, bore the following inscription; *The English Embassador carrying Tribute to the Emperor of China.*

We found the yachts that were destined to convey us exceedingly convenient, more so indeed than any I have seen on our canals of England. They are flat bottomed, and draw only about fifteen inches of water. Their upper works are high, appearing indeed like a floating house. They have three apartments for the accommodation of passengers; the first an antichamber for the servants and baggage; the middle a commodious sitting and dining room, about fifteen feet square; and the third divided into two or three sleeping rooms. Behind these is the kitchen; and still farther aft, small places like dog-kennels, for the boatmen. Sometimes there is a kind of second story, upon the apartments, divided into little cells, that are just the length and breadth of a man. A Chinese sailor requires no room for luggage, his whole wardrobe being generally on his back. In the different operations employed for making the yachts proceed, they give no interruption to the passengers. A projecting gangway on each side of the vessel, made of broad planks, serves as the passage from one end to the other.

The two officers that were sent from court, to conduct the Embassador to the capital, paid a visit to every yacht, and shewed the most earnest desire to please and to make us comfortable. Their names were *Van* and *Chou*, to which they annexed the title[70] of *Ta-gin*, or *great man*. *Van* had the rank of Lieutenant-General in the army, and *Chou* was the Governor of a district in *Pe-tche-lee*. We observed in their manners no indication of that stiff and ceremonious conduct, which custom obliges them to put on in public. On the contrary, they sat down to table with us, endeavouring to learn the use of the knife and fork, and made themselves extremely agreeable; lamented they were not able to hold conversation with us in our own language; and on going away, shook hands with us like Englishmen.

Provisions, fruit, and wines (such as the country affords) were sent on board in such profusion, that I really believe the Chinese boatmen, in the course of the passage up this river, were enabled to lay by their winter's stock from the surplus. In truth, as Sir George Staunton has observed, the hospitality, attention, and respect we hitherto experienced, were such as strangers meet with only in the Eastern parts of the world.

Nothing that could convey the idea of extraordinary wealth or comfort among the inhabitants, or of extraordinary abundance and fertility in the country, (unless in the copious supplies of our provisions) had yet occurred, either at *Chu-san* or in the first three days' sail up the *Pei-ho* towards the capital. The land on both sides was low and flat, and instead of hedge-rows, trenches were dug to mark the boundaries of property. A small proportion only was under cultivation. The greater part appeared to be sour swampy ground, covered with coarse grass, with bushes, and the common reed. There were few trees, except near the villages, which were of mean appearance,[71] the houses generally consisting of mud walls, one story in height, and thatched with straw or rushes. Here and there a solitary cottage intervened, but nothing that bore any resemblance to the residence of a gentleman, or that could even be called a comfortable farm-house. And although villages were numerous, no assemblage of houses were perceived, that properly could be classed under the name of a town, except that of *See-koo*, near the mouth of the river, and *Ta-koo*, a few miles higher, until we proceeded to the distance of about ninety miles, when we entered the suburbs of the large city of *Tien-sing*, stretching, like London on the Thames, for several miles along each bank of the river *Pei-ho*. But neither the buildings nor the river would bear any comparison, even with those parts about Redriffe and Wapping. Every thing, in fact, that we had hitherto seen wore an air of poverty and meanness. After a long confinement on board a ship, to those at least who are not accustomed to it, almost any country appears to possess the charms of a Paradise; yet on our first landing in this celebrated empire to the present place, which is no great distance from the capital, I am persuaded, that every individual of the embassy felt himself rather disappointed in the expectations he had formed. If any thing excited admiration, it was the vast multitudes of people that, from our first arrival, had daily flocked down to the banks of the river, of both sexes and of all ages. Their general appearance, however, was not such as to indicate any extraordinary degree of happiness or comfort. The best dressed men wore a sort of velvet cap on their heads; a short jacket, buttoned close round the neck, and folded across the breast, the sleeves remarkably wide; the materials cotton cloth, black, [72] blue, or brown silk, or European camblet; they wore quilted petticoats, and black sattin boots. The common people were dressed in large straw hats, blue or black cotton frocks, wide cotton trowsers, and thick clumsy shoes, sometimes made of straw. Some had coarse stockings of cotton cloth; the legs of others were naked. A single pair of drawers constituted indeed the whole clothing of a great portion of the crowd.

Never were poor women fitted out in a style so disadvantageous for setting off their charms as those who made their appearance on the banks of the *Pei-ho*, and we afterwards found that the dress of these, with some slight variations, was the common mode of the country. Bunches of large artificial flowers, generally resembling *asters*, whose colours were red, blue, or yellow, were stuck in their jet-black hair, which, without any pretensions to taste or freedom, was screwed up close behind, and folded into a ridge or knot across the crown of the head, not very unlike (except in the want of taste) to the present mode in which the young ladies of England braid their locks. Two bodkins of silver, brass, or iron, were conspicuously placed behind the head, in the form of an oblique cross, which is the common mode of Malay women. Their faces and necks were daubed with white paint, the eye-brows blackened, and on the center of the lower lip, and at the point of the chin, were two spots, about the size of a small wafer, of a deep vermillion colour. A blue cotton frock, like that of the men, reaching in some to the middle of the thigh, in others to the knee, was almost universal. A pair of wide trowsers, of different colours, but commonly either red, green, [73] or yellow, extended a little below the calf of the leg, where they were drawn close, in order the better to display an ankle and a foot, which for singularity at least, may challenge the whole world. This distorted and disproportionate member consists of a foot that has been cramped in its growth, to the length of four or five inches, and an ankle that is generally swollen in the same proportion that the foot is diminished. The little shoe is as fine as tinsel and tawdry can make it, and the ankle is bandaged round with party-coloured clothes, ornamented with fringe and tassels; and such a leg and foot, thus dressed out, are considered in China as superlatively beautiful.

The constant pain and uneasiness that female children must necessarily suffer, in the act of compressing, by means of bandages, the toes under the sole of the foot, and retaining them in that position until they literally grow into and become a part of it; and by forcing the heel forward, until it is entirely obliterated, make it the more wonderful how a custom, so unnatural and inhuman, should have continued for so many ages, at least such is the opinion, that its origin is entirely unknown, or explained by such fabulous absurdities as are too ridiculous to assign for its adoption.

Few savage tribes are without the unnatural custom of maiming or lopping off some part of the human body, as boring the lips and the cartilege of the nose, drawing or colouring the teeth, cutting off a joint from the fingers or toes, and otherwise practising, as they must suppose, improvements on nature. But on this consideration it would scarcely be fair [74] to conclude, that maiming the feet of the Chinese ladies derived its origin from a period of time when they were yet in a savage state, since we are in the daily habit of observing the most civilized and enlightened societies studying to find out beauties in defects, and creating them where nature had intended perfection. The Chinese would no doubt be equally surprized at, and consider as egregiously absurd, the custom of circumcision, as practiced by a great portion of Asiatic nations; nor have we any reason to think they would not condemn the refinement of docks and crops among our horses as an absurd custom, not less ridiculous in their eyes, than the little feet of their ladies are in ours. If they could not refrain from bursting into fits of laughter on examining the grease and powder with which our hair was disfigured; and if they sometimes lamented that so much oil and flour had unnecessarily been wasted, we might, perhaps, in the vanity of self-importance, affect to pity their taste; but setting custom and prejudice apart, we had certainly no great reason to despise and ridicule the Chinese, or indeed any other nation, merely because they differ from us in the little points of dress and manners, seeing how very nearly we can match them with similar follies and absurdities of our own.

The silence of the earliest travellers into China on so extraordinary a custom, would almost warrant a conjecture that, notwithstanding the pretended ignorance of the Chinese with regard to its origin, both the fashion and the sentiment of its being vulgar for ladies to be seen abroad, were only adopted within the period of a few centuries. The Venetian traveller, [75] although he makes frequent mention of the beauty and dress of the women, takes no notice of this singular fashion; and he observes that on the lake of *Hang-tchoo-foo* the ladies are accustomed to take their pleasure with their husbands and their families. The Embassadors also of Shah Rokh, the son of Tamerlane, who in the year 1419, were sent to congratulate the Emperor of China, state in the narrative of their expedition that, at their public reception, there stood two young virgins, one on each side of the throne, with their faces and bosoms uncovered; that they were furnished with paper and pencils and took down with great attention every word that the Emperor spoke. These Embassadors saw also numbers of women in open baths near the Yellow River; and, in one city, they remark that "there were many taverns, at the doors of which sat a number of young girls of extraordinary beauty." Nor do the travels of two Mahomedans into China in the ninth century, published by Mr. Renaudot, make any mention of the unnatural smallness of the women's feet; and they are not by any means deficient in their observations of the manners and customs of this nation, at that time so very little known to the rest of the world. Almost every thing they have related concerning China at this early period is found to be true at the present day, and as they particularly notice the dress and ornaments worn by the women, one would think they would not have omitted a custom so singular in its kind as that of maiming the feet, if it had then been as common as it now is. [76]

This monstrous fashion has generally been attributed to the jealousy of the men. Admitting this to have been the case, the Chinese must be allowed to be well versed in the management of the sex, to have so far gained the ascendancy over them, as to prevail upon them to adopt a fashion, which required a voluntary relinquishment of one of the greatest pleasures and blessings of life, the faculty of locomotion; and to contrive to render this fashion so universal that any deviation from it should be considered as disgraceful. The desire of being thought superior to the rest of his fellows sometimes, indeed, leads a man into strange extravagancies. Upon this principle the men of learning, as they are pleased to style themselves, suffer the nails of their little fingers to grow sometimes to the enormous length of three inches for the sole purpose of giving ocular demonstration of the impossibility of their being employed in any sort of manual labour; and upon the same principle, perhaps, the ladies of China may be induced to continue the custom of maiming their female infants, in order that their children may be distinguished from those of the peasantry, who, in most of the provinces, are condemned to submit to the drudgery of the field.

The interior wrappers of the ladies' feet are said to be seldom changed, remaining, sometimes, until they can no longer hold together; a custom that conveys no very favourable idea of Chinese cleanliness. This, indeed, forms no part of their character; on the contrary they are what Swift would call a *frowzy* people. The comfort of clean linen, or frequent change [77] of under-garments, is equally unknown to the Sovereign and to the peasant. A sort of thin coarse silk supplies the place of cotton or linen next the skin, among the upper ranks; but the common people wear a coarse kind of open cotton cloth. These vestments are more rarely removed for the purpose of washing than for that of being replaced with new ones; and the consequence of such neglect or economy is, as might naturally be supposed, an abundant increase of those vermin to whose production filthiness is found to be most favourable. The highest officers of state made no hesitation of calling their attendants in public to seek in their necks for those troublesome animals, which, when caught, they very composedly put between their teeth. They carry no pocket handkerchiefs, but generally blow their noses into small square pieces of paper which some of their attendants have ready prepared for the purpose. Many are not so cleanly, but spit about the rooms, or against the walls like the French, and they wipe their dirty hands in the sleeves of their gowns. They sleep at night in the same clothes they wear by day. Their bodies are as seldom washed as their articles of dress. They never make use of the bath, neither warm nor cold. Notwithstanding the vast number of rivers and canals, with which every part of the country is intersected, I do not remember to have seen a single groupe of boys bathing. The men, in the hottest day of summer, make use of warm water for washing the hands and face. They are unacquainted with the use of soap. We procured, in Pekin, a sort of Barilla with which and apricot oil we manufactured a sufficient quantity of this article to wash our linen, which, however, we were under the necessity of getting done by our own servants.[78]

On approaching the town of *Tien-sing* we observed a prodigious number of large stacks of salt, piled up in sacks of matting. The quantity thus stored was found, on rough calculation, to be sufficient for the consumption of thirty millions of people, for a whole year. Such a surprising aggregate of one of the useful and almost necessary, articles of life, was a preparative, in some measure, for the vast multitudes of people which appeared on our passing this northern emporium of China. The gabelle, or duty on salt, which the government here, as well as elsewhere, had found convenient to impose on one of the indispensable articles of life, partly accounted for such an extraordinary accumulation. The collector of the salt duties of *Tien-sing* held one of the most lucrative appointments in the gift of the crown.

The crowds of large vessels lying close together along the sides of the river; the various kinds of craft passing and re-passing; the town and manufactories and warehouses extending on each bank as far as the eye could reach, indicated a spirit of commerce far beyond any thing we had hitherto met with. The large vessels, the small craft, the boats, the shores, the walls surrounding the houses, the roofs were all covered with spectators. Our barges, being retarded in the narrow passages among the shipping, were at least two hours in reaching the head of the town. During the whole time the populace stood in the water, the front rank up to the middle, to get a peep at the strangers. Hitherto among the spectators there had generally appeared full as many of the fair sex as of the other; and the elderly dames, in[79] particular, had been so curious as to dip their little stumps into the water in order to have a peep into the barges as they glided slowly along; but here, among the whole crowd, not a single female was visible. Although the day was extremely sultry, the thermometer of Fahrenheit being 88° in the shade, as a mutual accommodation their heads were all uncovered, and their bald pates exposed to the scorching rays of the sun. It was an uncommon spectacle to see so many bronze-like heads stuck as close together, tier above tier, as Hogarth's groupe, intended to display the difference between character and caricature, but it lacked the variety of countenance which this artist has, in an inimitable manner, displayed in his picture.

The deep sounding *gong*, a sort of brazen kettle struck with a mallet, and used in the barges to direct the motions of the trackers on shore, the kettle-drums and the trumpets in the military band, the shrill music and squalling recitative in the theatre, which was entirely open in front, and facing the river in full view of the crowd; the number of temporary booths and buildings erected for the use of the viceroy, governor, judges, and other officers of government, and gaily decorated with ribbands and silken streamers; the buzz and merriment of the crowd had, altogether, so striking an affinity to the usual entertainments of Bartholomew fair, that no extraordinary stretch of the imagination was required to suppose ourselves for the moment to have been transported into Smithfield. We instantly acquitted the Chinese of any want of curiosity. The arrival of Elfi Bey in London drew not half the crowd; and yet the Chinese account[80] us much greater barbarians than we pretend to consider the mamelukes. The old viceroy of the province, a Tartar of mild and winning manners, had prepared for us a most magnificent entertainment with wine, fruits, and great variety of pastry and sweetmeats, together with presents of tea, silk, and nankins, not only to the Embassador and his suite, but also to the servants, musicians, and soldiers.

The cheerful and good-natured countenances of the multitude were extremely prepossessing; not less so their accommodating behaviour to one another. There was an innocence and simplicity in their features, that seemed to indicate a happy and contented turn of mind. This, however, being a sort of gala day, we might, on account of the extraordinary occasion, perhaps have viewed them to the best advantage; yet the same cheerful and willing mind had constantly shewn itself on all occasions, by all those who were employed in the service of the embassy. On board the yachts constant mirth and good humour prevailed among the seamen. When the weather was calm, the vessels were generally pushed on by means of two large sculls or oars turning upon pivots that were placed in projecting pieces of wood near the *bow* of the vessel, and not the stern, as is the practice of most other nations. From six to ten men are required to work one of these oars, which, instead of being taken out of the water, as in the act of rowing, are moved backwards and forwards under the surface, in a similar manner to what in England is understood by sculling. To lighten their labour, and assist in keeping time with the strokes, the following rude[81] air was generally sung by the master to which the whole crew used to join in chorus:

MIDI

On many a calm still evening, when a dead silence reigned upon the water, have we listened with pleasure to this artless and unpolished air, which was sung, with little alteration through the whole fleet. Extraordinary exertions of bodily strength, depending, in a certain degree, on the willingness of the mind, are frequently accompanied with exhilarating exclamations among the most savage people; but the Chinese song could not be considered in this point of view; like the exclamations of our seamen in hauling the ropes, or the oar song of the Hebridians, which, as Doctor Johnson has observed, resembled the proceleusmatick verse by which the rowers of Grecian[82] galleys were animated, the chief object of the Chinese chorus seemed to be that of combining chearfulness with regularity.

"Verse sweetens toil, however rude the sound."

Of their honesty, sobriety, and carefulness, we had already received convincing proofs. Of the number of packages, amounting to more than six hundred, of various sizes and descriptions, not a single article was missing nor injured, on their arrival at the capital, notwithstanding they had been moved about, and carried by land, and transhipped several times. Of the three state-officers, who had been deputed from court to attend the embassy, two of them were the most obliging and attentive creatures imaginable. The third, a Tartar, who first made his appearance at *Tien-sing*, was distant, proud, and imperious. The Chinese indeed were invariably more affable than the Tartars. In short, had we returned to Europe, without proceeding farther in the country than *Tien-sing*, a most lively impression would always have remained on my mind in favour of the Chinese. But a variety of incidents that afterwards occurred, and a more intimate acquaintance with their manners and habits, produced a woeful change of sentiment in this respect. Of such incidents, as may tend to illustrate the moral character of this extraordinary people, I shall relate a few that were the most striking, in taking a general view of their state of society, to which, and to the nature of the executive government, all their moral actions may be referred: and by the influence of which, the natural bent of their character evidently has undergone a complete change.[83]

Leaving *Tien-sing* on the 11th of August, we found the river considerably contracted in its dimensions, and the stream more powerful. The surface of the country, in fact, began to assume a less uniform appearance, being now partly broken into hill and dale; but nothing approaching to a mountain was yet visible in any direction. It was still however scantily wooded, few trees appearing except large willows on the banks, and knots of elms, or firs, before the houses of men in office, and the temples, both of which were generally found at the head of each village. More grain was here cultivated than on the plains near the mouth of the river. Two species of millet, the *panicum crus galli*, and the *italicum*, and two of a larger grain, the *holcus sorghum*, and the *saccharatus*, were the most abundant. We observed also a few patches of buck-wheat, and different sorts of kidney-beans; but neither common wheat, barley, nor oats. A species of nettle, the *urtica nivea* was also sown in square patches, for the purpose of converting its fibres into thread, of which they manufacture a kind of cloth. We saw no gardens nor pleasure-grounds, but considerable tracts of pasture or meadow-land intervened between the villages, on which however were few cattle, and those few remarkably small. Those we procured for the use of the ships along the coast of the gulph of *Pe-tche-lee*, seldom exceeded the weight of two hundred pounds. The few sheep we saw were of the broad-tailed species. The cottages of the peasantry were very mean, without any appearance of comfort, and thinly scattered; seldom standing alone, but generally collected into small villages.[84]

If, however, cities, towns, villages, and farm-houses, were less abundant so near the capital, than from the relations of travellers we had expected to find them, the multitudes of inhabitants whose constant dwelling was on the water, amply made up the apparent deficiency on shore. We passed, in one day, upon this river, more than six hundred large vessels, having each a range of ten or twelve distinct apartments built upon the deck, and each apartment contained a whole family. The number of persons in one of these vessels, we reckoned, on an average, to be about fifty, and we actually counted above one thousand vessels of this description, that were floating on that part of the river, between *Tien-sing* and *Tong-tchoo*. The different kinds of craft, besides these, that were perpetually passing and re-passing, or lying chained to the banks of the river, all of which were crowded with men, women, and children, contained full as many as the large vessels above mentioned; so that, in the distance of ninety miles, on this small branch of a river, there were floating on the water not fewer than one hundred thousand souls.

Among the different cargoes of cotton wool, copper-money, rice, silk, salt, tea, and other commodities for the supply of the capital, we observed an article of commerce, in several of the large open craft, that puzzled us not a little to find out for what it was intended. It consisted of dry brown cakes, not much larger but thicker than those we call crumpets. A close examination, however, soon discovered the nature of their composition, which, it seemed, was a mixture of every kind of filth and excrementitious substances, moulded into their present shape, and dried in the sun. In this form they are carried to[85] the capital as articles of merchandize, where they meet with a ready market from the gardeners in the vicinity; who, after dissolving them in urine, use them for manure.

Little occurred that was worthy of note, between *Tien-sing* and *Tong-tchoo*, except an instance in the exercise of arbitrary power, not less cruel than that of the Governor of *Chu-san*, and ill agreeing with the feelings of Englishmen. Some of our provisions happened one morning to be a little tainted, which could not be wondered at, considering the heat of the weather, the mercury, by Fahrenheit's scale, being from 82° to 88°. The officers, however, who had been commissioned to furnish the supply of provisions, were instantly deprived of their rank, and all their servants severely bambooed. The Embassador interceded with *Van* and *Chou* in favour of the degraded delinquents, was heard with great attention, but perceived that little indulgence or relaxation from strict discipline was to be expected on such occasions.

The whole distance, from the entrance of the *Pei-ho* to the city of *Tong-tchoo* is about one hundred and seventy miles. Here we found two buildings, that had been erected in the space of two days, for the temporary purpose of receiving the presents and baggage; and they were constructed of such large dimensions, that they were capable of containing at least ten times the quantity. The materials were wooden poles and mats, and a fence of wooden paling surrounded the whole.

We took up our lodging in a spacious temple in the suburbs, from whence the priests were turned out without the least[86] ceremony, to make room for us, consisting in the whole of one hundred persons nearly. And here it was settled we should remain until every article was landed, and coolies or porters procured sufficient to carry the whole at once to

Pekin, which was computed to be about twelve miles to the westward from this place. And although near three thousand men were required for this purpose, they were supplied the instant the goods were all on shore; nor did it appear that any difficulty would have been found in raising double that number, as there seemed to be ten times the number of idle spectators as of persons employed. The plain between the landing-place and the temple was like a fair, and cakes, rice, tea, and fruit upon masses of ice, and many other refreshments were exposed for sale, under large square umbrellas, that served instead of booths. A slice of water-melon, cooled on ice, was sold for one *tchen*, a piece of base copper coin, of the value of about three-tenths of a farthing. Not a single woman appeared among the many thousand spectators that were assembled on the plain.

CHAP. III.
Journey through the Capital to a Country Villa of the Emperor.
Return to Pekin. The Imperial Palace and Gardens
of Yuen-min-yuen, and the Parks of Gehol.

Order of Procession from Tong-choo to the Capital.—Crowd assembled on the Occasion.— Appearance of Pekin without and within the Walls.—Some Account of this City.—Proceed to a Country Villa of the Emperor.—Inconveniences of.—Return to Pekin.—Embassador proceeds to Tartary.— Author sent to the Palace of Yuen-min-yuen.—Miserable Lodgings of.—Visit of the President and Members of the Mathematical Tribunal.—Of the Bishop of Pekin, and others.—Gill's Sword-blades.— Hatchett's Carriages.—Scorpion found in a Cask packed at Birmingham.—Portraits of English Nobility.—Effects of Accounts from Tartary on the Officers of State in Pekin.—Emperor's return to the Capital.—Inspects the Presents.—Application of the Embassador for Leave to depart.—Short Account of the Palace and Gardens of Yuen-min-yuen.—Lord Macartney's Description of the Eastern and Western Parks of Gehol.—And his general Remarks on Chinese Landscape Gardening.

THE presents for the Emperor and our private baggage being[87] all landed, the packages repaired, and every article minutely noted down by the officers of government, the porters were directed to fix their bamboo bearing poles to each package, that no impediment might prevent our setting out at an early hour in the morning. In doing this, as well as in landing the articles from the vessels, the Chinese porters shewed such expedition, strength, and activity, as could not, I believe, be pa[88]rallel or procured in so short a time, in any other country. Every thing here, in fact, seems to be at the instant command of the state; and the most laborious tasks are undertaken and executed with a readiness, and even a chearfulness, which one could scarcely expect to meet with in so despotic a government.

According to the arrangement, on the 21st of August about three o'clock in the morning, we were prepared to set out, but could scarcely be said to be fairly in motion till five, and before we had cleared the city of *Tong-tchoo*, it was past six o'clock. From this city to the capital, I may venture to say, the road never before exhibited so motley a groupe. In front marched about three thousand porters, carrying six hundred packages; some of which were so large and heavy, as to require thirty-two bearers, with these were mixed a proportionate number of inferior officers, each having the charge and superintendence of a division. Next followed eighty-five waggons, and thirty-nine hand-carts, each with one wheel, loaded with wine, porter and other European provisions, ammunition, and such heavy articles as were not liable to be broken. Eight light field pieces, which were among the presents for the Emperor, closed this part of the procession. After these paraded the Tartar legate, and several officers from court, with their numerous attendants; some on horseback, some in chairs, and others on foot. Then followed the Embassador's guard in waggons, the servants, musicians, and mechanics, also in waggons; the gentlemen of the suite on horseback, the Embassador, the Minister Plenipotentiary, his son, and the interpreter, in four ornamented chairs; the rest of the suite in small covered carriages[89] on two wheels, not unlike in appearance to our funeral hearses, but only about half the length; and last of all *Van* and *Chou*, with their attendants, closed this motley procession.

Though the distance was only twelve miles, it was thought advisable by our conductors to halt for breakfast about half-way; for, as heavy bodies move slowly, what with the delay and confusion in first getting into order, and the frequent stoppages on the road, we found it was eight o'clock before the whole of the cavalcade had reached the half-way house. Here we had a most sumptuous breakfast of roast pork and venison, rice and made dishes, eggs, tea, milk, and a variety of fruits served up on masses of ice.

The porters and the heavy baggage moved forwards without halting; and having ended our comfortable repast, we followed without loss of time. We had scarcely proceeded three miles, till we found the sides of the road lined with spectators on horseback, on foot, in small carriages similar to those we rode in, in carts, waggons, and chairs. In the last were Chinese ladies but, having gauze curtains at the sides and front, we could see little of them. Several well-looking women in long silken robes, with a great number of children, were in the small carriages. These we understood to be Tartars. A file of soldiers now moved along with the procession on each side of the road, armed with whips, which they continually exercised in order to keep off the crowd that increased as we approached the capital, and, at length, was so great as to obstruct the road. We observed, however, that though the soldiers were very[90] active and noisy in brandishing their whips, they only struck them against the ground, and never let them fall upon the people. Indeed a Chinese crowd is not so tumultuous and unruly as it generally is elsewhere.

The excessive heat of the weather, the dustiness of the road, the closeness of the carriages, and the slow manner in which we moved along, would have made this short journey almost insupportable, but from the novelty of the scene, the smiles, the grins, the gestures of the multitude, and above all, the momentary expectation of entering the greatest city on the surface of the globe. Those also who had been so unlucky as to make choice of the little covered carriages, found themselves extremely uncomfortable, notwithstanding they are the best, the most easy and genteel sort of carriage that the country affords. Being fixed on the wheels without springs, and having no seats in the inside, they are to an European, who must sit on his haunches in the bottom, the most uneasy vehicles that can be imagined. Father Semedo, one of the earliest missionaries to China, asserts, that coaches were anciently in common use in this country, and that they were laid down on account of the great convenience and little expence of sedan chairs. The coaches alluded to by the reverend father were, in all probability, the little carts above mentioned, for not the vestige of any thing better is to be found among them; not the least appearance of any thing like a spring carriage. It is more probable that palanquins and chairs have been in common use here and in India, from the earliest period of their histories. The *lectica* of the Romans is supposed to have been brought to Rome[91] in the time of the Republic from some of the eastern nations.

The great road to the capital lay across an open country, sandy and ill cultivated, and the few houses on each side were of mean appearance, generally built with mud, or half burnt bricks, to the very gates of Pekin. The middle part of the road, for the width of eighteen or twenty feet, was paved with stones of granite from six to sixteen feet in length and broad in proportion. Every one of these enormous flag stones must have been brought, at least sixty miles, the nearest mountains where quarries of granite are found being those that divide China from Mantchoo Tartary, near the great wall.

A temple on the right of the road and a bridge of white marble having the balustrade ornamented with figures, meant to represent lions and other animals cut out of the same material, were the only objects that attracted any notice, until the walls and the lofty gates of the capital appeared in view. None of the buildings within, on this side of the city, overtopped the walls, though these did not appear to exceed twenty-five or at most thirty feet in height; they were flanked with square towers, and surrounded by a moat or ditch. These towers projected about forty feet from the line of the wall, and were placed at regular intervals of about seventy yards, being considered as bow-shot distance from each other. Each had a small guard-house upon its summit. The thickness of the base of the wall was about twenty-five feet, and the width across this top within[92] the parapets twelve feet; so that the sides of the wall have a very considerable slope, much more however within than without. The middle part was composed of the earth that had been dug out of the ditch; and was kept together by two retaining walls, part of which were of brick and part of stone. The famous barrier on the borders of Tartary, and the ramparts of all the cities in the country, are built in the same manner.

No cannon were mounted on the walls nor on the bastions; but in the high building which surmounted the gate, and which was several stories one above the other, the portholes were closed with red doors, on the outside of which were painted the representations of cannon, not unlike at a distance the sham ports in a ship of war. The gates of a Chinese city are generally double, and placed in the flanks of a square or semicircular bastion. The first opens into a large space, surrounded with buildings, which are appropriated entirely for military uses, being the depôt of provisions and ammunition, *place d'armes*, and barracks. Out of this place, in one of the flanks, the second gate, having a similar high building erected over it as the first, opens into the city.

The first appearance of this celebrated capital is not much calculated to raise high expectations, nor does it in the least improve upon a more intimate acquaintance. In approaching an European city it generally happens that a great variety of objects catch the eye, as the towers and spires of churches, domes, obelisks, and other buildings for public purposes towering above the rest; and the mind is amused in conjecturing the form, and[93] magnitude of their several constructions, and the uses to which they may be applied. In Pekin not even a chimney is seen rising above the roofs of the houses which, being all nearly of the same height, and the streets laid out in straight lines, have the appearance and the regularity of a large encampment. The roofs would only require to be painted white, instead of being red, green, or blue, to make the resemblance complete. Few houses exceed the height of one story, and none but the great shops have either windows or openings in the wall in front, but most of them have a sort of terrace, with a railed balcony or parapet wall in front, on which are placed pots of flowers, or shrubs, or stunted trees.

This city is an oblong square, the outward boundary of which is forty *lees*, each *lee* being six hundred yards, so that the inclosing wall is near fourteen English miles, and the area about twelve square miles, independent of the extensive suburbs at every gate. In the south wall are three gates, and in each of the other sides two, from whence it is sometimes called *The city with nine gates*; but its usual name is *Pe-ching*, or the Northern Court. The middle gate, on the south side, opens into the Imperial city, which is a space of ground within the general inclosure, in the shape of a parallelogram, about a mile in length from north to south, and three-fourths of a mile from east to west. A wall built of large red polished bricks, and twenty feet high, covered with a roof of tiles painted yellow and varnished, surrounds this space, in which are contained not only the imperial palace and gardens, but also all the tribunals, or public offices of government, lodgings for the mi[94]nisters, the eunuchs, artificers, and tradesmen belonging to the court. A great variety of surface, as well as of different objects, appear within this inclosure. A rivulet winding through it not only affords a plentiful supply of water, but adds largely to the beauties of the grounds, by being formed into canals and basons, and lakes, which, with the artificial mounts, and rocks, and groves, exhibit the happiest imitation of nature.

Between the other two gates, in the south wall, and the corresponding and opposite ones on the north side of the city, run two streets perfectly straight, each being four English miles in length, and about one hundred and twenty feet in width. One street also of the same width runs from one of the eastern to the opposite western gate, but the other is interrupted by the north wall of the imperial city, round which it is carried. The cross streets can be considered only as lanes branching from these main streets at right angles; are very narrow; but the houses in them are generally of the same construction as those in the great streets. The large houses of the state officers are in these lanes.

Although the approach to Pekin afforded little that was interesting, we had no sooner passed the gate and opened out the broad street, than a very singular and novel appearance was exhibited. We saw before us a line of buildings on each side of a wide street, consisting entirely of shops and warehouses, the particular goods of which were brought out and displayed in groupes in front of the houses. Before these were generally erected large wooden pillars, whose tops were much higher[95] than the eves of the houses, bearing inscriptions in gilt characters, setting forth the nature of the wares to be sold, and the honest reputation of the seller; and, to attract the more notice, they were generally hung with various coloured flags and streamers and ribbands from top to bottom, exhibiting the appearance of a line of shipping dressed, as we sometimes see them, in the colours of all the different nations in Europe. The sides of the houses were not less brilliant in the several colours with which they were painted, consisting generally of sky blue or green mixed with gold: and what appeared to us singular enough, the articles for sale that made the greatest show were coffins for the dead. The most splendid of our coffin furniture would make but a poor figure if placed beside that intended for a wealthy Chinese. These machines are seldom less than three inches thick, and twice the bulk of ours. Next to those our notice was attracted by the brilliant appearance of the funeral biers and the marriage cars, both covered with ornamental canopies.

At the four points where the great streets intersect one another were erected those singular buildings, sometimes of stone, but generally of wood, which have been called triumphal arches, but which, in fact, are monuments to the memory of those who had deserved well of the community, or who had attained an unusual longevity. They consist invariably of a large central gateway, with a smaller one on each side, all covered with narrow roofs; and, like the houses, they are painted, varnished, and gilt in the most splendid manner.[96]

The multitude of moveable workshops of tinkers and barbers, coblers and blacksmiths; the tents and booths where tea and fruit, rice and other eatables were exposed for sale, with the wares and merchandize arrayed before the doors, had contracted this spacious street to a narrow road in the middle, just wide enough for two of our little vehicles to pass each other. The cavalcade of officers and soldiers that preceded the embassy, the processions of men in office attended by their numerous retinues, bearing umbrellas and flags, painted lanterns, and a variety of strange insignia of their rank and station, different trains that were accompanying, with lamentable cries, corpses to their graves, and, with squalling music, brides to their husbands, the troops of dromedaries laden with coals from Tartary, the wheelbarrows and hand-carts stuffed with vegetables, occupied nearly the whole of this middle space in one continued line, leaving very little room for the cavalcade of the embassy to pass. All was in motion. The sides of the street were filled with an immense concourse of people, buying and selling and bartering their different commodities. The buzz and confused noises of this mixed multitude, proceeding from the loud bawling of those who were crying their wares, the wrangling of others, with every now and then a strange twanging noise like the jarring of a cracked Jew's harp, the barber's signal made by his tweezers, the mirth and the laughter that prevailed in every groupe, could scarcely be exceeded by the brokers in the Bank rotunda, or by the Jews and old women in *Rosemary-Lane*. Pedlars with their packs, and jugglers, and conjurers, and fortune-tellers, mountebanks and quack-doctors, comedians and musicians, left no space unoccupied. The Tartar soldiers, with[97] their whips, kept with difficulty a clear passage for the embassy to move slowly forwards; so slow, indeed, that although we entered the eastern gate at half-past nine, it was near twelve before we arrived at the western.

Although an extraordinary crowd might be expected to assemble on such a particular occasion, on the same principle of curiosity as could not fail to attract a crowd of spectators in London, yet there was a most remarkable and a striking difference observable between a London and a Pekin populace. In the former the whole attention and soul of the multitude would have been wrapt up in the novel spectacle; all would have been idlers. In Pekin, the shew was but an accessary; every one pursued his business, at the same time that he gratified his curiosity. In fact, it appeared that, on every day throughout the whole year, there was the same noise and bustle and crowd in the capital of China. I scarcely ever passed the western gate, which happened twice, or oftener, in the week, that I had not to wait a considerable time before the passage was free, particularly in the morning, notwithstanding the exertions of two or three soldiers with their whips to clear the way. The crowd, however, was entirely confined to the great streets, which are the only outlets of the city. In the cross lanes all was still and quiet.

Women in Pekin were commonly seen among the crowd, or walking in the narrow streets, or riding on horseback, which they crossed in the same manner as the men, but they were all Tartars. They wore long silken robes, reaching down to their feet; their shoes appeared to be as much above the common size,[98] as those of the Chinese are under it; the upper part was generally of embroidered satin, the sole consisted of folds of cloth or paper, about an inch thick; they were square in front, and a little turned up. The hair smoothed up on all sides, not very different from that of the Chinese; and though their faces were painted with white lead and vermillion, it was evident their skins were much fairer than those of the former. The Chinese women are more scrupulously confined to the house in the capital than elsewhere. Young girls were sometimes seen smoking their pipes in the doors of their houses, but they always retired on the approach of men.

All the streets were covered with sand and dust: none had the least pavement. The cross lanes were generally watered, which did not appear to be the case in the main streets. A large sheet of water, several acres in extent, within the northern wall, affords to that part of the city, and to the palace an abundant supply of that element, as does also a small stream which runs along the western wall to that neighbourhood. There are besides abundance of wells; but the water of some of these is so dreadfully nauseous, that we, who were unaccustomed to it, were under the necessity of sending to a distance to obtain such as was free from mineral or earthy impregnations. When mixed with tea, the well water was particularly disgusting.

Although Pekin cannot boast, like ancient Rome, or modern London, of the conveniences of common sewers to carry off the dirt and dregs that must necessarily accumulate in large cities, yet it enjoys one important advantage, which is rarely[99] found in capitals out of England: no kind of filth or nastiness, creating offensive smells is thrown out into the streets, a piece of cleanliness that perhaps may be attributed rather to the scarcity and value of manure, than to the exertions of the police officers. Each family has a large earthen jar, into which is carefully collected every thing that may be used as manure; when the jar is full, there is no difficulty of converting its contents into money, or of exchanging them for vegetables. The same small boxed carts with one wheel, which supply the city with vegetables, invariably return to the gardens with a load of this liquid manure. Between the palace of *Yuen-min-yuen* and Pekin, I have met many hundreds of these carts. They are generally dragged by one person, and pushed on by another; and they leave upon the road an odour that continues without intermission for many miles. Thus, though the city is cleared of its filth, it seldom loses its fragrance. In fact, a constant disgusting odour remains in and about all the houses the whole day long, from the fermentation of the heterogeneous mixtures kept above ground, which in our great cities are carried off in drains.

The medical gentlemen of China are not quite so ingenious, as we are told the faculty in Madrid were about the middle of the last century, when the inhabitants were directed, by royal proclamation, to build proper places of retirement to their houses, instead of emptying their nocturnal machines out of the windows into the streets. The inhabitants took it into their heads to consider this order as a great affront, and a direct violation of the rights of man; but the doctors were the most[100] strenuous opposers of the measure, having no doubt very cogent reasons for wishing the continuance of the practice. They assured the inhabitants, that if human excrement was no longer to be accumulated in the streets, to attract the putrescent particles floating in the air, they would find their way into the human body, and a pestilential sickness would be the inevitable consequence.

The police of the capital, as we afterwards found, is so well regulated, that the safety and tranquillity of the inhabitants are seldom disturbed. At the end of every cross street, and at certain distances in it, are a kind of cross bars, with sentry boxes at each of which is placed a soldier, and few of these streets are without a guard-house. Besides, the proprietor or inhabitant of every tenth house, like the ancient tythingmen of England, takes it in turn to keep the peace, and be responsible for the good conduct of his nine neighbours. If any riotous company should assemble, or any disturbances happen within his district, he is to give immediate information thereof to the nearest guard-house. The soldiers also go their rounds and instead of crying the hour like our watchmen, strike upon a short tube of bamboo, which gives a dull hollow sound, that for several nights prevented us from sleeping until we were accustomed to it.

It took us full two hours, as I before observed, in passing from the eastern to the western gate of Pekin. The clouds of dust raised by the populace were here much denser than on the road, and the smothering heat of the day, the thermometer in our little carts standing at 96°, was almost insupportable. Except[101] the great crowd on every side, we

34

saw little to engage the attention after the first five minutes. Indeed, a single walk through one of the broad streets is quite sufficient to give a stranger a competent idea of the whole city. He will immediately perceive that every street is laid out in the same manner, and every house built upon the same plan; and that their architecture is void of taste, grandeur, beauty, solidity, or convenience; that the houses are merely tents, and that there is nothing magnificent, even in the palace of the Emperor;—but we shall have occasion to speak on this subject hereafter. Ask a Chinese, however, what is to be seen that is curious or great in the capital, and he will immediately enter upon a long history of the beauties of the palace belonging to *Ta-whang-tee*, the mighty Emperor. According to his notions, every thing within the palace walls is gold and silver. He will tell you of gold and silver pillars, gold and silver roofs, gold and silver vases, in which are swimming gold and silver fishes. All, however, is not gold that glitters in China, more than elsewhere. The Emperor, as I shall hereafter have occasion to notice, has very little surplus revenue at his disposal, and is frequently distressed for money to pay his army and other exigences of the state. And, though China has of late years drawn from Europe a considerable quantity of specie, yet when this is scattered over so vast an extent of country, and divided among so many millions of people, it becomes almost as a drop thrown into the sea. Most of the money, besides, that enters China is melted down, and converted into articles of luxury or convenience. Few nations are better acquainted with the value of these precious metals than the Chinese; and few, if any, can surpass their in[102]genuity in drawing out the one into thin leaves, and the other into the finest wire.

We were not a little overjoyed in finding ourselves once more upon the flagged causeway, and in an open country, after passing a small suburb beyond the western gate of the city. They brought us to a villa which was a kind of appendage to one of the Emperor's palaces, about eight miles beyond Pekin. The buildings, consisting of a number of small detached apartments, straggling over a surface of ground, about fifteen acres in extent, were neither sufficiently numerous to lodge the suite, nor to contain the presents and our baggage; and were moreover so miserably out of repair and in so ruinous a condition, that the greater part was wholly uninhabitable. The officers were accordingly told that these were not accommodations suitable to the dignity of a British Embassador, and that he would not on any consideration put up with them; that it was a matter of indifference whether he was lodged in the city or the country, but that the lodgings should be convenient and proper. The superintending officers, upon this, caused a large temporary building to be erected with poles and mats, which, as by magic, was finished in the course of the night, hoping, by this exertion, to have removed all objections to the place. His Lordship, however, being determined not to remain where there was neither a decent room, nor any kind of comfort or convenience, every building being entirely unfurnished, and, as I said before, the greater number untenantable, insisted upon being removed to Pekin, where accordingly it was very soon announced there was a suitable house ready for his reception.[103]

On returning to the capital we passed through the great street of a town called *Hai-tien* in which most of the houses were of two stories, and before the upper of which was a kind of Véranda full of dwarf trees and flower-pots. A great proportion of the houses were either butchers' shops or coffin-makers. From the end of this street was a most extensive view of Pekin and the surrounding country. The eye from hence took in the whole length of the high straight wall with its two lofty gates and numerous square towers. At each angle of the wall is a large square building rising above the parapet to four heights or stories of port-holes, and covered with two roofs. In each row of the four fronts are fourteen windows or port-holes. These I understood to be the rice magazines or public granaries. Near the north-west angle is a tall pagoda, another high tower not unlike a glass-house, and towards the higher western gate appeared the upper part of a pyramidal building that terminated in a gilded flame, very like the summit of our Monument under which, instead of a gallery, was a most magnificent canopy or umbrella, painted and gilt with such brilliant colours, that from certain points of view, when the rays of the sun played upon it, the glittering appearance had a very good effect. It was said to be a temple, and seemed to be of the same kind of architecture as the *Shoo-ma-doo* described by Col. Symes in his embassy to Ava.

We found our new lodging sufficiently large, but the apartments were shamefully dirty, having been uninhabited for some time; very much out of repair, and totally unfurnished. This house, being considered be one of the best in the whole city, I shall have[104] occasion to take notice of hereafter, in speaking of the state of their architecture. It was built by the late *Ho-poo*, or Collector of the customs at Canton, from which situation he was preferred to the collectorship of salt duties at *Tien-sing*, where, it seems, he was detected in embezzling the public revenues, thrown into jail, and his immense property confiscated to the crown. The officers appointed to attend the embassy told us, that when it was proposed to the Emperor for the English Embassador to occupy this house, he immediately replied, "Most certainly, you cannot refuse the temporary occupation of a house to the Embassador of that nation which contributed so very amply towards the expense of building it." The inference to be drawn from such a remark, is, that the court of Pekin is well aware of the extortions committed against foreigners at Canton.

The Emperor being at this time in Tartary, where he meant to celebrate the festival of the anniversary of his birth-day, had given orders that the public introduction of the British Embassador should be fixed for that day, and should take place at Gehol, a small town 136 miles from Pekin, where he had a large palace, park, gardens, and a magnificent *Poo-ta-la*or temple of Budha. Accordingly a selection was made of such presents as were the most portable, to be sent forwards into Tartary; and the Embassador, with part of his suite, several officers of the court, and their retinue, set out from Pekin on the second of September. Some of the gentlemen, with part of the guard and of the servants, remained in Pekin, and Dr. Dinwiddie and myself, with two mechanics, had apartments allotted to us in the palace of *Yuen-min-yuen*, where the largest and most va[105]luable of the presents were to be fitted up for the inspection of the old Emperor on his return from Tartary.

Having already acquired some little knowledge of the language on the passage from England, by the assistance of two Chinese priests who had been sent by their superiors to Naples, for the purpose of being instructed in the Christian religion, I hoped to find this temporary banishment less irksome, particularly as I had previously stipulated with the officers belonging to that palace for an unconditional leave to visit the capital whenever I should find it necessary or proper, during the absence of the Embassador; and, it is but fair to say, they kept faith to their engagement in the strictest sense. A horse and one of the little covered carts were always at my disposal.

The gentlemen left in the city were less agreeably situated. At the outer gate of their lodgings a guard was stationed with orders to allow none of them to pass, and all their proceedings and movements were closely watched. Sometimes they were a little relieved by occasional visits from the European missionaries; but so suspicious were the officers of government of any communication with these gentlemen that they were invariably accompanied by some of them to act as spies, notwithstanding they could not comprehend one single word that was exchanged in the conversations they held together. A Chinese has no knowledge whatsoever of any of the European languages. But he watches the actions, and even the motions of the eye, and makes his report accordingly. The courts of the house were constantly filled with the inferior officers of government and[106] their servants, all of whom had some post or other assigned to them connected with the British Embassy. One was the superintendant of the kitchen, another furnished tea, one was appointed to supply us with fruit, another with vegetables, and another with milk.

During the time I should be required to reside in *Yuen-min-yuen*, I particularly wished to have none other than Chinese servants, that I might be under the necessity of extending the little knowledge I had already acquired of the spoken language. This is by no means difficult to learn except in the nice intonations or inflexions of voice, but the written character is, perhaps of all others, the most abstruse and most perplexing both to the eye and to the memory. The length of time that is usually required by the Chinese, together with the intense study and stretch of the memory which they find necessary in order to obtain a very small proportion of the characters that form the language, are serious obstructions to the progress of the arts and sciences, but favourable to the stability of the government of which indeed the language may be considered as one of the great bulwarks. But the observations I have to make on this subject will more properly be reserved for a separate chapter.

On arriving at *Yuen-min-yuen* I found a number of Chinese workmen busily employed in breaking open the packages, some in one place and some in another, to the no little danger of the globes, clocks, glass lustres, and such like frangible articles, many of which must inevitably have suffered under less careful and dexterous hands than those of the Chinese. As it was intended they[107] should be placed in one large room, the great hall in which the Emperor gives audience to his ministers, the first operation was to move them all thither, and carefully to unpack them; and we had the satisfaction to find that not a single article was either missing or injured.

We had not been long here, before a gentleman appeared who, notwithstanding his Chinese dress, I soon perceived to be an European. He introduced himself by saying, in the Latin language, that his name was Deodato a Neapolitan missionary, and that the court had appointed him to act as interpreter, hoped he might be useful to us, and offered his services in the most handsome manner; and, I have great pleasure in availing myself of this opportunity to acknowledge the friendly and unremitting attention I received from him during a residence of five weeks in this palace, and the very material assistance he afforded in explaining the nature, value, and use of the several pieces of machinery to those Chinese who were appointed to superintend them. Signor Deodato was an excellent mechanic; and in this capacity was employed in the palace to inspect and keep in order the numberless pieces of clock-work that had found their way thither, chiefly from London.

The officer appointed to attend us wore a light blue button in his cap, denoting the 4th degree of rank. When he shewed the apartments that were designed for us, I could not forbear observing to him, that they seemed fitter for hogs than for human creatures, and that rather than be obliged to occupy those, or any[108] other like them, I should for my own part prefer coming down from the capital every morning, and return in the evening. They consisted of three or four hovels in a small court, surrounded with a wall as high as their roofs. Each room was about twelve feet square, the walls completely naked, the ceiling broken in, the rushes or stems of *boleus*, that held the plaister, hanging down and strewed on the floor; the lattice work of the windows partially covered with broken paper; the doors consisting of old bamboo skreens; the floor covered with dust, and there was not the least furniture in any of them, except an old table and two or three chairs in the one which was intended, I suppose, for the dining-room. The rest had nothing in them whatsoever but a little raised platform of brick-work, which they told us was to sleep on, and that they should cover it with mats, and order proper bedding to be brought upon it. Yet these miserable hovels were not only within the palace wall, but scarcely two hundred yards from the great hall of audience. The officer assured us that they were the apartments of one of their *Ta-gin* (great men) but that, as I did not seem to like them, we should be accommodated with others. We were then carried a little farther, where there was a number of buildings upon a more extensive scale enclosed also by high walls. The apartments were somewhat larger, but miserably dirty both within and without, and wholly unfurnished; but as our attendant took care to tell us they belonged to one of the *ministers of state*, and that he lodged in them when the Emperor was at Yuen-min-yuen, we were precluded from further complaint. Had we refused those that were considered sufficient for a minister of state, the man might have thought that nothing[109] less than the Emperor's own would have satisfied us. If the menial servants of his Britannic Majesty's Ministers were no better lodged than the ministers themselves of his Chinese Majesty, they would be apt to think themselves very ill used. We accepted them, however, such as they were, and caused them to be swept out, an operation which had not been performed for many months before; a table and chairs were brought in, with mats, pillows, and silken mattresses; but for these we had no occasion, having fortunately brought with us from the ships our own cots.

To make amends for our uncomfortable lodging, we sat down to a most excellent dinner, wholly prepared in the Chinese style, consisting of a vast variety of made dishes very neatly dressed, and served in porcelain bowls. The best soup I ever tasted in any part of the world was made here from an extract of beef, seasoned with a preparation of soy and other ingredients. Their vermicelli is excellent, and all their pastry is unusually light and white as snow. We understood it to be made from the buck wheat. The luxury of ice, in the neighbourhood of the capital, is within the reach of the poorest peasant; and, although they drink their tea and other beverage warm, they prefer all kinds of fruit when cooled on ice.

The three first days, while the articles were unpacking and assorting, we remained tolerably quiet, being annoyed only with the interference and inquisitiveness of an old eunuch, who had in his train about a dozen of the same kind *simile aut secundum*. But no sooner were they taken out of their cases, and set up in[110] the room, than visitors of all ranks, from princes of the blood to plain citizens, came daily to look at the presents, but more particularly at us, whom I believe they considered by much the greatest curiosities. All the men of letters and rank, who held employments in the state, and whose attendance had been dispensed with at Gehol, flocked to *Yuen-min-yuen*.

Among the numerous visitors came one day in great state the president of a board in Pekin, on which the Jesuits have conferred the pompous but unmerited title of the *Tribunal of Mathematics*. He was accompanied by a Portuguese missionary of the name of *Govea*, who is the titular Bishop of Pekin, Padre Antonio, and his secretary, both Portuguese, and all three members of the said tribunal. The particular object of their visit was to make themselves fully acquainted with the nature and use of the several presents that related to science, and especially of the large planetarium, which had already made a great noise in China, in order that they might be able to give a proper description and explanation to his Imperial Majesty, both of this instrument, and of all the others connected with their department, and to answer any question concerning them that might be asked.

It created no sort of surprize to any of us, on finding that the Chinese who accompanied these reverend gentlemen were completely ignorant of the nature of a complicated machine, whose motions, regulated by the most ingenious mechanism that had ever been constructed in Europe, represented all those even of the most irregular and eccentric of the heavenly bodies;[111] nor in perceiving that they seemed to be rather disappointed in the appearance and operations of this instrument. It was obvious, from the few questions put by the president of this learned body, that he had conceived the planetarium to be something similar to one of those curious pieces of musical mechanism which, in the Canton jargon, are called *Sing-songs*, and that nothing more was necessary than to wind it up like a jack, when it would immediately spin round, and tell him every thing that he wanted to know.

But the difficulty of making the right reverend Bishop and his colleagues comprehend the principles upon which it was constructed, and the several phenomena of the heavenly bodies exhibited by it, conveyed almost as bad an opinion of their astronomical and mathematical knowledge as of that of their president. The prelate, however, appeared to be a man of mild and placid temper, pleasing manners, and of a modest and unassuming deportment. His secretary was a keen sharp fellow, extremely inquisitive, and resolved not to lose the little knowledge he might acquire, for he wrote down the answer to every question that was proposed.

The following day the Bishop came unattended by the Chinese part of their board, and gave us some account of the nature of their employ. The astronomical part of the national almanack, such as calculating eclipses, the times of new and full moon, the rising and setting of the sun, were, as he informed us, entrusted to him and his colleagues, but the astrological part was managed by a committee of the Chinese members. He candidly[112] avowed that neither he nor any of his European brethren were well qualified for the task, and that they had been hitherto more indebted to the *Connoissances de tems* of Paris than to their own calculations. That having exactly ascertained the difference of meridians between Pekin and Paris, they had little difficulty in reducing the calculations made for the latter, so as to answer for the situation of the former, at least to a degree of accuracy that was sufficiently near the truth not to be detected by any of the Chinese members.

The French revolution having put an end to future communications with that country was to them a severe blow in this respect, though the secretary thought he could now manage the calculation of an eclipse sufficiently correct to pass current with the Chinese. Fortunately, however, Doctor Dinwiddie had provided himself on leaving London with a set of the nautical almanacks, calculated for the meridian of Greenwich, up to the year 1800, which they considered as an invaluable present.

The grandsons of the Emperor were almost daily visitors. It seems there is a kind of college in the palace for their education. Though young men from the ages of sixteen to five-and-twenty, the old eunuch used frequently to push them by the shoulders out of the hall of audience; and, on expressing my surprise to Deodato at such insolence, he informed me that he was their *aya*, their governor!

We had also a great number of Tartar generals and military officers who had heard of sword-blades that would cut iron[113] bars without injuring the edge; and so great was their astonishment on proving the fact, that they could scarcely credit the evidence of their own eyes. We could not confer a more acceptable present on a military officer than one of Gill's sword-blades; and from the eager applications made for them, as we passed through the country, the introduction of them through Canton, in the regular course of trade, would, I should suppose, be no difficult task.

But the two elegant carriages made by Hatchett puzzled the Chinese more than any of the other presents. Nothing of the kind had ever been seen at the capital; and the disputes among themselves as to the part which was intended for the seat of the Emperor were whimsical enough. The hammer-cloth that covered the box of the winter carriage had a smart edging, and was ornamented with festoons of roses. Its splendid appearance and elevated situation determined it at once, in the opinion of the majority, to be the Emperor's seat; but a difficulty arose how to appropriate the inside of the carriage. They examined the windows, the blinds, and the screens, and at last concluded, that it could be for nobody but his ladies. The old eunuch came to me for information, and when he learned that the fine elevated box was to be the seat of the man who managed the horses, and that the Emperor's place was within, he asked me, with a sneer, if I supposed the *Ta-whang-tee* would suffer any man to sit higher than himself, and to turn his back towards him? and he wished to know if we could not contrive to have the coach-box removed and placed somewhere behind the body of the carriage.[114]

A remarkable circumstance, not easily to be accounted for, occurred in opening a cask of Birmingham hardware. Every one knows the necessity of excluding the sea-air as much as possible from highly polished articles of iron and steel, and accordingly all such articles intended to be sent abroad are packed with the greatest care. The casks, or cases, are made as tight as possible and covered with pitched canvas. Such was the cask in question. Yet, when the head was taken off, and a few of the packages removed, an enormous large scorpion was found in the midst of the cask, nearly in a torpid state, but it quickly recovered on exposure to the warm air.

"The thing we know is neither rich nor rare,
But wonder how the devil it got there?"

Among the presents carried into Tartary was a collection of prints, chiefly portraits of English nobility and distinguished persons; and to make the present more acceptable, they were bound up in three volumes in yellow Morocco. The Emperor was so pleased with this collection, that he sent it express to *Yuen-min-yuen* to have the name, rank, and office of each portrait translated into the Mantchoo and Chinese languages. The Tartar writer got on pretty well, but the Chinese secretary was not a little puzzled with the B, the D, and the R, that so frequently recurred in the English names. The Duke of Marlborough was *Too-ke Ma-ul-po-loo*, and Bedford was transformed to *Pe-te-fo-ul-te*. But here a more serious difficulty occurred than that of writing the name. The rank was also to be written down, and on coming to the portrait of this nobleman, (which was a proof impression of the print, engraved from a picture by[115] Sir Joshua Reynolds, when the late Duke of Bedford was a youth,) I told the Chinese to write him down a *Ta-gin*, or great man of the second order. He instantly observed that I surely meant his father was a *Ta-gin*. I then explained to him that, according to our laws, the son succeeded to the rank of the father, and that with us it was by no means necessary, in order to obtain the first rank in the country, that a man should be of a certain age, be possessed of superior talents, or suitable qualifications. That these were sometimes conducive to high honours, yet that a great part of the legislative body of the nation were entitled to their rank and situation by birth. They laughed heartily at the idea of a man being born a legislator, when it required so many years of close application to enable one of their countrymen to pass his examination for the very lowest order of state-officers. As, however, the descendants of Confucius continue to enjoy a sort of nominal rank, and as their Emperor can also confer an hereditary dignity, without entitling to office, emolument, or exclusive privilege, they considered his Grace might be one of this description, and wrote down his rank accordingly; but they positively refused to give him the title of *Ta-gin*, or great man, asking me, if I thought their Emperor was so stupid as not to know the impossibility of a little boy having attained the rank of a *great man*.

About the 14th of September, or three days before the Emperor's birth-day, *Padre Anselmo*, the procurator for the mission *de propaganda fide*, delivered me letters from Macao for the Embassador, which the Chinese refused to send to Gehol, though daily expresses went to and from that place. *Anselmo* hinted to[116] me that the late viceroy of Canton, who was no friend to the English, had arrived, and that he feared all was not right. That the Tartar legate had been degraded from his rank for deceiving the Emperor, and particularly for not paying his personal respects to the Embassador on board his ship when in *Tien-sing* roads. That the peacock's feather, which he wore in his cap as a mark of his master's favour, was exchanged for a crow's tail, the sign of great disgrace, and that the consideration of his age and his family had alone saved him from banishment. The Emperor, it seems, having heard that the Embassador had his picture in his cabin on board the Lion, asked the legate whether it was like him, upon which it came out that he had never been near the Lion, as his orders directed him.

On the 17th, being the Emperor's birth-day, all the princes and officers about the palace assembled in their robes of ceremony, to make their obeisance to the throne in the great hall of audience. On this occasion were placed on the floor before the throne, on three small tripods, a cup of tea, of oil, and of rice, perhaps as an acknowledgment of the Emperor being the proprietary of the soil, of which these are three material products. The old eunuch told me that I might remain in the hall during the ceremony, if I would consent to perform it with them, and offered to instruct me in it. He said that all the officers of government, in every part of the empire, made their prostrations to the name of the Emperor inscribed on yellow silk on that day.[117]

Two days after this, on going as usual in the morning to the hall of audience, I found the doors shut and the old eunuch, who kept the keys, walking about in so sullen a mood that I could not get from him a single word. Different groupes of officers were assembled in the court-yard, all looking as if something very dreadful either had occurred, or was about to happen. Nobody would speak to me, nor could I get the least explanation of this extraordinary conduct, till at length our friend Deodato appeared with a countenance no less woeful than those of the officers of government, and the old eunuch. I asked him what was the matter? His answer was, We are all lost, ruined, and undone! He then informed me that intelligence had arrived from Gehol, stating, that Lord Macartney had refused to comply with the ceremony of prostrating himself, like the Embassadors of tributary princes, nine times before the Emperor, unless one of equal rank with himself should go through the same ceremony before the portrait of his Britannic Majesty: that rather than do this they had accepted his offer to perform the same ceremony of respect to the Emperor as to his own sovereign. That although little was thought of this affair at Gehol, the great officers of state in the tribunal or department of ceremonies in Pekin were mortified, and perplexed, and alarmed; and that, in short, it was impossible to say what might be the consequence of an event unprecedented in the annals of the empire. That the Emperor, when he began to think more seriously on the subject, might possibly impeach those before the criminal tribunal who had advised him to accede to such a proposal, on reflecting how much his dignity had suffered by the compliance; and that the records of the country might hand it down to pos[118]terity, as an event that had tarnished the lustre of his reign, being nothing short of breaking through an ancient custom, and adopting one of a barbarous nation in its place. Deodato thought even that its ill effects might extend to them, as Europeans, and might injure the cause which was the first object of their mission.

I found it in vain to put into good humour that day either the officers of government, or the eunuchs, or even the missionaries; and our table was very materially affected by it, both in the number and the quality of dishes;—a criterion from which, more than any other, a judgment may be formed of the state of mind in which a Chinese happens to be.

Something of the same kind, it seems, occurred at Gehol. From the time the Embassador began to make conditions, his table was abridged, under an idea that he might be starved into an unconditional compliance. Finding this experiment fail, they had recourse to a different conduct, and became all kindness and complaisance.

The ill-humour occasioned by the news from Gehol gradually wore off, but I observed that the princes who had hitherto been daily visitors now kept entirely away; and the old eunuch, when put out of his way, used to apply to us the epithet of proud, headstrong Englishmen.

On the 26th the Embassador (during whose stay at Gehol in Tartary an account of all that passed there is given in Sir George Staunton's book) returned to Pekin, when the re[119]mainder of the presents were sent to Yuen-min-yuen. A number of Tartar princes and great officers of state came to look at those fitted up in the hall of audience, and seemed extremely solicitous that the whole should be got ready without delay. Notice was also given that, on the 30th the Emperor would inspect the presents. This was the day fixed for his return, and it was notified to the Embassador that it was an usual compliment for all public officers to meet him on the road, at the distance of ten or twelve miles from the capital. Accordingly, about four o'clock in the morning of the 30th, we were all mounted and arrived at our ground about six. The whole road had been newly made, rolled as level as a bowling-green, watered to keep down the dust and, on each side, at the distance of about fifty yards from each other, were small triangular poles erected, from which were suspended painted lanterns.

They brought us into a kind of guard-house, where tea and other refreshments were prepared, after which we took our station on a high bank on the left of the road. On each side, as far as the eye could reach, were several thousands of the great officers of state in their habits of ceremony; Tartar troops in their holiday dresses; standard-bearers without number, military music, and officers of the household, lining the two sides of the road. The approach of the Emperor was announced by a blast of the trumpet, followed by softer music, "and at that time when all the people heard the sound of the cornet, flutes, harp, sackbut, psaltery, and all kinds of music, then the princes, the governors, and captains, the judges, the treasurers, the counsellors, the sheriffs, and all the rulers of the[120] provinces, that were gathered together, fell down and worshipped," except certain strangers, who, being obstinately resolved to do no greater homage to any sovereign than what is required by their own sovereign, bent one knee only to the ground.

The Emperor was carried by eight men in a kind of sedan chair, which was followed by a clumsy state chariot upon two wheels, and without springs. He bowed very graciously to the Embassador as he passed, and sent a message to him to say that, understanding he was not well, he advised him to return immediately to Pekin, and not to stop at Yuen-min-yuen, as was intended.

The morning being very cold, we were desirous to get home as fast as we could; and accordingly galloped along with some of the Tartar cavalry. When we arrived under the walls of Pekin, we turned our horses towards a different gate to that through which we were accustomed to pass, in order to see a little more of the city. But one of our conductors, who had thought it his duty not to lose sight of us, in perceiving us making a wrong turn, hallowed out with all his might. We pushed forward, however, and got through the gate, but we were pursued with such a hue and cry, that we were glad to escape through one of the cross streets leading to our hotel, where we arrived with at least a hundred soldiers at our heels.[121]

On the 1st of October the Emperor, attended by a Tartar, inspected the presents in the hall of audience and examined them with minute attention. He desired the Tartar prince to tell us, through Deodato, that the accounts he had received of our good conduct at *Yuen-min-yuen* gave him great pleasure, and that he had ordered a present to be made to each of us, as a proof of his entire satisfaction. This present was brought, after his departure from the hall, by the old eunuch, who took care to tell us that before we received it we must make nine prostrations according to the Chinese custom. I made him no answer, but requested Deodato to explain to the Tartar prince, who was still present, that being under the orders of the Embassador we did not think ourselves authorized to do what he had found good to refuse, but that we had not the least objection to go through the same ceremony that he had done at Gehol. The Tartar prince immediately answered that nothing further was required. We accordingly placed one knee on the lowest step leading to the throne. The present consisted of rolls of silk and several pieces of silver cast in the form of a Tartar shoe, without any mark or inscription on them, and each about the weight of an ounce.

The presents being now all delivered, and the Embassador informed by the missionaries that preparations were making for our departure, the usual time being nearly expired, his Excellency was desirous of having the day fixed, and for this purpose dispatched a note to the first minister, who sent an answer by the Tartar legate to inform him that, to prevent any likelihood of being surprized by the approaching bad weather,[122] the Emperor had named the 7th instant for the beginning of our journey; and had given orders that every honour and distinction should be paid to the Embassy on the road.

But before I quit these renowned gardens of Yuen-min-yuen, it will naturally be expected I should say something on their subject. From all that I had heard and read of the grandeur and beauty of the scenery and the magnificence of the palaces, I had certainly expected to meet with a style of gardening and laying out of grounds superior, or at least equal, to any thing in the same line in Europe; and, perhaps indeed, I might have been fully gratified in all my expectation provided no restraint had been thrown upon our walks, which was far from being the case. All the little excursions I made were by stealth. Even in the short distance between the hall of audience and our lodgings, which might be about three hundred paces, we were continually watched. The idea of being stopped by an eunuch or some of the inferior officers belonging to the court, was sufficient to put us on our guard against meeting with any such mortification; pride, in such circumstances, generally gets the better of the desire, however strong, of gratifying curiosity. I sometimes, however, ventured to stroll from our lodging in the evening in order to take a stolen glance at these celebrated gardens.

The grounds of *Yuen-min-yuen* are calculated to comprehend an extent of at least ten English miles in diameter, or about sixty thousand acres, a great part of which, however, is wastes and woodland. The general appearance of those parts near where we lodged, as to the natural surface of the country, bro[123]ken into hill and dale, and diversified with wood and lawn, may be compared with Richmond park, to which, however, they add the very great advantage of abundance of canals, rivers, and large sheets of water, whose banks, although artificial, are neither trimmed, nor shorn, nor sloped, like the glacis of a fortification, but have been thrown up with immense labour in an irregular, and, as it were, fortuitous manner, so as to represent the free hand of nature. Bold rocky promontories are seen jutting into a lake, and vallies retiring, some choaked with wood, others in a state of high cultivation. In particular spots where pleasure-houses, or places of rest or retirement, were erected, the views appeared to have been studied. The trees were not only placed according to their magnitudes, but the tints of their foliage seemed also to have been considered in the composition of the picture, which some of the landscapes might be called with great propriety. But, if an opinion may be formed from those parts of them which I have seen, and I understood there is a great similarity throughout the whole, they fall very short of the fanciful and extravagant descriptions that Sir William Chambers has given of Chinese gardening. Much, however, has been done, and nothing that I saw could be considered as an offence to nature.

Thirty distinct places of residence for the Emperor, with all the necessary appendages of building to each, for lodging the several officers of state, who are required to be present on court days and particular occasions, for the eunuchs, servants, and artificers, each composing a village of no inconsiderable magnitude, are said to be contained within the inclosure of these gar[124]dens. These assemblages of buildings, which they dignify with the name of palaces, are, however, of such a nature as to be more remarkable for their number than for their splendour or magnificence. A great proportion of the buildings consists in mean cottages. The very dwelling of the Emperor and the grand hall in which he gives audience, when divested of the gilding and the gaudy colours with which they are daubed, are little superior, and much less solid, than the barns of a substantial English farmer. Their apartments are as deficient in proportion, as their construction is void of every rule and principle which we are apt to consider as essential to architecture. The principal hall of audience at Yuen-min-yuen stood upon a platform of granite, raised about four feet above the level of the court. A row of large wooden columns surrounding the building supported the projecting roof; and a second row within the first, and corresponding with it (the interstices between the columns being filled up with brick-work to the height of about four feet) served for the walls of the room. The upper part of these walls was a kind of lattice-work, covered over with large sheets of oiled paper, and was capable of being thrown entirely open on public occasions. The wooden columns had no capitals, and the only architrave was the horizontal beam that supported the rafters of the roof. This, in direct contradiction to the established mode in European architecture, was the uppermost member of what might be called the entablature or frize, which was a broad skreen of wood, fastened between the upper part of the columns, painted with the most vivid colours of blue, red, and green, and interlarded with gilding; and the whole had net-work of wire stretched[125] over it, to prevent its being defiled by swallows, and other birds frequenting human dwellings. The length of this room within was one hundred and ten feet, breadth forty-two, and height twenty feet: the ceiling painted with circles, squares, and polygons, whimsically disposed, and loaded with a great variety of colours. The floor was paved with grey marble flag stones laid chequer-wise. The throne, placed in a recess, was supported by rows of pillars painted red like those without. It consisted entirely of wood, not unlike mahogany, the carving of which was exquisitely fine. The only furniture was a pair of brass kettle-drums, two large paintings, two pair of ancient blue porcelain vases, a few volumes of manuscripts, and a table at one end of the room on which was placed an old English chiming clock, made in the seventeenth century by one Clarke of Leadenhall-street, and which our old friend the eunuch had the impudence to tell us was the workmanship of a Chinese. A pair of circular fans made of the wing feathers of the Argus pheasant, and mounted on long polished ebony poles stood, one on each side of the throne, over which was written in four characters, "true, great, refulgent, splendor;" and under these, in a lozenge, the character of *Happiness*. In the different courts were several miserable attempts at sculpture, and some bronze figures, but all the objects were fanciful, distorted, and entirely out of nature. The only specimen of workmanship about the palace, that would bear a close examination, besides the carving of the throne, was a brick wall enclosing the flower garden, which, perhaps, in no respect is exceeded by any thing of the sort in England.[126]

With regard to the architecture and gardening of the Chinese, it may be expected that I should give a more detailed description, or offer some opinion on those subjects. The little I have to say on the former will be reserved for another place; and, with respect to the latter, I regret that I had not an opportunity of seeing so much as I could have wished, and particularly the Emperor's great park at Gehol, which, from the description of the Embassador, seemed to be almost unrivalled for its features of beauty, sublimity, and amenity. But my own deficiency will be amply filled up with an extract or two from the Journal of his Lordship, whose taste and skill in landscape gardening are so well known. I have indeed much to regret that I could not enrich the present work with more extracts from it, but as it makes a complete picture of itself the partial selection of detached parts might have been injurious to it, by conveying wrong impressions, when unconnected with the rest. I am, therefore, the more obliged (and gladly embrace this opportunity of expressing the obligations I feel) to his Lordship, for what little he has allowed me to transcribe.

Speaking of the route from Pekin to Gehol in Tartary, Lord Macartney observes: "Our journey, upon the whole, has been very pleasant and, being divided into seven days, not at all fatiguing. At the end of every stage we have been lodged and entertained in the wings or houses adjoining to the Emperor's palaces. These palaces, which occur at short distances from each other on the road, have been built for his reception, on his annual visit to Tartary. They are constructed upon nearly the same plan and in the same taste.[127] They front the south, and are usually situated on irregular ground near the basis of gentle hills which, together with their adjoining vallies, are enclosed by high walls and laid out in parks and pleasure grounds, with every possible attention to picturesque beauty. Whenever water can be brought into the view it is not neglected; the distant hills are planted, cultivated, or left naked, according to their accompaniments in the prospect. The wall is often concealed in a sunk fence, in order to give an idea of greater extent. A Chinese gardener is the painter of nature, and though totally ignorant of perspective, as a science, produces the happiest effects by the management, or rather pencilling, of distances, if I may use the expression, by relieving or keeping down the features of the scene, by contrasting trees of a bright with those of a dusky foliage, by bringing them forward, or throwing them back, according to their bulk and their figure, and by introducing buildings of different dimensions, either heightened by strong colouring, or softened by simplicity and omission of ornament.

"The Emperor having been informed that, in the course of our travels in China we had shewn a strong desire of seeing every thing curious and interesting, was pleased to give directions to the first minister to shew us his park or garden at Gehol. It is called in Chinese *Van-shoo-yuen*, or Paradise of ten thousand (or innumerable) trees. In order to have this gratification (which is considered as an instance of uncommon favour) we rose this morning at three o'clock and went to the palace where we waited, mixed with all the great of [128] ficers of state, for three hours (such is the etiquette of the place) till the Emperor's appearance. At last he came forth, borne in the usual manner by sixteen persons on a high open palankeen, attended by guards, music, standards, and umbrellas without number; and observing us, as we stood in the front line, graciously beckoned us to approach, having ordered his people to stop; he entered into conversation with us; and, with great affability of manner, told us that he was on his way to the pagoda, where he usually paid his morning devotions; that as we professed a different religion from his he would not ask us to accompany him, but that he had ordered his first minister and chief Collaos to conduct us through his garden, and to shew us whatever we were desirous of seeing there.

Drawn by W^m. Alexander from a Sketch by Capt. Parish, Roy^l. Artil^l. Engraved by T. Medland.

View in the Eastern Side of the Imperial Park at Gehol.

Published by Messrs. Cadell, & Davies, Strand, London.
May 2, 1804.

"Having expressed my sense of this mark of his condescension in the proper manner, and my increasing admiration of every thing I had yet observed at Gehol, I retired and, whilst he proceeded to his adorations at the pagoda, I accompanied the ministers and other great Collaos of the court to a pavilion prepared for us, from whence, after a short collation, we set out on horseback to view this wonderful garden. We rode about three miles through a very beautiful park kept in the highest order and much resembling the approach to Luton in Bedfordshire; the grounds gently undulated and chequered with various groupes of well contrasted trees in the offskip. As we moved onward an extensive lake appeared before us, the extremities of which seemed to lose themselves in distance and obscurity. Here was a large and [129] magnificent yacht ready to receive us, and a number of smaller ones for the attendants, elegantly fitted up and adorned with numberless vanes, pendants, and streamers. The shores of the lake have all the varieties of shape, which the fancy of a painter can delineate, and are so indented with bays, or broken with projections, that almost every stroke of the oar brought a new and unexpected object to our view. Nor are islands wanting, but they are situated only where they should be, each in its proper place and having its proper character: one marked by a pagoda, or other building; one quite destitute of ornament; some smooth and level; some steep and uneven; and others frowning with wood, or smiling with culture. Where any things particularly interesting were to be seen we disembarked, from time to time, to visit them, and I dare say that, in the course of our voyage, we stopped at forty or fifty different palaces or pavilions. These are all furnished in the richest manner with pictures of the Emperor's huntings and progresses, with stupendous vases of jasper and agate; with the finest porcelain and Japan, and with every kind of European toys and *sing-songs*; with spheres, orreries, clocks, and musical automatons of such exquisite workmanship, and in such profusion, that *our* presents must shrink from the comparison, and *hide their diminished heads*; and yet I am told, that the fine things we have seen are far exceeded by others of the same kind in the apartments of the ladies, and in the European repository at *Yuen-min-yuen*. In every one of the pavilions was a throne, or imperial state, and a *Eu-jou*, or symbol of peace and prosperity, placed at[130] one side of it resembling that which the Emperor delivered to me yesterday for the king.

"It would be an endless task were I to attempt a detail of all the wonders of this charming place. There is no beauty of distribution, no feature of amenity, no reach of fancy which embellishes our pleasure grounds in England, that is not to be found here. Had China been accessible to Mr. Browne or Mr. Hamilton, I should have sworn they had drawn their happiest ideas from the rich sources, which I have tasted this day; for in the course of a few hours I have enjoyed such vicissitudes of rural delight, as I did not conceive could be felt out of England, being at different moments enchanted by scenes perfectly similar to those I had known there, to the magnificence of Stowe, the softer beauties of Wooburn, and the fairy-land of Paine's Hill.

"One thing I was particularly struck with, I mean the happy choice of situation for ornamental buildings. From attention to this circumstance they have not the air of being crowded or disproportioned; they never intrude upon the eye; but wherever they appear always shew themselves to advantage, and aid, improve, and enliven the prospect.

"In many places the lake is overspread with the Nenuphar or lotus (Nelumbium) resembling our broad leaved water lilly. This is an accompaniment which, though the Chinese are passionately fond of, cultivating it in all their pieces of water,[131] I confess I don't much admire. Artificial rocks and ponds with gold and silver fish are perhaps too often introduced, and the monstrous porcelain figures of lions and tygers, usually placed before the pavilions, are displeasing to an European eye; but these are trifles of no great moment; and I am astonished that now, after a six hours critical survey of these gardens, I can scarcely recollect any thing besides to find fault with.

"At our taking leave of the minister, he told us that we had only seen the eastern side of the gardens, but that the western side, which was the larger part still remained for him to shew us, and that he should have that pleasure another day.

"Accordingly, on the day of the Emperor's anniversary festival, after the ceremony was ended, the first or great Collao *Ho-chun-tong*, the *Foo-leou*, the *Foo-leou*'s brothers *Foo-chan-tong*, and *Song-ta-gin*, with the other great men who attended us two days since, in our visit to the eastern garden, now proposed to accompany us to the western, which forms a strong contrast with the other, and exhibits all the sublimer beauties of nature in as high a degree as the part which we saw before possesses the attractions of softness and amenity. It is one of the finest forest-scenes in the world; wild, woody, mountainous and rocky, abounding with stags and deer of different species, and most of the other beasts of the chase, not dangerous to man.[132]

"In many places immense woods, chiefly oaks, pines, and chesnuts, grow upon almost perpendicular steeps, and force their sturdy roots through every resistance of surface and of soil, where vegetation would seem almost impossible. These woods often clamber over the loftiest pinnacles of the stony hills, or gathering on the skirts of them, descend with a rapid sweep, and bury themselves in the deepest vallies. There, at proper distances, you find palaces, banquetting houses, and monasteries, (but without bonzes) adapted to the situation and peculiar circumstances of the place, sometimes with a rivulet on one hand, gently stealing through the glade, at other with a cataract tumbling from above, raging with foam, and rebounding with a thousand echoes from below, or silently engulphed in a gloomy pool, or yawning chasm.

"The roads by which we approached these romantic scenes are often hewn out of the living rock, and conducted round the hills in a kind of rugged stair-case, and yet no accident occurred in our progress, not a false step disturbed the regularity of our cavalcade, though the horses are spirited and all of them unshod. From the great irregularity of the ground, and the various heights to which we ascended, we had opportunities of catching many magnificent points of view by detached glances, but after wandering for several hours (and yet never wearied with wandering) we at last reached a covered pavilion open on all sides, and situated on a summit so elevated as perfectly to command the whole surrounding country to a vast extent. The radius of the ho[133]rizon I should suppose to be at least twenty miles from the central spot where we stood; and certainly so rich, so various, so beautiful, so sublime a prospect my eyes had never beheld. I saw every thing before me as on an illuminated map, palaces, pagodas, towns, villages, farm-houses, plains, and vallies, watered by innumerable streams, hills waving with woods, and meadows covered with cattle of the most beautiful marks and colours. All seemed to be nearly at my feet, and that a step would convey me within reach of them.

"I observed here a vast number of what we call in England *sheet* cows, also sheet horses, many pyeballs, dappled, mottled, and spotted, the latter chiefly strawberry.

"From hence was pointed out to us by the minister a vast enclosure below, which, he said, was not more accessible to him than to us, being never entered but by the Emperor, his women, or his Eunuchs. It includes within its bounds, though on a smaller scale, most of the beauties which distinguish the eastern and the western gardens which we have already seen; but from every thing I can learn it falls very short of the fanciful descriptions which Father Attiret and Sir William Chambers have intruded upon us as realities. That within these private retreats, various entertainments of the most novel and expensive nature are prepared and exhibited by the Eunuchs, who are very numerous (perhaps some thousands) to amuse the Emperor and his ladies, I have no doubt; but that they are carried to all the lengths of extravagance and improbability those gentle[134]men have mentioned, I very much question, as from every enquiry I have made (and I have not been sparing to make them) I have by no means sufficient reason to warrant me in acceding to, or confirming, the accounts which they have given us.

"If any place in England can be said in any respect to have similar features to the western park, which I have seen this day, it is Lowther Hall in Westmoreland, which (when I knew it many years ago) from the extent of prospect, the grand surrounding objects, the noble situation, the diversity of surface, the extensive woods, and command of water, I thought might be rendered by a man of sense, spirit, and taste, the finest scene in the British dominions."

After the descriptive and interesting detail of the beauties of the two sides of the imperial park or gardens of Gehol, his Lordship makes a few general observations on Chinese gardening, and the ornamental edifices that are usually employed to aid the effect, as well as contribute to use and convenience. He observes,

"Whether our style of gardening was really copied from the Chinese, or originated with ourselves, I leave for vanity to assert, and idleness to discuss. A discovery which is the result of good sense and reflexion may equally occur to the most distant nations, without either borrowing from the other. There is certainly a great analogy between our gardening[135] and the Chinese, but our excellence seems to be rather in improving nature, theirs to conquer her, and yet produce the same effect. It is indifferent to a Chinese where he makes his garden, whether on a spot favoured, or abandoned, by the rural deities. If the latter, he invites them, or compels them to return. His point is to change every thing from what he found it, to explode the old fashion of the creation, and introduce novelty in every corner. If there be a waste, he adorns it with trees; if a dry desert, he waters it with a river, or floats it with a lake. If there be a smooth flat, he varies it with all possible conversions. He undulates the surface, he raises it in hills, scoops it into vallies, and roughens it with rocks. He softens asperities, brings amenity into the wilderness, or animates the tameness of an expanse, by accompanying it with the majesty of a forest. Deceptions and eye-traps the Chinese are not unacquainted with, but they use them very sparingly. I observed no artificial ruins, caves, or hermitages. Though the sublime predominates in its proper station, you are insensibly led to contemplate it, not startled by its sudden intrusion, for in the plan cheerfulness is the principal feature, and lights up the face of the scene. To enliven it still more, the aid of architecture is invited; all the buildings are perfect of their kind, either elegantly simple, or highly decorated, according to the effect that is intended to arise, erected at suitable distances, and judiciously contracted, never crowded together in confusion, nor affectedly confronted, and staring at each other without meaning. Proper edifices in proper places. The[136] summer-house, the pavilion, the pagodas, have all their respective situations, which *they* distinguish and improve, but which any other structures would injure or deform. The only things disagreeable to my eye are the large porcelain figures of lions, tygers, &c.

46

and the rough hewn steps, and huge masses of rock work, which they seem studious of introducing near many of their houses and palaces. Considering their general good taste in the other points, I was much surprised at this, and could only account for it, by the expence and the difficulty of bringing together such incongruities, for it is a common effect of enormous riches to push every thing they can procure to bombast and extravagance, which are the death of taste. In other countries, however, as well as in China, I have seen some of the most boasted feats, either outgrowing their beauty from a plethora of their owner's wealth, or becoming capricious and hypocondriacal by a quackish application of it. A few fine places, even in England, might be pointed out that are labouring under these disorders; not to mention some celebrated houses where twisted stair-cases, window-glass cupolas, and embroidered chimney-pieces, convey nothing to us but the whims and dreams of sickly fancy, without an atom of grandeur, taste, or propriety.

"The architecture of the Chinese is of a peculiar style, totally unlike any other, irreducible to our rules, but perfectly consistent with its own. It has certain principles, from which it never deviates, and although, when examined ac[137]cording to ours, it sins against the ideas we have imbibed of distribution, composition, and proportion; yet, upon the whole, it often produces a most pleasing effect, as we sometimes see a person without a single good feature in his face have, nevertheless, a very agreeable countenance."

CHAP. IV.
Sketch of the State of Society in China.—Manners, Customs, Sentiments, and Moral Character of the People.

Condition of Women, a Criterion of the State of Society.—Degraded State of in China.—Domestic Manners unfavourable to Filial Affection.—Parental Authority.—Ill Effects of Separating the Sexes.—Social Intercourse unknown, except for gaming.—Their Worship Solitary.—Feasts of New Year.—Propensity to gaming.—Influence of the Laws seems to have destroyed the natural Character of the People.—Made them indifferent, or cruel.—Various Instances of this Remark in public and in private Life.—Remarks on Infanticide.—Perhaps less general than usually thought.—Character of Chinese in Foreign Countries.—Temper and Disposition of the Chinese.—Merchants.—Cuckoo-Clocks.—Conduct of a Prince of the Blood.—Of the Prime Minister.—Comparison of the Physical and Moral Characters of the Chinese and Mantchoo Tartars.—General Character of the Nation illustrated.

IT may, perhaps, be laid down as an invariable maxim, that[138] the condition of the female part of society in any nation will furnish a tolerable just criterion of the degree of civilization to which that nation has arrived. The manners, habits, and prevailing sentiments of women, have great influence on those of the society to which they belong, and generally give a turn to its character. Thus we shall find that those nations, where the moral and intellectual powers of the mind in the female sex are held in most estimation, will be governed by such laws as are[139] best calculated to promote the general happiness of the people; and, on the contrary, where the personal qualifications of the sex are the only objects of consideration, as is the case in all the despotic governments of Asiatic nations, tyranny, oppression, and slavery are sure to prevail; and these personal accomplishments, so far from being of use to the owner, serve only to deprive her of liberty, and the society of her friends; to render her a degraded victim, subservient to the sensual gratification, the caprice, and the jealousy of tyrant man. Among savage tribes the labour and drudgery invariably fall heaviest on the weaker sex.

The talents of women, in our own happy island, began only in the reign of Queen Elizabeth to be held in a proper degree of consideration. As women, they were admired and courted, but they scarcely could be said to participate in the society of men. In fact, the manners of our forefathers, before that reign, were too rough for them. In Wales, wives were sold to their husbands. In Scotland, women could not appear as evidences in a court of justice. In the time of Henry the Eighth, an act was passed prohibiting women and apprentices from reading the New Testament in the English language. Among the polished Greeks, they were held in little estimation. Homer degrades all his females: he makes the Grecian princesses weave the web, spin, and do all the drudgery of a modern washerwoman; and rarely allows them any share of social intercourse with the other sex. Yet the very foundations on which he has constructed his two matchless poems are women. It appears also from all the dramatic writers of ancient Greece, whose aim[140] was "to hold as 'twere the mirror up to nature, to shew the very age and body of the time its form and pressure," that notwithstanding their extreme delicacy of taste, and rapid progress in the fine arts, their manners were low and coarse, and that they were entire strangers to any other gratification arising from the society of women, than the indulgence of the sensual appetite. Even the grave Herodotus mentions, in the highest terms of approbation, the custom of Babylon of selling by auction, on a certain fixed day, all the young women who had any pretensions to beauty, in order to raise a sum of money for portioning off the rest of the females, to whom nature had been less liberal in bestowing her gifts, and who were knocked down to those who were satisfied to take them with the least money. This degradation of women would seem to be as impolitic as it is extraordinary since, under their guidance, the earliest, and sometimes the most indelible (I believe I may safely add, the best and most amiable) impressions are stamped on the youthful mind. In infancy their protection is indispensably necessary, and in sickness, or in old age, they unquestionably afford the best and kindest relief: or, as a French author has neatly observed, "*Sans les femmes, les deux extrémités de la vie seraient sans secours, et le milieu sans plaisirs.*" "Without woman the two extremities of life would be helpless, and the middle of it joyless."

The Chinese, if possible, have imposed on their women a greater degree of humility and restraint than the Greeks of old, or the Europeans in the dark ages. Not satisfied with the physical deprivation of the use of their limbs, they have contrived, in order to keep them the more confined, to make it a moral[141] crime for a woman to be seen abroad. If they should have occasion to visit a friend or relation, they must be carried in a close sedan chair: to walk would be the height of vulgarity. Even the country ladies, who may not possess the luxury of a chair, rather than walk, suffer themselves to be sometimes rolled about in a sort of covered wheelbarrow. The wives and daughters, however, of the lower class are neither confined to the house, nor exempt from hard and slavish labour, many being obliged to work with an infant upon the back, while the husband, in all probability, is gaming, or otherwise idling away his time. I have frequently seen women assisting to drag a sort of light plough, and the harrow. Nieuwhoff, in one of his prints, taken from drawings supposed to be made in China, yokes, if I mistake not, a woman to the same plough with an ass. Should this be the fact, the Chinese are not singular, if we may credit the Natural Historian of Antiquity[a], who observes that, to open the fertile fields of *Byzacium* in Africa, it was necessary to wait until the rains had soaked into the ground; "after which a little weakly ass, and an old woman, attached to the same yoke, were sufficient to drag the plough through the soil," *post imbres vili asello, et a parte altera jugi anu vomerem trahente vidimus scindi.*

In the province of *Kiang-see* nothing is more common than to see a woman drawing a kind of light plough, with a single handle, through ground that has previously been prepared. The easier task of directing the machine is left to the husband, [142]who, holding the plough with one hand, at the same time with the other casts the seed into the drills.

The advantages which those women possess in a higher sphere of life, if any, are not much to be envied. Even at home, in her family, a woman must neither eat at the same table, nor sit in the same room with her husband. And the male children, at the age of nine or ten, are entirely separated from their sisters. Thus the feelings of affection, not the instinctive products of nature, but the offspring of frequent intercourse and of a mutual communication of their little wants and pleasures, are nipped in the very bud of dawning sentiment. A cold and ceremonious conduct must be observed on all occasions between the members of the same family. There is no common focus to attract and concentrate the love and respect of children for their parents. Each lives retired and apart from the other. The little incidents and adventures of the day, which furnish the conversation among children of many a long winter's evening, by a comfortable fire-side, in our own country, are in China buried in silence. Boys, it is true, sometimes mix together in schools, but the stiff and ceremonious behaviour, which constitutes no inconsiderable part of their education, throws a restraint on all the little playful actions incident to their time of life and completely subdues all spirit of activity and enterprize. A Chinese youth of the higher class is inanimate, formal, and inactive, constantly endeavouring to assume the gravity of years.[143]

To beguile the many tedious and heavy hours, that must unavoidably occur to the secluded females totally unqualified for mental pursuits, the tobacco-pipe is the usual expedient. Every female from the age of eight or nine years wears, as an appendage to her dress, a small silken purse or pocket to hold tobacco and a pipe, with the use of which many of them are not unacquainted at this tender age. Some indeed are constantly employed in working embroidery on silks, or in painting birds, insects, and flowers on thin gauze. In the ladies' apartments of the great house in which we lived at Pekin, we observed some very beautiful specimens of both kinds in the pannels of the partitions, and I brought home a few articles which I understand have been much admired; but the women who employ their time in this manner are generally the wives and daughters of tradesmen and artificers, who are usually the weavers both of cottons and silks. I remember asking one of the great officers of the court, who wore a silken vest beautifully embroidered, if it was the work of his lady, but the supposition that his wife should condescend to use her needle seemed to give him offence.

Their manners in domestic life are little calculated to produce that extraordinary degree of filial piety, or affection and reverence towards parents, for which they have been eminently celebrated, and to the salutary effects of which the Jesuits have attributed the stability of the government. Filial duty is, in fact, in China, less a moral sentiment, than a precept which by length of time has acquired the efficacy of a positive law; and it may truly be said to exist more in the maxims of the go[141]vernment, than in the minds of the people. Had they, indeed, considered filial piety to be sufficiently strong when left to its own natural influence, a precept or law to enforce it would have been superfluous. The first maxim inculcated in early life is the entire submission of children to the will of their parents. The tenor of this precept is not only "to honour thy father and thy mother, that thy days may be long in the land;" but to labour for thy father and thy mother as long as they both shall live, to sell thyself into perpetual servitude for their support, if necessary, and to consider thy life at their disposal. So much has this sentiment of parental authority gained ground by precept and habit, that to all intents and purposes it is as binding as the strongest law. It gives to the parent the exercise of the same unlimited and arbitrary power over his children, that the Emperor, the common father, possesses by law over his people. Hence, as among the Romans, the father has the power to sell his son for a slave; and this power, either from caprice, or from poverty, or other causes, is not unfrequently put in force.

A law that is founded in reason or equity seldom requires to be explained or justified. The government of China, in sanctioning an act of parental authority that militates so strongly against every principle of nature, of moral right and wrong, seems to have felt the force of this remark. Their learned men have been employed in writing volumes on the subject, the principal aim of which appears to be that of impressing on the minds of the people the comparative authority of the Emperor over his subjects and of a parent over his children. The rea[145]sonableness and justice of the latter being once established, that of the former, in a patriarchal government, followed of course; and the extent of the power delegated to the one could not in justice be withheld from the other. And for the better allaying of any scruples that might be supposed to arise in men's consciences, it was easy to invent any piece of sophistry to serve by way of justification for those unnatural parents who might feel themselves disposed, or who from want might be induced, to part with their children into perpetual slavery. A son, says one of their most celebrated lawgivers, after the death of his father, has the power of selling his services for a day, or a year, or for life; but a father, while living, has unlimited authority over his son; a father has, therefore, the same right of selling the services of his son to another for any length of time, or even for life.

Daughters may be said to be invariably sold. The bridegroom must always make his bargain with the parents of his intended bride. The latter has no choice. She is a lot in the market to be disposed of to the highest bidder. The man, indeed, in this respect, has no great advantage on his side, as he is not allowed to see his intended wife until he arrives in formal procession at his gate. If, however, on opening the door of the chair, in which the lady is shut up, and of which the key has been sent before, he should dislike his bargain, he can return her to her parents; in which case the articles are forfeited that constituted her price; and a sum of money, in addition to them, may be demanded, not exceeding, however, the value of[146] these articles. These matrimonial processions, attended with pomp and music, are not unlike those used by the Greeks when the bride was conducted to her husband's house in a splendid car; only, in the former instance, the lady is completely invisible to every one.

To what a degraded condition is a female reduced by this absurd custom! How little inducement, it would be supposed, she could have to appear amiable or elegant, or to study her dress, or cramp her feet, or paint her face, knowing she will be consigned into the hands of the first man who will give the price that her parents have fixed upon her charms. No previous conversation is allowed to take place, no exchange of opinions or comparison of sentiments with regard to inclinations or dislikes; all the little silent acts of attention and kindness, which so eloquently speak to the heart, and demonstrate the sincerity of the attachment, are utterly unfelt. In a word, that state of the human heart, occasioned by the mutual affection between the sexes, and from whence proceed the happiest, the most interesting, and sometimes also, the most distressing moments of life, has no existence in China. The man takes a wife because the laws of the country direct him to do so, and custom has made it indispensable; and the woman, after marriage, continues to be the same piece of inanimate furniture she always was in her father's house. She suffers no indignity, nor does she feel any jealousy or disturbance (at least it is prudent not to shew it) when her husband brings into the same house a second, or a third woman. The first is contented with the honour of[147] presiding over, and directing the concerns of, the family within doors, and in hearing the children of the others calling her mother.

It might be urged, perhaps, on the part of the husband, that it would be highly unreasonable for the woman to complain. The man who purchased her ought to have an equal right in the same manner to purchase others. The case is materially different where parties are united by sentiments of love and esteem, or bound by promises or engagements; under such circumstances the introduction of a second wife, under the same roof, could not fail to disturb the harmony of the family, and occasion the most poignant feelings of distress to the first. But a Chinese wife has no such feelings, nor does the husband make any such engagements.

Although polygamy be allowed by the government, as indeed it could not well happen otherwise where women are articles of purchase, yet it is an evil that, in a great degree, corrects itself. Nine-tenths of the community find it difficult to rear the offspring of one woman by the labour of their hands; such, therefore, are neither in circumstances, nor probably feel much inclination, to purchase a second. The general practice would, besides, be morally impossible. In a country where so many female infants are exposed, and where the laws or custom oblige every man to marry, any person taking to himself two wives must leave some other without one, unless indeed it be supposed with the author of *L'Esprit des Loix*, what there seems to be no grounds for supposing, that a much greater[148] number of females are born than of males. But all the observations of this lively and ingenious author with regard to China, and particularly the inferences he draws with respect to climate, fall to the ground. It is not the vigour of natural propensities, as he has supposed, that destroys the moral ones; it is not the effect of climate that makes it to be considered among these people "as a prodigy of virtue for a man to meet a fine woman in a retired chamber without offering violence to her,"—it is the effect of studiously pampering the appetite, nurturing vicious notions, considering women as entirely subservient to the pleasures of man; and, in short, by fancying those pleasures in the head, rather than feeling them in the heart, that have led them to adopt a sentiment which does the nation so little credit. The climate being every where temperate, and the diet of the majority of the people moderate, I might say scanty, these have little influence in promoting a vehement desire for sexual intercourse. It is indeed among the upper ranks only and a few wealthy merchants (whom the sumptuary laws, prohibiting fine houses, gardens, carriages, and every kind of external shew and grandeur, have encouraged secretly to indulge and pamper their appetite in every species of luxury and voluptuousness) where a plurality of wives are to be found. Every great officer of state has his haram consisting of six, eight, or ten women, according to his circumstances and his inclination for the sex. Every merchant also of Canton has his seraglio; but a poor man finds one wife quite sufficient for all his wants, and the children of one woman as many, and sometimes more, than he is able to support.[149]

The unsociable distance which the law (or custom, stronger than law) prescribes to be observed between the sexes, and the cool and indifferent manner of bargaining for a wife, are not calculated to produce numerous instances of criminal intercourse. These, however, sometimes happen, and the weight of punishment always fall heaviest on the woman. The husband finds no difficulty in obtaining a sentence of divorce, after which he may sell her for a slave and thus redeem a part at least of his purchase-money. The same thing happens in case a wife should elope, instances of which I fancy are still more rare; as if she be of any fashion, her feet are ill calculated to carry her off with speed; and if a young girl should chance to lose what is usually held to be the most valuable part of female reputation, she is sent to market by her parents and publicly sold for a slave. In cases of mutual dislike, or incompatibility of temper, the woman is generally sent back to her parents. A woman can inherit no property, but it may be left to her by will. If a widow has no children, or females only, the property descends to the nearest male relation on the deceased husband's side, but he must maintain the daughters until he can provide them with husbands.

The prohibition against the frequent intercourse with modest females, for there are public women in every great city, is not attended here with the effect of rendering the pursuit more eager; nor does it increase the ardour, as among the ancient Spartans who were obliged to steal, as it were, the embraces of their lawful wives. In China it seems to have the contrary effect of promoting that sort of connexion which, being one of[150] the greatest violations of the laws of nature, ought to be considered among the first of moral crimes—a connexion that sinks the man many degrees below the brute. The commission of this detestable and unnatural act is attended with so little sense of shame, or feelings of delicacy, that many of the first officers of state seemed to make no hesitation in publicly avowing it. Each of these officers is constantly attended by his pipe-bearer, who is generally a handsome boy from fourteen to eighteen years of age, and is always well dressed. In pointing out to our notice the boys of each other, they made use of signs and motions, the meaning of which was too obvious to be misinterpreted. The two Mahomedans, I observe, who were in China in the ninth century, have also taken notice of this circumstance: and I find in the journal of Mr. Hittner, a gentleman who was in that part of the suite who accompanied the British Embassador into Tartary, in speaking of the palaces of Gehol, the following remark: "Dans l'un de ces palais, parmi d'autres chefs-d'œuvres de l'art, on voyait deux statues de garçons, en marbre, d'un excellent travail; ils avaient les pieds et les mains liés, et leur position ne laissait point de doute que le vice des Grecs n'eût perdu son horreur pour les Chinois. Un vieil eunuque nous les fit remarquer avec un sourire impudent."

It has been remarked that this unnatural crime prevails most in those countries where polygamy is allowed, that is to say, in those countries where the affections of women are not consulted, but their persons purchased for gold—a remark which may lead to this conclusion, that it is rather a moral turpitude[151] than a propensity arising from physical or local causes. The appetite for female intercourse soon becomes glutted by the facility of enjoyment; and where women, so circumstanced, can only receive the embraces of their proprietors from a sense of duty, their coldness and indifference, the necessary consequence of such connections, must also increase in the men the tendency to produce satiety. I think it has been observed that, even in Europe, where females in general have the superior advantage of fixing their own value upon themselves, it is the greatest rakes and debauchees, who,

"——bred at home in idleness and riot,
Ransack for mistresses th' unwholesome stews,
And never know the worth of virtuous love."

fly sometimes in search of fresh enjoyment in the detestable way here alluded to[2].

I have already observed that the state of domestic society in China was ill calculated to promote the affection and kindness which children not only owe to, but really feel for, their parents in many countries of Europe. A tyrant, in fact, to command, and a slave to obey, are found in every family; for, where the father is a despot, the son will naturally be a slave; and if all the little acts of kindness and silent attentions, that create [152]mutual endearments, be wanting among the members of the same family, living under the same roof, it will be in vain to expect to find them in the enlarged sphere of public life. In fact, they have no kind of friendly societies nor meetings to talk over the transactions and the news of the day. These can only take place in a free government. A Chinese having finished his daily employment retires to his solitary apartment. There are, it is true, a sort of public houses where the lower orders of people sometimes resort for their cup of tea or of *seau-tchoo* (a kind of ardent spirit distilled from a mixture of rice and other grain) but such houses are seldom, if at all, frequented for the sake of company. They are no incitement, as those are of a similar kind in Europe, to jovial pleasures or to vulgar ebriety. From this odious vice the bulk of the people are entirely free. Among the multitudes which we daily saw, in passing from one extremity of the country to the other, I do not recollect having ever met with a single instance of a man being disguised in liquor. In Canton, where the lower orders of people are employed by Europeans and necessarily mix with European seamen, intoxication is not infrequent among the natives, but this vice forms no part of the general character of the people. Whenever a few Chinese happen to meet together, it is generally for the purpose of gaming, or to eat a kettle of boiled rice, or drink a pot of tea, or smoke a pipe of tobacco.

The upper ranks indulge at home in the use of opium. Great quantities of this intoxicating drug are smuggled into the country, notwithstanding all the precautions taken by the government to prohibit the importation of it; but it is too expensive[153] to be used by the common people. The officers of the customs are not beyond a bribe. After receiving the sum agreed upon between the importer and themselves they frequently become the purchasers of the prohibited article. Most of the country ships from Bengal carry opium to China; but that of Turkey sent from London in the China ships is preferred, and sells at near double the price of the other. The governor of Canton, after describing in one of his late proclamations on the subject the pernicious and fatal effects arising from the use of opium, observes, "Thus it is that foreigners by the means of a vile excrementitious substance derive from this empire the most solid profits and advantages; but that our countrymen should blindly pursue this destructive and ensnaring vice, even till death is the consequence, without being undeceived, is indeed a fact odious and deplorable in the highest degree." Yet the governor of Canton very composedly takes his daily dose of opium.

The young people have no occasional assemblies for the purpose of dancing and of exercising themselves in feats of activity which, in Europe, are attended with the happy effects of shaking off the gloom and melancholy that a life of constant labour or seclusion from society is apt to promote. They have not even a fixed day of rest set apart for religious worship. Their acts of devotion partake of the same solitary cast that prevails in their domestic life. In none of the different sects of religion, which at various times have been imported into, and adopted in China, has congregational worship been[154] inculcated, which, to that country in particular, may be considered as a great misfortune. For, independent of religions considerations, the sabbatical institution is attended with advantages of a physical as well as of a moral nature; and humanity is not less concerned than policy in consecrating one day out of seven, or some other given number, to the service of the great Creator, and to rest from bodily labour. When the government of France, in the height of her rage for innovation, fell into the hands of atheistical demagogues, when her temples were polluted and every thing sacred was invaded and profaned, the seventh day was considered as a relic of ancient superstition and the observance of it accordingly abolished; and, about the same time, it became the fashion among a certain description of people to use specious arguments against its continuance in our own country; as being, for example, a day for the encouragement of idleness, drunkenness, and dissipation. Such a remark could only be applied to large cities and towns; and in crowded manufacturing towns the mechanic, who can subsist by working three days in the week, would be at no loss in finding opportunities, were there no sabbath day, in the course of the other four to commit irregularities. And who, even for the sake of the mechanic and artificer, would wish to see the labouring peasant deprived of one day's rest, out of seven, which to him is more precious than the wages he has hardly earned the other six? What man, possessed of common feelings of humanity, in beholding the decent and modest husbandman, accompanied by his family in their best attire attending the parish-church, does not participate in the smile of content which on this day particularly beams on his countenance,[155] and bespeaks the serenity of his mind? Having on this day discharged his duty to God, refreshed his body with rest, enjoyed the comfort of clean clothing, and exercised his mind in conversing with his neighbours, he returns with double vigour to his daily labour; having, as Mr. Addison observes in one of his Spectators, rubbed off the rust of the week.

The first of the new year in China, and a few succeeding days, are the only holidays, properly speaking, that are observed by the working part of the community. On these days the poorest peasant makes a point of procuring new clothing for himself and his family; they pay their visits to friends and relations, interchange civilities and compliments, make and receive presents; and the officers of government and the higher ranks give feasts and entertainments. But even in those feasts there is nothing that bears the resemblance of conviviality. The guests never partake together of the same service of dishes, but each has frequently his separate table; sometimes two, but never more than four, sit at the same table; and their eyes must constantly be kept upon the master of the feast, to watch all his motions, and to observe every morsel he puts into his mouth, and every time he lifts the cup to his lips; for a Chinese of good-breeding can neither eat nor drink without a particular ceremony, to which the guests must pay attention. If a person invited should, from sickness or any accident, be prevented from fulfilling his engagement, the portion of the dinner that was intended to be placed on his table is sent in procession to his own house; a custom that strongly points out the very little notion[156] they entertain of the *social* pleasures of the table. It is customary to send after each guest the remains even of his dinner. Whenever in the course of our journey we visited a governor or viceroy of a province, we generally found him at the head of a range of tables, covered with a multitude of dishes, which invariably were marched after us to the yachts. Martial, if I mistake not, has some allusion to a similar custom among the Romans. Each carried his own napkin to a feast, which being filled with the remains of the entertainment was sent home by a slave; but this appears to have been done more out of compliment to the host, to shew the great esteem in which they held his cheer, than for the sake of the viands; for the Romans loved conviviality.

The Chinese also, like the ancient Egyptians as exemplified in the enormous mess which Joseph gave to little Benjamin above the rest of his brothers, testify, on all occasions, that they consider the measure of a man's stomach to depend more upon the rank of its owner than either his bulk or appetite. The Embassador's allowance was at least five times as great as that of any person in his suite. In this particular, however, these nations are not singular, neither in ancient nor in modern times. The kings of Sparta, and indeed every Grecian hero, were always supposed to eat twice the quantity of a common soldier; and the only difference with regard to our heroes of the present day consists in their being enabled to convert quantity into quality, an advantage for which they are not a little indebted to the invention of money, into which all other articles can be commuted.[157]

Whatever may be the occasion of bringing together a few idlers, they seldom part without trying their luck at some game of chance for which a Chinese is never unprepared. He rarely goes abroad without a pack of cards in his pocket or a pair of dice. Both of these, like almost every thing else in the country, are different from similar articles elsewhere. Their cards are much more numerous than ours, and their games much more complicated. Nor are they at any loss, even if none of the party should happen to be furnished with cards or dice; on such an emergency their fingers are employed to answer the purpose, which are all that is required to play the game of *Tsoi-moi*, a game of which the lower class of people is particularly fond. Two persons, sitting directly opposite to each other, raise their hands at the same moment, when each calls out the number he guesses to be the sum of the fingers expanded by himself and his adversary. The closed fist is none, the thumb one, the thumb and forefinger two, &c. so that the chances lie between 0 and 5, as each must know the number held out by himself. The middling class of people likewise play at this game when they give entertainments where wine is served, and the loser is always obliged to drink off a cup of wine. At this childish game two persons will sometimes play to a very late hour, till he who has had the worst of the game has been obliged to drink so much wine that he can no longer see either to count his own or his adversary's fingers. I have thus particularly noticed the Chinese *Tsoi-moi*, on account of the extraordinary coincidence between it and a game in use among the Romans, to which frequent allusion is made by Cicero. In a note by Melancthon on Cicero's Offices it is thus described. "*Micare digitis,* ludi genus est. Sic ludentes, simul digitos alterius[158] manus quot volunt citissime erigunt, et simul ambo divinant quot simul erecti sint; quod qui definivit, lucratus est: unde acri visu opus est, et multa fide, ut cum aliquo in tenebris mices." "*Micare digitis,* is a kind of game. Those who play at it stretch out, with great quickness, as many fingers of one hand each, as they please, and at the same instant both guess how many are held up by the two together; and he who guesses right wins the game: hence a sharp sight is necessary, and also great confidence when it is played in the dark."

The Chinese have certainly the *acer visus*, but I doubt much whether they have faith enough in each other's integrity to play at the game of fingers in the dark, which, in the opinion of Cicero, was a strong test of a truly honest man. The same game is said to be still played in Italy under the name of *Morra.*[8]

The officers about Yuen-min-yuen used to play a kind of chess, which appeared to me to be essentially different from that game as played by the Persians, the Indians, and other oriental nations, both with regard to the lines drawn on the board, the form of the chess-men, and the moves, from which I should rather conclude it to be a game of their own invention, than an introduction either from India or by the army of *Gengis-khan,* as some authors have conjectured.

[159]
The spirit of gaming is so universal in most of the towns and cities, that in almost every bye-corner, groupes are to be found playing at cards or throwing dice. They are accused even of frequently staking their wives and children on the hazard of a die. It may easily be conceived that where a man can sell his children into slavery, there can be little remorse, in the breast of a gamester reduced to his last stake, to risk the loss of what the law has sanctioned him to dispose of. Yet we are very gravely assured by some of the reverend missionaries, that "the Chinese are entirely ignorant of all games of chance;" that "they can enjoy no amusements but such as are authorized by the laws." These gentlemen surely could not be ignorant that one of their most favourite sports is cock-fighting, and that this cruel and unmanly *amusement,* as they are pleased to consider it, is full as eagerly pursued by the upper classes in China as, to their shame and disgrace be it spoken, it continues to be by those in a similar situation in some parts of Europe. The training of quails for the same cruel purpose of butchering each other furnishes abundance of employment for the idle and dissipated. They have even extended their enquiries after fighting animals into the insect tribe, in which they have discovered a species of *gryllus,* or locust, that will attack each other with such ferocity as seldom to quit their hold without bringing away at the same time a limb of their antagonist. These little creatures are fed and kept apart in bamboo cages; and the custom of making them devour each other is so common that, during the summer months, scarcely a boy is seen without his cage and his grasshoppers.[160]

I have already had occasion to observe that the natural disposition of the Chinese should seem to have suffered almost a total change by the influence of the laws and maxims of government, an influence which, in this country more than elsewhere, has given a bias to the manners, sentiments, and moral character of the people; for here every ancient proverb carries with it the force of a law. While they are by nature quiet, passive, and timid, the state of society and the abuse of the laws by which they are governed, have rendered them indifferent, unfeeling, and even cruel, as a few examples, which among many others occurred, will but too clearly bear evidence; and as the particular instances, from which I have sometimes drawn an inference, accorded with the common actions and occurrences of life, I have not hesitated to consider them as so many general features in their moral character; at the same time I am aware that allowances ought to be made for particular ways of thinking, and for customs entirely dissimilar from our own, which are, therefore, not exactly to be appreciated by the same rule as if they had occurred in our own country. The public feasts of Sparta, in which the girls danced naked in presence of young men, had not the same effect on the Lacedemonian youth, as they might be supposed to produce in Europe; nor is the delicacy of the Hindoo women offended by looking on the Lingam. Thus the Chinese are entitled to our indulgence by the peculiar circumstances under which they are placed, but I leave it in the breast of the reader to make what allowance he may think they deserve.[161]

The common practice of flogging with the bamboo has generally been considered by the missionaries in the light of a gentle correction, exercised by men in power over their inferiors, just as a father would chastise his son, but not as a punishment to which disgrace is attached. However lightly these gentlemen may chuse to treat this humiliating chastisement, to which all are liable from the prime minister to the peasant, it is but too often inflicted in the anger and by the caprice of a man in office, and frequently with circumstances of unwarrantable cruelty and injustice. Of the truth of this remark we had several instances. In our return down the *Pei-ho*, the water being considerably shallower than when we first sailed up this river, one of our accommodation barges got aground in the middle of the night. The air was piercing cold, and the poor creatures belonging to the vessel were busy until sun-rise in midst of the river, using their endeavours to get her off. The rest of the fleet had proceeded, and the patience of the superintending officer at length being exhausted, he ordered his soldiers to flog the whole crew; which was accordingly done in a most unmerciful manner and this was their only reward for the use of the yacht, their time and labour for two days. The instance of degrading an officer and flogging all his people, because the meat brought for our use was a little tainted when the temperature was at 88° in the shade, I have already had occasion to notice.

Whenever the wind was contrary, or it was found necessary to track the vessels against the stream, a number of men were employed for this purpose. The poor creatures were always[162] pressed into this disagreeable and laborious service, for which they were to receive about six-pence a day so long as they tracked, without any allowance being made to them for returning to the place from whence they were forced. These people knowing the difficulty there was of getting others to supply their places, and that their services would be required until such should be procured, generally deserted by night, disregarding their pay. In order to procure others, the officers dispatched their soldiers to the nearest village, taking the inhabitants by surprize and forcing them out of their beds to join the yachts. Scarcely a night occurred in which some poor wretches did not suffer the lashes of the soldiers for attempting to escape, or for pleading the excuse of old age, or infirmity. It was painful to behold the deplorable condition of some of these creatures. Several were half naked and appeared to be wasting and languishing for want of food. Yet the task of dragging along the vessels was far from being light. Sometimes they were under the necessity of wading to the middle in mud; sometimes to swim across creeks, and immediately afterwards to expose their naked bodies to a scorching sun; and they were always driven by a soldier or the lictor of some petty police officer carrying in his hand an enormous whip, with which he lashed them with as little reluctance as if they had been a team of horses.

The Dutch Embassy proceeded by land to the capital, in the middle of winter, when the rivers and canals were frozen. The thermometer was frequently from 8 to 16 degrees below the freeing point, and the face of the country was mostly covered with ice and snow; yet they were often under the neces[163]sity of travelling all night; and the peasantry, who were pressed to carry the presents and their baggage, notwithstanding their heavy loads, were obliged to keep up with them as long as they could. In the course of two nights, Mr. Van Braam observes, not less than eight of these poor wretches actually expired under their burdens, through cold, hunger, fatigue, and the cruel treatment of their drivers.

It had been the practice of some of the gentlemen of the British embassy, in their return through the country, to walk during a part of the day, and to join the barges towards the hour of dinner. One day an officer of high rank took it into his head to interrupt them in their usual walk, and for this purpose dispatched after them nine or ten of his soldiers, who forced them in a rude manner to return to the vessels. Our two conductors *Van* and *Chou*, coming up at the time, and being made acquainted with the circumstance, gave to each of the soldiers a most severe flogging. One of these, who had been particularly insolent, had his ears bored through with iron wire, and his hands bound to them for several days. The viceroy of Canton was at this time with the embassy, and being in rank superior to the offending officer, he ordered the latter to appear before him, gave him a severe reprimand, and sentenced him to receive forty strokes of the bamboo as a *gentle correction*. Our two

Chinese friends were particularly pressing that the gentlemen insulted should be present at the punishment of the officer, and it was not without difficulty they could be persuaded that such a scene would not afford them any gratification. It happened also, in the Dutch embassy, that an inferior officer was flogged and[164] disgraced by their conductors for not having in readiness a sufficient number of coolies or porters to proceed with the baggage, and to carry the sedan chairs in which they travelled.

The tyranny that men in office exercise over the multitude, and each other, is perfectly agreeable to the systematic subordination which the law has sanctioned. But as authority is a dangerous deposit in the hands of the wisest, and leads sometimes the most wary to

"Play such fantastic tricks before high heaven
As make the angels weep,"

what must the effects of it be when vested in an illiterate Chinese or rude Tartar who has no other talent or recommendation for his authority than the power alone which his office allows him to exercise?

Several instances however occurred in the course of our journey through the country, which seemed to mark the same unfeeling and hard-hearted disposition to exist between persons of equal condition in life, as in men in office over their inferiors. One of these afforded an extraordinary trait of inhumanity. A poor fellow at Macao, in the employ of the British factory there, fell by accident from a wall and pitched upon his skull. His companions took him up with very little appearance of life and, in this state, were carrying him away towards the skirts of the town, where they were met by one of the medical gentlemen belonging to the embassy. He interrogated them what they meant to do with the unfortunate man, and was very[165] coolly answered, they were going to bury him. Having expressed his astonishment that they should think of putting a man into the grave before the breath was out of his body, they replied that they were of opinion he never could recover, and that if they carried him home he would only be a trouble and expence to his friends so long as he remained in a situation which rendered him unable to assist himself. The man, however, by the humanity and attention of Doctor Scott, was restored again to his family and to those friends who knew so well to appreciate the value of his life.

The doctor however was not aware of the risk he ran in thus exercising his humanity, as by a law of the country, which appears to us extraordinary, if a wounded man be taken into the protection and charge of any person with a view to effect his recovery, and he should happen to die under his hands, the person into whose care he was last taken is liable to be punished with death, unless he can produce undeniable evidence to prove how the wound was made, or that he survived it forty days. The consequence of such a law is, that if a person should happen to be mortally wounded in an affray, he is suffered to die in the streets, from the fear (should any one take charge of him) of being made responsible for his life.

A striking instance of the fatal effects of such a law happened at Canton lately. A fire broke out in the suburbs and three Chinese, in assisting to extinguish it, had their limbs fractured and were otherwise dreadfully wounded by the falling of a wall. The surgeon of the English factory, with all the alacrity to ad[166]minister relief to suffering humanity, which characterizes the profession in Britain, directed them to be carried to the factory, and was preparing to perform amputation, as the only possible means of saving their lives, when one of the Hong merchants having heard what was going on ran with great haste to the place, and entreated the surgeon by no means to think of performing any operation upon them, but rather to suffer them to be taken away from the factory as speedily as possible; adding that, however good his intentions might be, if any one of the patients should die under his hands, he would inevitably be tried for murder, and the most mitigated punishment would be that of banishment for life into the wilds of Tartary. The wounded Chinese were accordingly removed privately, and, no doubt, abandoned to their fate.

The operation of such a barbarous law (for so it appears to us) will serve to explain the conduct of the Chinese in the following instance. In the course of our journey down the grand canal we had occasion to witness a scene, which was considered as a remarkable example of a want of fellow-feeling. Of the number of persons who had crowded down to the banks of the canal several had posted themselves upon the high projecting stern of an old vessel which, unfortunately, breaking down with the weight, the whole groupe tumbled with the wreck into the canal, just at the moment when the yachts of the embassy were passing. Although numbers of boats were sailing about the place, none were perceived to go to the assistance of those that were struggling in the water. They even seemed not to know that such an accident had happened, nor could the shrieks of the boys, [167] floating on pieces of the wreck, attract their attention. One fellow was observed very busily employed in picking up, with his boat-hook, the hat of a drowning man. It was in vain we endeavoured to prevail on the people of our vessel to heave to and send the boat to their assistance. It is true, we were then going at the rate of seven miles an hour, which was the plea they made for not stopping. I have no doubt that several of these unfortunate people must inevitably have perished.

Being thus insensible to the sufferings of their companions and countrymen, little compassion is to be expected from them towards strangers. From a manuscript journal, kept by a gentleman in the suite of the Dutch Embassador, it appears that, on their route to the capital, the writer felt an inclination to try his skaits on a sheet of ice that they passed by the road-side; he was also urged to it by the conducing officers. Having proceeded to some distance from the shore, the ice gave way and he fell in up to the neck. The Chinese, instead of rendering him any assistance, in the absence of his own countrymen who had gone forwards, ran away laughing at this accident and left him to scramble out as well as he could, which was not effected without very great difficulty.

But, if further proofs were wanting to establish the insensible and incompassionate character of the Chinese, the horrid practice of infanticide, tolerated by custom and encouraged by the government, can leave no doubt on this subject.—I venture to say encouraged, because where the legislature does not interfere to prevent crimes, it certainly may be said to lend them its [168] countenance. No law, however, allows, as I observe it noticed in a modern author of reputation, a father to expose all the daughters and the third son. I believe the laws of China do not suppose such an unnatural crime to exist, and have therefore provided no punishment for it. It is true, they have left a child to the entire disposal of the father, concluding, perhaps, that if his feelings will not prevent him from doing an injury, no other consideration will. Thus, though the commission of infanticide be frequent in China, it is considered as more prudent to wink at it as an inevitable evil which natural affection will better correct than penal statues; an evil that, on the other hand, if publicly tolerated, would directly contradict the grand principle of filial piety, upon which their system of obedience rests, and their patriarchal form of government is founded.

It is, however, tacitly considered as a part of the duty of the police of Pekin to employ certain persons to go their rounds, at an early hour in the morning, with carts, in order to pick up such bodies of infants as may have been thrown out into the streets in the course of the night. No inquiries are made, but the bodies are carried to a common pit without the city walls, into which all those that may be living, as well as those that are dead, are said to be thrown promiscuously. At this horrible pit of destruction the Roman Catholic missionaries, established in Pekin, attend by turns as a part of the duties of their office, in order, as one of them expressed himself to me on this subject, to chuse among them those that are the most *lively*, to make future proselytes, and by the administration of baptism to such of the [169] rest as might be still alive, *pour leur sauver l'âme*. The Mahomedans who, at the time that their services were useful in assisting to prepare the national calendar, had a powerful influence at Court, did much better: these zealous bigots to a religion, whose least distinguishing feature is that of humanity, were, however, on these occasions, the means of saving the *lives* of all the little innocents they possibly could save from this maw of death, which was an humane act, although it might be for the purpose of bringing them up in the principles of their own faith. I was assured by one of the Christian missionaries, with whom I had daily conversation during a residence of five weeks within the walls of the Emperor's palace at *Yuen-min-yuen*, and who took his turn in attending, *pour leur sauver l'âme*, that such scenes were sometimes exhibited on these occasions as to make the feeling mind shudder with horror. When I mention that dogs and swine are let loose in all the narrow streets of the capital, the reader may conceive what will sometimes necessarily happen to the exposed infants, before the police-carts can pick them up.

The number of children thus unnaturally and inhumanly slaughtered, or interred alive, in the course of a year, is differently stated by different authors, some making it about ten and others thirty thousand in the whole empire. The truth, as generally happens, may probably lie about the middle. The missionaries, who alone possess the means of ascertaining nearly the number that is thus sacrificed in the capital, differ very materially in their statements: taking the mean, as given by those with whom we conversed on the subject, I should conclude that[170] about twenty-four infants were, on an average, in Pekin, daily carried to the pit of death where the little innocents that have not yet breathed their last are condemned without remorse,

"——to be stifled in the vault,
To whose foul mouth no healthsome air breathes in,
And there die."

This calculation gives nine thousand nearly for the capital alone, where it is supposed about an equal number are exposed to that of all the other parts of the empire. Those, whose constant residence is upon the water, and whose poverty, or superstition, or total insensibility, or whatever the cause may be that leads them to the perpetration of an act against which nature revolts, sometimes, it is said, expose their infants by throwing them into the canal or river with a gourd tied round their necks, to keep the head above water, and preserve them alive until some humane person may be induced to pick them up. This hazardous experiment, in a country where humanity appears to be reduced to so low an ebb, can only be considered as an aggravation of cruelty. I have seen the dead body of an infant, but without any gourd, floating down the river of Canton among the boats, and the people seemed to take no more notice of it than if it had been the carcase of a dog: this, indeed, would in all probability have attracted their attention, dogs being an article of food commonly used by them; the miserable half-famished Chinese, living upon the water, are glad to get any thing in the shape of animal food, which they will even eat in a state of putrefaction. Yet, little scrupulous as they are with[171] regard to diet, I am not credulous enough to believe the information of a Swedish author[9] to be correct in his statement of a cure for a certain disease, though "he has no reason to doubt of the fact," *per τεκνοφαγιαν alternis diebus, alternis jejunio—by eating children every other day!*

A picture so horrid in its nature as the exposing of infants presents to the imagination is not to be surpassed among the most savage nations. The celebrated legislator of Athens made no law to punish parricide, because he considered it as a crime against nature, too heinous ever to be committed, and that the bare supposition of such a crime would have disgraced the country. The Chinese, in like manner, have no positive law against infanticide. The laws of the rude and warlike Spartans allowed infanticide, of which, however, the parents were not the perpetrators, nor the abettors. Nor, among these people, were the weak and sickly children, deemed by the magistrates unlikely ever to become of use to themselves, or to the public, thrown into the αποθηκη, or common repository of the dead bodies of children, until life had been previously extinguished, we will charitably suppose, by gentle and the least painful means.

The exposing of children, however, it must be allowed, was very common among the ancients. The stern and rigid virtues of the Romans allowed this among many other customs, that were more unnatural than amiable, and such as in civilized societies of the present day would have been considered among the most atrocious of moral crimes. A Roman father, if his in[172]fant was meant to be preserved, lifted it from the ground in his arms; if he neglected that ceremony, the child, it would seem, was considered as doomed to exposure in the highway. Thus, in the Andrian of Terence, where, though the scene is not laid in Rome, Roman customs are described, "quidquid peperisset, decreverunt tollere." "Let it be boy or girl they have resolved to lift it from the ground." Nor indeed is secret infanticide unknown in modern Europe, although it may be owing to a different principle. In such cases, the sense of shame and the fear of encountering the scorn and obloquy of the world have determined the conduct of the unhappy mother, before the feelings of nature could have time to operate. For I am willing to hope that none who had ever experienced a mother's feelings and a mother's joy would consent by any means, direct or indirect, or under any impression of fear of shame, of scorn, or biting penury, to the destruction of a new-born babe. And I may venture to say with confidence, that a British cottager, however indigent, would divide his scanty pittance among a dozen children rather than consent to let some of them perish, that he and the rest might fare the better, were even our laws as tacit on this subject as those of China.

Some of the Christian missionaries, in their accounts of this country, have attempted to palliate the unnatural act of exposing infants, by attributing it to the midwife, who they pretend to say, from knowing the circumstances of the parents, strangle the child without the knowledge of the mother, telling her that the infant was still-born. Others have ascribed the practice to a belief in the metempsycosis, or transmigration of souls into [173] other bodies, that the parents, seeing their children must be doomed to poverty, think it is better at once to let the soul escape in search of a more happy asylum, than to linger in one condemned to want and wretchedness. No degree of superstition, one would imagine, could prevail upon a parent to reason thus, in that most anxious and critical moment when the combined efforts of hope and fear, of exquisite joy and severe pain, agitate by turns the mother's breast. Besides, the Chinese trouble themselves very little with superstitious notions, unless where they apprehend some personal danger. Nor is it more probable that the midwife should take upon herself the commission of a concealed and voluntary murder of an innocent and helpless infant, for the sake of sparing those feelings in another, of which the supposition implies she could not possibly partake; and if she should be encouraged by the father, whose affections for an infant child may be more gradually unfolded than the mother's, to perpetrate so horrid an act, we must allow that to the evidence of unnatural and murtherous parents must be added that of hired ruffians; so that Chinese virtue would gain little by such a supposition.

It is much more probable that extreme poverty and hopeless indigence, the frequent experience of direful famines, and the scenes of misery and calamity occasioned by them, acting on minds whose affections are not very powerful, induce this unnatural crime which common custom has encouraged, and which is not prohibited by positive law. That this is the case, and that future advantages are not overlooked, will appear from the circumstance of almost all the infants that are exposed being fe[171]males, who are the least able to provide for themselves, and the least profitable to their parents; and the practice is most frequent in crowded cities, where not only poverty more commonly prevails, but so many examples daily occur of inhumanity, of summary punishments, acts of violence and cruelty, that the mind becomes callous and habituated to scenes that once would have shocked, and is at length scarcely susceptible of the enormity of crimes.

I am afraid, however, it is but too common a practice even in the remotest corners of the provinces. A respectable French missionary, now in London, who was many years in *Fo-kien*, told me that he once happened to call on one of his converts just at the moment his wife was brought to-bed. The devoted infant was delivered to the father in order to be plunged into a jar of water that was prepared for the purpose. The missionary expostulated with the man on the heinousness of an act that was a crime against God and nature. The man persisted that, having already more than he could support, it would be a greater crime to preserve a life condemned to want and misery, than to take it away without pain. The missionary, finding that no argument of his was likely to divert him from his purpose, observed "that, as a Christian, he could not refuse him the satisfaction of saving the infant's soul by baptism." During the ceremony, as the father held the infant in his arms he happened to fix his eyes on its face, when the missionary thought he perceived the feelings of nature begin to work; and he protracted the ceremony to give time for the latent spark of parental affection to kindle into flame. When the ceremony was ended; "Now," [175] says the missionary, "I have done my duty in saving a soul from perishing." "And I," rejoined the man, "will do mine, by saving its life," and hurried away with the infant to deposit it in the bosom of its mother.

How very weak then, in reality, must be the boasted filial affection of the Chinese for their parents, when they scruple not to become the murderers of their own children, towards whom, according to the immutable laws of nature, the force of affection will ever be stronger than for those whom the laws of China, in preference, have commanded to be protected and supported when rendered incapable of assisting themselves. The truth of this observation, which I believe few will call in question, is a strong proof that, as I have already remarked, filial piety among the Chinese may rather be considered in the light of an ancient precept, carrying with it the weight of a positive law, than the effect of sentiment.

It is right to mention here (what however is no palliation of the crime, though a diminution of the extent of it) a circumstance which I do not recollect to have seen noticed by any author, and the truth of which I have too good authority to call in question. As every corpse great and small must be carried to a place of burial at a considerable distance without the city, and as custom requires that all funerals should be conducted with very heavy expences, people in Pekin, even those in comfortable circumstances, make no hesitation in laying in baskets still-born children, or infants who may die the first month, knowing that they will be taken up by the police.[176] This being the case, we may easily conceive that, in a city said to contain three millions of people, a great proportion of the nine thousand, which we have supposed to be annually exposed, may be of the above description. According to the rules of political arithmetic, and supposing half of those who died to be exposed, the number would be diminished to about 4000. The expence attending a Chinese funeral is more extravagant than an European can well conceive. A rich Hong merchant at Canton is known to have kept his mother near twelve months above ground, because it was not convenient for him to bury her in a manner suitable to his supposed wealth and station.

I am informed also that foundling hospitals do exist in China, but that they are on a small scale, being raised and supported by donations of individuals, and their continuance is therefore as precarious as the wealth of their charitable founders.

These unfavourable features in the character of a people, whose natural disposition is neither ferocious nor morose; but, on the contrary, mild, obliging, and cheerful, can be attributed only to the habits in which they have been trained, and to the heavy hand of power perpetually hanging over them. That this is actually the case may be inferred from the general conduct and character of those vast multitudes who, from time to time, have emigrated to the Philippine islands, Batavia, Pulo Pinang and other parts of our East Indian settlements. In those places they are not less remarkable for their honesty, than for their peaceable and industrious habits. To the Dutch in Batavia they are[177] masons, carpenters, tailors, shoemakers, shopkeepers, bankers, and, in short, every thing. Indolence and luxury are there arrived to such a height that, without the assistance of the Chinese, the Dutch would literally be in danger of starving. Yet the infamous government of that place, in the year 1741, caused to be massacred, in cold blood, many thousands of these harmless people who offered no resistance; neither women nor children escaped the fury of these blood-hounds.

In these places it appears also, that their quickness at invention is not surpassed by accuracy of imitation, for which they have always been accounted remarkably expert in their own country. Man is, by nature, a hoarding animal; and his endeavours to accumulate property will be proportioned to the security and stability which the laws afford for the possession and enjoyment of that property. In China, the laws regarding property are insufficient to give it that security: hence the talent of invention is there seldom exercised beyond suggesting the means of providing for the first necessities and the most pressing wants. A man, indeed, is afraid here to be considered as wealthy, well knowing that some of the rapacious officers of the state would find legal reasons to extort his riches from him.

The exterior deportment of every class in China is uncommonly decent, and all their manners mild and engaging; but even these among persons of any rank are considered as objects worthy the interference of the legislature; hence it follows that they are ceremonious without sincerity, studious of the forms only of politeness[178] without either the ease or elegance of good-breeding. An inferior makes a sham attempt to fall on his knees before his superior, and the latter affects a slight motion to raise him. A common salutation has its mode prescribed by the court of ceremonies; and any neglect or default in a plebeian towards his superior is punishable by corporal chastisement, and in men in office by degradation or suspension. In making thus the exterior and public manners of the people a concern of the legislature, society in many respects was considerably benefited. Between equals, and among the lower orders of people, abusive language is very unusual, and they seldom proceed to blows. If a quarrel should be carried to this extremity, the contest is rarely attended with more serious consequences than the loss of the long lock of hair growing from the crown of the head, or the rent of their clothes. The act of drawing a sword, or presenting a pistol, is sufficient to frighten a common Chinese into convulsions; and their warriors shew but few symptoms of bravery. The Chinese may certainly be considered among the most timid people on the face of the earth; they seem to possess neither personal courage, nor the least pretence of mind in dangers or difficulties; consequences that are derived probably from the influence of the moral over the physical character. Yet there is perhaps no country where acts of suicide occur more frequently than in China, among the women as well as the men: such acts being marked with no disgrace, are not held in any abhorrence. The government, indeed, should seem to hold out encouragement to suicide, by a very common practice of mitigating the sentence of death, in allowing the criminal to be his own executioner. [179] The late viceroy of Canton, about two years ago, put an end to his life by swallowing his stone snuff-bottle, which stuck in the oesophagus; and he died in excruciating agonies.

In a government, where every man is liable to be made a slave, where every man is subject to be flogged with the bamboo at the nod of one of the lowest rank of those in office, and where he is compelled to kiss the rod that beats him or, which amounts to the same thing, to thank the tyrant on his knees for the trouble he has taken to correct his morals, high notions of honour and dignified sentiments are not to be expected. Where the maxims of the government commanding, and the opinions of the people agreeing, that corporal punishment may be inflicted, on the ground of a favour conferred upon the person punished, a principle of humiliation is admitted that is well calculated to exclude and obliterate every notion of the dignity of human nature.

A slave, in fact, cannot be dishonoured. The condition itself of being dependent upon and subject to the caprice of another, without the privilege of appeal, is such a degraded state of the human species, that those who are unfortunately reduced to it have no further ignominy or sense of shame to undergo. The vices of such a condition are innumerable, and they appear on all occasions among this people celebrated (rather undeservedly I think) for their polished manners and civilized government. A Chinese merchant will cheat, whenever an opportunity offers him the means, because he is considered to be [180] incapable of acting honestly; a Chinese peasant will steal when ever he can do it without danger of being detected, because the punishment is only the bamboo, to which he is daily liable; and a Chinese prince, or a prime minister, will extort the property of the subject, and apply it to his private use, whenever he thinks he can do it with impunity. The only check upon the rapacity of men in power is the influence of fear, arising from the possibility of detection: the love of honour, the dread of shame, and a sense of justice, seem to be equally unfelt by the majority of men in office.

It would be needless to multiply instances to those already on record of the refined knavery displayed by Chinese merchants in their dealings with Europeans, or the tricks that they play off in their transactions with one another. They are well known to most nations, and are proverbial in their own. A merchant with them is considered as the lowest character in the country, as a man that will cheat if he can, and whose trade it is to create and then supply artificial wants. To this general character, which public opinion has most probably made to be what it is, an exception is due to those merchants who, acting under the immediate sanction of the government, have always been remarked for their liberality and accuracy in their dealings with Europeans trading to Canton. These men who are styled the *Hong* merchants, in distinction to a common merchant whom they call *mai-mai-gin, a buying and selling man*, might not unjustly be compared with the most eminent of the mercantile class in England. [181]

But as traders in general are degraded in all the state maxims, and consequently in public opinion, it is not surprising they should attach so little respect to the character of foreign merchants trading to their ports, especially as several knavish tricks have been practised upon them, in spite of all their acuteness and precaution. The gaudy watches of indifferent workmanship, fabricated purposely for the China market and once in universal demand, are now scarcely asked for. One gentleman in the Honourable East India Company's employ took it into his head that cuckoo clocks might prove a saleable article in China, and accordingly laid in a large assortment, which more than answered his most sanguine expectations. But as these wooden machines were constructed for sale only, and not for use, the cuckoo clocks became all mute long before the second arrival of this gentleman with another cargo. His clocks were now not only unsaleable, but the former purchasers threatened to return theirs upon his hands, which would certainly have been done, had not a thought entered his head, that not only pacified his former customers but procured him also other purchasers for his second cargo—he convinced them by undeniable authorities, that the cuckoo was a very odd kind of bird which sung only at certain seasons of the year, and assured them that whenever the proper time arrived, all the cuckoos they had purchased would once again "tune their melodious throats." After this it would only be fair to allow the Chinese sometimes to trick the European purchaser with a wooden ham instead of a real one.

But as something more honourable might be expected in a prince of the blood, a grandson of the Emperor, I shall just[182] mention one anecdote that happened during my abode in the palace of *Yuen-min-yuen*. This gentleman, then about five-and-twenty years of age, having no ostensible employment, came almost daily to the hall of audience, where we were arranging the presents for the Emperor. He had frequently desired to look at a gold time-piece which I wore in my pocket; one morning I received a message from him, by one of the missionaries, to know if I would sell it and for what price. I explained to the missionary that, being a present from a friend and a token of remembrance, I could not willingly part with it, but that I would endeavour to procure him one equally good from our artificers who I thought had such articles for sale. I soon discovered, however, that his Royal Highness had already been with these people, but did not like their prices. The following morning a second missionary came to me, bringing a present from the prince consisting of about half a pound of common tea, a silk purse, and a few trumpery trinkets, hinting at the same time, that he was expected to carry back the watch in return as an equivalent. I requested the missionary immediately to take back the princely present, which he did with considerable reluctance, dreading his Highness's displeasure. The poor fellow happened to have a gold watch about him, which he was desired to shew; and the same day he had a visit from one of the prince's domestics to say, that his master would do him the honour to accept his watch; which he was not only under the necessity of sending, but was obliged to thank him, on his knees, for this extraordinary mark of distinction. He told me, moreover, that this same gentleman had at least a dozen watches which had been procured in the same honourable way.[183]

In the list of presents carried by the late Dutch Embassador were two grand pieces of machinery, that formerly were a part of the curious museum of the ingenious Mr. Coxe. In the course of the long journey from Canton to Pekin they had suffered some slight damage. On leaving the capital they discovered, through one of the missionaries, that while these pieces were under repair, the prime minister *Ho-tchung-tang* had substituted two others of a very inferior and common sort to complete the list, reserving the two grand pieces of clockwork for himself, which, at some future period, he would, perhaps, take the merit of presenting to the Emperor in his own name.

These examples but too clearly illustrate a great defect in the boasted moral character of the Chinese. But the fault, as I before observed, seems to be more in the system of government than in the nature and disposition of the people. The accession of a foreign power to the throne, by adopting the language, the laws, and the customs of the conquered, has preserved with the forms all the abuses of the ancient government. The character of the governors may differ a little, but that of the governed remains unchanged. The Tartars, by assuming the dress, the manners, and the habits of the Chinese, by being originally descended from the same stock, and by a great resemblance of features, are scarcely distinguishable from them in their external appearance. And if any physical difference exist, it seems to be in stature only, which may have arisen from local causes. The Chinese are rather taller, and of a more slender and delicate form than the Tartars, who are in general[184] short, thick, and robust. The small eye, elliptical at the end next to the nose, is a predominating feature in the cast of both the Tartar and the Chinese countenance, and they have both the same high cheek bones and pointed chins, which, with the custom of shaving off the hair, gives to the head the shape of an inverted cone, remarkable enough in some subjects, but neither so general, nor so singular, as to warrant their being considered among the *monsters* in nature, *Homo monstrosus,macrocephalus, capite conico, Chinensis*[10]. The head of our worthy conductor *Van-ta-gin*, who was a real Chinese, had nothing in its shape different from that of an European, except the eye. The portrait of this gentleman, drawn by Mr. Hickey, is so strong a likeness, and he was deservedly so great a favourite of every Englishman in the train of the British Embassador, that I am happy in having in opportunity of placing it at the head of this work.

The natural colour both of the Chinese and Tartars seems to be that tint between a fair and dark complexion, which we distinguish the word *brunet* or *brunette*; and the shades of this complexion are deeper, or lighter, according as they have been more or less exposed to the influence of the climate. The women of the lower class, who labour in the fields or who dwell in vessels, are almost invariably coarse, ill-featured, and of a deep brown complexion, like that of the Hottentot. But this we find to be the case among the poor of almost every nation. Hard labour, scanty fare, and early and frequent parturi[185]tion, soon wither the delicate buds of beauty. The sprightliness and expression of the features, as well as the colour of the skin, which distinguish the higher ranks from the vulgar, are the effects of ease and education. We saw women in China, though very few, that might pass for beauties even in Europe. The Malay features however prevail in most; a small black or dark brown eye, a short rounded nose, generally a little flattened, lips considerably thicker than in Europeans, and black hair, are universal.

The Mantchoo Tartars would appear to be composed of a mixed race: among these we observed several, both men and women, that were extremely fair and of florid complexions: some had light blue eyes, straight or aquiline noses, brown hair, immense bushy beards, and had much more the appearance of Greeks than of Tartars. It is certainly not improbable that the Greeks of Sogdiana, whose descendants must have blended with the western Tartars and with whom the Mantchoos were connected, may have communicated this cast of countenance. *Tchien-lung*, whose nose was somewhat aquiline and complexion florid, used to boast of his descent from *Gengis-khan*: these, however, are exceptions to the general character, which is evidently the same as that of the Chinese.

But although their appearance and manners are externally the same, a closer acquaintance soon discovers that in disposition they are widely different. Those who are better pleased with a blunt sincerity bordering on rudeness than a studied complaisance approaching to servility; who may think it better to be[186] robbed openly than cheated civilly, will be apt to give the preference to the Tartar character. Yet those Tartars of distinction, who fill some of the higher situations in the state, soon lose their native roughness and are scarcely distinguishable in their manners and demeanour from the Chinese.

The ease, politeness, and dignified carriage of the old viceroy of *Pe-tche-lee*, who was a Mantchoo, could not be exceeded by the most practiced courtier in modern Europe: the attention he shewed to every thing that concerned the embassy, the unaffected manner in which he received and entertained us at *Tien-sing*; the kindness and condescension with which he gave his orders to the inferior officers and to his domestics, placed him in a very amiable point of view. He was a very fine old man of seventy-eight years of age, of low stature, with small sparkling eyes, a benign aspect, a long silver beard, and the whole of his appearance calm, venerable, and dignified. The manners of *Sun-ta-gin*, a relation of the Emperor and one of the six ministers of state, were no less dignified, easy, and engaging; and *Chung-ta-gin*, the new viceroy of Canton, was a plain, unassuming, and good-natured man. The prime minister *Ho-chang-tong*, the little Tartar legate, and the ex-viceroy of Canton, were the only persons of rank among the many we had occasion to converse with that discovered the least ill-humour, distant hauteur, and want of complaisance. All the rest with whom we had any concern, whether Tartars or Chinese, when in our private society, were easy, affable, and familiar, extremely good-humoured, loquacious, communicative. It was in public only, and towards each other, that they assumed their ceremonious[187] gravity, and practised all the tricks of demeanour which custom requires of them.

The general character, however, of the nation is a strange compound of pride and meanness, of affected gravity and real frivolousness, of refined civility and gross indelicacy. With an appearance of great simplicity and openness in conversation, they practise a degree of art and cunning against which an European is but ill prepared. Their manner of introducing the subject of the court ceremonies in conversation with the Embassador is no bad specimen of their sly address in managing matters of this sort. Some of them observed, by mere accident as it were, how curious it was to see the different modes of dress that prevailed among different nations: this naturally brought on a comparison between theirs and ours, the latter of which they pretended to examine with critical attention. After a good deal of circumlocutory observations, they thought their own entitled to the preference, being more convenient, on account of its being made wide and loose and free from tight ligatures; whereas ours must be exceedingly uneasy and troublesome in any other posture than that of standing upright; and particularly so in making the genuflections and prostrations which were customary and indeed necessary to be performed by all persons whenever the Emperor appeared in public. No notice being taken of this broad hint, so artfully introduced, they proceeded to compare their wide petticoats with our breeches, and to contrast the play and freedom of their knee-joints with the obstruction that our knee-buckles and garters must necessarily occasion. This brought them directly to the point, and they finished by[188] recommending, in the warmth of their friendship, that we should disencumber ourselves of our breeches, as they would certainly be inconvenient to appear in at court.

Of perseverance in negociation, or more properly speaking, *in driving a bargain*, the Tartar legate gave no bad specimen of his talent. Having in vain practiced every art to obtain from the Embassador an unconditional compliance with the court ceremony, he was sent at length by the Prime Minister to inform him, that the important point was finally decided and that the English mode was to be adopted; but, he observed, that as it was not the custom of China to kiss the Emperor's hand, he had something to propose to which there could be no objection, and which was that, in lieu of that part of the English ceremony, he should put the second knee upon the ground and, instead of bending one knee, to kneel on both. In fact, they negociate on the most trifling point with as much caution and preciseness, as if they were forming a treaty of peace, and with more address than some treaties of peace have been negociated.

As a direct refusal to any request would betray a want of good breeding, every proposal finds their immediate acquiescence; they promise without hesitation, but generally disappoint by the invention of some sly pretence or plausible objection. They have no proper sense of the obligations of truth. So little scrupulous indeed are they with regard to veracity, that they will assert and contradict without blushing, as it may best suit the purpose of the moment.[189]

The vanity of an usurped national superiority and a high notion of self-importance never forsake them on any occasion. Those advantages in others which they cannot avoid feeling, they will affect not to see. And although they are reduced to the necessity of employing foreigners to regulate their calendar and keep their clocks in order, although they are in the habit of receiving yearly various specimens of art and ingenuity from Europe, yet they pertinaciously affect to consider all the nations of the earth as barbarians in comparison of themselves. A Chinese merchant of Canton, who, from the frequent opportunities of seeing English ships, was not insensible of their advantages over those of his own nation which traded to Batavia and other distant ports, resolved, and actually began, to construct a vessel according to an English model; but the *Hoo-poo* or collector of the customs being apprized of it, not only obliged him to relinquish his project but fined him in a heavy penalty for presuming to adopt the modes of a barbarous nation. So great is their national conceit that not a single article imported into the country, as I have elsewhere observed, retains its name. Not a nation, nor person, nor object, that does not receive a Chinese appellation: so that their language, though poor, is pure.

The expressions made use of in salutation, by different nations, may perhaps be considered as deriving their origin from features of national character. *Lau-ye, Old sir*, is a title of respect, with which the first officers of state may be addressed, because the maxims of government have inculcated the doctrine of obedience, respect, and protection to old age. The common salutation among the lower orders of people in some of the[190] southern provinces is *Ya fan, Have you eaten your rice?* the greatest happiness that the common class of people in China can hope to enjoy consisting in their having a sufficiency of rice. Thus also the Dutch, who are considered as great eaters, have a morning salutation which is common among all ranks, *Smaakelyk eeten! May you eat a hearty dinner!* Another universal salutation among this people is, *Hoe vaart uwe? How do you sail?* adopted no doubt in the early periods of the Republic, when they were all navigators and fishermen. The usual salutation at Cairo is, How do you sweat? a dry hot skin being a sure indication of a destructive ephemeral fever. I think some author has observed, in contrasting the haughty Spaniard with the frivolous Frenchman, that the proud steady gait and inflexible solemnity of the former were expressed in his mode of salutation, *Come esta? How do you stand?* whilst the *Comment vous portez vous? How do you carry yourself?* was equally expressive of the gay motion and incessant action of the latter.

The Chinese are so ceremonious among themselves, and so punctilious with regard to etiquette, that the omission of the most minute point established by the court of ceremonies is considered as a criminal offence. Visiting by tickets, which with us is a fashion of modern refinement, has been a common practice in China some thousand years; but the rank of a Chinese visitor is immediately ascertained by the size, colour, and ornaments of his ticket, which also varies in all these points according to the rank of the person visited. The old Viceroy of *Pe-tche-lee's* ticket to the Embassador contained as much crimson-coloured paper as would be sufficient to cover the walls of a moderate-sized room.

CHAP. V.
Manners and Amusements of the Court—Reception of Embassadors—Character
and private Life of the Emperor—His Eunuchs and Women.

General Character of the Court—Of the Buildings about the Palace—Lord Macartney's *Account of his Introduction—Of the Celebration of the Emperor's Anniversary Festival—Of a Puppet-Shew—Comedy and Pantomime—Wrestling—Conjuring and Fire-Works—Reception and Entertainment of the Dutch Embassadors from a Manuscript Journal—Observations on the State of the Chinese Stage—Extraordinary Scene in one of their Dramas—Gross and indelicate Exhibitions—Sketch of* Kien-Long's *Life and Character—Kills his Son by an unlucky Blow—conceives himself immortal—Influence of the Eunuchs of the Tartar Conquest—their present State and Offices—Emperor's Wife, Queens, and Concubines—How disposed of at his Death.*

AFTER the sketch I have exhibited of the state of society[191] among the different ranks in China, a tolerable notion may be formed of the general character and complexion of the court. It is, as Lord Macartney has justly observed, "a singular mixture of ostentatious hospitality and inbred suspicion, ceremonious civility and real rudeness, shadowy complaisance and substantial perverseness; and this prevails through all the departments connected with the Court, although somewhat modified by the personal disposition of those at their head; but as[192] to that genuine politeness, which distinguishes our manners, it cannot be expected in Orientals, considering among other things the light in which they are accustomed to regard the female part of society." Whether the great ministers of state, who have daily intercourse in the different tribunals, sometimes relax from the stiff and formal deportment observed towards each other in public, I am not able to say, but when at Court they invariably observe certain stated forms and expression as studied and ceremonious as if they had never met before. It appeared to us highly ridiculous to see our friends, the two colleagues *Van-ta-gin* and *Chou-ta-gin,* on meeting in the precincts of the palace, performing to each other all the genuflexions and motions of the body which the ceremonial institutes of the empire require.

I rather suspect, however, that where any degree of confidence prevails among these people they sometimes enjoy their moments of conviviality. Our two worthy conductors met at Canton an old acquaintance who was governor of a city in Fo-kien. He gave them an evening entertainment on the river in a splendid yacht to which I was privately invited. On entering the great cabin I found the three gentlemen with each a young girl by his side very richly dressed, the cheeks, lips, and chin highly *rouged*, the rest of the face and neck whitened with a preparation of cerate. I was welcomed by a cup of hot wine from each of the ladies who first sipped by way of pledging me. During supper, which for number and variety of dishes exceeded any thing I had hitherto met with in the country, the girls played on the flute and sung several airs, but there was no[193]thing very captivating either in the vocal or instrumental part of the music. We passed a most convivial evening free from any reserve or restraint, but on going away I was particularly desired by *Van* not to take any notice of what I had seen, apprehensive, I suppose, that their brother officers might condemn their want of prudence in admitting a barbarian to witness their relaxation from good morals. The yacht and the ladies it seemed were hired for the occasion.

The incalculable numbers of the great officers of state and their attendants, all robed in the richest silks, embroidered with the most brilliant colours, and tissued with gold and silver, the order, silence, and solemnity with which they arrange and conduct themselves on public court-days are the most commanding features on such occasions.

This sober pomp of Asiatic grandeur is exhibited only at certain fixed festivals; of which the principal is the anniversary of the Emperor's birth-day, the commencement of a new year, the ceremonial of holding the plough, and the reception of foreign embassadors, most of whom they contrive to be present at one or other of those festivals. The birth-day is considered to be the most splendid; when all the Tartar princes and tributuaries, and all the principal officers of government both civil and military, are expected to be present.

For reasons of state, which will be noticed hereafter, the Emperor rarely shews himself in public among the Chinese part[194] of his subjects, except on such occasions; and even then the exhibition is confined within the precincts of the palace from which the populace are entirely excluded. Consistent with their system of sumptuary laws there is little external appearance of pomp or magnificence in the establishment of the Emperor. The buildings that compose the palace and the furniture within them, if we except the paint, the gilding, and the varnish, that appear on the houses even of plebeians, are equally void of unnecessary and expensive ornaments. Those who should rely on the florid relations, in which the missionaries and some travellers have indulged in their descriptions of the palaces of Pekin and those of *Yuen-min-yuen*, would experience on visiting them a woful disappointment. These buildings, like the common habitations of the country, are all modelled after the form of a tent, and are magnificent only by a comparison with the others and by their number, which is sufficient, indeed, to form a town of themselves. Their walls are higher than those of ordinary houses, their wooden columns of greater diameter, their roofs are immense, and a greater variety of painting and gilding may be bestowed on the different parts; but none of them exceeds one story in height, and they are jumbled and surrounded with mean and insignificant hovels. Some writer has observed that the King of England is worse lodged at Saint James's palace than any sovereign in Europe. Were I to compare some of the imperial palaces in China to any royal residence in Europe it would certainly be to Saint James's; but the apartments, the furniture, and conveniences of the latter, bad as they are, infinitely transcend any of those in China. The stone or clay floors are indeed sometimes covered with a[195] carpet of English broad-cloth, and the walls papered; but they have no glass in the windows, no stoves, fire-places, or fire-grates in the rooms; no sofas, bureaux, chandeliers, nor looking-glasses; no book-cases, prints, nor paintings. They have neither curtains nor sheets to their beds; a bench of wood, or a platform of brick-work, is raised in an alcove, on which are mats or stuffed mattresses, hard pillows, or cushions, according to the season of the year; instead of doors they have usually skreens, made of the fibres of bamboo. In short, the wretched lodgings of the state-officers at the court of Versailles, in the time of the French monarchy, were princely palaces in comparison of those allotted to the first ministers of the Emperor of China, in the capital as well as at *Yuen-min-yuen*.

When attending the court, on public occasions, each courtier takes his meal alone in his solitary cell on a small square table crowded with bowls of rice and various stews; without table-linen or napkins, without knife, fork, or spoon; a pair of small sticks, or the quills of a porcupine, are the only substitutes for these convenient articles: placing the bowl under his chin, with these he throws the rice into his mouth and takes up the pieces of meat in his soup or stews. Having finished his lonely meal, he generally lies down to sleep. In a government so suspicious as that of China, if parties were known to meet together, the object of them might be supposed something beyond that of conviviality, which however mutual jealousy and distrust have prevented from growing into common use.

As the ready compliance of the late Dutch Embassadors with all the degrading ceremonies required by the Chinese, added to [196] their constant residence in the capital, gave them more opportunities of observing the manners and the amusements of the court than occurred to the British embassy, I shall here avail myself of that part of a journal relating to this subject, which was kept by a young gentleman in the suite of the former, and whose accuracy of observation may be depended on. The account given by him of the New Year's festival, added to Lord Macartney's description of his introduction and the birth-day solemnities, which his Lordship has obligingly permitted me to extract from his journal, together with my own observations at the palace of *Yuen-min-yuen*, will serve to convey a tolerably exact idea of the state, pleasures, and amusements of the great Monarch of China.

"On the 14th September," observes his Lordship, "at four o'clock in the morning we set out for the court, under the convoy of *Van-ta-gin*, and *Chou-ta-gin*, and reached it in little more than an hour, the distance being about three miles from our hotel. We alighted at the park gate, from whence we walked to the Imperial encampment, and were conducted to a large handsome tent prepared for us, on one side of the Emperor's. After waiting there about an hour, his approach was announced by drums and music, on which we quitted our tent and came forward upon the green carpet. He was seated in an open Palankeen, carried by sixteen bearers, attended by numbers of officers bearing flags, standards, and umbrellas; and as he passed we paid him our compliments, by kneeling on one knee, whilst all the Chinese made their usual prostrations. As soon as he had ascended his throne I came to the entrance of his tent, and [197] holding in both my hands a large gold box, enriched with diamonds, in which was enclosed the King's letter, I walked deliberately up and, ascending the steps of the throne, delivered it into the Emperor's own hands, who, having received it, passed it to the Minister by whom it was placed on the cushion. He then gave me, as the first present from him to his Majesty, the *Eu-shee*, or symbol of peace and prosperity, and expressed his hopes that my Sovereign and he should always live in good correspondence and amity. It is a whitish agate-looking stone, perhaps serpentine, about a foot and a half long, curiously carved, and highly prized by the Chinese; but to me it does not appear in itself to be of any great value.

"The Emperor then presented me with an *Eu-shee* of a greenish-coloured serpentine stone, and of the same emblematic character; at the same time he very graciously received from me a pair of beautiful enamelled watches, set with diamonds which, having looked at, he passed to the Minister.

"Sir George Staunton (whom, as he had been appointed Minister plenipotentiary, to act in case of my death or departure, I introduced to him as such) now came forward, and after kneeling upon one knee, in the same manner as I had done, presented to him two elegant air-guns, and received from him an *Eu-shee* of greenish stone nearly similar to mine. Other presents were sent, at the same time, to all the gentlemen of my train. We then descended from the steps of the [198] throne, and sat down upon cushions at one of the tables on the Emperor's left hand. And at other tables, according to their different ranks, the chief Tartar princes and the Mandarins of the court at the same time took their places; all dressed in the proper robes of their respective ranks. These tables were then uncovered and exhibited a sumptuous banquet. The Emperor sent us several dishes from his own table, together with some liquors, which the Chinese call wine; not however expressed from the grape, but distilled or extracted from rice, herbs, and honey.

"In about half an hour he sent for Sir George Staunton and me to come to him and gave to each of us, with his own hands, a cup of warm wine, which we immediately drank in his presence, and found it very pleasant and comfortable, the morning being cold and raw. Among other things he asked me the age of my Sovereign and, being informed of it, said he hoped he might live as many years as himself which were then eighty-three. His manner was dignified, but affable and condescending; and his reception of us was very gracious and satisfactory.

"The order and regularity in serving and removing the dinner was wonderfully exact, and every function of the ceremony performed with such silence and solemnity as in some measure to resemble the celebration of a religious mystery.

"There were present on this occasion three Embassadors from *Ta-tze* or Pegu, and six Mahomedan Embassadors[199] from the Kalmucs of the south-west, but their appearance was not very splendid. During the ceremony, which lasted five hours, various entertainments of wrestling, tumbling, wire-dancing, together with dramatic representations, were exhibited opposite the Emperor's tent, but at a considerable distance from it.

"The 17th of September, being the Emperor's birth day, we set out for the court at three o'clock in the morning, conducted by *Van-ta-gin, Chou-ta-gin,* and our usual attendants. We reposed ourselves about two hours in a large saloon at the entrance of the palace enclosure, where fruit, tea, warm milk, and other refreshments were brought to us. At last notice was given that the festival was going to begin, and we immediately descended into the garden, where we found all the great men and mandarins in their robes of state, drawn up before the Imperial pavilion. The Emperor did not shew himself, but remained concealed behind a screen, from whence I presume he could see and enjoy the ceremonies without inconvenience or interruption. All eyes were turned towards the place where his Majesty was imagined to be enthroned, and seemed to express an impatience to begin the devotions of the day. Slow, solemn music, muffled drums, and deep-toned bells, were heard at a distance;—on a sudden the sounds ceased, and all was still—again they were renewed, and then intermitted with short pauses; during which several persons passed backwards and forwards, in the proscenium or foreground of the tent, at if engaged in preparing some *grand coup-de-theatre.*[200]

"At length the great band, both vocal and instrumental, struck up with all their powers of harmony, and instantly the whole court fell flat upon their faces before this invisible Nebuchadnezzar, whilst

"He in his cloudy tabernacle shrined
Sojourned the while."

"The music might be considered as a sort of birth-day ode, or state anthem, the burthen of which was, '*Bow down your heads all ye dwellers upon earth, bow down your heads before the great Kien-long, the great Kien-long.*' And then all the dwellers upon China earth there present, except ourselves, bowed down their heads and prostrated themselves upon the ground at every renewal of the chorus. Indeed, in no religion either ancient or modern has the divinity ever been addressed, I believe, with stronger exterior marks of worship and adoration than were this morning paid to the phantom of his Chinese majesty. Such is the mode of celebrating the Emperor's anniversary festival, according to the court ritual. We saw nothing of him the whole day, nor did any of his ministers, I imagine, approach him, for they all seemed to retire at the same moment that we did.

"In the course of a tour we made in the gardens with the prime minister and other great officers of state, whom the Emperor had directed to attend us, we were entertained at one of the palaces with a collation of petitpatis, salt relishes, and other savoury dishes, with fruits and sweetmeats, milk[201] and ice-water; and as soon as we rose from table, a number of yellow boxes, or drawers, were carried in procession before us, containing several pieces of silk and porcelain, which we were told were presents to us from the Emperor, and we consequently made our bows as they passed. We were also amused with a Chinese puppet-shew which differs but little from an English one. There are a distressed princess confined in a castle, and a knight-errant, who, after fighting wild beasts and dragons, sets her at liberty and marries her; wedding-feasts, jousts, and tournaments. Besides these, there was also a comic drama, in which some personages not unlike punch and his wife, Bandemeer and Scaramouch performed capital parts. This puppet-shew, we were told, properly belongs to the ladies' apartments, but was sent out as a particular compliment to entertain us; one of the performances was exhibited with great applause from our conductors, and I understand it is a favourite piece at court.

"On the morning of the 18th September we again went to court, in consequence of an invitation from the Emperor, to see the Chinese comedy and other diversions given on occasion of his birth-day. The comedy began at eight o'clock and lasted till noon. The Emperor was seated on a throne, opposite the stage, which projected a good deal into the pit. The boxes were on each side without seats or divisions. The women were placed above, behind the lattices, so that they might enjoy the amusements of the theatre without being observed.[202]

"Soon after we came in, the Emperor sent for Sir George Staunton and me to attend him, and told us, with great condescension of manner, that we ought not to be surprised to see a man of his age at the theatre, for that he seldom came there except upon a very particular occasion like the present, for that, considering the extent of his dominions and the number of his subjects, he could spare but little time for such amusements. I endeavoured, in the turn of my answer, to lead him towards the subject of my embassy, but he seemed not disposed to enter into it farther than by delivering me a little box of old japan, in the bottom of which were some pieces of agate and other stones much valued by the Chinese and Tartars; and at the top a small book written and painted by his own hand, which he desired me to present to the king my master as a token of his friendship saying, that the old box had been 800 years in his family. He, at the same time, gave me a book for myself also written and painted by him, together with several purses for Areca nut. He likewise gave a purse of the same sort to Sir George Staunton, and sent some small presents to the other gentlemen of the embassy. After this several pieces of silk or porcelain, but seemingly of no great value, were distributed among the Tartar princes and chief courtiers, who appeared to receive them with every possible demonstration of humility and gratitude.

"The theatrical entertainments consisted of great variety, both tragical and comical; several distinct pieces were acted in succession, though without any apparent connexion with one an[203]other. Some of them were historical, and others of pure fancy, partly in *recitativo*, partly in singing, and partly in plain speaking, without any accompaniment of instrumental music, but abounding in battles, murders, and most of the usual incidents of the drama. Last of all was the grand pantomime which, from the approbation it met with, is, I presume, considered as a first-rate effort of invention and ingenuity. It seemed to me, as far as I could comprehend it, to represent the marriage of the ocean and the earth. The latter exhibited her various riches and productions, dragons, and elephants, and tygers, and eagles, and ostriches, oaks and pines, and other trees of different kinds. The ocean was not behind hand, but poured forth on the stage the wealth of his dominions, under the figures of whales and dolphins, porpesses and leviathans, and other sea monsters, besides ships, rocks, shells, spunges, and corals, all performed by concealed actors, who were quite perfect in their parts, and performed their characters to admiration. These two marine and land regiments, after separately parading in a circular procession for a considerable time, at last joined together and, forming one body, came to the front of the stage when, after a few evolutions, they opened to the right and left, to give room for the whale, who seemed to be the commanding officer, to waddle forward; and who, taking his station exactly opposite to the Emperor's box, spouted out of his mouth into the pit several tons of water, which quickly disappeared through the perforations of the floor. This ejaculation was received with the highest applause, and two or three of the great men at my elbow desired me to take par[204]ticular notice of it; repeating, at the same time, '*Hao. kung hao!*—'*charming, delightful!*

"A little before one o'clock in the afternoon we retired, and at four we returned to court to see the evening's entertainments, which were exhibited on the lawn, in front of the great tent or pavilion, where we had been first presented to the Emperor. He arrived very soon after us, mounted his throne, and gave the signal to begin. We had now wrestling and dancing, and tumbling and posture-making, which appeared to us particularly awkward and clumsy, from the performers being mostly dressed according to the Chinese *costume*, one inseparable part of which is a pair of heavy quilted boots with the soles of an inch thick. The wrestlers, however, seemed to be pretty expert and afforded much diversion to such as were admirers of the *Palæstra*.

"A boy climbed up a pole or bamboo thirty or forty feet high, played several gambols, and balanced himself on the top of it in various attitudes, but his performance fell far short of what I have often met with in India of the same kind.

"A fellow lay down on his back, and then raised his feet, legs, and thighs from his middle, perpendicularly, so as to form a right angle with his body. On the soles of his feet was placed a large round empty jar, about four feet long and from two and a half to three feet diameter. This he balanced for some time, turning it round and round horizon[205]tally, till one of the spectators put a little boy into it, who, after throwing himself into various postures at the mouth of it, came out and sat on the top. He then stood up, then fell flat upon his back, then shifted to his belly, and after shewing a hundred tricks of that sort, jumped down upon the ground and relieved his coadjutor.

"A man then came forward and after fastening three slender sticks to each of his boots took six porcelain dishes of about eighteen inches diameter, and balancing them separately at the end of a little ivory rod, which he held in his hand, and twirling them about for some time, put them one after the other upon the points of the six bootsticks abovementioned, they continuing to turn round all the while. He then took two small sticks in his left hand, and put dishes upon them in the same manner as upon the other, and also one more upon the little finger of his right hand, so that he had nine dishes annexed to him at once, all twirling together, which in a few minutes he took off one by one and placed them regularly on the ground, without the slightest interruption or miscarriage.

"There were many other things of the same kind, but I saw none at all comparable to the tumbling, rope-dancing, wire-walking, and straw balancing of Sadler's-Wells; neither did I observe any seats of equitation in the style of Hughes's and Ashley's amphitheatres, although I had been always told that the Tartars were remarkably skilful in the instruction and discipline of their horses. Last of all were[206] the fire-works which, in some particulars, exceeded any thing of the kind I had ever seen. In grandeur, magnificence, and variety, they were, I own, inferior to the Chinese fire-works we had seen at Batavia, but infinitely superior in point of novelty, neatness, and ingenuity of contrivance. One piece of machinery I greatly admired; a green chest of five feet square was hoisted up by a pulley to the height of fifty or sixty feet from the ground; the bottom was so constructed as then suddenly to fall out, and make way for twenty or thirty strings of lanterns inclosed in the box to descend from it, unfolding themselves from one another by degrees so as at last to form a collection of at least five hundred, each having a light of a beautifully coloured flame burning brightly within it. This devolution and developement of lanterns (which appeared to me to be composed of gauze and paper) were several times repeated, and every time exhibited a difference of colour and figure. On each side was a correspondence of smaller boxes, which opened in like manner as the others, and let down an immense network of fire, with divisions and compartments of various forms and dimensions, round and square, hexagons, octagons and lozenges, which shone like the brightest burnished copper, and flashed like prismatic lightning, with every impulse of the wind. The diversity of colours indeed with which the Chinese have the secret of cloathing fire seems one of the chief merits of their pyrotechny. The whole concluded with a volcano, or general explosion and discharge of suns and stars, squibs, bouncers, crackers, rockets, and grenades, which involved the gardens for above an hour after in a cloud of intolerable[207] smoke. Whilst these entertainments were going forward the Emperor sent to us a variety of refreshments, all which, as coming from him, the etiquette of the court required us to partake of, although we had dined but a short time before.

"However meanly we must think of the taste and delicacy of the court of China, whose most refined amusements seem to be chiefly such as I have now described, together with the wretched dramas of the morning, yet it must be confessed, that there was something grand and imposing in the general effect that resulted from the whole *spectacle*. The Emperor himself being seated in front upon his throne, and all his great men and officers attending in their robes of ceremony, and stationed on each side of him, some standing, some sitting, some kneeling, and the guards and standard-bearers behind them in incalculable numbers. A dead silence was rigidly observed, not a syllable articulated, nor a laugh exploded during the whole performance."

70

Such was the reception and the entertainment of the British Embassador at the court of Gehol, in *Mantchoo* Tartary, during the days of the festival of the Emperor's anniversary. I now proceed to give some account of the manner in which the Dutch Embassadors were received, and the entertainments that took place on the occasion of the festival of the new year, as related in the manuscript journal above alluded to.[208]

This journalist observes that, on approaching the capital of the empire, they were not a little astonished to find that the farther they advanced the more miserable and poor was the apparent condition of the people, and the face of the country; the clay-built huts and those of ill-burnt bricks were crumbling to dust; the temples were in ruins, the earthen gods were demolished, and their fragments strewed on the ground; and the district was thinly inhabited. The following day they entered Pekin but were turned out again to take up their lodgings in the suburbs, in a sort of stable. From this place they were ordered to proceed to the palace in their old travelling dresses, as their baggage was not yet arrived. They were drawn in small carts as crazy and as much out of order as their own dresses. Sitting in the bottom of these carts, without any seats, they waited within the walls of the palace a full hour, while an empty room was swept out for their reception. Having remained here for some time, a few planks were brought in, on which were arranged a number of dishes of meat and fish, stewed in different ways. Having finished their repast, thus ended their first day's visit.

The following morning, at five o'clock, they were again summoned to court, and ushered into a small room like that of the preceding day, without any kind of furniture. The weather being extremely cold, the thermometer many degrees below the freezing point, the Embassadors prevailed on the people to make a little fire which after some time was brought in, not however without letting them understand that it was an extra[209]ordinary mark of favour, it being the custom of the Chinese to let all Embassadors wait the arrival of the Emperor in the open air.

At length the Emperor made his appearance, carried by eight men in a yellow sedan chair. On his approaching the place where the Embassadors and their suite were standing, they were directed by the master of the ceremonies to fall down on their knees, and in this posture the first Embassador was instructed to hold in both his hands, above his head, the gold box in which was contained the letter for the Emperor: the second minister then stepped forwards, and took the letter out of his hands, which he delivered to the Emperor; and, at the same time, they were directed to bow their heads nine times to the ground, in token of acknowledgment for the gracious reception they had met with from his Chinese Majesty.

This ceremony being ended, they were desired to follow the Emperor's chair, which was carried to the side of a pond or bason in the gardens, then frozen over. From this place the Emperor was drawn on a sledge to a tent pitched on the ice, whilst the Embassador and his suite were conducted into a dirty hovel little better than a pig-stye, where they were desired to sit down on a sort of bench built of stone and mortar; for, like the room they were put into on a former day, it was destitute of the least furniture; and they were told that something presently would be brought for them to eat. On complaining to their conductors that this was not the manner in which they were accustomed to sit down to meat, and that they did not con[210]ceive such apartments to be at all suitable to the situation they had the honour to hold, they were shortly afterwards conducted into another room, little better however than the first, but partly furnished with a few old chairs and tables. The candlesticks were small blocks of wood, to which the candles were fastened with a couple of nails. A few dishes of stewed meat were served up and, as a great delicacy from the Emperor's table, were brought in, without any dish, a pair of stag's legs, which the Chinese threw down upon the naked table; and for this mark of imperial favour they were required to make the customary genuflections and nine prostrations.

Van Braam, in the journal which he or some of his friends published in Paris, gives a curious account of the manner in which they were fed from the Emperor's table: "La viande consistait en un morceau de côtes sur lequelles il n'y avait point un demi-pouce d'épaisseur d'une chair maigre, en un petit os de l'épaule ou il n'y avait presque pas de chair, et en quatre ou cinq autres ossemens fournis par le dos ou par les pattes d'un mouton, et qui semblaient

avoir été déja rongés. Tout ce dégoûtant ensemble était sur un plat sale et paraissait plutôt destiné à faire le regal d'un chien que le repas d'un homme. En Holland le dernier des mendians recevrait, dans un hôpital, une pittance plus propre, et cependant c'est une marque d'honneur de la part d'un Empereur envers un Ambassadeur! Peut-être même etait-ce le reste du Prince, et dans ce cas, selon l'opinion des Chinois, c'était le dernier terme de la faveur, puisque nous pouvions achever l'os que sa Majesté avait commencé à nettoyer."—
"The meat consisted of a[211] small piece of the ribs, on which there was not half an inch in thickness of lean flesh, and a small shoulder-blade almost without any upon it; and in four or five other pieces of bones from the back, or the legs of a sheep, which appeared to have been already gnawed. The whole of this disgusting mess was brought upon a dirty plate, and seemed much rather intended to feast a dog than as a refreshment for man. In Holland the meanest beggar would receive in an hospital his allowance in a neater manner; and yet it was intended as a mark of honour on the part of an Emperor towards an Embassador! Perhaps it was even the remains of the Sovereign, and in that case, according to the opinion of the Chinese, it was the greatest possible act of favour, since we should then have had an opportunity of finishing the bone which his Imperial Majesty had begun to pick."

The Dutch gentlemen, equally disgusted with the meanness and filthiness of the place, and with the pride and haughtiness of the people, became now reconciled to the shabby appearance of their old travelling dresses, which they began to consider as fully good enough for the occasion.

Having finished their elegant repast, the amusements of the day commenced on the ice. The Emperor made his appearance in a sort of sledge, supported by the figures of four dragons. This machine was moved about by several great Mandarins, some dragging before, and others pushing behind. The four principal ministers of state were also drawn upon the ice in their sledges by inferior mandarins. Whole troops of civil[212] and military officers soon appeared, some on sledges, some on skaits, and others playing at football upon the ice, and he that picked up the ball was rewarded by the Emperor. The ball was then hung up in a kind of arch, and several mandarins shot at it, in passing on skaits, with their bows and arrows. Their skaits were cut off short under the heel, and the forepart was turned up at right angles. Owing to this form, or to the inexpertness of the skaiters, they could not stop themselves on a sudden, but always tumbled one over the other whenever they came near the edge of the ice, or towards the quarter where the Emperor happened to be.

Leaving this place, they were carried through several narrow streets, composed of miserable houses, forming a surprising contrast with the proud walls of the palace. They were conducted into a small room of one of these houses, almost void of furniture, in order to pay their compliments to *Ho-tchung-tang*, the Collao, or prime minister, whom they found sitting cross-legged on a truckle bedstead with cane bottom. Before this creature of fortune, whose fate I shall have occasion hereafter to notice, they were obliged to go down on their knees. Like a true prime minister of China, he waved all conversation that might lead towards business, talked to them of the length of their journey, was astonished how they bore the cold weather in such scanty clothing, and such like general topics, which, in fact, signified nothing. From the first minister they paid their visit to the second, whom they found lodged in a similar manner; after which they returned to their mean apartments in the city, more satisfied on a comparison with[213] the miserable little chambers in which they had found the two first ministers of this far-famed empire lodged, and the mean hovels which they met with in the very center of the space shut in by the walls of the imperial palace. The impressions that the events and transactions of this day made on the minds of the visitors were those of utter astonishment, on finding every thing so very much the reverse of what they had been led to expect.

The following day they were again drawn to court in their little carts, before four o'clock in the morning, where, after having waited about five hours in empty rooms, similar to those of the preceding day, two or three great men (*Ta-gin*) called upon them, but behaved towards them in a distant, scornful, and haughty manner. "We had once more," observes the Dutch journalist, from which I quote, "an occasion to remark the surprising contrast of magnificence and meanness in the buildings, and of pride and littleness in the persons belonging to the imperial palace."

After these interviews, they were suffered to remain a day or two at home; but on a bag of dried grapes being brought by a mandarin from the Emperor, they were required to thank him for the present with nine prostrations, as usual. Another time a little pastry from the imperial kitchen demanded the same ceremony. In short, whether at home or in the palace, the Chinese were determined they should be kept in the constant practice of the *koo-too*, or ceremony of genuflexion and prostration.[214]

On the 26th of January, the Embassadors received notice that it was expected they should attend the procession of the Emperor to the temple, where he was about to make an offering to the God of Heaven and of earth. Having waited accordingly by the road side, from three o'clock in the morning till six, the weather dismally cold, Fahrenheit's thermometer standing at 16° below the freezing point, the Emperor at length passed in his chair, when they made the usual prostrations and returned home.

The next morning they were again required to proceed to the same place, and at the same early hour, to witness his return and again to go through the usual ceremony.

On the 29th, they were again summoned to attend by the road side to do homage before the Emperor, as he passed them on his way to a pagoda or *Poo-ta-la*, a kind of temple or monastery, where a great number of priests, clothed in yellow, lived together in a state of celibacy; and here he made his burnt-offerings. The mystical rates performed, presents were brought out for the Embassador and suite, and also for the *King* of *Holland*, consisting of little purses, flimsey silks, and a coarse stuff somewhat similar to that known by seamen under the name of *bunting*; and, in token of gratitude for this mark of imperial kindness, they were directed again to *bow down their heads to the ground*.

On the 30th, it was announced to them that the Emperor intended to pay a visit to his palace at *Yuen-min-yuen*, and that[215] it would be necessary for them to follow him thither; after having, as usual, paid their respects in the Chinese manner by the road side as he passed.

On the 31st, they were conducted round the grounds of *Yuen-min-yuen* by several Mandarins, and received great satisfaction in viewing the vast variety of buildings, and the good taste in which the gardens and pleasure grounds were laid out, and which wore an agreeable aspect, even in the depth of winter. In one of the buildings they saw the several presents deposited, which had been carried the preceding year by the Earl of Macartney. They were stowed away with no great care, among many other articles, in all probability never more to see the light of day. It seems the elegant carriages of Hatchett, that were finished with so much care and objects of admiration even in London, were here carelessly thrown behind one of their mean and clumsy carts, to which they pretended to bestow a preference. Capricious as children, the toy once played with must be thrown aside and changed for something new; or, in this instance, it would not be out of character to suppose, that the two vehicles had designedly been placed together to point out to Europeans of how little estimation the Chinese considered their articles of ostentation, when they could perform the same services by simpler and less expensive means.

The Dutch Embassadors and their suite were now to have a specimen of the court entertainments, and the polite amusements of this grand empire. They consisted chiefly of the contortions of the human body, practiced by posture-masters; of [216] rope-dancing, and a sort of pantomimic performance, the principal characters of which were men dressed in skins, and going on all-fours, intended to represent wild beasts; and a parcel of boys habited in the dresses of mandarins, who were to hunt them. This extraordinary chace, and the music, and the rope-dancing, put the Emperor into such good humour, that he rewarded the performers very liberally. And the Empress and the ladies, who were in an upper part of the house concealed behind a sort of venetian blinds, appeared from their tittering noise to be highly entertained. The whole concluded, though in the middle of the day, with a variety of fire-works; and the Chinese part of the company departed seemingly well satisfied with these diversions.

An eclipse of the moon happening on the fourth of February gave occasion to the Embassadors to enjoy a little rest at home, though they were summoned to attend the palace at a very early hour in the morning. The Emperor and his mandarins were engaged the whole day in devoutly praying the gods that the moon might not be eaten up by the great dragon that was hovering about her. Recovered from their apprehensions, an entertainment was given the following day, at which the Embassadors were required to be present. After a number of juggling tricks and infantine sports, a pantomime, intended to be an exhibition of the battle of the dragon and the moon, was represented before the full court. In this engagement two or three hundred priests, bearing lanterns suspended at the ends of long sticks, performed a variety of evolutions, dancing and capering about, sometimes over the plain, and then over chairs[217] and tables, affording to his Imperial Majesty and to his courtiers the greatest pleasure and satisfaction.

On the fifteenth of February the Dutch Embassadors left Pekin, having remained there thirty-six days, during which they were scarcely allowed to have a single day's rest, but were obliged, at the most unseasonable hours, in the depth of winter, when the thermometer was seldom higher than 10 or 12 degrees below the freezing point, to dance attendance upon the Emperor and the great officers of state, whenever they might think fit to call upon them; and to submit to the degrading ceremony of knocking the head nine times against the ground, at least on thirty different occasions, and without having the satisfaction of gaining by this unconditional compliance any one earthly thing, beyond a compliment from the Emperor,*that they went through their prostrations to admiration*! And they were finally obliged to leave the capital without being once allowed to speak on any kind of business, or even asked a single question as to the nature of their mission, which, indeed, the Chinese were determined to take for granted was purely complimentary to their great Emperor.

The manuscript I quote from describes minutely all the pantomimic performances, the tricks of conjurors and jugglers, and the feats of posture-masters, but as they seem to be pretty much of the same kind as were exhibited before the British Embassy in Tartary, as described by Lord Macartney, I forbear to relate them. Enough has been said to shew the taste of the court in this respect, and the state of the drama in China.[218]

I suspect, however, that the amusements of the theatre have in some degree degenerated at court since the time of the Tartar conquest. Dancing, riding, wrestling, and posture-making, are more congenial to the rude and unpolished Tartar than the airs and dialogue of a regular drama, which is better suited to the genius and spirit of the ceremonious and effeminate Chinese. I am led to this observation from the very common custom among the Chinese officers of state of having private theatres in their houses, in which, instead of the juggling tricks above mentioned, they occasionally entertain their guests with regular dramatic performances. In the course of our journey through the country and at Canton, we were entertained with a number of exhibitions of this kind; and as "the purpose of playing," as our immortal bard has observed, "both at the first, and now, was, and is, to hold as 'twere the mirror up to nature," it may not be foreign to the present subject to take a brief notice of such performances.

The subjects of the pieces exhibited are for the most part historical, and relate generally to the transactions of remote periods, in which cases the dresses are conformable to the ancient*costume* of China. There are others, however, that represent the Tartar conquest, but none built on historical events subsequent to that period. But the ancient drama is preferred by the critics. They have also comic pieces, in which there is always a buffoon, whose grimaces and low jests, like those of the buffoons in our own theatres, obtain from the audience the greatest share of applause. The dialogue in all their dramas, whether serious or comic, is conducted in a kind of mono[219]tonous recitative, sometimes however rising or sinking a few tones, which are meant to be expressive of passionate or querulous cadences. The speaker is interrupted at intervals by shrill harsh music, generally of wind instruments, and the pauses are invariably filled up with a loud crash, aided by the sonorous and deafening gong, and sometimes by the kettle drum. An air or song generally follows. Joy, grief, rage, despair, madness, are all attempted to be expressed in song on the Chinese stage. I am not sure that a vehement admirer of the Italian opera might not take umbrage at the representation of a Chinese drama, as it appears to be something so very like a burlesque on that fashionable species of dramatic entertainment; nor is the Chinese stage wanting in those vocal warblers, the nature of whom, as we are told by the ingenious and very entertaining Martin Sherlock, a French lady explained to her little inquisitive daughter, by informing her, that there was the same difference between them and men, as between an ox and a bull.

Such creatures are indeed more necessary to the Chinese theatre, as the manners of the country prohibit women from appearing in public.

The unity of action is so far preserved, that they have actually no change of scene; but change of place must frequently be supposed. To assist the imagination in this respect, their management is whimsical enough. If it be necessary to send a general on a distant expedition, he mounts a stick, takes two or three turns round the stage, brandishes a little whip, and sings a song; when this is ended, he stops short, and recommences his recitative, when the journey is supposed to be performed.[220] The want of scenery is sometimes supplied by a very unclassical figure, which, just the reverse of the *prosopopoeia* or personification of grammarians, considers persons to represent things. If, for instance, a walled city is to be stormed, a parcel of soldiers, piling themselves on a heap across the stage, are supposed to represent the wall over which the storming party is to scramble. This puts one in mind of the shifts of Nick Bottom. "Some man or other must present wall," and, "let him have some plaister, or some lome, or some rough-cast about him to signify wall."

The audience is never left in doubt as to the character which is produced before it. Like the ancient Greek drama and, in imitation thereof, all our old plays, the *dramatis personæ* introduce themselves in appropriate speeches to the acquaintance of the spectators.

As to the time of action, a single drama will sometimes include the transactions of a whole century, or even of a dynasty more than twice the length of that period; which, among other absurdities, gave Voltaire occasion to compare what he thought to be a literal translation of the *Orphan of the House of Tchao*, "to those monstrous farces of Shakespear, which have been called tragedies;" farces, however, which will continue to be read by those who understand them, which *he* did not, with heartfelt emotion and delight, when his *Orphan of China* shall have sunk into the neglect even of his own admiring countrymen.[221]

In this miserable composition of *Father Prémare*, for it can scarcely be called a translation, there is neither diction, nor sentiment, nor character; it is a mere tissue of unnatural, or at least very improbable events, fit only for the amusement of children, and not capable of raising one single passion, but that of contempt for the taste of those who could express an admiration of such a composition. The denouement of the piece is materially assisted by means of a dog: but this part of the story is told, and not exhibited; the Chinese taste not being quite so depraved, in this instance, as to admit the performance of a four-footed animal on the stage.

This drama, with ninety-nine others, published together in one work, are considered as the classical stock-pieces of the Chinese stage; but like ourselves, they complain that a depraved taste prevails for modern productions very inferior to those of ancient date. It is certainly true, that every sort of ribaldry and obscenity are encouraged on the Chinese stage at the present day. A set of players of a superior kind travel occasionally from Nankin to Canton; at the latter of which cities, it seems, they meet with considerable encouragement from the Hong merchants, and other wealthy inhabitants. At these exhibitions the English are sometimes present. The subject and the conduct of one of their stock pieces, which being a great favourite is frequently repeated, are so remarkable, that I cannot forbear taking some notice of it. A woman being tempted to murder her husband performs the act whilst he is asleep, by striking a small hatchet into his forehead. He appears on the stage with a large gash just above the eyes, out of which issues a prodigious[222] effusion of blood, reels about for some time, bemoaning his lamentable fate in a song, till exhausted by loss of blood, he falls, and dies. The woman is seized, brought before a magistrate, and condemned to be flayed alive. The sentence is put in execution; and, in the following act, she appears upon the stage not only naked, but completely excoriated. The thin wrapper with which the creature (an eunuch) is covered, who sustains the part, is stretched so tight about the body, and so well painted, as to represent the disgusting object of a human being deprived of its skin; and in this condition the character sings or, more properly speaking, whines nearly half an hour on the stage, to excite the compassion of three infernal or malignant spirits who, like Æacus, Minos, and Rhadamanthus, sit in judgment on her future destiny. I have been informed that it is scarcely possible to conceive a more obscene, indelicate, and disgusting object, than this favourite exhibition, which, if intended "to hold the mirror up to nature," it is to nature in its most gross, rude, and uncivilized state, ill-agreeing with the boasted morality, high polish, refined delicacy, and ceremonious exterior of the Chinese nation; but it tends, among other parts of their real conduct in life, to strengthen an observation I have already made with regard to their filial piety, and which, with few exceptions, may perhaps be extended to most of their civil and moral institutions, "that they exist more in state maxims, than in the minds of the people." As, however, a Chinese might be led to make similar reflexions on the exhibition of Harlequin Skeleton, and those numerous representations that of late years have crept upon our own stage, where ghosts, hobgoblins, and bleeding statues are called in aid of the *spectacle*,[223] I should hesitate to draw any general conclusion, with regard to their taste, from the particular exhibition of a woman flayed alive, were they not in the constant practice of performing other pieces that, in point of immorality and obscenity, are still infinitely worse; so vulgarly indelicate and so filthy, that the European part of the audience is sometimes compelled by disgust to leave the theatre. These are such as will not bear description, nor do I know to what scenic representations they can with propriety be compared, unless to those gross indecencies of Theodora, which Procopius has described to have been exhibited on the Roman stage, in the reign of Justinian[11]. The people who encourage them must be sunk very deep in intellectual grossness, and have totally lost sight of all decency. These and similar scenes may be considered among the ill effects of excluding women from their due share of influence in society.

It would be impossible to compliment the court of Pekin on the elegance and refinement of its entertainments, but at the expence of truth and reason. Those of Tartar origin will no more bear a comparison with the noble contests of strength and agility displayed by the old hardy Romans in the Circensian games, than the regular drama of the Chinese will admit of being measured by the softer, but more refined and rational amusements of a similar kind in Europe. It is true the scenic representations in the decline of the Roman empire, as they are described to us, appear to have been as rude and barbarous as those of the Chinese. They began by exhibiting in their vast [224]amphitheatre the rare and wonderful productions of nature. Forests enlivened with innumerable birds; caverns pouring forth lions, and tygers, and panthers, and other beasts of prey; plains covered with the elephant, the rhinosceros, the zebra, the ostrich, and other curious animals, which the wilds of Africa furnished, were all brought together within the circuit of the *arena*. Not satisfied with the rich productions of the earth, the sea must also become tributary to their amusements. The arena was convertible into a sheet of water; and, at length, the two elements concluding a marriage, as on the Chinese theatre, produced a race of monsters which, according to the Latin poet's[12] description, might vie with those of China.

"Non solum nobus sylvestria cernere monstra
Contigit, æquoreos ego cum certantibus ursis
Spectavi vitulos, et equorum nomine dignum
Sed difforme genus."——

Where Sylvan monsters not alone appear,
But sea-cows struggle with the shaggy bear,
And horses of the deep, a shapeless race.——

In short, the greater part of the amusements of the Chinese are, at the present day, of a nature so very puerile, or so gross and vulgar, that the tricks and the puppet-shews which are occasionally exhibited in a common fair of one of the country towns of England, may be considered as comparatively polished, interesting, and rational. In slight-of-hand, in posture-making, rope-dancing, riding, and athletic exercises, they are much inferior to Europeans; but in the variety of their fire-works they, perhaps, may carry the palm against the whole[225]world. In every other respect the amusements of the capital of China appear to be of a low and trifling nature, neither suited to the affected gravity of the government nor to the generally supposed state of civilization among the people.

The old Emperor, as he observed to Lord Macartney, seldom partook of such amusements. Considering, indeed, all the circumstances connected with the reign of the present dynasty on the throne, the government of an empire of such vast magnitude, stored with an almost incalculable population, must necessarily be a task of inconceivable vigilance and toil; a task that must have required all the time, the talents, and the attention of the four sovereigns to ensure the brilliant and unparalleled successes that have distinguished their long reign. *Tchien Lung*, at the age of eighty-three, was so little afflicted with the infirmities of age, that he had all the appearance and activity of a hale man of sixty. His eye was dark, quick, and penetrating, his nose rather aquiline, and his complexion, even at this advanced age, was florid. His height I should suppose to be about five feet ten inches, and he was perfectly upright. Though neither corpulent nor muscular at eighty-three, it was not difficult to perceive that he once had possessed great bodily strength. He always enjoyed a vigorous constitution, which the regularity of his life did not impair. Like all the Mantchoo Tartars he was fond of hunting, an exercise that during the summer months he never neglected. He had the reputation of being an expert bowman, and inferior only in drawing this weapon to his grandfather *Caung-shee*, who boasts, in his last[226] will, that he drew a bow of the weight or strength of one hundred and fifty pounds.

Nor were the faculties of his mind less active, or less powerful, than those of his body. As prompt in conceiving as resolute in executing his plans of conquest, he seemed to command success. Kind and charitable, as on all occasions he shewed himself to his subjects, by remitting the taxes, and administering relief in seasons of distress, he was no less vindictive and relentless to his enemies. Impatient of restraint or reverses, he has sometimes been led to act with injustice, and to punish with too great severity. His irascible temper was once the cause of a severe and lasting affliction to himself, and the circumstances connected with it are said to have produced a gloom and melancholy on his mind which never entirely forsook him. About the middle part of his reign, he made a circuit through the heart of his empire. At *Sau-tchoo-foo*, a city that is celebrated for its beautiful ladies which, being purchased when infants, are educated there for sale to the opulent, he was captivated with a girl of extraordinary beauty and talents, whom he intended to carry back with him to his capital. The Empress, by means of an eunuch, was made acquainted with his new amour, and dreading his future neglect, her spirits were depressed to such a degree, that a few days after receiving the intelligence she put an end to her existence with a cord. The Emperor, on hearing this melancholy news, was greatly distressed and repaired without delay to Pekin. One of his sons, a very amiable youth, fearful of incurring his father's displeasure, had entertained some doubts whether it would be most proper[227] to appear before him in deep mourning for his mother, which might be construed as an insult to the father, who had been the cause of her death, or in his robes of ceremony, which would be disrespectful to the memory of his deceased mother. In this dilemma he consulted his schoolmaster, who, like a true Chinese, advised him to put on both. He did so and, unfortunately for him, covered the mourning with the ceremonial habit. *Tchien-Lung*, whose affection had now returned for his deceased Empress, and whose melancholy fate he was deeply lamenting, on perceiving his son at his feet without mourning, was so shocked and exasperated at the supposed want of filial duty that, in the moment of rage, he gave him a violent kick in an unfortunate place which, after his languishing a few days, proved fatal.

None of his four surviving sons ever possessed any share of his confidence or authority which, of late years, were wholly bestowed on his first minister *Ho-chung-tong*. He had a due sense of religious duties, which he regularly performed every morning. Having made a vow at the early part of his reign that, should it please heaven to grant him to govern his dominions for a complete cycle, or sixty years, he would then retire, and resign the throne to his successor, he religiously observed it on the accomplishment of the event. The sincerity of his faith may partly be inferred from the numerous and splendid temples he built and endowed in different parts of oriental Tartary, of which the *Poo-ta-la*, or convent of Budha at Gehol, is the most magnificent. It is said indeed, from the circumstance of his long and fortunate reign, he had, in his later years, entertained[228] an idea, that the Lama, or Budha, or Fo, for they are all the same personage, had condescended to become incarnate in his person. "However wild and extravagant," observes Lord Macartney, "such a conceit may be regarded, we know from history how much even the best understandings may be perverted by prosperity, and that human nature, not satisfied with the good things of this world, sometimes wishes to anticipate the condition and felicity of the next. If Alexander scorned to own less than Jupiter Ammon for his father, if many Roman Emperors extorted altars and sacrifices in their lifetime, if, even in the reign of Queen Elizabeth, an English nobleman[13] encouraged the belief of his descent from a swan, and was complimented in a dedication upon his feathered pedigree, a similar infatuation may be the less inexcusable in *Kien-Long*, a monarch, the length and happiness of whose reign, the unlimited obedience of whose incalculable number of subjects, and the health and vigour of whose body, have hitherto kept out of his view most of those circumstances that are apt to remind other men of their misery and mortality."

Till his last illness he continued to rise at three o'clock in the morning, both in winter and summer. He usually took some cordial to fortify his stomach, and then repaired to his private devotions at one of his temples. After this he read the dispatches of his great officers, both civil and military, who from their different stations were ordered to write to him directly, [229]and not to the tribunals as had usually been the case. About seven he took his breakfast of tea, wines, and confectionary, when he transacted business with the first minister, consulting with, or directing, him in the weighty matters of state, previous to their appearing in regular form before the respective departments to which they belonged. He had then a kind of levee, which was usually attended by the Collaos, or ministers, and the presidents of the departments or public boards. At eleven refreshments were again served up and, after business was over, he either amused himself in the women's apartments, or walked round his palace or gardens. Between three and four he usually dined, after which he retired to his private rooms and employed himself in reading or writing till bed-time, which was always regulated by, and seldom later than, the setting of the sun.

He was fully persuaded that his uninterrupted health was chiefly owing to his early retiring to rest, and early rising; an observation, indeed, that in our country has grown into a maxim, and maxims are generally grounded on truth. The late Lord Mansfield made a point for many years of enquiring from all the aged persons, that at any time appeared before him to give evidence, into their particular mode of living, in order that he might be able to form some general conclusion with regard to the causes of their longevity. The result of his observations was, that he could draw no inference from their intemperance or abstemiousness with regard to diet or drinking, but that they all agreed in one point, that of being early risers.[230]

Tchien-Lung resigned the throne of China to his fifteenth son, the present *Kia-king*, in February 1796, having completed a reign of sixty years; and he died in the month of February 1799, at the advanced age of eighty-nine years.

When the Tartars conquered China, they found all the great offices of state filled by eunuchs, and the palace swarmed with these creatures; the greater part was immediately displaced, and other Chinese of talent and education were put into their places. Having, however, adopted the laws and customs of the conquered, it became necessary to keep up the usual establishment of women in the palace, the inevitable consequence of which was the retention of a certain number of eunuchs to look after them. And they are at this moment as numerous, perhaps, in all the palaces, as they were at the conquest, but none of them are dignified with any office of trust or importance in the state. They consider themselves, however, as elevated far above the plebeian rank; and a bunch of keys or a birch broom gives them all the airs and insolence of office.

Of these eunuchs there are two kinds. The one is so far emasculated as never to have the consolation of being a father; the other must submit to lose every trace of manhood. The first are entrusted with the inspection and superintendance of the buildings, gardens, and other works belonging to the imperial palaces, which they are required to keep in order. The *Rasibus*, as the missionaries call them, are admitted into the interior of the palace. These creatures paint their faces, study[231] their dress, and are as coquettish as the ladies, upon whom indeed it is their chief business to attend. The greatest favourite sleeps in the same room with the Emperor, to be ready to administer to his wishes; and in this capacity he finds numberless opportunities to prejudice his master against those for whom he may have conceived a dislike; and instances are not wanting where the first officers in the state have been disgraced by means of these creatures.

They are equally detested and feared by the princes of the blood who reside in the palace, by the court officers, and by the missionaries in the employ of government. The latter find it necessary to make frequent, and sometimes expensive, presents to those in

78

particular about the person of his Imperial Majesty. Should any of these gentlemen happen to carry about with him a watch, snuff-box, or other trinket, which the eunuch condescends to admire, there is no alternative; the missionary takes the hint, and begs his acceptance of it, knowing very well that the only way to preserve his friendship is to share with him his property. An omission of this piece of civility has been productive of great injury to the European. The gentleman who regulates and keeps in order the several pieces of clock-work in the palace assured me, that the old eunuch, who was entrusted with the keys of the rooms, used to go in by night and purposely derange and break the machinery, that he might be put to the trouble and expence of repairing it. This happened to him so often that, at length, he became acquainted with the secret of applying the proper preventive, which although expensive was still less vexatious than[232] the constant reparation of the mischief done to the articles of which he had the superintendance.

The Chinese eunuchs are addicted to all the vices that distinguish these creatures in other countries. There is scarcely one about the palace, whether of the class of porters and sweepers, or of that which is qualified for the inner apartments, but have women in their lodgings, who are generally the daughters of poor people, from whom they are purchased, and are consequently considered as their slaves. It is difficult to conceive a condition in life more humiliating, or more deplorable, than that of a female slave to an eunuch; but happily for such females, in this country the mental powers are not very active. Several of the missionaries assured me of the truth of this fact, which indeed I have strong reasons for believing even of the *Rasibus*. The keeper of the hall of audience once took me to his lodgings, but on coming to the door he desired me to wait till he had made some arrangements within; the meaning of which was, until he had removed his lady out of the way; nor was he in the least displeased at my hinting this to him. Being one of the favourite attendants of the ladies of the court, he was of course a *black eunuch*. He was the most capricious creature in the world; being sometimes extremely civil and communicative, sometimes sullen, and not deigning to open his lips: and whenever he took it into his head to be offended, he was sure to practice some little revenge. I fancy he was clerk of the kitchen, for the quality and the quantity of our dinner generally depended on the state of his humour. When the report of the Embassador's making conditions with regard to the[233] ceremony of introduction first reached *Yuen-min-yuen*, he was more than usually peevish, and conceived, as he thought, a notable piece of revenge. Some pains had been taken to arrange the presents in such a manner in the great hall as to fill the room well, and set them off to the best advantage. The old creature, determined to give us additional trouble and to break through the arrangement that had been made, desired that the whole might be placed at one end of the room. On my objecting to this he pretended to have received the Emperor's order, and that at all events it must be obeyed; and the reason he assigned for the change was, "that his Majesty might see them at once from his throne, without being at the trouble of turning his head."

The great number of these creatures about the palace of *Yuen-min-yuen* made my residence there extremely disagreeable. They seemed, indeed, to be placed as spies on our conduct. If I attempted to move ever so little beyond the court of our apartments, I was sure of being watched and pursued by some of them; to persist in my walk would have thrown the whole palace in an uproar. I one day happened inadvertently to stray through a thicket, which it seems led towards the apartments of the ladies, but I had not proceeded far before I heard several squalling voices in the thicket, which I soon recognised to be those of eunuchs. They had run themselves out of breath in seeking me, and my old friend of the kitchen was not to be pacified for putting him to the hazard, as he pretended, of losing his head by my imprudence.[234]

The eunuchs and the women are the only companions of the Emperor in his leisure hours: of the latter, one only has the rank of Empress, after whom are two Queens and their numerous attendants, which constitute the second class of the establishment; and the third consists of six Queens, and their attendants. To these three ranks of his wives are attached one hundred ladies, who are usually called his concubines, though they are as much a legal part of his establishment as the others. They would seem to be of the same description, and to hold the same rank as the handmaids of the ancient Israelites. Their children are all considered as branches of the Imperial family, but the preference to the succession is generally given to the male issue of the first Empress, provided there should be any. This however is entirely a matter of choice, the Emperor having an uncontrouled power of nominating his successor, either in his own family or out of it. The daughters are usually married to Tartar princes, and other Tartars of distinction, but rarely, if ever, to a Chinese.

On the accession of a new Emperor, men of the first rank and situation in the empire consider themselves as highly honoured and extremely fortunate, if the graces of their daughters should prove sufficient to provide them a place in the list of his concubines; in which case, like the nuns in some countries of Europe, they are doomed for ever to reside within the walls of the palace. Such a fate, however, being common in China in a certain degree to all women-kind, is less to be deplored than the similar lot of those in Europe, where one sex is supposed to be entitled to an equal degree of liberty with[255] the other; and as the custom of China authorizes the sale of all young women by their parents or relations to men they never saw, and without their consent previously obtained, there can be no hardship in consigning them over to the arms of the prince; nor is any disgrace attached to the condition of a concubine, where every marriage is a legal prostitution. At the death of the sovereign all his women are removed to a separate building, called by a term which, divested of its metaphor, implies the *Palace of Chastity*, where they are doomed to reside during the remainder of their lives.

CHAP. VI.
Language.—Literature, and the fine Arts.—Sciences.—Mechanics, and Medicine.

Opinion of the Chinese Language being hieroglyphical erroneous.—Doctor Hager's mistakes.—Etymological Comparisons fallacious.—Examples of.—Nature of the Chinese written Character.—Difficulty and Ambiguity of.—Curious Mistake of an eminent Antiquarian.—Mode of acquiring the Character.—Oral Language.—Mantchoo Tartar Alphabet.—Chinese Literature.—Astronomy.—Chronology.—Cycle of sixty Years.—Geography.—Arithmetic.—Chemical Arts.—Cannon and Gunpowder.—Distillation.—Potteries.—Silk Manufactures.—Ivory.—Bamboo.—Paper.—Ink.—Printing.—Mechanics.—Music.—Painting.—Sculpture.—Architecture.—Hotel of the English Embassador in Pekin.—The Great Wall.—The Grand Canal.—Bridges.—Cemeteries.—Natural Philosophy.—Medicine.—Chinese Pharmacopoeia.—Quacks.—Contagious Fevers.—Small pox.—Opthalmia.—Venereal Disease.—Midwifery.—Surgery.—Doctor Gregory's Opinion of their Medical Knowledge.—Sir William Jones's Opinion of their general Character.

IF no traces remained, nor any authorities could be produced,[256] of the antiquity of the Chinese nation, except the written character of their language, this alone would be sufficient to decide that point in its favour. There is so much originality in this language, and such a great and essential difference between it and that of any other nation not immediately derived from the[257] Chinese, that not the most distant degree of affinity can be discovered, either with regard to the form of the character, the system on which it is constructed, or the idiom, with any other known language upon the face of the globe. Authors, however, and some of high reputation, have been led to suppose that, in the Chinese character, they could trace some relation to those hieroglyphical or sacred inscriptions found among the remains of the ancient Egyptians; others have considered it to be a modification of hieroglyphic writing, and that each character was the symbol or comprehensive form of the idea it was meant to express, or, in other words, an abstract delineation of the object intended to be represented. To strengthen such an opinion, they have ingeniously selected a few instances where, by adding to one part, and curtailing another, changing a straight line into a curved one, or a square into a circle, something might be made out that approached to the picture, or the object of the idea conveyed by the character as, for example, the character 田, representing *a cultivated piece of ground*, they supposed to be the picture of an inclosure, turned up in ridges; yet it so happens that, in this country, there are no inclosures; the character, 口 *a mouth*, has been considered by them as a very close resemblance of that object; 上 and 下 *above* and *below*, distinctly marked these points of position; the character 人, signifying *man*, is, according to their opinion, obviously an abbreviated representation of the human figure; yet the very same character, with an additional line[238] across, thus 大, which by the way approaches nearer to the human figure, having now arms as well as legs, signifies the abstract quality *great*; and with a second line thus 天 the material or visible *heaven*, between either of which and *man* it would be no easy task to find out the analogy; and still less so to trace an affinity between any of them, and 犬 which signifies *a dog*.

It is true certain ancient characters are still extant, in which a rude representation of the image is employed; as for instance, a circle for the sun, and a crescent for the moon, but these appear to have been used only as abbreviations, in the same manner as these objects are still characterized in our almanacks, and in our astronomical calculations. Thus also the *kingdom of China* is designed by a square, with a vertical line drawn through the middle, in conformity perhaps with their ideas of the earth being a square, and China placed in its center; so far these may be considered as symbols of the objects intended to be represented. So, also, the numerals one, two, three, being designed by 一 二 三, would naturally suggest themselves as being fully as convenient for the purpose, and perhaps more so than any other; and where the first series of numerals ended, which according to the universal custom of counting by the fingers was at *ten*, the very act of placing the index of the right hand on the little finger of the left would suggest the form of the[239] vertical cross 十 as the symbol or representation of the number ten.

I cannot avoid taking notice in this place of a publication of Doctor Hager, which he calls an "*Explanation of the Elementary Characters of the Chinese*." In this work he has advanced a most extraordinary argument to prove an analogy between the ancient Romans and the Chinese, from the resemblance which he has fancied to exist between the numeral characters and the numeral sounds made use of by those two nations. The Romans, he observes, expressed their numerals one, two, three, by a corresponding number of vertical strokes I. II. III. which the Chinese place horizontally 一 二 三. The Romans designed the number ten by an oblique cross X, and the Chinese by a vertical one 十. This resemblance in the forming of their numerals, so simple and natural that almost all nations have adopted it, is surely too slight a coincidence for concluding, that the people who use them must necessarily, at some period or other, have had communication together. The Doctor however seems to think so, and proceeds to observe, that the three principal Roman cyphers, I. V. X. or one, five and ten, are denoted in the Chinese language by the same sounds that they express in the Roman alphabet. This remark, although ingenious, is not correct. *One* and *five*, it is true, are expressed in the Chinese language by the *y* and *ou* of the French, which it may be presumed, were the sounds that the letters I. and V. obtained in the ancient Roman alphabet; but with regard to the *ten*, or X, which, he says, the Chinese pronounce *xe*, he is entirely mistaken, the Chinese word for *ten* in Pekin being *shee*,[240] and in Canton *shap*. This error the Doctor appears to have been led into by consulting some vocabulary in the Chinese and Portuguese languages; in the latter of which the letter X is pronounced like our *sh*. But admitting, in its fullest extent, the resemblance of some of the numerals used by the two nations, in the shape of the character, and of others in the sound, it certainly cannot be assumed to prove any thing beyond a mere accidental coincidence.

The earliest accounts of China, after the doubling of the Cape of Good Hope, being written by Portuguese missionaries, and the Chinese proper names still remaining to be spelt in the letters of that alphabet, have led several etymologists into great errors, not only with regard to the letter X, but more particularly in the *m* final, and the *h* incipient, the former being pronounced *ng*, and the latter with a strong aspirate, as *sh*. Thus the name of the second Emperor of the present dynasty is almost universally written in Europe *Cam-hi*, whereas it is as universally pronounced in China *Caung-shee*.

The learned Doctor seems to be still less happy in his next conjecture, where he observes that, as the Romans expressed their *five* by simply dividing the X, or ten, so also the ancient character signifying *five* with the Chinese was X or ten between two lines thus   indicating, as it were, that the number ten was divided in two; the Doctor seems to have forgotten that he has here placed his cross in the *Roman* form, and not as the Chinese write it; and it is certainly a strange way of cutting a thing in two, by enclosing it between two lines; but the learned[241] seldom baulk at an absurdity, when a system is to be established. The Chinese character for five is 五.

Of all deductions, those drawn from etymological comparisons are, perhaps, the most fallacious. Were these allowed to have any weight, the Chinese spoken language is of such a nature, that it would be no difficult task to point out its relationship to that of every nation upon earth. Being entirely monosyllabic, and each word ending in a vowel or a liquid, and being, at the same time, deprived of the sounds of several letters in our alphabet, it becomes necessarily incapable of supplying any great number of distinct syllables. Three hundred are, in fact, nearly as many as an European tongue can articulate, or ear distinguish. It follows, of course, that the same sound must have a great variety of significations. The syllable *ching*, for example, is actually expressed by fifty-one different characters, each having a different, unconnected, and opposite meaning; but it would be the height of absurdity to attempt to prove the coincidence of any other language with the Chinese, because it might happen to possess a word something like the sound of *ching*, which might also bear a signification not very different from one of those fifty-one that it held in the Chinese.

The Greek abounds with Chinese words. κυον, a *dog*, is in Chinese both *keou* and *keun*, expressive of the same animal; έυ, *good*, is not very different from the Chinese *hau*, which signifies the same quality; and the article τὸ is not far remote from *ta*,[242] *he*, or *that*. Both Greeks and Romans might recognise their first personal pronoun έγω or *ego* in *go*, or as it is sometimes written *ngo*. The Italian affirmative *si* is sufficiently near the Chinese *shee*, or *zee*, expressing assent. The French *étang*, and the Chinese *tang*, a pond or lake, are nearly the same, and their two negatives *pas* and *poo* are not very remote. *Lex*, *loi*, *le*, *law*, compared with *leu*, *lee*, *laws* and *institutes*, are examples of analogy that would be decisive to the etymological inquirer. The English word *mien*, the countenance, and the Chinese *mien*, expressing the same idea, are nothing different, and we might be supposed to have taken our *goose* from their *goo*. To *sing* is *chaung*, which comes very near our *chaunt*. The Chinese call a cat *miau*, and so does the Hottentot. The Malay word *to know* is *tau*, and the Chinese monosyllable for the same verb is also *tau*, though in conversation they generally use the compound *tchee-tau*, each of which separately have nearly the same meaning. The Sumatrans have *mau* for mother, the Chinese say *moo*. On grounds equally slight with these have many attempts been made to form conclusions from etymological comparisons. If I mistake not, the very ingenious Mr. Bryant makes the word *gate* a derivative from the Indian word *ghaut*, a pass between mountains. Surely this is going a great deal too far for our little monosyllable. Might we not with as great a degree of propriety fetch our *shallow* or *shoal* from China, where *sha-loo* signifies a flat sand, occasionally covered with the tide? A noted antiquarian has been led into some comical mistakes in his attempt to establish a resemblance between the Chinese and the Irish languages, frequently by his having considered the letters of the continental alphabets, in which the Chinese[243] vocabulary he consulted was written, to be pronounced in the same manner as his own[14].

Whatever degree of affinity may be discovered between the[244] sounds of the Chinese language and those of other nations, their written character has no analogy whatsoever, but is entirely peculiar to itself. Neither the Egyptian inscriptions, nor the[245] nail-headed characters, or monograms, found on the Babylonian bricks, have any nearer resemblance to the Chinese than the Hebrew letters have to the Sanscrit; the only analogy that can be said to exist between them is, that of their being composed of points and lines. Nor are any marks or traces of alphabetic writing discoverable in the composition of the Chinese character; and, if at any time, hieroglyphics have been employed to convey ideas, they have long given way to a collection of arbitrary signs settled by convention, and constructed on a system, as regular and constant as the formation of sounds[246] in any of the European languages arises out of the alphabets of those languages.

The history of the world affords abundant evidence that, in the dawn of civilization, most nations endeavoured to fix and to perpetuate ideas by painting the figures of the objects that produced them. The Egyptian priesthood recorded the mysteries of their

82

religion in graphic emblems of this kind; and the Mexicans, on the first arrival of the Spaniards, informed their prince Montezuma of what was passing by painting their ideas on a roll of cloth. There is no way so natural as this of expressing, and conveying to the understanding of others, the images that pass in the mind, without the help of speech. In the course of the present voyage, an officer of artillery and myself were dispatched to make observations on the small island of *Collao*, near the coast of *Cochin-China*. In order to make the natives comprehend our desire to procure some poultry, we drew on paper the figure of a hen, and were immediately supplied to the extent of our wants. One of the inhabitants taking up the idea drew close behind the hen the figure of an egg, and a nod of the head obtained us as many as we had occasion for. The Bosjesmen Hottentots, the most wild and savage race perhaps of human beings, are in the constant habit of drawing, on the sides of caverns, the representations of the different animals peculiar to the country. When I visited some of those caverns I considered such drawings as the employment of idle hours; but, on since reflecting that in almost all such caverns are also to be seen the figures of Dutch boors (who hunt these miserable creatures like wild beasts) in a variety of[217] attitudes, some with guns in their hands, and others in the act of firing upon their countrymen; waggons sometimes proceeding and at others standing still, the oxen unyoked, and the boors sleeping; and these representations generally followed by a number of lines scored like so many tallies; I am inclined to think they have adopted this method of informing their companions of the number of their enemies, and the magnitude of the danger. The animals represented were generally such as were to be met with in the district where the drawings appeared; this, to a people who subsist by the chace and by plunder, might serve as another piece of important information.

The Chinese history, although it takes notice of the time when they had no other method of keeping their records, except, like the Peruvians, by knotting cords, makes no mention of any hieroglyphical characters being used by them. If such were actually the case, the remains of symbolical writing would now be most discoverable in the radical, or elementary characters, of which we shall presently have occasion to speak, and especially in those which were employed to express some of the most remarkable objects in nature. Out of the two hundred and twelve, or thereabout, which constitute the number of the radical signs, the following are a few of the most simple, in none of which, in my opinion, does there appear to be the least resemblance between the picture and the object.[218]

人 *gin*, man

口 *koo*, a mouth

土 *tee*, earth

子 *tsé*, a son

艸 *tsau*, a plant

山 *shan*, a mountain

心 *sin*, a heart

手 *shoo*, a hand

方 *fang*, space, or a square of ground

月 *yué*, the moon

日 *jee*, the sun

木 *moo*, a tree

水 *swee*, water

火 *ho*, fire

石 *shee*, a stone.

The rest of the elementary characters are, if possible, still more unlike the objects they represent. There seems, therefore, to be no grounds for concluding that the Chinese ever made use of hieroglyphics or, more properly speaking, that their present character sprung out of hieroglyphics. They have a tradition, which is universally believed, that their prince *Fo-shee* was the inventor of the system upon which their written character is formed, and which, without any material alteration, there is every reason to suppose has continued in use to this day. To *Fo-shee*, however, they ascribe the invention of almost every thing they know, which has led Mr. Baillie ingeniously to conjecture that *Fo-shee* must have been some foreigner who first[249] civilized China; as arts and sciences do not spring up and bear fruit in the life of one man. Many changes in the form of characters may have taken place from time to time, but the principle on which they are constructed seems to have maintained its ground. The redundancies of particular characters have been removed for the sake of convenience; and the learned in their epistolary writing have adopted a sort of running hand, in which the form is so very materially altered, by rounding off the angles, connecting some parts and wholly omitting others, as to make it appear to a superficial observer a totally different language. But I may venture to observe, that it has not only not undergone any material alteration for more than two thousand years, but that it has never borrowed a *character*, or a syllable, from any other language that now exists. As a proof of this, it may be mentioned, that every new article that has found its way into China since its discovery to Europeans has acquired a Chinese name, and entirely sunk that which it bore by the nation who introduced it. The proper names even of countries, nations, and individuals are changed, and assume new ones in their language. Thus Europe is called *See-yang*, the western country; Japan *Tung-yang*, the eastern country; India *Siau-see-yang*, the little western country. The English are dignified by the name of *Hung-mou*, or *Red-heads*, and the French, Spanish, Portuguese, and others, who visit China, have each a name in the language of the country totally distinct from that they bear in Europe. This inflexibility in retaining the words of their own poor language has frequently made me think, that Doctor Johnson had the Chinese in his mind when, in that inimitable piece of fine writing which prefaces his diction[250]ary, he made this remark: "The language most likely to continue long without alteration, would be that of a nation raised a little, and but a little, above barbarity, secluded from strangers, and totally employed in procuring the conveniences of life."

The invention of the Chinese character, although an effort of genius, required far less powers of the mind than the discovery of an alphabet; a discovery so sublime that, according to the opinion of some, nothing less than a divine origin ought to be ascribed to it. It may, however, be considered as the nearest approximation to an universal character that has hitherto been attempted by the learned and ingenious of any nation; each character conveying at once to the eye, not only simple, but the most combined ideas. The plan of our countryman, Bishop Wilkins, for establishing an universal character is, in all respects, so similar to that upon which the Chinese language is constructed, that a reference to the former will be found to convey a very competent idea of the nature of the latter. The universal character of our countryman is, however, more systematic, and more philosophical, than the plan of the Chinese character.

Certain signs expressing simple objects or ideas may be considered as the roots or primitives of this language. These are few in number, not exceeding two hundred and twelve, one of which, or its abbreviation, will be found to compose a part of every character in the language; and may, therefore, be considered as the *key* to the character into which it enters. The[251]eye soon becomes accustomed to fix upon the particular key, or root, of the most complicated characters, in some of which are not fewer than sixty or seventy distinct lines and points. The right line, the curved line, and a point are the rudiments of all the characters. These, variously combined with one another, have been extended from time to time, as occasion might require, to nearly eighty thousand different characters.

To explain the manner in which their dictionaries are arranged will serve to convey a correct notion of the nature of this extraordinary language. All the two hundred and twelve roots or keys are drawn fair and distinct on the head of the page, beginning with the most simple, or that which contains the fewest number of lines or points, and proceeding to the most complicated; and on the margins of the page are marked the numeral characters one, two, three, &c. which signify, that the *root* or *key* at the top will be found to be combined on that page with one, two, three, &c. lines or points. Suppose, for example, a learner should meet with an unknown character, in which he perceives that the simple sign expressing *water* is the *key* or *root*, and that it contains, besides this root, *six* additional points and lines. He immediately turns over his dictionary to the place where the

84

character *water* stands on the top of the page, and proceeding with his eye directed to the margin, until the numeral character *six* occurs, he will soon perceive the one in question; for all the characters in the language, belonging to the *root water*, and composed of *six* other lines and points, will follow successively in this place. The name or sound of the character is placed immediately after it,[252] expressed in such others as are supposed to be most familiar; and, in the method made use of for conveying this information, the Chinese have discovered some faint and very imperfect idea of alphabetic writing, by splitting the monosyllabic sound into a dissyllable, and again compressing the dissyllable into a simple sound. One instance will serve to explain this method. Suppose the name of the character under consideration to be *ping*. If no single character be thought sufficiently simple to express the sound *ping*, immediately after it will be placed two well-known characters *pe* and *ing*; but, as every character in the language has a monosyllabic sound, it will readily be concluded, that *pe* and *ing*, when compressed into one syllable, must be pronounced *ping*. After these, the meaning or explanation follows, in the clearest and most easy characters that can be employed.

When, indeed, a considerable progress has been made in the language, the general meaning of many of the characters may be pretty nearly guessed at by the eye alone, as they will mostly be found to have some reference, either immediate or remote, though very often in a figurative sense, to the signification of the *key* or *root*; in the same manner as in the classification of objects in natural history, every species may be referred to its proper genus. The signs, for instance, expressing the *hand* and the *heart*, are two *roots*, and all the works of art, the different trades and manufactures, arrange themselves under the first, and all the passions, affections, and sentiments of the mind under the latter. The root of an *unit* or *one* comprehends all the characters expressive of unity, concord, harmony, and the[253] like. Thus, if I observe a character compounded of the two simple *roots*, *one* and *heart*, I have no difficulty in concluding that its signification is *unanimity*, but, if the sign of a *negative* should also appear in the same character, the meaning will be reversed to *discord* or *dissention*, literally *not one heart*. Many proper names of persons have the character signifying *man* for their key or root, and all foreign names have the character *mouth* or *voice* annexed, which shews at once that the character is a proper name employed only to express sound without any particular meaning.

Nor are these keys or roots, although sometimes placed on the right of the character, sometimes on the left, now at the top, and then at the bottom, so very difficult to be discovered to a person who knows but a little of the language, as Doctor Hager has imagined. This is by far the easiest part of the language. The abbreviations in the compound characters, and the figurative sense in which they are sometimes used, constitute the difficulty, by the obscurity in which they are involved, and the ambiguity to which they are liable.

The Doctor is equally unfortunate in the discovery which he thinks he has made of a want of order in classing the elements according to the number of lines they contain. The instances he gives of such anomaly are in the two characters of 母 *moo*, mother; and 田 *tien*, cultivated ground: the first of which he is surprised to find among the elementary characters of *four* lines, and the latter (which he asserts to be still more simple) among those of *five*. The Chinese, however, are[254] not quite so much out of order as the Doctor seems to be out of his province in attempting a critique on a language, of which he really possesses a very superficial knowledge. The first character 母 *moo* is composed of and the second 田 *tien* of ; the one of four and the other of five lines according to the arrangement of Chinese dictionaries, and their elementary treatises.

Among the roots or primitives that most frequently occur are those expressing the *hand*, *heart*, *mouth*, and the five elements, *earth*, *air*, *fire*, *wood*, and *water*. *Man* is also a very common root.

The composition of characters is capable of exercising a very considerable degree of ingenuity, and the analysis of them is extremely entertaining to a foreigner. As in a proposition of Euclid it is necessary to go through the whole demonstration before the figure to which it refers can be properly understood, so, in the Chinese character, the sense of the several component parts must first be known in order to comprehend the meaning of the compound. To endeavour to recollect them without this knowledge would be a laborious and almost impossible effort of the mind. Indeed, after this knowledge is acquired, the sense is sometimes so hid in metaphor, and in allusions to particular customs or ways of thinking, that when all the component parts of a character are well understood, the meaning may yet remain in obscurity. It may not be difficult to conceive, for instance, that in a figurative language, the union of[255] the *sun* and *moon* might be employed to express any extraordinary degree of *light* or *brilliancy*; but it would not so readily occur, that the character *foo* or *happiness*, or *supreme felicity*, should be designed by the union of the characters expressing a spirit or demon, the number *one* or *unity*, a *mouth*, and a piece of *cultivated ground*, thus 福. This character in the Chinese language is meant to convey the same idea as the word *comfort* does in our own. The character implying the *middle* of any thing, annexed to that of *heart*, was not inaptly employed to express *a very dear friend*, nor that with the *heart* surmounted by a *negative*, to imply *indifference*, *no heart*; but it is not so easy to assign any reason why the character *ping*, signifying rank or order, should be expressed by the character *mouth*, repeated thrice, and placed like the three balls of a pawnbroker, thus 品, or why four of these mouths arranged as under, with the character *ta*, *great*, in the center, should imply an instrument, or piece of mechanism. 器. Nor would it readily occur why the character 男 *nan*, *masculine*, should be made up of *tien*, a *field*, and *lee*, *strength*, unless from the idea that the *male sex* possesses *strength*, and only can inherit *land*. But that a *smoothness* or *volubility* of *speech* 唫 should be designed by *koo*, *mouth*, and *kin*, *gold*, we can more easily conceive, as we apply the epithet *silver tongue* pretty nearly on the same occasion.

If the Chinese had rigidly adhered to the ingenious and philosophical mechanism they originally employed in the construc[256]tion of their characters, it would be the most interesting of all languages. But such is far from being the case. New characters are daily constructed, in which convenience, rather than perspicuity, has been consulted.

It will follow from what has been said, that every compounded character is not only a word, but also a *definition*, comprehending in visible marks its full explanation; but no character, however compounded, can have more than a monosyllabic sound, though each part when alone has a distinct sound, as well as sense. Thus, "Happiness," though compounded of four distinct characters, *shee*, a demon; *ye*, one; *koo*, a mouth, and *tien*, a piece of cultivated ground, has only the simple monosyllabic sound *foo*, which is unlike that of any one of its compounds.

The sounds and various inflexions incidental to languages in general, are not necessary to be attended to in the study of the Chinese characters. They speak equally strong to a person who is deaf and dumb, as the most copious language could do to one in the full enjoyment of all his senses. It is a language addressed entirely to the eye, and not to the ear. Just as a piece of music laid before several persons of different nations of Europe would be played by each in the same key, the same measure, and the same air, so would the Chinese characters be equally understood by the natives of Japan, Tunquin, and Cochin-China; yet each would give them different names or sounds, that would be wholly unintelligible to one another. When, on the present voyage, we stopped at Pulo Condore,[257] the inhabitants, being Cochin-Chinese, had no difficulty in corresponding, by writing, with our Chinese interpreters, though they could not interchange one intelligible word.

Although, with the assistance of a good dictionary and a tolerable memory, a knowledge of such of the Chinese characters, as most frequently occur, may be obtained by a foreigner; yet the ambiguity to which they are liable, on account of the frequent figurative expressions and substitution of metaphor for the literal meaning, renders their best compositions extremely obscure. Another, and not the least, difficulty to a learner of this language arises from the abridgment of the characters for the sake of convenience, by which the eye is deprived of the chain that originally connected the component parts. In short, it is a language where much is to be made out that is not expressed, and particularly so in what is called fine writing; and a thorough knowledge of it can only be acquired from a familiar acquaintance with the manners, customs, habits, and opinions of the people. Those missionaries even, who have resided in the country the best part of their lives, and accepted employments about the palace, are frequently at a loss in translating and composing the official papers that are necessary to be made out on the occasion of an European embassy.

It is, however, a matter of surprize that, after all that has been published in Europe by the Jesuits of the grandeur, the magnificence, the learning, and the philosophy of the Chinese, so very few persons should have taken the trouble to make themselves acquainted with the language of this extraordinary nation. So little was a *professor* of Chinese, at Rome, versed[258] in the language he professed to know, that he is said[16] to have mistaken some characters found on a bust of Isis for Chinese, which bust and the characters were afterwards proved to be the work of a modern artist of Turin, made after his own fancy. In Great Britain we have known still less of the Chinese language and Chinese literature than on the continent. It is not many years ago, that one of the small copper coins of China, stamped in the reign, and with the name, of the late *Tchien-lung* (or as he is usually called in the southern dialect of China *Kien-long*) was picked up in a bog in Ireland, and being considered as a great curiosity, was carried to an indefatigable antiquary, whose researches have been of considerable use in investigating the ancient history and language of that island. Not knowing the Chinese character, nor their coin, it was natural enough for him to compare them with some language with which he was acquainted; and the conclusion he drew was, that the four following characters on the face were ancient Syriac; and that the reverse (which are Mantchoo letters) appeared to be astronomical, or talismanic characters, of which he could give no explanation.

F

ace.

Tch *ien-lung.* *Pao-tung.*

(Emperor's name.) Current value.

R

everse.

po *tchin.*

House, or dynasty, of *Tchin.*

[259]

The Mantchoo Tartar characters of another coin he supposed to signify *p u r*, which is construed into *sors*, or lot; and it is concluded, that these coins must either have been imported into Ireland by the Phœnicians, or manufactured in the country; in which case, the Irish must have had an oriental alphabet. "In either case," it is observed, "these medals contribute more to authenticate the ancient history of Ireland than all the volumes that have been written on the subject."

I have noticed this circumstance, which is taken from the *Collectanea Hibernica*, in order to shew how little is known of the Chinese character and language among the learned, when so good a scholar and eminent antiquary committed so great a mistake.

The youth of China generally begin to study the language when they are about six years of age. Their first employment is to learn by name a certain number of easy characters, without any regard to the signification, or without understanding the meaning of one of them, consequently, without adding to the mind one single idea, for five or six years, except that of labour and difficulty. For the *name* of a character, it may be recollected, has no reference whatsoever to its *meaning*. Thus fifty-one different characters, of as many distinct significations, have the same name of *ching*; and if ten or a dozen characters, bearing the sound of *ching*, should occur in the same page, the learner, in this stage of his education, is not instructed in the several meanings; his object is to acquire the sound, but to neglect the sense. I have been told, that a regular-bred scholar[260] is required to get by heart a very large volume of the works of Confucius so perfectly, that he may be able to turn to any passage or sentence from hearing the sound of the characters only, without his having one single idea of their signification. The next step is to form the characters, commencing by tracing, or going over, a certain number that are faintly drawn in red ink. As soon as they are able to cover these with tolerable accuracy, without deviating from the lines of the original, they then endeavour to imitate them on fresh paper. These operations employ at least four years more of their life. Thus, a young man of fourteen or sixteen years of age, although he may be able to write a great number of characters, for each of which he can also give a name, yet, at the same time, he can affix no distinct idea to any one of them. The contrary method would appear advisable of teaching them first the signification of the simple roots, and the analysis of the compound characters, and afterwards the sounds, or, perhaps, to let the one accompany the other.

Objections of a similar nature to those now mentioned against the mode of Chinese education, have, it is true, been frequently stated with regard to the plan of educating youths in the public grammar schools of our own country; that some of the most precious years of their lives, when the faculties were in growing vigour, and the plastic mind most susceptible of receiving and retaining impressions, are wasted in poring over the metaphysics of a Latin Grammar, which they cannot possibly comprehend; and in learning by heart a number of declinations, conjugations, and syntax rules, which serve only[261] to puzzle and disgust, instead of affording instruction or amusement: that the grammar, or philosophical part of a language, is useful only for the niceties and perfection of that language, and not a subject for boys. In all instances, perhaps, where the language to be learned is made the common colloquial language of the pupil, the objections stated against the use of the grammar may have some weight. But as this is not the case with regard to the Greek and Latin languages in Europe, nor to the written character in China, which differs widely from the colloquial, long experience may, perhaps, in both cases, have led to the adoption of the most eligible method[17].

But a youth of Europe has a very material advantage over one of China, during the time in which he is said to be poring over his Latin Grammar. He is in the daily habit of acquiring new ideas, from his knowledge of other languages. His mother-tongue supplies him with books, which he is able to comprehend, and from which he derives both entertainment and instruction. Without enumerating the great variety of these that daily engage his attention, I deem it sufficient to observe, [262] that his Robinson Crusoe (the best book, with few exceptions, that can be put into a boy's hand) shews the numberless difficulties to which he is liable in the world, when the anxious cares of his parents have ceased to watch over him; it is there pointed out to him that, arduous as many undertakings may appear to be, few are insurmountable; that the body and the mind of man are furnished with resources which, by patience, diligence, prudence, and reflexion, will enable him to overcome the greatest difficulties, and escape the most imminent dangers. His Tom Jones, however exceptionable in those parts where human failings are represented under an amiable and alluring dress, leaves, upon the whole, a lively impression in favour of generosity and virtue, and seldom fails to excite an indignant glow against perfidy, selfishness, and brutality. The young Chinese has no such relief from his dry study of acquiring the names and representations of things that to him have as yet no meaning. He knows not a word of any language but his own.

The last step in the education of a Chinese is to analyse the characters, by the help of the dictionary, in the manner already mentioned, so that he now first begins to comprehend the use of the written character. Extracts from the works of their famous philosopher *Cong-foo-tse* (the Confucius of the missionaries) are generally put into his hands; beginning with those that treat on moral subjects, in which are set forth, in short sentences, the praises of virtue, and the odiousness of vice, with rules of conduct to be observed in the world. The *eternal mean*, in the style and manner of the maxims of Seneca, next follows;[263] and the art of government, with an abridgment of the laws, completes him for taking his first degree, which generally happens when he has attained his twentieth year; but in order to be qualified for any high employment, he must study at least ten years longer.

From this view of the written character, and the mode of education, it will readily occur, that little progress is likely to be made in any of the speculative sciences; and more especially as their assistance is not necessary to obtain the most elevated situations in the government. The examinations to be passed for the attainment of office are principally confined to the knowledge of the language; and as far as this goes, they are rigid to the utmost degree. The candidates are put into separate apartments, having previously been searched, in order to ascertain that they have no writing of any kind about them. They are allowed nothing but pencils, ink, and paper, and within a given time they are each to produce a theme on the subject that shall be proposed to them. The excellence of the composition, which is submitted to the examining officers, or men of letters, depends chiefly on the following points.

That every character be neatly and accurately made.

That each character be well chosen, and not in vulgar use.

That the same character do not occur twice in the same composition.

The subject and the manner of treating it are of the least[264] consideration, but those on morality, or history, are generally preferred. If the following story, as communicated by one of the missionaries, and related, I believe, by the Abbé Grozier, be true, there requires no further illustration of the state of literature in China. "A candidate for preferment having inadvertently made use of an abbreviation in writing the character *ma* (which signifies a *horse*) had not only the mortification of seeing his composition, very good in every other respect, rejected solely on that account; but, at the same time, was severely rallied by the censor, who, among other things, asked him how he could possibly expect his horse to walk without having all his legs!"

The construction of the colloquial, or spoken language, is extremely simple. It admits of no inflexion of termination, either in the verb, or in the noun, each word being the same invariable monosyllable in number, in gender, in case, mood, and tense; and, as most of these monosyllables begin with a consonant and end with a vowel, except a few that terminate in *l*, *n*, or *ng*, the number of such sounds, or simple syllables, is very limited. To an European they do not exceed three hundred and fifty. But a Chinese, by early habit, has acquired greater power over the organs of speech, and can so modulate his voice as to give to the same monosyllable five or six distinct tones of sound; so that he can utter at least twelve or thirteen hundred radical words, which, with the compounds, are found to be fully sufficient for expressing all his wants.[265]

On this curious subject I am enabled to speak with great accuracy, through the kindness of Sir George Staunton, to whom, indeed, I am indebted for more information in this work than I am allowed to acknowledge. From the best manuscript Chinese dictionary in his possession, he has obligingly taken the trouble to draw out the following abstract of all the simple sounds, or words, in the Chinese language, together with their inflexions or accentuations, by which they are extended as far as any tongue can possibly articulate, or the nicest ear discriminate. The first column shews all the initial letters, or their powers in the language; the second, the number of terminations, or the remaining part of the monosyllable beside the initial; and the third, expresses the number of monosyllabic sounds that may be given to each by inflexion, or modulation of voice, and by making use of aspirates.

Initials Power.	Number of terminations to each.	Number of inflexions or accentuations.
Ch. as in Child.	20	131 including aspirates.
F.	10	30 no aspirates.

	G.	11	32 no aspirates.
	bet ween H. & S.	36	114 all strong aspirates.
	Y.	16	61 no aspirates.
	J as in French *Jour*	14	34 no aspirates.
	K.	37	206 including aspirates.
	L.	25	66 no aspirates.
	M.	22	58 no aspirates.
0	N.	23	56 no aspirates.
1	O.	1	2 no aspirates.
2	P.	21	104 including aspirates.
3	S.	29	86 no aspirates.
4	T.	17	105 including aspirates.
5	Ts.	28	147 including aspirates.
6	bet ween V. and W.	13	39 no aspirates.
7	Sh.	19	60 no aspirates.

So that in the whole colloquial language of China, an European[266] may make out 342 simple monosyllabic sounds, which by the help of aspirates, inflexions of voice, or accentuations, are capable of being increased by a Chinese to 1331 words. And as the written language is said to contain 80,000 characters, and each character has a name, it will follow, that, on an average, 60 characters, of so many different significations, must necessarily be called by the same monosyllabic name. Hence, a composition if read would be totally unintelligible to the ear, and must be seen to be understood. The monosyllabic sound assigned to each charter is applied to so many different meanings, that in its unconnected state it may be said to have no meaning at all.

In the business of common life, the nice inflexions or modulations, that are required to make out these thirteen hundred words, may amply be expressed in about fifteen thousand characters, so that each monosyllabic sound will, in this case, on an average, admit of about twelve distinct significations. This recurrence of the same words must necessarily cause great ambiguity in conversation, and it frequently indeed leads to ridiculous mistakes, especially by foreigners. Thus, a sober missionary, intending to pass the night at a peasant's house, asked as he thought for a *mat*, but was very much surprised on seeing his host presenting him with a *young girl*; these two objects, so very different from one another, being signified by two words whose pronunciations are not distinguishable, and consequently one or the other requires to be used with an adjunct.[267]

It was a source of daily amusement to our conductors, to hear the *equivoques* we made in attempting to speak their language. A Chinese, when the sense is doubtful, will draw the character, or the root of it, in the air with his finger or fan, by which he makes himself at once understood.

But as some of these monosyllabic words, as I have observed of *ching*, have not less than fifty distinct significations, which the nicest tones and inflexions, even of a Chinese voice, are not able to discriminate, such words are generally converted into compounds, by adding a second syllable, bearing some relative sense to the first, by which the meaning is at once determined. Among the significations, for instance, of the monosyllable *foo* is that of *father*, to which, for the sake of distinction, as *foo* has many significations beside that of father, they add the syllable *chin*, implying *kindred*; thus, a Chinese in speaking of his parents invariably says *foo-chin* for father, and *moo-chin* for mother; but, in writing, the character of *chin* would be considered as an unnecessary expletive, that of *foo* being very differently made from any other called by the same name.

The grammar of this language may briefly be explained. The noun, as observed, is indeclinable; the particles *te* or *tié*, mark the genitive, and always follow the noun; *eu* the dative, which it precedes, and *tung* or *tsung* the ablative, before which they are also placed. As for example,[268]

Nom. *gai* love.
Gen. *gai-te* of love.
Dat. *eu-gai* to love.
Acc. *gai* love.
Abl. *tung* or *tsung gai*, from or by love. And the same in the plural.
Give me *your* book,
Keu go NE-TE *shoo*.
Dear *to* men,
Quei EU *jin.*
Come you *with* him,
Ne-lai TUNG *ta.*

The adjective is also formed from the genitive of the noun as *pai*, whiteness; *pai-tié* white; *je* heat; *je-tié* hot; *lee*, reason; *lee-tié*, rational; *hau* goodness; *hau tié*, good. But when the adjective precedes the noun, as it generally does, the particle *tié* is omitted as, *hau jin*, a good man.

pai-ma, a white horse.

je-swee, hot water.

The plural of nouns is expressed by prefixing some word signifying plurality, as *to-jin*, many men; *to-to jin*, a multitude of men; *chung jin*, all men; and sometimes by a repetition of the word as *jin-jin*, men.

Adjectives are compared by placing the particle *keng* before the comparative, as *yeou*, soft; *keng yeou*, softer.

hau, good; *keng hau*, better.

My book is *newer* than yours,

Go-te shoo KENG *sin ne-te*.

The superlative is marked by various particles, sometimes preceding,[269] and sometimes following, the adjective, and it is also formed by repeating the positive, as

hau, hau tié, very good.

whang-whang-tié, very yellow.

The personal pronouns are,

ngo (nasal) or *go, ne, ta, go-men, ne-men, ta-men.*

I, thou, he, we, ye, they.

And they become possessives, in the same manner as nouns are changed into adjectives, by the addition of *te* or *tié*, as

go-te, ne-te, ta-te, go-men-te, ne-men-te, ta-men-te.

mine, thine, his, ours, yours, theirs.

The verb has likewise neither conjugation nor inflection; and the tenses, or times of action or passion, are limited to three; the present, the past, and the future. The present is signified simply by the verb, as *go lai*, I come; the past, is expressed by the particle *leo*, as *go lai leo*, I did come, or I have come; and the future is formed by placing the particle *yau* before the verb, as *go yau lai*, I will come; or, when something very determined is meant to be expressed, the compound *yuen-y* precedes the verb, as *go yuen-y-lai*, I am determined to come. It may be observed, however, that although these, and other particles signifying the time and mode of action, are necessary in common speech, yet, in fine writing, they are entirely omitted, which is another cause of the obscurity and difficulty that occur to strangers in the study of the Chinese character.[270]

The two negatives *mo* and *poo*, are of great use in the spoken language. The first is generally used with the verb *yeu* to have, and always implies a want or deficiency, as, *mo yeu nai*, there is no milk; *mo yeu tcha*, you can have no tea, I have no tea, there is no tea, &c. *Poo* is generally used to express qualities of an opposite nature, as, *hau*, good, *poo hau*, bad; *je*, hot; *poo je*, cold; *ta*, great; *poo ta*, little. The usual salutation between friends is *hau-poo-hau*, well, or not well?

The limits I have prescribed for the present work will not allow me to enter into a more detailed account of this singular language. What has been said may serve to convey a general idea of the written character, and the simple construction of the spoken language. I shall now endeavour, in a few words, to explain the nature and construction of the Mantchoo Tartar character, which, if the present family continue on the throne for a century longer, will, in all probability, supplant the Chinese, or will at least become the court language. In the enunciation it is full, sonorous, and far from being disagreeable, more like the Greek than any of the oriental languages; and it abounds with all those letters which the Chinese have rejected, particularly with the letters B and R. It is alphabetic, or, more properly speaking, syllabic, and the different parts of speech are susceptible of expressing number, case, gender, time, modes of action, passion, and other accidents, similar to those of European languages. This is effected either by change of termination, preposition, or interposition. The character is extremely beautiful, and it is written, like the Chinese, in perpendicular[271] columns, but beginning on the left side of the paper instead of the right, as is the case in writing the former language.

The elements of the language are comprized in twelve classes of simple sounds or monosyllables, from the different combinations of which all the words of the Mantchoo language are formed.

These classes are distinguished by the terminations.

The first class ends in a, e, i, o, u, pronounced exactly as the Italian.

The second, in ai, ei, iei, oi, ui.

The third, in ar, er, ir, or, ur, air, &c.

The fourth, in an, en, in, &c.

The fifth, in ang, eng, ing, &c.

The sixth, in ak, ek, ik, &c.

The seventh, in as, es, is, &c.

The eighth, in at, et, it, &c.

The ninth, in ap, ep, ip, &c.

The tenth, in au, eu, iu, ou.

The eleventh, in al, el, il, &c.

The twelfth, in am, em, im, &c.

The initials are, A. E. F. H. I. K. L. M. N. O. P. R. S. T. U. Y.

To give some idea of the character, I subjoin the written elements.[272]

The initial characters are represented by respective marks,[273] which being joined to these elementary terminations, generally at the upper extremity, give all the monosyllabic sounds, and the junction of these according to their various combinations all the words in the Mantchoo language. One example will be sufficient to shew the nature of such composition; thus the initials P. T. L. S. F. set before the 12th class of radicals, will stand as follows:

And if each of these syllables be respectively added to the 5th[274] class, they will stand thus:

Of the state of their literature, and progress in science, I have little to observe. The nature of the language will almost itself determine these points. With respect to any branch of polite literature, or speculative science, little improvement seems to have been made in the last two thousand years. Indeed, there are no works in the whole empire, modern or ancient, that are so much esteemed, so much studied, and I may perhaps add, so little comprehended, as the five classical books collected and commented upon by their great philosopher *Cong-foo-tse*, who lived about 450 years before the Christian æra; and these certainly are very extraordinary productions for the time in which they were written. These works and a few writings of their favourite master, according to the annals of the country, escaped the general destruction of books, when the barbarous *She-whang-te* ordered all the monuments of learning to be burnt, except such as treated of medicine and agriculture, about 200 years before Christ, for the absurd purpose, as they state, that he might be considered by posterity as the first civilized Emperor which had governed China, and that the records of its history might, by this mean artifice, appear to commence with his reign.[275]

Admitting such an event to have happened which, however, may be considered as doubtful, the supposition involves in it this necessary consequence, that the stock of learning at that time must have been very confined. It is scarcely possible, otherwise, how one person, near the end of his reign, could have contrived to assemble together all the works of art and literature, dispersed through so large a tract of country and so enlightened as it was then supposed to be. There were, besides, other independent sovereigns in the country, over whom he had little or no controul, so that it is very probable the commonwealth of letters suffered no great loss by the burning of the Chinese books. When the Caliph Omar commanded the Alexandrian library to be destroyed, which the pride and the learning of the Ptolemy family had collected from every part of the world, literature sustained an irreparable loss; but, although the tyrant had the power to consign to eternal oblivion the works of science, yet he had no power over the principles upon which these works were constructed.

These principles had spread themselves wide over the world. The expedition of Alexander carried the learning of the Egyptians and the Greeks into various countries of Asia, where they continued to flourish. And when the tyranny and oppression of the seventh Ptolemy (Physcon) forced the Alexandrians to abandon a city that was perpetually streaming with the blood of its citizens, they found an asylum in the Grecian states and in different parts of Asia. And as this sanguinary tyrant, in the midst of his cruelties, pretended and indeed shewed a fondness for literature, the arts and the sciences flourished even in his reign: the migrations, therefore, at this time, from the capital of Egypt, were|276| of the greatest importance and use to those nations among whom the refugees settled. Unluckily for China, the wild mountainous forests towards the south, and the wide sandy deserts to the north, that render any communication extremely difficult between this empire and the rest of Asia, together with their dislike for foreigners, seem, at this time, to have checked the progress of those arts and sciences which had long flourished in Europe and in Africa. Their history, at least, is silent as to any communication with India, till a century nearly after the commencement of the Christian æra, when the religion of Budha found its way from Thibet into China.

Whether the burning of the works of the learned in China did or did not happen, appears, as already observed, to admit of some doubt; but the antiquity, and the authenticity, of the five *king*, or classics, seem to be sufficiently established. And considering the early periods in which they were written, they certainly demonstrate a very superior degree of civilization. It has been observed that, in this country, the arts, the sciences, and literature, are not progressive; and the five *king* would lead one to conclude, that they have rather even been retrograde than stationary. The names of these works are:

1. *Shoo-king*. A collection of records and annals of various princes, commencing more than 2000 years before Christ.

2. *Shee-king*. Odes, sonnets, and maxims; most of them so abundant in metaphor, and so obscure, that much of the sense is to be made out by the translator.|277|

3. *Ye-king*. The perfect and the broken lines of *Fo-shee*; the most ancient relict in China, and perhaps the first attempt at written language: now perfectly incomprehensible.

4. *Chung-choo*. Spring and autumn. The history of some of the kings of *Loo*: the work principally of *Cong-foo-tse*.

5. *Lee-kee*. Ceremonies and moral duties. A compilation of *Cong-foo-tse*.

The lines of *Fo-shee* puzzled even the great philosopher of the country, who declared himself dissatisfied with all the explanations of the commentators. The learned and ingenious Leibnitz fancied he discovered in them a system of binary arithmetic, by which all the operations and results of numbers might be performed, with the help of two figures only, the cypher or zero 0, and an unit 1, the former being considered as the constant multiple of the latter, as 10 is of the unit. Thus 1 would stand for 1, 10 for two, 11 for three, 100 for four, and so on. It is unnecessary to observe, with how many inconveniences such a system would be attended when reduced to practice. This discovery of the binary series, which the mathematician, in all probability, considered only as a philosophical plaything, was communicated to Father Bouvet the Jesuit who, happening at that time to be engaged in decyphering the lines of *Fo-shee*, caught the idea and in an extacy of joy proclaimed to the world that Leibnitz had solved the *Fo-sheean* riddle.|278|

The missionaries of the Romish church are so accustomed to the mysteries with which their religion abounds, that every thing they meet with, and do not understand, among a strange people, is also resolved into a mystery. Thus, the following figure, which the Chinese, in allusion to the regular lines described on the back-shell of some of the tortoises, metaphorically call the mystic tortoise, has been supposed by some of these gentlemen to contain the most sublime doctrines of Chinese philosophy; that they embrace a summary of all that is perfect and imperfect, represent the numbers of heaven and earth, and such like jargon, which, it obviously appears, is no less unintelligible to themselves than to their readers.

These famous lines, supposed to be found on the back of a tortoise, are the following:

Who does not perceive, at a single glance, in this figure the common schoolboy's trick of the magic square, or placing the nine digits so that they shall make the sum of fifteen every way, thus,[279]

and what are the perfect and imperfect numbers, but the odd and even digits distinguished by open and close points? In like manner, I am inclined to believe, the several ways of placing these open and close points that occur in Chinese books are literally nothing more than the different combinations of the nine numerical figures, for which they are substituted.

Most of the other *king* have been translated, wholly or in part, and published in France. It may be observed, however, that all the Chinese writings, translated by the missionaries, have undergone so great a change in their European dress, that they ought rather to be looked upon as originals than translations. It is true, a literal translation would be nonsense, but there is a great difference between giving the meaning of an author, and writing a commentary upon him. Sir William Jones observes that the only method of doing justice to the poetical compositions of the Asiatics, is to give first a verbal and then a metrical version. The most barren subject, under his elegant pen, becomes replete with beauties. The following stanza, from one of the odes of the *Shee-king*, is an instance of this remark. It is calculated to have been written about the age of Homer; and it consists of fifteen characters.

123456
The peach-tree, how fair, how graceful, its leaves, how blooming,
7891011
how pleasant; such is a bride, when she enters her bridegroom's
12131415
house, and attends to her whole family.

This is a fair translation, as no more expletives are inserted[280] than such as were necessary to make up the sense, and it is thus paraphrased by Sir William Jones.

"Gay child of Spring, the garden's queen,
Yon peach-tree charms the roving fight;
Its fragrant leaves how richly green!
Its blossoms, how divinely bright!

"So softly smiles the blooming bride,
By love and conscious virtue led,
O'er her new mansion to preside,
And placid joys around her spread."

The late Emperor *Kien-Long* was considered among the best poets of modern times, and the most celebrated of his compositions is an ode in praise of Tea, which has been painted on all the teapots in the empire. The following is a verbal translation, with such auxiliaries only as were necessary to make the sense complete.

"On a slow fire set a tripod, whose colour and texture shew its long use; fill it with clear snow water, boil it as long as would be necessary to turn fish white, and crayfish red; throw it upon the delicate leaves of choice tea, in a cup of *yooé* (a particular sort of porcelain). Let it remain as long as the vapour rises in a cloud, and leaves only a thin mist floating on the surface. At your ease, drink this precious liquor, which will chase away the five causes of trouble. We[281] can taste and feel, but not describe, the state of repose produced by a liquor thus prepared."

He wrote, likewise, a long descriptive poem on the city and country of Moukden, in Mantchoo Tartary, which has been translated by some of the missionaries, and appears to possess much more merit than his ode on tea, of which, however, it is difficult to judge without a thorough knowledge of the language, as the ode may owe its chief beauties and its fame more to the choice of the characters than to the sounds, literal sense, or versification. To an European the Chinese language appears to have few elegancies: it wants all the little auxiliaries that add grace and energy to those of Europe. In the Chinese the beauty of an expression depends entirely on the choice of the character, and not on any selection or arrangement of the monosyllabic sounds. A character uniting a happy association of ideas has the same effect upon the eye of the Chinese, as a general theorem expressed in symbols has on a mathematician; but in both cases a man must be learned to feel the beauties of the concise expression. Even in speaking the language has few expletives. "English good, Chinese better,"—"to-day go, to-morrow come,"—"sea no bound, Kiang no bottom;"—"well, not well;"—are modes of expression in which an European will not find much elegance.

In addition to the defects of the language, there is another reason why poetry is not likely ever to become a favourite pursuit, or to be cultivated with success, among the Chinese. The state of society we have seen to be such as entirely to exclude[282] the passion of love. A man, in this country, marries only from necessity, or for the sake of obtaining an heir to his property, who may sacrifice to his manes, or because the maxims of the government have made it disgraceful to remain in a state of celibacy. The fine sentiments that arise from the mutual endearment of two persons enamoured of each other can therefore have no place in the heart of a Chinese: and it is to the effusions of a heart thus circumstanced, that poetry owes some of its greatest charms. Nor can they be considered as a nation of warriors; and war, next to love, has ever been the favourite theme of the muses.

The language is much better adapted to the concise style of ethics, than the sublime flights of poetry. The moral precepts of Cong-foo-tse display an excellent mind in the writer, and would do honour to any age and nation. The following will serve as a specimen of his subjects, style, and manner.

"There is one clear rule of conduct: to act with sincerity; and to conform with all one's soul, and with all one's strength, to this universal rule—do not any thing to another, that you would not wish another should do to you."

How conformable is this sentiment as well as the words in which it is expressed, to that of the great Author of our religion; a religion whose "ways are ways of pleasantness, and all whose paths are peace."[283]

"Five things ought to be well observed in the world. Justice between the prince and the subject; affection between father and son; fidelity between man and wife; subordination among brothers; concord among friends."

"There are three radical virtues: prudence to discern; universal benevolence to embrace (all mankind); courage to sustain."

"What passes in a man's mind is unknown to others: if you are wise, take great care of what none but yourself can see."

"Examples are better for the people than precepts."

"A wise man is his own most severe censor: he is his own accuser, his own evidence, and his own judge."

"A nation may accomplish more by bravery than by fire and water. I never knew a people perish, who had courage for their support."

"An upright man will not pursue a crooked path; he follows the straight road, and walks therein secure."

Having taken this short view of their language and literature, I shall now proceed to shew the present state of the arts and sciences, as far as the communications I had not only with the missionaries, but also with some of the most learned Chinese, will allow me to pronounce on these points. The observations[284] I have to make must of course be very general; minute particulars will not be expected in a work of this nature. There is no branch of science which the Chinese affect to value so much, and understand so little, as astronomy. The necessity indeed of being able to mark, with some degree of precision, the returns of the seasons and certain periods, in so large a community, must have directed an early attention of the government to this subject; and accordingly we find, that an astronomical board has formed one of the state establishments from the earliest periods of their history. Yet so little progress have they made in this science, that the only part of its functions, which can be called astronomical, has long been committed to the care of foreigners, whom they affect to hold in contempt and to consider as barbarians. The principal object of this board is to frame and to publish a national calendar, and to point out to the government the suitable times and seasons for its important undertakings. Even when the marriage of a prince or princess of the blood is about to take place, the commissioners of astronomy must appoint a fortunate day for the celebration of the nuptials, which is announced in form in the Pekin Gazette.

In this important almanack, as in the Greek and Roman calendars, are inserted all the supposed lucky and unlucky days in the year, predictions of the weather, days proper for taking medicine, commencing journies, taking home a wife, laying the foundation of a house, and other matters of moment, for entering upon which particular times are assigned. To the superintendency of the Chinese members of this august tribunal is committed the astrological part, a committee of whom is selected[285] annually for the execution of this important task. Whether the men of letters, as they call themselves, really believe in the absurdities of judicial astrology, or whether they may think it necessary to encourage the observance of popular superstitions, on political considerations, I will not take upon me to decide. If, however, they should happen to possess any such superior knowledge, great credit is due to them for acting the farce with such apparent earnestness, and with so much solemnity. The duration of the same system has certainly been long enough for them to have discovered, that the multitude are more effectually governed by opinion than by power.

The phenomena of the heavenly bodies, to an enlightened and intelligent mind, furnish the most grand and sublime spectacle in nature; to the ignorant and superstitious, the most awful. The common people of all countries, and in all ages, have considered the occasional privation of the light of the two great luminaries of heaven as the forerunners of some extraordinary event, whilst the more intelligent part of the community have turned these superstitious notions to their advantage. Thales is said to have been able to calculate the returns of eclipses six hundred years before the birth of Christ; of course, he was well acquainted with the causes by which they were produced; yet his countrymen were always filled with superstition and terror on the event of an eclipse. Plutarch has observed that Pericles learned from Anaxagoras to overcome the terrors which the various phenomena of the heavens inspired into those who knew not their causes; and he mentions a strik[286]ing proof which he gave of this knowledge, on his expedition against Peloponnesus, when there happened an eclipse of the sun. The sudden darkness, being considered as an omen unfavourable to the object of the expedition, occasioned a general consternation. Pericles, observing the pilot of his own galley to be frightened and confused, took his cloak and placed it before his eyes, asking him at the same time if he found any thing alarming, or of evil presage, in what he then did? and upon his answering in the negative: "Where then is the difference," said Pericles, "between this covering and the other, except that something of greater extent than my cloak deprives us of the light of the sun?" Nor can it be doubted that Alexander when, on a like occasion, previous to the battle of Arbêla, he commanded a sacrifice to be made to the sun, the moon, and the earth, as being the three powers to which eclipses were owing, did it merely to appease the superstitious notions of his army. To suppose him ignorant of their causes, would be paying an ill compliment to his great master. Thus it might have been with regard to the Chinese government, which, whether through ignorance or policy, still continues to observe with the greatest solemnity the same ceremonies, or nearly so, on the event of an eclipse, which were in use among the Egyptians, Greeks, and Romans, near two thousand years ago. When the moon was darkened by an eclipse, their drums and clarions and trumpets were sounded, under the notion that, by their shrill and loud noise, they might assist in relieving the labouring goddess.[287]

"A vast eclipse darkens the neighbouring planet,
Sound there, sound all our instruments of war;
Clarions and trumpets, silver, brass, and iron,
And beat a thousand drums to help her labour."

The brazen gong is violently beat by the Chinese on the same occasion; and that such an event may not pass unobserved, and the luminary thereby be deprived of the usual assistance of music, to frighten away or to charm the dragon, which they suppose to have seized upon it, the great officers of state in every city and principal town are instructed to give public notice of the time it will happen, according to the calculations of the national almanack. A rude projection of a lunar eclipse, that happened whilst we were at *Tong-choo*, was stuck up in the corners of the streets; all the officers were in mourning, and all business was suspended for that day. When the Dutch Embassadors were in Pekin, the sun was eclipsed on the 21st of January 1795, which happened to be the first day of their new year: a day observed through the whole empire with the greatest festivity and rejoicing; and almost the only day on which the bulk of the people refrain from their respective occupations. The Embassador and his suite were summoned to court at the usual hour of three in the morning. On arriving at the palace they were told that, in consequence of an eclipse of the sun, which was about to happen on that day and which was a most unfortunate event, portending an unhappy year to their country, the Emperor would not be visible for three days, during which time the whole court would go into mourning; that the amusements, feasts, and entertainments usual on this parti[288]cular day would be suspended from one end of the empire to the other.

Before an eclipse happens, the members of the mathematical board and other learned men in office assemble near the palace, each having in his hand a sketch of the obscuration, in order to witness the truth of the astronomer's calculation. But if these people were not all interested in making the calculation to agree with the time and other circumstances of the eclipse, the astronomers would run no great hazard of being detected in an error, provided it was not a very glaring one, as they have no instruments for measuring time with any tolerable degree of accuracy. The moment the eclipse begins, they all fall down on their knees, and bow their heads nine times to the ground, during which is struck up a horrible crash of gongs, kettle-drums, trumpets, and other noisy instruments, intended to scare the devouring dragon.

From the observance of such extravagant ceremonies it would not be fair to infer their total ignorance of the principles of astronomy; but that such is really the case, the latter part of their history furnishes abundant testimony. In the thirteenth century, when Gengis-Khan the Mongul Tartar first entered China, and his successor Kublai-Khan effected the conquest of the country, the greatest disorder and confusion prevailed in their chronology. They were neither able to regulate the reckoning of time, nor to settle the limits of the different provinces, nor even to ascertain the divisions of lands as allotted to the several districts. Kublai, according to their own annals, held out en[289]couragement for learned men to frequent his court from every part of the world, and through the means of the missionaries, both of the Christian and Mahomedan faith, but principally the latter, and perhaps still more through the descendants of the Greeks, who anciently settled in Bactriana, many important improvements were then introduced into China. He caused a regular survey to be taken of the whole empire. He adjusted their chronology, and corrected the errors of their astronomical observations; he imported various mathematical and astronomical instruments from Balk and Samarcand; such as were then in use among the Chinese being of a rude construction, and unfit to make observations of the heavenly bodies with any tolerable degree of accuracy; and he repaired the grand communication by water that connects the northern with the southern extremities of the empire, a work, in the contemplation of which the mind is not more strongly impressed with the grandeur and magnitude of the object, than with the pleasing sense of its important utility.

In some of the early accounts of China, published in Europe, we find the description of certain instruments, said to have been discovered on a mountain near the city of Nankin, and afterwards placed by the Chinese partly in that capital and partly in Pekin. On a more accurate examination of those instruments it appeared, that they had all been constructed for some particular place lying under the 37th parallel of latitude; from whence it followed, that all the observations made with them at Pekin, which is in 39° 55'. north, as well as all those made at Nankin in 32° 4'. north, must have been entirely false:[290] and the very act of placing them so distant from the parallel for which they were constructed, is in itself a sufficient proof of the ignorance of the Chinese in matters of this kind. Mr. Pauw has given the most probable conjecture respecting those instruments. He supposes them to have been made at Balk, in Bactriana, by some of those Greeks who obtained the government of that province under the successors of Alexander, and that they had passed into China during the period of the Mongul government.

The death of Kublai-Khan was speedily followed by the total expulsion of the Tartars from China; and most probably, at the same time, of all those learned men they had been the means of introducing into the country; for when the empire was again subdued by the Mantchoo Tartars, whose race now fills the throne, *Sun-chee*, the first Emperor of the present dynasty, observes in an edict published by him in 1650, that since the expulsion of the Monguls, the Chinese had not been able to make a correct almanack; and that error had been accumulating on error in their astronomical observations and chronology. At this time, some Mahomedans were again found to superintend the construction of the calendar; but the office devolving, at length, upon a Chinese, the unfortunate almanack-maker happened to insert a false intercalation, assigning thirteen months to the year 1670, when it should have contained no more than twelve. This mistake was an event too fortunate to be overlooked by some Catholic missionaries who, at that time, happened to be in the capital. They saw the advantages to be derived from convincing the Tartars of the ignorance of the[291] Chinese in a matter of the last importance to the government, and they had little doubt of success, where prejudice was already operating in their favour. In short, the Europeans succeeded; the almanacks of that year were declared defective, were called in, a new edition printed off, and the poor almanack-maker is said to have been strangled.

Four German Jesuits were then appointed to fill the vacant places in the tribunal of mathematics; and, being men of learning, they proved of no small use at court. After these the Portuguese succeeded to the appointments of regulating the calendar, three of whom, as already observed, are now entrusted with this important office. Fortunately for these gentlemen, the Chinese have no means of detecting any little inaccuracies that may happen in their calculations. I saw, and conversed with, numbers of their learned men at the palace of *Yuen-min-yuen*, but I can safely say, that not a single Chinese, nor a Tartar, who shewed themselves there, were possessed of the slightest knowledge of astronomy, nor one who could explain any of the various phenomena of the heavenly bodies. Astronomy with them consists entirely in a certain jargon of judicial astrology; and they remain firmly attached to the belief of the doctrines of their great philosopher, delivered more than two thousand years ago, which teach them that "the heaven is round, the earth a square fixed in the middle; the other four elements placed at its four sides: water to the north; fire to the south; wood to the east; and metal to the west:" and they believe the stars to be stuck, like so many nails, at equal distances from the earth, in the blue vault of heaven.[292]

As to the numerous eclipses taken notice of in the records of the country, they are mere registers, noted down whenever they happened, and not predictions or the result of calculations. It does not appear, indeed, that the Chinese were, at any time, able to predict an eclipse, notwithstanding all that has been said in their favour on this subject. The reputed Chinese tables, published by Father Couplet, have been detected to be those of Tycho Brahe; and Cassini found the chronology of their eclipses, published by Martinus, to be erroneous, and their returns impossible. It could not indeed be otherwise; the defectiveness of the calendar must necessarily falsify all their records as to time.

Had the missionaries been disposed to confer a real service on the Chinese, instead of misleading the world by their strange and wonderful accounts of this people; instead of bestowing so much time in translating into Chinese a set of logarithm tables for the use of *Kaung-shee*, the second Emperor of the present dynasty, of which they pretend he was so fond that he always carried them about with him suspended to his girdle, they should rather have taught them the use, and the convenience, of the Arabic numbers, of whose combinations and results their own language is not capable, and have instructed a few of their youth in the principles of arithmetic and the mathematics. For such an omission, however, human nature can readily find an excuse. It would be too great an instance of self-denial, to relinquish the advantages and the credit which their superior skill had gained them over a vast empire, by making the individuals of that empire participate in their knowledge.[293]

When we reflect, for a moment, how many perplexities and difficulties were occasioned by the irregular coincidences of the solar and lunar periods, in the calendars of Europe, from the time of Julius Cæsar to the altering of the style by Pope Gregory, we may readily conceive how great must be the errors in the chronology of a country, where the inhabitants are entirely ignorant even of the first principles of astronomy, and where they depended on the adventitious aid of foreigners, to enable them to carry into execution one of the most important concerns of the government.

Every thing of their own invention and discovery carries with it such strong marks of originality, as cannot easily be mistaken. The language declares itself to be most unquestionably the production of the country; so does the mariner's compass; and they have a cycle, or period, to assist their chronology, of which I think none will dispute with them the invention. In their records it is carried back to the time of the Emperor *Whang-tee*, the third from *Fo-shee*. This cycle, consisting of sixty years, has no reference to the periods of the motions or coincidences of the sun and moon, as one of the same period among the Hindus, but is used merely as our century, to distinguish time into eras or ages. Instead of denominating any given year the first, second, or third year of such a cycle, they have assumed two sets of characters, one set consisting of ten, and the other of twelve; the first are called the ten roots, and the second the twelve branches. The combination of a root and a branch gives a name for the year; and the different permutations, of which they are capable, supply them with[294]sixty distinct titles, making the complete cycle of sixty years. The nature of this period may be rendered familiar to such as are not conversant with the combination of numbers, by assuming the numerals from 1 to 10 for the ten roots, and the letters of the alphabet from *a* to *m*, for the twelve branches, and by placing them in a circle, in the following manner, where the cycle begins with the letter *a*.

Supposing these letters and figures to be Chinese characters, the first year of any cycle would be called 1*a*, the second 2*b*, the third 3*c*, and so on to 10*k*, the tenth year; the eleventh would be 1*l*, the twelfth 2*m*, the thirteenth 3*a*, and the sixtieth[295] 10*m*, when the whole revolution would be completed. This cycle, though always used in the records of their history, never appears in the date of public acts. These only specify the time of the reign under which they are given, as the 1st. 2d. or 3d. day of the 1st. 2d. or 3d. moon, of the 1st. 2d. or 3d. year of the reign of such or such an Emperor.

Little progress as they appear to have made in the science of astronomy, their knowledge of geography, which supposes indeed an acquaintance with the former, is equally limited. Their own empire was considered to occupy the middle space of the square surface of the earth, the rest of which was made up of islands. When the Jesuits first entered China, they found the charts, even of their own country, rude and incorrect sketches, without any scale or proportion, wherein a ridge of mountains covered a whole province, and a river swept away half of another. At present they have neat and accurate maps of the country, copied after the original survey of the whole empire, undertaken and completed by the Jesuits, after several years of indefatigable labour.

Although the Chinese language be unfavourable for numerical combinations it is admirably adapted for the concise operations of algebra, and the terse demonstrations of geometry, to neither of which, however, has it ever been made subservient, both the one and the other being totally unknown in the country. Their arithmetic is mechanical. To find the aggregate of numbers, a machine is in universal use, from the man of letters, to the meanest shopman behind his counter. By this machine, which is called a *Swan-pan*, arithmetical operations are rendered palpable. It consists of a frame of[296] wood, divided into two compartments by a bar running down the middle: through this bar, at right angles, are inserted a number of parallel wires, and on each wire, in one compartment, are five moveable balls, and in the other two. These wires may be considered as the ascending and descending powers of a numeration table, proceeding in a tenfold proportion; so that if a ball upon any of the wires, in the larger compartment, be placed against the middle bar, and called unity or one, a ball on the wire next above it will represent ten, and one on the next one hundred; so, also, a ball on the wire next below that expressing unity will be one-tenth, the next lower one hundredth, and the third one thousandth, part of an unit; and the balls on the corresponding wires in the smaller compartment will be five, fifty, five hundred, five-tenths, five hundredths, five thousandths; the value or power of each of these, in the smaller division, being always five times as much as of those in the larger. In the following figure,

100

suppose X be assumed as the line of units, the lines to the right will be integers decimally increasing, and those to the left fractional parts decimally decreasing; and the *Swan-pan* in the present position of the balls, will represent the number 573916 0705/10000.

This is clearly a system of decimal arithmetic, which, for the[297] ease, simplicity, and convenience of its operations, it were to be wished was generally adopted in Europe, instead of the endless ways in which the integer is differently divided in different countries, and in the different provinces of the same country. The *Swan-pan* would be no bad instrument for teaching to a blind person the operations of arithmetic. Yet, paradoxical as it may seem, these operations, as performed by the Chinese, like their written characters, require more the exercise of the eye than of the mind. The simple addition or subtraction of the little balls to, or from, the middle bar, shews at once by their disposition on the board the result of any required combination. The invention of it I think may fairly be attributed to the Chinese; though it has been compared, how justly I cannot pretend to say, to the Roman *abacus*.

It has been observed, and perhaps with a great deal of truth, that the arts which supply the luxuries, the conveniences, and the necessaries of life, have derived but little advantage in the first instance from the labours and speculations of philosophers; that the ingenuity of artists, the accidental or progressive discoveries of common workmen, in any particular branch of business, have frequently afforded *data*, from which, by the reasonings and investigations of philosophers, hints have sometimes been struck out for arriving at the same ends by a shorter way; that the learned are therefore more properly to be considered as improvers than inventors. Of this mortifying truth, the Chinese afford many strong examples in their arts and manufactures, and particularly in some of those operations that have a reference to chemistry, which cannot here be said to[298] exist as a science, although several branches are in common practice as chemical arts. Without possessing any theory concerning the affinities of bodies, or attractions of cohesion or aggregation, they clarify the muddy waters of their rivers, for immediate use, by stirring them round with a piece of alum in a hollow bamboo; a simple operation which, experience has taught them, will cause the clayey particles to fall to the bottom: and having ascertained the fact, they have given themselves no further trouble to explain the phenomenon.

In like manner, they are well acquainted with the effect of steam upon certain bodies that are immersed in it; that its heat is much greater than that of boiling water. Yet, although for ages they have been in the constant practice of confining it in close vessels, something like *Papin's digester*, for the purpose of softening horn, from which their thin, transparent, and capacious lanterns are made, they seem not to have discovered its extraordinary force when thus pent up; at least, they have never thought of applying that power to purposes which animal strength has not been adequate to effect. They extract from the three kingdoms of nature the most brilliant colours, which they have also acquired the art of preparing and mixing, so as to produce every intermediate tint; and, in their richest and most lively hues, they communicate these colours to silks, cottons, and paper; yet they have no theory on colours.

The process of smelting iron from the ore is well known to them; and their cast ware of this metal is remarkably thin and light. They have also an imperfect knowledge of converting[299] it into steel, but their manufactures of this article are not to be mentioned with those of Europe, I will not say of England, because it stands unrivalled in this and indeed almost every other branch of the arts. Though their cast-iron wares appear light and neat, and are annealed in heated ovens, to take off somewhat of their brittleness, yet their process of rendering cast iron malleable is imperfect, and all their manufactures of wrought iron are consequently of a very inferior kind, not only in workmanship but also in the quality of the metal. In most of the other metals their manufactures are above mediocrity. Their trinkets of silver fillagree are extremely neat, and their articles of tootanague are highly finished.

With the use of cannon they pretend to have been long acquainted. When Gengis-Khan entered China, in the thirteenth century, artillery and bombs and mines are said to have been employed on both sides; yet when the city of Macao, in the year 1621, made a present to the Emperor of three pieces of artillery, it was found necessary to send along with them three men to instruct the Chinese how to use them. The introduction of matchlocks, I am inclined to think, is of no very ancient date; they wear no marks of originality about them, like other articles of Chinese invention; on the contrary, they are exact models of the old Portugueze matchlock; and differ in nothing from those which still continue to be carried, as an article of commerce, by this nation to Cochin-China. There can be no doubt, however, of the use of gunpowder being known to the Chinese long before the Christian era.[300]

In a very ancient treatise on the military art, there is a detailed account of the manner how to annoy an enemy's camp, by springing a mine with gunpowder; but this treatise makes no mention of cannon. Fire-works, made generally of gunpowder, filings of zinc, camphor, and other ingredients, are described in various old tracts. It is easily conceived, that the deflagration of nitre was likely to be first noticed in those countries where it is the spontaneous and abundant production of the earth, which is the case on the elevated desarts of Tartary and Thibet, and on the low and extensive plains of India and China. The gunpowder, however, made by the Chinese is extremely bad. They have no particular manufactory, but each individual makes his own. It is in fact one part of the soldier's employment to prepare his own gunpowder. The usual proportions, according to *Van-ta-gin*'s information are,

      50 pounds of nitre,
25 —— sulphur,
25 —— charcoal.

They know not the art of granulating the paste, as in Europe, but use it in a coarse powder, which sometimes cakes together into a solid mass; and from the impurity of the nitre, (no means appearing to be employed for extracting the common salt it usually contains) the least exposure to the air, by attracting the moisture, makes it unfit for service. This may be one reason for their objection to firelocks.

It has been remarked, that the three great discoveries of the magnetic needle, of gunpowder, and of printing, in Europe, followed close upon the return of the famous traveller Marco[301]Polo. It was the boast indeed of *Caung-shee* to the Jesuits, when they instructed him in some of the sciences of Europe, that the latter country was neither acquainted with the mariner's compass, nor with the art of printing, nor with gunpowder, till they had been in common use in China near two thousand years. As to gunpowder, it is pretty obvious, that our countryman Roger Bacon was well acquainted with the ingredients that enter into its composition. In more than one part of his works he observes, that with saltpetre and other articles may be made a fire that will inflame to a great distance; and in one place he states, that with sulphur, saltpetre, and something else, which he disguises under two or three barbarous words, a composition may be made, by which the effects of thunder and of lightning may be imitated. Bacon died in the year 1292, and Marco Polo returned to Europe in 1295; so that he could not possibly have received any hint to lead towards the discovery through the channel of the Venetian traveller[18].

If the Chinese had, at any period of their history, been acquainted with the art of casting large cannon, and of making [302]use of them in their wars, it is scarcely probable they would ever have lost it. Yet it is very certain the two Jesuits, Schaal and Verbiest, took great pains to instruct them in the method of casting cannon; in which, however, they have not made any progress or improvement. I observed, near one of the gates of Pekin, a few rude, ill-shapen, and disproportionate pieces, lying unmounted on the ground, and these, with some of the same kind on the frontiers of Canton, and a few pieces, apparently twelve pounders, at *Hang-tcheu-foo*, which had wooden pent-houses erected over each, were the only cannon that we noticed in the whole country. Whether the specimens, exhibited in the annexed plate, which were drawn by the late Captain Parish of the Royal Artillery, be originally of Chinese invention, or borrowed from some other nation, I cannot take upon me to decide; but such are the pieces which are sometimes found, scattered about the gates of some of their cities.

Mr. Bell, who visited China in the suite of the Russian Embassador, near a century ago, remarks, that "towards the western extremity of the Great Wall, he observed some hundreds of old cannon piled up in one of the towers, each composed of three or four pieces of hammered iron, joined and fastened together with hoops of the same metal." It is probable indeed that the Chinese, like the Hindoos, before the time of Schaal and Verbiest, made use of cannon of wrought iron, which were hooped together like those mentioned by Mr. Bell.

Sketches of Chinese Artillery.

REFERENCES.

Fig. 1 Iron four Pounder about 8 feet long at Han cheu Fou
2. Iron four Pounder about 8 feet long at Chong san chien
3. A Field Piece about the Calibre and length of our Wall Piece
but of much greater thickness of Metal
4. Half Pounder Field Piece
5. A Platform of Masonry with irregular Pieces about 2 pounders
probably for throwing stones. They are thus placed in the open
Spaces at the Gate Ways at **PEKIN** *and Ton cheu*
6. A Stand for Field Pieces at Cou pe keou

Neele sculp. 352 Strand.

Published May 1st. 1804 by Cadell & Davies Strand.

In making their salutes, of which they are not sparing, they[303] invariably employ three small petards, or pistol-barrels rather, which are stuck erect in the ground; and in firing these small pieces the soldiers are so afraid, that they are discharged by a train laid from one to the other. When Captain Parish caused a few rounds to be fired from two field-pieces, which were among the presents for the Emperor, in as quick succession as possible, the Chinese officers very coolly observed, that their own soldiers could do it just as well, and perhaps better. And when Lord Macartney asked the Ex-viceroy of Canton if he would wish to see his guard go through the different evolutions as practised in Europe, he replied with equal indifference, "That they could not possibly be new to him, who had been so much engaged in the wars on the frontiers of Tartary;" though the chances are, that he had never before seen a firelock: with such ridiculous affectation of superiority, and contempt for other nations, does the unconquerable pride of this people inspire them. It seems, indeed, to be laid down as a general principle, never to be caught in the admiration of any thing brought among them by foreigners. Whenever a man of rank came to look at the presents, if observed by any of us, he would carelessly glance his eye over them, and affect as much indifference as if he was in the daily habit of viewing things of the same kind.

A French physician, who travelled in China, says he never saw an alembic or distillatory apparatus in the whole country. The art of distillation, however, is very well known, and in common practice. Their *Sau-tchoo*, (literally burnt wine), is[304] an ardent spirit distilled from various kinds of grain, but most commonly from rice, of a strong empyreumatic flavour, not unlike the spirit known in Scotland by the name of whiskey. The rice is kept in hot water till the grains are swollen; it is then mixed up with water in which has been dissolved a preparation called *pe-ka*, consisting of rice-flour, liquorice-root, anniseed, and garlic; this not only hastens fermentation, but is supposed to give it a peculiar flavour. The mixture then undergoes distillation. The *Sau-tchoo*, thus prepared, may be considered as the basis of the best arrack, which in Java is exclusively the manufacture of Chinese, and is nothing more than a rectification of the above spirit, with the addition of molasses and juice of the cocoa-nut tree. Before distillation the liquor is simply called *tchoo*, or wine, and in this state is a very insipid and disagreeable beverage. The vine grows extremely well in all the provinces, even as far north as Pekin, but the culture of it seems to meet with little encouragement, and no wine is made from the juice of the grape, except by the missionaries near the capital.

The manufacture of earthen ware, as far as depends upon the preparation of the materials, they have carried to a pitch of perfection not hitherto equalled by any nation, except the Japanese, who are allowed to excel them, not only in this branch, but also in all articles of lacquered and varnished ware, which fetch exorbitant prices even in China. The beauty of their porcelain, in a great degree, depends upon the extreme labour and attention that is paid to the assortment, and the preparation of the different articles employed. These are in[305] general a fine sort of clay called *Kao-lin* which is a species of Soap-rock, and a granite called *Pe-tun-tse*, composed chiefly of quartz, the proportion of mica being very small. These materials are ground down and washed with the greatest care; and when the paste has been turned or moulded into forms, each piece is put into a box of clay before it goes into the oven; yet with every precaution, it frequently happens (so much is this art still a work of chance) that a whole oven runs together and becomes a mass of vitrified matter. Neither the Chinese nor the Japanese can boast of giving to the materials much elegance of form. With those inimitable models from the Greek and Roman vases, brought into modern use by the ingenious Mr. Wedgwood, they will not bear a comparison. And nothing can be more rude and ill-designed than the grotesque figures and other objects painted, or rather daubed, on their porcelain, which however are generally the work of the wives and children of the labouring poor. That they can do better we have evident proof; for if a pattern be sent out from England, the artists in Canton will execute it with scrupulous exactness; and their colours are inimitable.

The manufacture of glass was totally unknown among them until the last century when, at the recommendation of the Jesuits, a family was engaged to go from France to Pekin, for the purpose of introducing the art of glass-making into the country. The attempt failed of success, and the concern, at the death of the manager, was broken up. In Canton they melt old broken glass and mold it into new forms; and they have been taught to coat plates of glass with silver, which are partially used as[306] looking-glasses; but their common mirrors are of polished metal, which is apparently a composition of copper and zinc.

The pride, or the policy, of the government affecting to despise any thing new or foreign, and the general want of encouragement to new inventions, however ingenious, have been greatly detrimental to the progress of the arts and manufactures. The people discover no want of genius to conceive, nor of dexterity to execute; and their imitative powers have always been acknowledged to be very great. Of the truth of this remark we had several instances at *Yuen-min-yuen*. The complicated glass lustres, consisting of several hundred pieces, were taken down, piece by piece, in the course of half an hour, by two Chinese, who had never seen any thing of the kind before, and were put up again by them with equal facility; yet Mr. Parker thought it necessary for our mechanics to attend at his warehouse several times to see them taken down and again put together, in order to be able to manage the business on their arrival in China. A Chinese undertook to cut a slip of glass from a large curved piece, intended to cover the great dome of the planetarium, after our two artificers had broken three similar pieces in attempting to cut them with the help of the diamond. The man performed it in private, nor could he be prevailed on to say in what manner he accomplished it. Being a little jagged along the margin, I suspect it was not cut but fractured, perhaps by passing a heated iron over a line drawn with water, or some other fluid. It is well known that a Chinese in Canton, on being shewn an European watch, undertook, and succeeded, to make one like it, though he had never seen any thing of the[307] kind before, but it was necessary to furnish him with a main spring, which he could not make: and they now fabricate in Canton, as well as in London, and at one third of the expence, all those ingenious pieces of mechanism which at one time were sent to China in such vast quantities from the repositories of Coxe and Merlin. The mind of a Chinese is quick and apprehensive, and his small delicate hands are formed for the execution of neat work.

The manufacture of silks has been established in China at a period so remote, as not to be ascertained from history; but the time when the cotton plant was first brought from the northern parts of India into the southern provinces of China is known, and noticed in their annals. That species of the cotton plant, from which is produced the manufacture usually called nankin cotton, is said to loose its peculiar yellow tint in the course of two or three years when cultivated in the southern provinces, owing, in all probability, to the great heat of the weather and continued sunshine. I have raised this particular species at the Cape of Good Hope where, upon the same plant, as well as on others produced from its seed, the pods were as full and the tint of as deep a yellow in the third year as in the first. As is generally the case in most of their manufactures, those of silk and cotton do not appear to have lately undergone progressive improvement. The want of proper encouragement from the government, and the rigid adherence to ancient usage, have rendered indeed all their fabrics stationary.[308]

Of all the mechanical arts that in which they seem to have attained the highest degree of perfection is the cutting of ivory. In this branch they stand unrivalled, even at Birmingham, that great nursery of the arts and manufactures where, I understand, it has been attempted by means of a machine to cut ivory fans and other articles, in imitation of those of the Chinese; but the experiment, although ingenious, has not hitherto succeeded to that degree, so as to produce articles fit to vie with those of the latter. Nothing can be more exquisitely beautiful than the fine open work displayed in a Chinese fan, the sticks of which would seem to be singly cut by the hand, for whatever pattern may be required, or a shield with coat of arms, or a cypher, the article will be finished according to the drawing at the shortest notice. The two outside sticks are full of bold sharp work, undercut in such a manner as could not be performed any other way than by the hand. Yet the most finished and beautiful of these fans may be purchased at Canton for five to ten Spanish dollars[19]. Out of a solid ball of ivory, with a hole in it not larger than half an inch in diameter, they will cut from nine to fifteen distinct hollow globes, one within another, all loose and capable of being turned round in every direction, and each of them carved full of the same kind of open work that appears on the fans. A very small sum of money is the price of one of these difficult trifles. Models of temples, [309]pagodas, and other pieces of architecture, are beautifully worked in ivory; and from the shavings, interwoven with pieces of quills, they make neat baskets and hats, which are as light and pliant as those of straw. In short, all kinds of toys for children, and other trinkets and trifles, are executed in a neater manner and for less money in China, than in any other part of the world.

The various uses, to which that elegant species of reed called the bamboo is applied, would require a volume to enumerate. Their chairs, their tables, their skreens, their bedsteads and bedding, and many other household moveables, are entirely constructed of this hollow reed, and some of them in a manner sufficiently ingenious and beautiful. It is used on board ships for poles, for sails, for cables, for rigging, and for caulking. In husbandry for carts, for wheelbarrows, for wheels to raise water, for fences, for sacking to hold grain, and a variety of other utensils. The young shoots furnish an article of food; and the wicks of their candles are made of its fibres. It serves to embellish the garden of the prince, and to cover the cottage of the peasant. It is the instrument, in the hand of power, that keeps the whole empire in awe. In short, there are few uses to which a Chinese cannot apply the bamboo, either entire or split into thin laths, or further divided into fibres to be twisted into cordage, or macerated into a pulp to be manufactured into paper.

That "there is nothing new under the sun," was the observation of a wise man in days of yore. Impressed with the[310] same idea an ingenious and learned modern author[20] has written a book to prove, that all the late discoveries and inventions of Europe were known to the ancients. The discovery of making paper from straw, although new, perhaps, in Europe, is of very ancient date in China. The straw of rice and other grain, the bark of the mulberry-tree, the cotton shrub, hemp, nettles, and various other plants and materials, are employed in the paper manufactories of China, where sheets are prepared of such dimensions, that a single one may be had to cover the whole side of a moderate sized room. The finer sort of paper for writing upon has a surface as smooth as vellum, and is washed with a strong solution of alum to prevent the ink from sinking. Many old persons and children earn a livelihood by washing the ink from written paper, which, being afterwards beaten and boiled to a paste, is re-manufactured into new sheets; and the ink is also separated from the water, and preserved for future life. To this article of their manufacture the arts in our own country owe so many advantages, that little requires to be said in its favour. The Chinese, however, acknowledge their obligations to the Coreans for the improvements in making ink, which, not many centuries ago, were received from them.

As to the art of printing, there can be little doubt of its antiquity in China, yet they have never proceeded beyond a wooden block. The nature, indeed, of the character is such, that moveable types would scarcely be practicable. It is true, [311]the component parts of the characters are sufficiently simple and few in number; but the difficulty of putting them together upon the frame, into the multitude of forms of which they are capable, is perhaps not to be surmounted.

Like the rest of their inventions the chain-pump which, in Europe, has been brought to such perfection as to constitute an essential part of ships of war and other large vessels, continues among the Chinese nearly in its primitive state, the principal improvement since its first invention consisting in the substitution of boards or basket-work for wisps of straw. Its power with them has never been extended beyond that of raising a small stream of water up an inclined plane, from one reservoir to another, to serve the purposes of irrigation. They are of different sizes, some worked by oxen, some by treading in a wheel, and others by the hand.

The great advantages attainable from the use of mechanical powers are either not understood or, purposely, not employed. In a country of such vast population, machinery may perhaps be considered as detrimental especially as, at least, nine-tenths of the community must derive their subsistence from manual labour. It may be a question, not at all decided in their minds, whether the general advantages of facilitating labour, and gaining time by means of machinery, be sufficient to counterbalance the individual distress that would, for a time, be occasioned by the introduction of such machinery. Whatever the reason may be, no such means are to be met with in the country. Among the presents that were carried out for the Empe[312]ror were an apparatus for the air pump, various articles for conducting a set of experiments in electricity, and the models of a complete set of mechanical powers placed upon a brass pillar. The Emperor, happening to cast his eye upon them, enquired of the eunuch in waiting for what they were intended. This mutilated animal, although he had been daily studying the nature and use of the several presents, in order to be able to say something upon them when they should be exhibited to his master, could not succeed in making his Imperial Majesty comprehend the intention of the articles in question. "I fancy," says the old monarch, "they are meant as playthings for some of my great grandchildren."

The power of the pulley is understood by them, and is applied on board all their large vessels, but always in a single state; at least, I never observed a block with more than one wheel in it. The principle of the lever should also seem to be well known, as all their valuable wares, even silver and gold, are weighed with the steelyard: and the tooth and pinion wheels are used in the construction of their self-moving toys, and in all their rice-mills that are put in motion by a water wheel. But none of the mechanical powers are applied on the great scale to facilitate and to expedite labour. Simplicity is the leading feature in all their contrivances that relate to the arts and manufactures. The tools of every artificer are of a construction the most simple that it should seem possible to make them, and yet each tool is so contrived as to answer several purposes. Thus, the bellows of the blacksmith, which is nothing more than a hollow cylinder of wood, with a valvular piston,[313] beside blowing the fire, serves for his seat when set on end, and as a box to contain the rest of his tools. The barber's bamboo basket, that contains his apparatus, is also the seat for his customers. The joiner makes use of his rule as a walking stick, and the chest that holds his tools serves him as a bench to work on. The pedlar's box and a large umbrella are sufficient for him to exhibit all his wares, and to form his little shop.

Little can be said in favour of the state of the fine arts in this country. Of their poetry, modern and ancient, I have given a specimen; but I think it right once more to observe that, with regard to Asiatic compositions, Europeans cannot form a proper judgment, and more especially of those of the Chinese, which, to the mysterious and obscure expressions of metaphor, add the disadvantage of a language that speaks but little to the ear; a whole sentence, or a combination of ideas, being sometimes shut up in a short monosyllable, whose beauties are most studiously addressed to the sense of seeing alone.

Of the other two sister arts, painting and music, a more decided opinion may be passed. Of the latter I have little to observe. It does not seem to be cultivated as a science: it is neither learned as an elegant accomplishment, nor practiced as an amusement of genteel life, except by those females who are educated for sale, or by such as hire themselves out for the entertainment of those who may be inclined to purchase their favours. And as the Chinese differ in their ideas from all other nations, these[311] women play generally upon wind instruments, such as small pipes and flutes; whilst the favourite instrument of the men is the guittar or something not very unlike it, some of which have two strings, some four, and others seven. Eunuchs, and the lowest class of persons, are hired to play; and the merit of a performance should seem to consist in the intenseness of the noise brought out of the different instruments. The gong or, as they call it, the *loo* is admirably adapted for this purpose. This instrument is a sort of shallow kettle, or rather the lid of a kettle, which they strike with a wooden mallet covered with leather. The composition is said to be copper, tin, and bismuth. They have also a kind of clarinet, three or four different sorts of trumpets, and a stringed instrument not unlike a violoncello. Their *sing* is a combination of uneven reeds of bamboo, not unlike the pipe of Pan; the tones are far from being disagreeable, but its construction is so wild and irregular, that it does not appear to be reducible to any kind of scale. Their kettle drums are generally shaped like barrels; and these, as well as different-sized bells fixed in a frame, constitute parts in their sacred music. They have also an instrument of music which consists of stones, cut into the shape of a carpenter's square, each stone suspended by the corner in a wooden frame. Those which I saw appeared to belong to that species of the silicious genus usually called Gneiss, a sort of slaty granite. In the Keswick museum are musical stones of the same kind, which were picked up in a rivulet at the foot of Skiddaw mountain; but these seem to contain small pieces of black shorl or tourmaline. It is indeed the boast of their historians, that the whole empire of na[315]ture has been laid under contribution in order to complete their system of music: that the skins of animals, the fibres of plants, metals, stones, and baked earths, have all been employed in the production of sounds. Their instruments, it is true, are sufficiently varied, both as to shape and materials, but I know of none that is even tolerable to an European ear. An English gentleman in Canton took some pains to collect the various instruments of the country, of which the annexed plate is a representation, but his catalogue is not complete.

A sheet of bell Metal
A pot of bell Metal
The Great Bell of Canton 20 feet diameter 8-16 Inches thick.
A Barrel drum sometimes of Wood & sometimes Metal.
A Log of Wood shaped like a Skull and used in Temples.
A Metal Bell.
A Lyre of silken Strings.
A small Flute.
A Muffled Drum.
The Metal Gong or Loo
Cymbals.
Uncertain
A Pair of Rattles or Castanets.
Cymbals struck with a rod.
Alommon Flute.
Two Stringed Violins
A Three Stringed Guitar.
A Pipe of inequal reeds or bamboos.
Four Stringed Guitars.
Three Trumpets.
A Lyre of 11 Metallic Strings.
Metal Plates an Instrument used in Sacred Music.
A small barrell Drum.
A fixed Drum used in Sacred Music.
A small Gong or Loo.

Neele sc. Strand

Published May 10th, 1804 by Cadell and Davies Strand.

A Chinese band generally plays, or endeavours to play, in unison, and sometimes an instrument takes the octave; but they never attempt to play in separate parts, confining their art to the melody only, if I may venture to apply a name of so much sweetness to an aggregation of harsh sounds. They have not the least notion of counter-point, or playing in parts: an invention indeed to which the elegant Greeks had not arrived, and which was unknown in Europe as well as Asia, until the monkish ages.

I never heard but one single Chinese who could be said to sing with feeling or plaintiveness. Accompanied with a kind of guittar, he sung the following air in praise of the flower*Moo-lee*, which it seems is one of the most popular songs in the whole country. The simple melody was taken down by Mr. Hittner, and I understand has been published in London, with head and tail-pieces, accompaniments, and all the refined arts of European music; so that it ceases to be a specimen of the plain melody of[316] China. I have therefore given it in its unadorned state, as sung and played by the Chinese, together with the words of the first stanza, and their literal translation.

MIDI

MOO-LEE-WHA.

I.

12345
Hau ye-to sien wha,

678910111213
Yeu tchau yeu jie lo tsai go kia

141516171819
Go pun tai, poo tchoo mun

202122232425
Twee tcho sien wha ul lo.

II.

123456
Hau ye to Moo-lee-wha

7891011121314
Man yuen wha kai soy poo quee ta

151617181920
Go pun tai tsai ye ta

21222324252627
Tai you kung kan wha jin ma.
[317]

Literal Translation.

I.

108

12345
How delightful this branch of fresh flowers

678910111213
One morning one day it was dropped in my house

141516171819
I the owner will wear it not out of doors

202122232425
But I will hold the fresh flower and be happy.

II.

123456
How delightful this branch of the *Moo-lee* flower

7891011121314
In the full plot of flowers blowing freely none excels it

151617181920
I the owner will wear this gathered branch

21222324252627
Wear it yet fear, the flower seen, men will envy.

I have thought it not amiss to subjoin a few other airs of the popular kind, which were written by the same gentleman at Canton, who made the drawings of their musical instruments.[318]

CHINESE POPULAR AIRS.

MIDI

MIDI

[319]

MIDI

[320]

MIDI

MIDI

[321]

[322]

They have no other notion of noting down music than that of employing a character expressing the name of every note in the scale; and even this imperfect way they learned from Pereira the Jesuit. They affected to dislike the Embassador's band which they pretended to say produced no music, but a confusion of noises; yet the Emperor's chief musician gave himself a great deal of trouble in tracing out the several instruments on large sheets of paper, each of its particular size, marking the places of the holes, screws, strings, and other parts, which they conceived necessary to enable them to make others of a similar construction.

It would be difficult to assign the motive that induced Father Amiot to observe, that "the Chinese, in order to obtain their[323] scale of notes or gamut perfect, were not afraid of submitting to the most laborious operations of geometry, and to the most tedious and disgusting calculations in the science of numbers;" as he must have known, that they were altogether ignorant of geometry, and that their arithmetic extended not beyond their *Swan-pan*. Of the same nature is the bold and unfounded assertion of another of the Jesuits, "that the musical system of the Chinese was borrowed from them by the Greeks and Egyptians, anterior to the time of Hermes or Orpheus!"

With regard to painting, they can be considered in no other light than as miserable daubers, being unable to pencil out a correct outline of many objects, to give body to the same by the application of proper lights and shadows, and to lay on the nice shades of colour, so as to resemble the tints of nature. But the gaudy colouring of certain flowers, birds, and insects, they imitate with a degree of exactness and brilliancy to which Europeans have not yet arrived. To give distance to objects on canvas, by diminishing them, by faint colouring, and by perspective, they have no sort of conception. At *Yuen-min-yuen* I found two very large paintings of landscapes which, as to the pencilling, were done with tolerable execution, but they were finished with a minuteness of detail, and without any of those strong lights and masses of shade, which give force and effect to a picture; none of the rules of perspective were observed, nor any attempt to throw the objects to their proper distances; yet I could not help fancying that I discovered in them the hand of an European. The[324] old eunuch, who carried the keys of the room, frequently asked me, when looking at these pictures, if I did not think his countrymen were excellent painters; and having one day expressed great admiration for the talents of the artist, he led me into a recess of the room, and opening a chest, supported upon a pedestal, he observed, with a significant look, he was now going to produce something that would astonish me. He then took out several large volumes, which were full of figures, drawn in a very superior style and tinted with water colours, representing the several trades and occupations carried on in the country; but they seemed to be stuck against the paper, having neither shadow nor foreground, nor distance, to give them any relief. On the opposite page to each figure was a description, in the Mantchoo Tartar and the Chinese languages. Having turned over one of the volumes, I observed, on the last page, the name of *Castaglione*, which at once solved the riddle. On re-examining the large pictures in the hall, I found the same name in the corner of each. While going through the volume, the old eunuch frequently asked, if any one in Europe could paint like the Chinese? but, on my pointing to the name, and repeating the word *Castaglione*, he immediately shut the book and returned them all into the chest, nor, from that time, could I ever prevail upon him to let me have another sight of them. On enquiry, I found that Castaglione was a missionary in great repute at court, where he executed a number of paintings, but was expressly directed by the Emperor to paint all his subjects after the Chinese manner, and not like those of Europe, with broad masses of shade and the distant objects scarcely visible, observing to him, as one of the missionaries told me, that the[325] imperfections of the eye afforded no reason why the objects of nature should also be copied as imperfect. This idea of the Emperor accords with a remark made by one of his ministers, who came to see the portrait of His Britannic Majesty, "that it was great pity it should have been spoiled by the dirt upon the face," pointing, at the same time, to the broad shade of the nose.

Ghirrardini, an European painter, published an account of his voyage to China, where, it appears, he was so disgusted that, having observed how little idea they possess of the fine arts, he adds, with rather more petulancy than truth, "these Chinese are fit for nothing but weighing silver, and eating rice." Ghirrardini painted a large colonnade in vanishing perspective, which struck them so very forcibly that they concluded he must certainly have dealings with the Devil; but, on approaching the canvas and feeling with their hands, in order to be fully convinced that all they saw was on a flat surface, they persisted that nothing could be more unnatural than to represent distances, where there actually neither was, nor could be, any distance.

It is scarcely necessary to add any thing further with regard to the state of painting in China. I shall only observe, that the Emperor's favourite draughtsman, who may of course be supposed as good or better than others of the same profession in the capital, was sent to make drawings of some of the principal presents to carry to his master, then in Tartary, as elucidations of the descriptive catalogue. This man, after various unsuc[326]cessful attempts to design the elegant time-pieces of Vulliamy, supported by beautiful figures of white marble, supplicated my assistance in a matter which he represented as of the last importance to himself. It was in vain to assure him that I was no draughtsman; he was determined to have the proof of it; and he departed extremely well satisfied in obtaining a very mean performance with the pencil, to copy after or cover with his China ink. Every part of the machines, except the naked figures which supported the time-piece and a barometer, he drew with neatness and accuracy, but all his attempts to copy these were unsuccessful. Whether it was owing to any real difficulty that exists in the nice turns and proportions of the human figure, or that by being better acquainted with it we more readily perceive the defects in the imitation of it, or from the circumstance of the human form being concealed in this country in loose folding robes, that caused the Chinese draughtsman so completely to fail, I leave to the artists of our own country to determine: but the fact was as I state it; all his attempts to draw these figures were preposterous.

As to those specimens of beautiful flowers, birds, and insects, sometimes brought over to Europe, they are the work of artists at Canton where, from being in the habit of copying prints and drawings, carried thither for the purpose of being transferred to porcelain, or as articles of commerce, they have acquired a better taste than in the interior parts of the country. Great quantities of porcelain are sent from the potteries to Canton perfectly white, that the purchaser may have them painted to his own pattern: and specimens of these bear testimony that[327] they are no mean copyists. It has been observed, however, that the subjects of natural history, painted by them, are frequently incorrect; that it is no unusual thing to meet with the flower of one plant set upon the stalk of another, and having the leaves of a third. This may formerly have been the case, from their following imperfect patterns, or from supposing they could improve nature; but having found that the representations of natural objects are in more request among foreigners, they pay a stricter attention to the subject that may be required; and we found them indeed such scrupulous copyists, as not only to draw the exact number of the petals, the stamina, and pistilla of a flower, but also the very number of leaves, with the thorns or spots on the foot-stalk that supported it. They will even count the number of scales on a fish, and mark them out in their representations, and it is impossible to imitate the brilliant colours of nature more closely. I brought home several drawings of plants, birds, and insects, that have been greatly admired for their accuracy and close colouring; but they want that effect which the proper application of light and shade never fails to produce. The coloured prints of Europe that are carried out to Canton are copied there with wonderful fidelity. But in doing this, they exercise no judgment of their own. Every defect and blemish, original or accidental, they are sure to copy, being mere servile imitators, and not in the least feeling the force or the beauty of any specimen of the arts that may come before them; for the same person who is one day employed in copying a beautiful European print, will sit down the next to a Chinese drawing replete with absurdity.[328]

Whatever may be the progress of the arts in the port of Canton, they are not likely to experience much improvement in the interior parts of the country, or in the capital. It was the pride rather of the monarch, and of his ministers, that made them reject the proposal of Castaglione to establish a school for the arts, than the apprehension, as stated by the missionaries, that the rage for painting would become so general, as to be prejudicial to useful labour.

In a country where painting is at so low an ebb, it would be in vain to expect much execution from the chissel. Grotesque images of ideal beings, and monstrous distortions of nature, are sometimes seen upon the ballustrades of bridges, and in their temples, where the niches are filled with gigantic gods of baked clay, sometimes painted with gaudy colours, and sometimes plastered over with gold leaf, or covered with a coat of varnish. They are as little able to model as to draw the human figure with any degree of correctness. In the whole empire there is not a statue, a hewn pillar, or a column that deserves to be mentioned. Large four-sided blocks of stone or wood are frequently erected near the gates of cities, with inscriptions upon them, meant to perpetuate the memory of certain distinguished characters; but they are neither objects of grandeur nor ornament, having a much closer resemblance to a gallows than to triumphal arches, as the missionaries, for what reason I know not, have thought fit to call them.

The intention of these monumental erections will appear from some of their inscriptions.[329]

I.

Honour granted by the Emperor.
The grateful odour of one hundred years.
Retirement. Tranquillity.

II.

Emperor's order.
Peace and Happiness,
The balm of Life.
On a fortunate day, in the 8th month of the 50th year of the
reign of Kien-Long, this monument was erected by the
Emperor's order, in honour of Liang-tien-pe, aged
102 years.

The two following are inscriptions on monuments that have been erected to chaste women, a description of ladies whom the Chinese consider to be rarely met with.

III.

Honour granted by the Emperor.
Icy coldness. Hard frost.

IV.

The Emperor's order.
The sweet fragrance of piety and virginity.
Sublime chastity. Pure morals.

The whole of their architecture, indeed, is as unsightly[330] as unsolid; without elegance or convenience of design, and without any settled proportion; mean in its appearance, and clumsy in the workmanship. Their pagodas of five, seven, and nine rounds, or roofs, are the most striking objects; but though they appear to be the imitations or, perhaps, more properly speaking, the models of a similar kind of pyramids found in India, they are neither so well designed, nor so well executed: they are, in fact, so very ill constructed that half of them, without any marks of antiquity, appear in ruins; of these useless and whimsical edifices His Majesty's garden at Kew exhibits a specimen, which is not inferior in any respect to the very best I have met with in China. The height of such structures, and the badness of the materials with which they are usually built, contradict the notion that they assign as a reason for the lowness of their houses, which is, that they may escape being thrown down by earthquakes. In fact, the tent stands confessed in all their dwellings, of which the curved roof and the wooden pillars (in imitation of the poles) forming a colonnade round the ill-built brick walls, clearly denote the origin; and from this original form they have never ventured to deviate. Their temples are mostly constructed upon the same plan, with the addition of a second, and sometimes a third roof, one above the other. The wooden pillars that constitute the colonnade are generally of larch fir, of no settled proportion between the length and the diameter, and they are invariably painted red and sometimes covered with a coat of varnish.[331]

As custom and fashion are not the same in any two countries, it has been contended by many that there can be no such thing as true taste. The advocates for taste arising out of custom will say, that no solid reason can be offered why the pillar which supports the Doric capital should be two diameters shorter than that which sustains the Corinthian; and that it is the habit only of seeing them thus constructed that constitutes their propriety. Though the respective beauties of these particular columns may, in part, be felt from the habit of observing them always retaining a settled proportion, yet it must be allowed that, in the most perfect works of nature, there appears a certain harmony and agreement of one part with another, that without any settled proportion seldom fail to please. Few people will disagree in their ideas of a handsome tree, or an elegant flower, though there be no fixed proportion between the trunk and the branches, the flower and the foot-stalk. Proportion, therefore, alone, is not sufficient to constitute beauty. There must be no stiffness, no sudden breaking off from a straight line to a curve; but the changes should be easy, not visible in any particular part, but running imperceptibly through the whole. Utility has also been considered as one of the constituent parts of beauty. In the Chinese column, labouring under an enormous mass of roof, without either base or capital, there is neither symmetry of parts, nor ease, nor particular utility. Nor have the large ill-shapen and unnatural figures of lions, dragons, and serpents, grinning on the tops and corners of the roofs, any higher pretensions to good taste, to utility, or to beauty.[332]

"The architecture of the Chinese," says one of their encomiasts, "though it bears no relation to that of Europe; though it has borrowed nothing from that of the Greeks, has a certain beauty peculiar to itself." It is indeed peculiar to itself, and the missionaries may be assured they are the only persons who will ever discover "real palaces in the mansions of the Emperor," or to whom, "their immensity, symmetry, and magnificence, will announce the grandeur of the master who inhabits them."

113

The house of a prince, or a great officer of state, in the capital, is not much distinguished from that of a tradesman, except by the greater space of ground on which it stands, and by being surrounded by a high wall. Our lodgings in Pekin were in a house of this description. The ground plot was four hundred by three hundred feet, and it was laid out into ten or twelve courts, some having two, some three, and others four, tent-shaped houses, standing on stone terraces raised about three feet above the court, which was paved with tiles. Galleries of communication, forming colonnades of red wooden pillars, were carried from each building and from one court to another, so that every part of the house might be visited without exposure to the sun or the rain. The number of wooden pillars of which the colonnades were formed was about 900. Most of the rooms were open to the rafters of the roof; but some had a slight ceiling of bamboo laths covered with plaster; and the ladies apartments consisted of two stories; the upper however had no light, and was not so good as our common attics. The floors were laid with bricks or clay. The windows had no[333] glass; oiled paper, or silk gauze, or pearl shell, or horn, were used as substitutes for this article. In the corners of some of the rooms were holes in the ground, covered over with stones or wood, intended for fire-places, from whence the heat is conveyed, as in the houses of ancient Rome, through flues in the floor, or in the walls, the latter of which are generally whitened with lime made from shells and imported from the sea coast. One room was pointed out to us as the theatre. The stage was in the middle, and a sort of gallery was erected in front of it. A stone room was built in the midst of a piece of water, in imitation of a passage yacht, and one of the courts was roughened with rocks, with points and precipices and excavations, as a representation of nature in miniature. On the ledges of these were meant to be placed their favourite flowers and stunted trees, for which they are famous.

There is not a water-closet, nor a decent place of retirement in all China. Sometimes a stick is placed over a hole in a corner, but in general they make use of large earthen jars with narrow tops. In the great house we occupied was a walled inclosure, with a row of small square holes of brick-work sunk in the ground.

Next to the pagodas, the most conspicuous objects are the gates of cities. These are generally square buildings, carried several stories above the arched gateway and, like the temples, are covered with one or more large projecting roofs. But the most stupendous work of this country is the great wall that divides it from northern Tartary. It is built exactly upon the same plan as the wall of Pekin, being a mound of earth cased on[334] each side with bricks or stone. The astonishing magnitude of the fabric consists not so much in the plan of the work, as in the immense distance of fifteen hundred miles over which it is extended, over mountains of two and three thousand feet in height, across deep vallies and rivers. But the elevations, plans, and sections of this wall and its towers have been taken with such truth and accuracy by the late Captain Parish, of the Royal Artillery, that all further description would be superfluous. They are to be found in Sir George Staunton's valuable account of the embassy to China.

The same Emperor, who is said to have committed the barbarous act of destroying the works of the learned, raised this stupendous fabric, which has no parallel in the whole world, not even in the pyramids of Egypt, the magnitude of the largest of these containing only a very small portion of the quantity of matter comprehended in the great wall of China. This indeed is so enormous, that admitting, what I believe has never been denied, its length to be fifteen hundred miles, and the dimensions throughout pretty much the same as where it was crossed by the British Embassy, the materials of all the dwelling-houses of England and Scotland, supposing them to amount to one million eight hundred thousand, and to average on the whole two thousand cubic feet of masonry or brick-work, are barely equivalent to the bulk or contents of the great wall of China. Nor are the projecting massy towers of stone and brick included in this calculation. These alone, supposing them to continue throughout at bow-shot distance, were calculated to contain as much masonry and brick-work as all London. To[335] give another idea of the mass of matter in this stupendous fabric, it may be observed, that it is more than sufficient to surround the circumference of the earth on two of its great circles, with two walls, each six feet high and two feet thick! It is to be understood, however, that in this calculation is included the earthy part in the middle of the wall.

114

Turning from an object, which the great Doctor Johnson was of opinion would be an honour to any one to say that his grandfather had seen, another presents itself scarcely inferior in point of grandeur, and greatly excelling it in general utility. This is what has usually been called the imperial or grand canal, an inland navigation of such extent and magnitude as to stand unrivalled in the history of the world. I may safely say that, in point of magnitude, our most extensive inland navigation of England can no more be compared to the grand trunk that intersects China, than a park or garden fish-pond to the great lake of Winandermere. The Chinese ascribe an antiquity to this work higher by many centuries than to that of the great wall; but the Tartars pretend it was first opened in the thirteenth century under the Mongul government. The probability is, that an effeminate and shameful administration had suffered it to fall into decay, and that the more active Tartars caused it to undergo a thorough repair: at present it exhibits no appearances of great antiquity. The bridges, the stone piers of the flood-gates, the quays, and the retaining walls of the earthen embankments are comparatively new. Whether it has originally been constructed by Chinese or Tartars, the conception of such an undertaking, and the manner in which it is executed,|336| imply a degree of science and ingenuity beyond what I suspect we should now find in the country, either in one or the other of these people. The general surface of the country and other favourable circumstances have contributed very materially to assist the projector, but a great deal of skill and management, as well as of immense labour, are conspicuous throughout the whole work.

I shall endeavour to convey, in a few words, a general idea of the principles on which this grand undertaking has been carried on. All the rivers of note in China fall from the high lands of Tartary, which lie to the northward of Thibet, crossing the plains of this empire in their descent to the sea from west to east. The inland navigation being carried from north to south cuts these rivers at right angles, the smaller streams of which terminating in it afford a constant supply of water; and the three great rivers, the *Eu-ho* to the north, the *Yellow River* towards the middle, and the *Yang-tse-kiang* to the south, intersecting the canal, carry off the superfluous water to the sea. The former, therefore, are the *feeders*, and the latter the *dischargers*, of the great trunk of the canal. A number of difficulties must have arisen in accommodating the general level of the canal to the several levels of the feeding streams; for notwithstanding all the favourable circumstances of the face of the country, it has been found necessary in many places to cut down to the depth of sixty or seventy feet below the surface; and, in others, to raise mounds of earth upon lakes and swamps and marshy grounds, of such a length and magnitude that nothing short of the absolute command over multitudes could have ac|337|complished an undertaking, whose immensity is only exceeded by the great wall. These gigantic embankments are sometimes carried through lakes of several miles in diameter, between which the water is forced up to a height considerably above that of the lake; and in such situations we sometimes observed this enormous aqueduct gliding along at the rate of three miles an hour. Few parts of it are level: in some places it has little or no current; one day we had it setting to the southward at the rate of one, two, or three miles an hour, the next to the northward, and frequently on the same day we found it stationary, and running in opposite directions. This balancing of the level was effected by flood-gates thrown across at certain distances to elevate or depress the height of the water a few inches, as might appear to be necessary; and these stoppages are simply planks sliding in grooves, that are cut into the sides of two stone abutments, which in these places contract the canal to the width of about thirty feet. There is not a lock nor, except these, a single interruption to a continued navigation of six hundred miles.

The most remarkable parts of this extraordinary work will be noticed in a following chapter, descriptive of our journey through the empire.

Over this main trunk, and most of the other canals and rivers, are a great variety of bridges, some with arches that are pointed not unlike the gothic, some semicircular, and others shaped like a horse-shoe: some have the piers of such an extraordinary height that the largest vessels, of two hundred tons, sail under them without striking their masts. Some of their bridges, of three,|358| five, and seven arches[21], that cross the canal, are extremely light and beautiful to the eye, but the plan on which they are usually constructed does not imply much strength. Each stone, from five to ten feet in length, is cut so as to form a segment of the arch, and as, in such cases, there is no key-stone, ribs of wood fitted to the convexity of the arch are bolted through the stones by iron bars, fixed fast into the solid parts of the bridge. Sometimes, however, they are without wood, and the curved stones are morticed into long transverse blocks of stone, as in the annexed plate, which was drawn with great accuracy by Mr. Alexander.

In this Plate,

No. 1. Are stones cut to the curve of the arch 10 feet long.

2. An immense stone, 2 feet square, of the whole
depth of the arch.

3. Curved stones,7 feet long.

4. Ditto,5 feet.

5. Ditto,3½ feet.

6. Ditto,3 feet.

7. Ditto,3 feet.

8.8. Stones similar to No. 2. being each one entire
piece running through the bridge, and intended,
it would seem, to bind the fabric together as the
pillars 9.9. are morticed into them.

Construction of the Arch of a
CHINESE BRIDGE
Neele sc. 352, Strand.
Pub. May 10ᵗʰ., 1804, by Cadell, & Davies Strand.

There are, however, other arches wherein the stones are smaller and pointed to a centre as in ours. I have understood from [339]the late Captain Parish, that no masonry could be superior to that of the great wall, and that all the arched and vaulted work in the old towers was exceedingly well turned. This being the case, we may probably be not far amiss in allowing the Chinese to have employed this useful and ornamental part of architecture before it was known to the Greeks and the Romans. Neither the Egyptians nor the Persians appear at any time to have applied it in their buildings. The ruins of Thebes and of Persepolis have no arches, nor have those of Balbec and Palmyra; nor do they seem to have been much used in the magnificent buildings of the Romans antecedent to the time of Augustus. The grand and elegant columns of all these nations were connected by straight architraves of stone, of dimensions not inferior to the columns themselves. In the Hindoo excavations are arches cut out of the solid mountain; but when loose stones were employed, and a building was intended to be superstructed on columns, the stones above the capitals were overlaid like inverted steps, till they met in a point in the middle above the two columns, appearing at a little distance exactly like the gothic arch, of which this might have given the first idea. If then the antiquity be admitted which the Chinese ascribe to the building of the great wall, and no reason but a negative one, the silence of Marco Polo, has been offered against it (an objection easily refuted), they have a claim to the invention of the arch founded on no unsolid grounds.

The cemeteries, or repositories of the dead, exhibit a much greater variety of monumental architecture than the dwellings of the living can boast of. Some indeed deposit the remains of[340]their ancestors in houses that differ in nothing from those they inhabited while living, except in their diminutive size; others prefer a square vault, ornamented in such a manner as fancy may suggest; some make choice of a hexagon to cover the deceased, and others of an octagon. The round, the triangular, the square, and multangular column, is indifferently raised over the grave of a Chinese; but the most common form of a monument to the remains of persons of rank consists in three terraces, one above another, inclosed by circular walls. The door or entrance of the vault is in the centre of the uppermost terrace, covered with an appropriate inscription; and figures of slaves and horses and cattle, with other creatures that, when living, were subservient to them and added to their pleasures, are employed after their death to decorate the terraces of their tombs.

116

"Quæ gratia currûm
Armorumque fuit vivis, quæ cura nitentes
Pascere equos, eadem sequitur tellure repostos."
VIRGIL, ÆNEID vi.

"Those pleasing cares the heroes felt, alive,
For chariots, steeds, and arms, in death survive."   PITT.

It may be considered as superfluous, after what has been said, to observe, that no branch of natural philosophy is made a study, or a pursuit in China. The practical application of some of the most obvious effects produced by natural causes could not escape the observation of a people who had, at an early period, attained so high a degree of civilization, but, satisfied with the practical part, they pushed their enquiries no farther. Of pneumatics, hydrostatics, electricity, and magnetism, [341] they may be said to have little or no knowledge; and their optics extend not beyond the making of convex and concave lenses of rock crystal to assist the sight in magnifying, or throwing more rays upon, small objects and, by collecting to a focus the rays of the sun, to set fire to combustible substances. These lenses are cut with a saw and afterwards polished, the powder of crystal being used in both operations. To polish diamonds they make use of the powder of adamantine spar, or the corundum stone. In cutting different kinds of stone into groups of figures, houses, mountains, and sometimes into whole landscapes, they discover more of persevering labour, of a determination to subdue difficulties, which were not worth the subduing, than real ingenuity. Among the many remarkable instances of this kind of labour, there is one in the possession of the Right Honourable Charles Greville, that deserves to be noticed. It is a group of well formed, excavated, and highly ornamented bottles, covered with foliage and figures, raised in the manner of the antique *Cameos*, with moveable ring-handles, standing on a base or pedestal, the whole cut out of one solid block of clear rock crystal. Yet this laborious trifle was probably sold for a few dollars in China. It was bought in London for about thirty pounds, where it could not have been made for many times that sum, if, indeed, it could have been made at all. All their spectacles that I have seen were crystal set in horn, tortoise-shell, or ivory. The single microscope is in common use, but they have never hit upon the effect of approximating objects by combining two or more lenses, a discovery indeed to which in Europe we are more indebted to chance than to the result of scientific enquiry. I observed at *Yuen-min-yuen* [342] a rude kind of magic lantern, and a camera obscura, neither of which, although evidently of Chinese workmanship, appeared to wear the marks of a national invention. I should rather conclude, that they were part of those striking and curious experiments which the early Jesuits displayed at court, in order to astonish the Emperor with their profound skill, and raise their reputation as men of learning. Of the *ombres Chinoises* they may, perhaps, claim the invention, and in pyrotechny their ingenuity may be reckoned much superior to any thing which has hitherto been exhibited in that art in Europe.

A convex lens is among the usual appendages to the tobacco pipe. With these they are in the daily habit of lighting their pipes. Hence the great burning lens made by Mr. Parker of Fleet-Street, and carried out among the presents for the Emperor, was an object that excited no admiration in the minds of the Chinese. The difficulty of making a lens of such magnitude perfect, or free from flaw, and its extraordinary powers could not be understood, and consequently not appreciated by them: and although in the short space of four seconds it completely melted down one of their base copper coins, when the sun was more than forty degrees beyond the meridian, it made no impression of surprize on their uninformed minds. The only enquiry they made about it was, whether the substance was crystal; but being informed it was glass, they turned away with a sort of disdain, as if they would say, Is a lump of glass a proper present to offer to our great *Whang-tee*? The prime minister, *Ho-tchung-tang*, in order to convince us how very familiar articles of such a nature were to him, lighted his pipe very [343] composedly at the focus, but had a narrow escape from singeing his sattin sleeve, which would certainly have happened had I not given him a sudden push. He seemed, however, to be insensible of his danger, and walked off without the least concern.

Indeed, in selecting the many valuable presents relating to science, their knowledge and learning had been greatly overrated. They had little esteem for what they could not comprehend, and specimens of art served only to excite their jealousy, and to wound their pride. Whenever a future embassy shall be sent to Pekin, I should recommend articles of gold, silver, and steel, children's toys and trinkets, and perhaps a few specimens of Derbyshire spar, with the finest broad-cloth and kerseymeres, in preference to all others; for in their present state, they are totally incapable of appreciating any thing great or excellent in the arts and sciences.

To alleviate the afflictions of mankind, and to assuage the pains which the human frame is liable to suffer, must have been among the earliest studies of civilized society; and accordingly, in the history of ancient kingdoms, we find the practitioners of the healing art regarded even to adoration. Chiron, the preceptor of Achilles, and the master of Æsculapius, was transferred to the heavens, where he still shines under the name of Sagittarius. Among these nations, indeed, which we call savage, there is usually shewn a more than ordinary respect for such of their countrymen as are most skilled in removing obstructions, allaying tumours, healing bruises, and, generally[311] speaking, who can apply relief to misery. But the Chinese, who seem to differ in their opinions from all the rest of mankind, whether civilized or savage, pay little respect to the therapeutick art. They have established no public schools for the study of medicine, nor does the pursuit of it lead to honours, rank, or fortune. Such as take up the profession are generally of an inferior class; and the eunuchs about the palace are considered among their best physicians. According to their own account, the books on medicine escaped the fire, by which they pretend the works of learning were consumed, in the reign of *Shee-whang-tee*, two hundred years before the Christian era; and yet the best of their medical books of the present day are little better than mere herbals, specifying the names and enumerating the qualities of certain plants. The knowledge of these plants and of their supposed virtues goes a great way towards constituting a physician. Those most commonly employed are Gin-sing, rhubarb, and China-root. A few preparations are also found in their pharmacopœia from the animal and the mineral kingdoms. In the former they employ snakes, beetles, centipedes, and the aureliæ of the silk worm and other insects; the meloe and the bee are used for blisters. In the latter, saltpetre, sulphur, native cinnabar, and a few other articles are occasionally prescribed. Opium is taken as a medicine, but more generally as a cordial to exhilarate the spirits. Though the importation of this drug is strictly prohibited, yet, as I have before observed, vast quantities are annually smuggled into the country from Bengal and from Europe, through the connivance of the custom-house officers.[345]

The physiology of the human body, or the doctrine which explains the constitution of man, is neither understood, nor considered as necessary to be known; and their skill in pathology, or in the causes and effects of diseases, is extremely limited, very often absurd, and generally erroneous. The seat of most diseases are, in fact, supposed to be discoverable by feeling the pulse, agreeably to a system built upon principles the most wild and extravagant. Having no knowledge whatsoever of the circulation of the blood, notwithstanding the Jesuits have made no scruple in asserting it was well known to them long before Europeans had any idea of it, they imagine, that every particular part of the human body has a particular pulse assigned to it, and that these have all a corresponding and sympathetic pulse in the arm; thus, they suppose one pulse to be situated in the heart, another in the lungs, a third in the kidneys, and so forth; and the skill of the doctor consists in discovering the prevailing pulse in the body, by its sympathetic pulsations in the arm; and the mummery made use of on such occasions is highly ludicrous.

By eating too freely of unripe fruit at *Chu-san* I had a violent attack of *cholera morbus*, and on application being made to the governor for a little opium and rhubarb, he immediately dispatched to me one of his physicians. With a countenance as grave and a solemnity as settled, as ever was exhibited in a consultation over a doubtful case in London or Edinburgh, he fixed his eyes upon the ceiling, while he held my hand, beginning at the wrist, and proceeding towards the bending of[346] the elbow, pressing sometimes hard with one finger, and then light with another, as if he was running over the keys of a harpsicord. This performance continued about ten minutes in solemn silence, after which he let go my hand and pronounced my complaint to have arisen from eating something that had disagreed with the stomach. I shall not take upon me to decide whether this conclusion was drawn from his skill in the pulse, or from a conjecture of the nature of the complaint from the medicines that had been demanded, and which met with his entire approbation, or from a knowledge of the fact.

Le Compte, who had less reason to be cautious, from his having left the country, than other missionaries who are doomed to remain there for life, positively says, that the physicians always endeavour to make themselves secretly acquainted with the case of the patient, before they pronounce upon it, as their reputation depends more on their assigning the true cause of the disorder than on the cure. He then proceeds to tell a story of a friend of his who, being troubled with a swelling, sent for a Chinese physician. This gentleman told him very gravely, that it was occasioned by a small worm which, unless extracted by his skill, would ultimately produce gangrene and certain death. Accordingly one day after the tumour, by the application of a few poultices, was getting better, the doctor contrived to drop upon the removed poultice a little maggot, for the extraction of which he assumed to himself no small degree of merit. Le Compte's stories, however, are not always to be depended on.[347]

The priests are also a kind of doctors, and make plaisters for a variety of purposes, some to draw out the disease to the part applied, some as charms against the evil spirit, and others which they pretend to be aphrodisiac; all of which, and the last in particular, are in great demand among the wealthy. In this respect the Chinese agree with most nations of antiquity, whose priests were generally employed as physicians. The number of quacks and venders of nostrums is immense in every city who gain a livelihood by the credulity of the multitude. One of this description exhibited in the public streets of Canton a powder for sale as a specific for the bite of a snake; and to convince the crowd of its immediate efficacy, he carried with him a species of this reptile, whose bite was known to be extremely venemous. He applied the mouth of the animal to the tip of his tongue, which began to swell so very rapidly, that in a few minutes the mouth was no longer able to contain it. The intumescence continued till it seemed to burst, and exhibited a shocking sight of foam and blood, during which the quack appeared in extreme agonies, and excited the commiseration of all the bye-standers. In the height of the paroxysm he applied a little of his powder to the nose and the inflamed member, after which it gradually subsided, and the disorder disappeared. Though the probability in the city of any one person being bit with a snake was not less perhaps than a hundred thousand to one, yet every person present bought of the miraculous powder, till a sly fellow maliciously suggested that the whole of this scene might probably have been performed by means of a bladder concealed in the mouth.[348]

But the usual remedy for the bite of a snake is a topical application of sulphur, or the bruised head of the same animal that gave the wound. The coincidence of such an extravagant idea among nations as remote from each other as the equator from the pole is sufficiently remarkable. A Roman poet observes,

"Quum nocuit serpens, fertur caput illius apte
Vulneribus jungi: sanat quem sauciat ipsa."
Q. Serenus de Medicina.

If to a serpent's bite its head be laid,
'Twill heal the wound which by itself was made.

The naked legs of the Hottentots are frequently stung by scorpions, and they invariably endeavour to catch the animal, which they bruise and apply to the wound, being confident of the cure; the Javanese, or inhabitants of Java, are fully persuaded of the efficacy of such application; and the author above quoted observes with regard to the sting of this insect,

"Vulneribusque aptus, fertur revocare venenum."

Being applied to the wound, it is said to draw out the poison.

As it is a violation of good morals for a gentleman to be seen in company with ladies, much more so to touch the hands of the fair, the faculty rather than lose a fee, though it commonly amounts only to fifty *tchen*, or the twentieth part of six shillings and eight-pence, have contrived an ingenious way of feeling a lady's pulse: a silken cord being made fast to the wrist of the patient is passed through a hole in the wainscot into another apartment where the doctor, applying his hand to the cord,[349] after a due observance of solemn mockery, decides upon the case and prescribes accordingly. About court, however, a particular class of eunuchs only are entrusted with feeling the pulse of the ladies.

The crowded manner in which the common people live together in small apartments in all the cities, the confined streets and, above all, the want of cleanliness in their persons, beget sometimes contagious diseases that sweep off whole families, similar to the plague. In Pekin incredible numbers perish in these contagious fevers, which more frequently happen there than in other parts of the empire, notwithstanding the moderate temperature of the climate. In the southern provinces they are neither so general, nor so fatal as might be expected, owing, I believe, in a very great degree, to the universal custom among the mass of the people of wearing vegetable substances next the skin which, being more cleanly, are consequently more wholesome than clothing made from animal matter. Thus, linen and cotton are preferable to silk and woollen next the skin, which should be worn only by persons of the most cleanly habits. Another antidote to the ill effects that might be expected from want of cleanliness in their houses and their persons, is the constant ventilation kept up in the former both by day and night: during warm weather, they have no other door but an open matted skreen, and the windows are either entirely open or of thin paper only. Notwithstanding their want of personal cleanliness, they are little troubled with leprous or cutaneous diseases, and they pretend to be totally ignorant of gout, stone, or gravel, which they ascribe to the preventive effects of tea.[350] In favour of this opinion, it has been observed by some of our physicians, that since the introduction of tea into common use, cutaneous diseases have become much more rare in Great Britain than they were before that period, which others have ascribed, perhaps with more propriety, to the general use of linen; both, however, may have been instrumental in producing the happy effect.

The ravages of the small-pox, wherever they make their appearance, are attended with a general calamity. Of these they pretend to distinguish above forty different species, to each of which they have given a particular name. If a good sort breaks out, inoculation or, more properly speaking, infection by artificial means becomes general. The usual way of communicating the disease is by inserting the matter, contained in a little cotton wool, into the nostrils, or they put on the clothes of, or sleep in the same bed with, such as may have had a favourable kind; but they never introduce the matter by making any incision in the skin. This fatal disease, as appears from the records of the empire, was unknown before the tenth century, when it was perhaps introduced by the Mahomedans of Arabia who, at that period, carried on a considerable commerce with Canton from the Persian gulph, and who not long before had received it from the Saracens, when they invaded and conquered the Eastern Empire. The same disease was likewise one of those blessings which the mad crusades conferred upon Europe; since which time, to the close of the eighteenth century, not a hope had been held out of its extirpation when, happily, the invaluable discovery of the cow-pock, or rather the general[351] application of that discovery, which had long been confined to a particular district, has furnished abundant grounds to hope, that this desirable event may now be accomplished.

In some of the provinces the lower orders of people are said to be dreadfully afflicted with sore eyes, and this endemic complaint has been supposed to proceed from the copious use of rice; a conjecture, apparently, without any kind of foundation, as the Hindus and other Indian nations, whose whole diet consists almost exclusively of this grain, are not particularly subject to the like disease: and in Egypt, both in ancient and modern times, the opthalmia and blindness were much more prevalent than in China; yet rice was neither cultivated nor known in that part of Africa until the reign of the caliphs, when it was introduced from the eastward. The disease in China, if prevalent there, may more probably be owing to their living in crowded and low habitations, wherein there is a perpetual smoke from the fire, from tapers made of sandal wood dust employed for marking the divisions of the day, from the general use of tobacco, and from the miasma or noxious vapours exhaling from the dirt and offals which are collected in or near their habitations. The organ of sight may also be relaxed, and rendered more susceptible of disease, by the constant practice of washing the face, even in the middle of summer, with warm water. I must observe, however, that in the course of our long journey, we saw very few blind people, or persons afflicted with sore eyes.[352]

It will readily be inferred, from the short view which has been taken of the state of society, that the disease occasioned by an unrestrained and promiscuous intercourse of the sexes cannot be very common in China. In fact, it is scarcely known, and the treatment of it is so little understood, in the few cases which do occur, that it is allowed to work its way into the system, and is then considered by them as an incurable leprosy. On arriving at the northern extremity of the province of Canton, one of our conductors had imprudently passed the night in one of those houses where, by the license of government, females are allowed to prostitute their persons in order to gain a livelihood. Here, it seems, he had caught the infection, and after suffering a considerable degree of pain, and not less alarm, he communicated to our physician the symptoms of his complaint, of the nature and cause of which he was entirely ignorant. He was a man of forty years, of a vigorous constitution and a gay cheerful temper, and had served as an officer in several campaigns from the different provinces of northern Tartary to the frontiers of India, yet such a disease did not consist with his knowledge. From this circumstance, and many others of a similar kind, I conclude that, although it may sometimes make its appearance in the capital, and even here but very rarely, it has originally, and no long time ago, found its way thither through the ports of Chusan, Canton, and Macao, where numbers of abandoned woman obtain their subsistence by selling their favours to such of every nation as may be disposed to purchase them. It is, in fact, sometimes called by the Chinese the *Canton-ulcer*.[353]

No male physician is ever allowed to prescribe for pregnant women; and they consider it so great a breach of delicacy for a man to be in the same room with a woman when in labour that, whatever difficulties may occur, the case is left entirely to the woman who attends her. There is not a man-midwife in all China, and yet the want of them does not appear to be injurious to population. They could scarcely believe it possible that, in Europe, men should be allowed to practice a profession which, in their minds, belonged exclusively to the other sex.

As a due knowledge of the organization of the human body, of the powers and functions of the several parts, is attainable only by the study of practical anatomy, a study that would shock the weak nerves of a timid Chinese, it will not be expected that their surgical operations should either be numerous or neatly performed. The law indeed which I have had occasion to notice, and the effects produced by it in two or three instances that occurred to our knowledge, will sufficiently explain the very low ebb of chirurgical skill. No one will readily undertake to perform the most simple operation, where not only all the direct consequences, but the contingencies for forty days must lie at his door. They sometimes succeed in reducing a dislocation, and in setting a simple fracture; but in difficult and complicated cases, the patient is generally abandoned to chance. Amputation is never practised. In the course of our whole journey, wherein we passed through millions of people, I do not recollect to have seen a single individual that had sustained the loss of a limb, and but very few in any way maimed; from whence I conclude, that accidents are uncommon, or that[354] serious ones usually terminate in the loss of life. A Chinese is so dreadfully afraid of a sharp cutting instrument, that he has not even submitted to the operation of bloodletting; though the principle is admitted, as they are in the practice of drawing blood by scarifying the skin, and applying cupping vessels. In certain complaints they burn the skin with small pointed irons made hot, and sometimes, after puncturing the part with silver needles, they set fire to the leaves of a species of Artemisia upon it, in the same manner as the Moxa in Japan is made use of to cure and even prevent a number of diseases, but especially the gout and rheumatism, the former of which is said to be unknown in China. Cleansing the ears, cutting corns, pulling the joints till they crack, twitching the nose, thumping on the back, and such like operations, are annexed to the shaving profession, by which thousands in every city gain a livelihood. In short, the whole medical skill of the Chinese may be summed up in the words of the ingenious Doctor Gregory from the information he obtained from his friend Doctor Gillan. "In the greatest, most ancient, and most civilized empire on the face of the earth, an empire that was great, populous, and highly civilized two thousand years ago, when this country was as savage as New Zealand is at present, no such good medical aid can be obtained among the people of it, as a smart boy of sixteen, who had been but twelve months apprentice to a good and well employed Edinburgh Surgeon, might reasonably be expected to afford." "If," continues the Doctor, "the Emperor of China, the absolute monarch of three hundred and thirty-three millions of people, more than twice as many as all Europe contains,[355] were attacked with a pleurisy, or got his leg broken, it would be happy for him to get such a boy for his first physician and serjeant-surgeon. The boy (if he had seen his master's practice in but one or two similar cases) would certainly know how to set his Imperial Majesty's leg, and would probably cure him of his pleurisy, which none of his own subjects could do."

Having thus given a slight sketch of the state of some of the leading branches in science, arts, and manufactures, omitting purposely that of agriculture, which will be noticed among the subjects of a future section, I think, upon the whole, it may fairly be concluded, that the Chinese have been among the first nations, now existing in the world, to arrive at a certain pitch of perfection, where, from the policy of the government, or some other cause, they have remained stationary: that they were civilized, fully to the same extent they now are, more than two thousand years ago, at a period when all Europe might be considered, comparatively, as barbarous; but that they have since made little progress in any thing, and been retrograde in many things: that, at this moment, compared with Europe, they can only be said to be great in trifles, whilst they are really trifling in every thing that is great. I cannot however exactly subscribe to an opinion pronounced on them by a learned and elegant writer[22], who was well versed in oriental literature, as being rather too unqualified; but he was less acquainted with their character than that of any other Asiatic nation, and totally ignorant of their language. "Their letters," says he, [356]"if we may so call them, are merely the symbols of ideas; their philosophy seems yet in so rude a state, as hardly to deserve the appellation; they have no ancient monuments from which their origin can be traced, even by plausible conjecture; their sciences are wholly exotic; and their mechanical arts have nothing in them characteristic of a particular family; nothing which any set of men, in a country so highly favoured by nature, might not have discovered and improved."

CHAP. VII.
Government—Laws—Tenures of Land and Taxes—Revenues—Civil and Military Ranks, and Establishments.

Opinions on which the Executive Authority is grounded.—Principle on which an Emperor of China seldom appears in public.—The Censorate.—Public Departments.—Laws.—Scale of Crimes and Punishments.—Laws regarding Homicide.—Curious Law Case.—No Appeal from Civil Suits.—Defects in the Executive Government.—Duty of Obedience and Power of personal Correction.—Russia and China compared.—Fate of the Prime Minister Ho-chang-tong.—Yearly Calendar and Pekin Gazette, engines of Government.—Freedom of the Press.—Duration of the Government attempted to be explained.—Precautions of Government to prevent Insurrections.—Taxes and Revenues.—Civil and Military Establishments.—Chinese Army, its Numbers and Appointments.—Conduct of the Tartar Government at the Conquest.—Impolitic Change of late Years, and the probable Consequences of it.

THE late period at which the nations of Europe became first[357] acquainted with the existence even of that vast extent of country comprehended under the name of China, the difficulties of access to any part of it when known, the peculiar nature of the language which, as I have endeavoured to prove, has no relation with any other either ancient or modern, the extreme jealousy of the government towards foreigners, and the contempt in which they were held by the lowest of the people, may[358] serve, among other causes, to account for the very limited and imperfect knowledge we have hitherto obtained of the real history of this extraordinary empire: for their records, it seems, are by no means deficient. For two centuries at least before the Christian era, down to the present time, the transactions of each reign are amply detailed without any interruption. They have even preserved collections of copper coins, forming a regular series of the different Emperors that have filled the throne of China for the last two thousand years. Such a collection, though not quite complete, Sir George Staunton brought with him to England.

Before this time, when China consisted of a number of petty states or principalities, the annals of the country are said to abound with recitals of wars and battles and bloodshed, like those of every other part of the world. But, in proportion as the number of those distinct kingdoms diminished, till at length they were all melted and amalgamated into one great empire, the destruction of the human race by human means abated, and the government, since that time, has been less interrupted by foreign war, or domestic commotion, than any other that history has made known. But whether this desirable state of public tranquillity may have been brought about by the peculiar nature of the government being adapted to the genius and habits of the people, which in the opinion of Aristotle is the best of all possible governments, or rather by constraining and subduing the genius and habits of the people to the views and maxims of the government, is a question that may admit of some dispute. At the present day, however, it is sufficiently evident, that[350] the heavy hand of power has completely overcome and moulded to its own shape the physical character of the people, and that their moral sentiments and actions are swayed by the opinions, and almost under the entire dominion, of the government.

These opinions, to which it owes so much of its stability, are grounded on a principle of authority which, according to maxims industriously inculcated and now completely established in the minds of the people, is considered as the natural and unalienable right of the parent over his children; an authority that is not supposed to cease at any given period of life or years, but to extend, and to be maintained with undiminished and uncontrouled sway, until the death of one of the parties dissolves the obligation. The Emperor being considered as the common father of his people is accordingly invested with the exercise of the same authority over them, as the father of a family exerts on those of his particular household. In this sense he takes the title of the *Great Father*, and by his being thus placed above any earthly controul, he is supposed to be also above earthly descent, and therefore, as a natural consequence, he sometimes styles himself the *sole ruler of the world* and the *Son of Heaven*. But that no inconsistency might appear in the grand fabric of filial obedience the Emperor, with solemn ceremony at the commencement of every new year, makes his prostrations before the Empress Dowager, and on the same day he demands a repetition of the same homage from all his great officers of state. Conformable to this system, founded entirely on parental authority, the governor of a province is considered as the father of that province; of a city, the father of that city; and the head[360] of any office or department is supposed to preside over it with the same authority, interest, and affection, as the father of a family superintends and manages the concerns of domestic life.

It is greatly to be lamented that a system of government, so plausible in theory, should be liable to so many abuses in practice; and that this fatherly care and affection in the governors, and filial duty and reverence in the governed would, with much more propriety, be expressed by the terms of tyranny, oppression, and injustice in the one, and by fear, deceit, and disobedience in the other.

The first grand maxim on which the Emperor acts is, seldom to appear before the public, a maxim whose origin would be difficultly traced to any principle of affection or solicitude for his children; much more easily explained as the offspring of suspicion. The tyrant who may be conscious of having committed, or assented to, acts of cruelty and oppression, must feel a reluctance to mix with those who may have smarted under the lash of his power, naturally concluding that some secret hand may be led, by a single blow, to avenge his own wrongs, or those of his fellow subjects. The principle, however, upon which the Emperor of China seldom shews himself in public, and then only in the height of splendor and magnificence, seems to be established on a policy of a very different kind to that of self-preservation. A power that acts in secret, and whose influence is felt near and remote at the same moment, makes a stronger impression on the mind, and is regarded with more[361] dread and awful respect, than if the agent was always visible and familiar to the eye of every one. The priests of the Eleusinian mysteries were well acquainted with this feature of the human character, which is stronger in proportion as the reasoning faculties are less improved, and which required the enlightened mind of a Socrates to be able to disregard the terror they inspired among the vulgar. Thus also *Deiôces*, as Heredotus informs us, when once established as king in Ecbatana, would suffer none of the people, for whom before he was the common advocate, to be now admitted to his presence, concluding that all those who were debarred from seeing him, would easily be persuaded that his nature, by being created king, was transformed into something much superior to theirs. A frequent access indeed to men of rank and power and talents, a familiar and unrestrained intercourse with them, and a daily observance of their ordinary actions and engagements in the concerns of life, have a tendency very much to diminish that reverence and respect which public opinion had been willing to allow them. It was justly observed by the great Condé, that no man is a hero to his valet-de-chambre.

Considerations of this kind, rather than any dread of his subjects, may probably have suggested the custom which prohibits an Emperor of China from making his person too familiar to the multitude, and which requires that he should exhibit himself only on particular occasions, arrayed in pomp and magnificence, and at the head of his whole court, consisting of an assemblage of many thousand officers of state, the agents of his[362] will, all ready, at the word of command, to prostrate themselves at his feet.

The power of the sovereign is absolute; but the patriarchal system, making it a point of indispensable duty for a son to bring offerings to the spirit of his deceased parent in the most public manner, operates as some check upon the exercise of this power. By this civil institution, the duties of which are observed with more than a religious strictness, he is constantly put in mind that the memory of his private conduct, as well as of his public acts, will long survive his natural life; that his name will, at certain times in every year, be pronounced with a kind of sacred and reverential awe, from one extremity of the extensive empire to the other, provided he may have filled his station to the satisfaction of his subjects; and that, on the contrary, public execrations will rescue from oblivion any arbitrary act of injustice and oppression, of which he may have been guilty. It may also operate as a motive for being nice and circumspect in the nomination of a successor, which the law has left entirely to his choice.

The consideration, however, of posthumous fame, would operate only as a slender restraint on the caprices of a tyrant, as the history of this, as well as other countries, furnishes abundant examples. It has, therefore, been thought necessary to add another, and perhaps a more effectual check, to curb any disposition to licentiousness or tyranny that might arise in the breast of the monarch. This is the appointment of the Censo[363]rate, an office filled by two persons, who have the power of remonstrating freely against any illegal or unconstitutional act about to be committed, or sanctioned by the Emperor. And although it may well be supposed, that these men are extremely cautious in the exercise of the power delegated to them, by virtue of their office, and in the discharge of this disagreeable part of their duty, yet they have another task to perform, on which their own posthumous fame is not less involved than that of their master, and in the execution of which they run less risk of giving offence. They are the historiographers of the empire; or, more correctly speaking, the biographers of the Emperor. Their employment, in this capacity, consists chiefly in collecting the sentiments of the monarch, in recording his speeches and memorable sayings, and in noting down the most prominent of his private actions, and the remarkable occurrences of his reign. These records are lodged in a large chest, which is kept in that part of the palace where the tribunals of government are held, and which is supposed not to be opened until the decease of the Emperor; and, if any thing material to the injury of his character and reputation is found to be recorded, the publication of it is delayed, out of delicacy to his family, till two or three generations have passed away, and sometimes till the expiration of the dynasty; by that indulgence they pretend, that a more faithful relation is likely to be obtained, in which neither fear nor flattery could have operated to disguise the truth.

An institution, so remarkable and singular in its kind in an arbitrary government, could not fail to carry with it a very[364] powerful influence upon the decisions of the monarch, and to make him solicitous to act, on all occasions, in such a manner, as would be most likely to secure a good name, and to transmit his character unsullied and sacred to posterity. The records of their history are said to mention a story of an Emperor, of the dynasty or family of *Tang*, who, from a consciousness of having, in several instances, transgressed the bounds of his authority, was determined to take a peep into the historical chest, where he knew he should find all his actions recorded. Having made use of a variety of arguments, in order to convince the two censors that there could be nothing improper in the step he was about to take, as, among other things, he assured them, he was actuated with the desire only of being made acquainted with his greatest faults, as the first step to amendment, one of these gentlemen is said to have answered him very nobly, to this effect: "It is true your Majesty has committed a number of errors, and it has been the painful duty of our employment to take notice of them; a duty," continued he, "which further obliges us to inform posterity of the conversation which your Majesty has this day, very improperly, held with us."

To assist the Emperor in the weighty affairs of state, and in the arduous task of governing an empire of so great an extent, and such immense population, the constitution has assigned him two councils, one ordinary, and the other extraordinary; the ordinary council is composed of his principal ministers, under the name of Collao, of which there are six. The extraordinary council consists entirely of the princes of the blood.[305]

For the administration of the affairs of government, there are six boards or departments, consisting of,

1. The Court of Appointments to vacancies in the offices of government, being composed of the minister and learned men, qualified to judge of the merits of candidates.

2. The Court of Finance.

3. The Court of Ceremonies, presiding over the direction of ancient customs, and treating with foreign Embassadors.

4. The Court for regulating military affairs.

5. The Tribunal of Justice.

6. The Board of Works.

These public functionaries resolve upon, recommend, and report to the Emperor, all matters belonging to their separate jurisdictions, who, with the advice of his ordinary and, if considered to be necessary, of his extraordinary council, affirms, amends, or rejects their decrees. For this purpose, the late Emperor never omitted to give regular audience in the great hall of the palace every morning at the hours of four or five o'clock. Subordinate to these supreme courts held in the capital, are others of similar constitution established in the different pro[306]vinces and great cities of the empire, each of which corresponds with its principal in Pekin.

It would far exceed the limits of the present work, were I to enter into a detail of their code of laws, which indeed I am not sufficiently prepared to do. They are published for the use of the subject, in the plainest characters that the language will admit, making sixteen small volumes, a copy of which is now in England; and I am encouraged to hold out a reasonable hope, that this compendium of the laws of China may, ere long, appear in an able and faithful English translation, which will explain, more than all the volumes that have hitherto been written on the subject of China, in what manner a mass of people, more than the double of that which is found in all Europe, has been kept together through so many ages in one bond of union. This work[23] on the laws of China, for perspicuity and method, may justly be compared with Blackstone's Commentaries on the Laws of England. It not only contains the laws arranged under their respective heads, but to every law is added a short commentary and a case.

I have been assured, on the best authority, that the laws of China define, in the most distinct and perspicuous manner, almost every shade of criminal offences, and the punishment awarded to each crime: that the greatest care appears to have been taken in constructing this scale of crimes and punishments; that they are very far from being sanguinary: and that if the practice was equal to the theory, few nations could boast[307] of a more mild, and, at the same time, a more efficacious dispensation of justice. Of all the despotic governments existing, there is certainly none where the life of man is held so sacred as in the laws of China. A murder is never overlooked, except in the horrid practice of exposing infants: nor dares the Emperor himself, all-powerful as he is, to take away the life of the meanest subject, without the formality at least of a regular process, though, as will be seen in the case of the late prime minister of *Kien-Long*, the chance of escaping must be very slender, where he himself becomes the accuser. So tenaciously however do they adhere to that solemn declaration of God delivered to Noah—"At the hand of every man's brother will I require the life of man. Whoso sheddeth man's blood, by man shall his blood be shed,"—that the good intention is oftentimes defeated by requiring, as I have elsewhere observed, from the person last seen in company with one who may have received a mortal wound, or who may have died suddenly, a circumstantial account, supported by evidence, in what manner his death was occasioned.

In attempting to proportion punishments to the degrees of crimes, indeed of awarding the same punishment for stealing a loaf of bread and taking away the life of man, the Chinese legislators, according to our notions, seem to have made too little distinction between accidental manslaughter and premeditated murder. To constitute the crime, it is not necessary to prove the intention or malice aforethought; for though want of intention palliates the offence, and consequently mitigates the[368] punishment, yet it never entirely excuses the offender. If a man should kill another by an unforeseen and unavoidable accident, his life is forfeited by the law, and however favourable the circumstances may appear in behalf of the criminal, the Emperor alone is invested with the power of remitting the sentence, a power which he very rarely if ever exercises to the extent of a full pardon but, on many occasions, to a mitigation of the punishment awarded by law. Strictly speaking, no sentence of death can be carried into execution until it has been ratified by the monarch. Yet in state crimes, or in acts of great atrocity, the viceroy of a province sometimes takes upon himself to order summary punishment, and prompt execution has been inflicted on foreign criminals at Canton when guilty only of homicide. Thus, about the beginning of the last century, a man belonging to Captain Shelvocke had the misfortune to kill a Chinese on the river. The corpse was laid before the door of the English factory, and the first person that came out, who happened to be one of the supercargoes, was seized and carried as a prisoner into the city, nor would they consent to his release till the criminal was given up, whom, after a short inquiry, they strangled. The recent affair of the unfortunate gunner is well known. An affray happened in Macao a few years ago, in which a Chinese was killed by the Portuguese. A peremptory demand was made for one of the latter, to expiate the death of the former. The government of this place, either unable or unwilling to fix on the delinquent, proposed terms of compromise, which were rejected and force was threatened to be used. There happened to be a merchant from Manilla then residing at Macao, a man of excellent cha[369]racter, who had long carried on a commerce between the two ports. This unfortunate man was selected to be the innocent victim to appease the rigour of Chinese justice, and he was immediately strangled[24].

The process of every trial for criminal offences, of which the punishment is capital, must be transmitted to Pekin, and submit[370]ted to the impartial eye of the supreme tribunal of justice, which affirms or alters, according to the nature of the case. And where any peculiar circumstances appear in favour of the accused, an order for revising the sentence is recommended to the Emperor, who, in such cases, either amends it himself, or directs the proceedings to be returned to the provincial court, with the sentiments of the supreme tribunal on the case. The proceedings are then revised, and if the circumstances are found to apply to the suggestions of the high court, they alter[371] or modify their former sentence accordingly[25].

As in some of the Grecian states, and other nations of modern times, the punishment of treason was extended to the relations of the criminal, so in China, even to the ninth genera[372]tion, a traitor's blood is supposed to be tainted, though they usually satisfy the law by including only the nearest male relations, then living, in the guilt of the culprit, and by mitigating[373] their punishment to that of exile. Nothing can be more unjust and absurd, however politic, than such a law, absurd, because it considers a non-entity capable of committing a crime; and[374] unjust, because it punishes an innocent person. The lawgiver of Israel, in order to intimidate his stiff-necked and rebellious subjects, found it expedient to threaten the visitation of God on[375] the children, for the sins of the fathers, unto the third and fourth generation, a sentiment however which, it would seem, lapse of time had rendered less expedient, for the prophet Eze[376]kiel, who on this subject had more elevated notions of moral right than either the Greeks or the Chinese, spurns it with great indignation. In allusion to such an idea, which it seems had become a proverb among the Jews, he breaks out into this sublime exclamation: "What mean ye that ye use this proverb concerning the land of Israel, saying, The fathers have eaten sour grapes, and the children's teeth are set on edge? As I live, saith the Lord, ye shall not have occasion any more to use this proverb in Israel. Behold all souls are mine; as the soul of the father, so also the soul of the son, is mine. The soul that sinneth, *it* shall die. The son shall not bear the iniquity of the father, neither shall the father bear the iniquity of the son: the righteousness of the righteous shall be upon *him*, and the wickedness of the wicked shall be upon *him*."

In most causes, except those of high treason, it may be presumed, the high tribunal of Pekin will act with strict impar[377]tiality. And it is greatly to be lamented, that all civil causes have not been made subject to a similar revision as those of a criminal nature, which would strike at the root of an evil that is most grievously felt in China, where the officers of justice are known, in most cases, to be corrupted by bribery. They have, however, wisely separated the office of judge from that of the legislator. The former, having found the fact, has only to refer to the code of laws, in which he is supplied with a scale of crimes and their punishments. Such a mode of distributing justice is not however without its inconveniences. Tender as the government has shewn itself, where the life of a subject is concerned, having once established the proportion of punishment to the offence it has supposed an appeal, in civil causes and misdemeanors, to be unnecessary. The sentence in such causes being thus left in the breast of a single judge, how great soever may be the nicety by which the penalty is adapted to the offence, the exclusion from appeal is in itself a bar to the just and impartial administration of the laws. The subject being refused the benefit of carrying his cause into a higher, and on that account more likely to be a more impartial, court, has no security against the caprice, malice, or corruption of his judge.

It may not perhaps be thought unworthy of notice that the legislators of China, among the various punishments devised for the commission of crimes, have given the criminal no opportunity, either by labouring at any of the public works, or in solitary confinement, to make some reparation for the injury he has committed against society. Confinement in prison, as a[378] punishment, is not known. Exile or personal chastisement are decreed for all irregularities not approaching to capital offences.

Executions for capital crimes are not frequently exhibited; when found guilty the criminals are remanded to prison till a general gaol delivery, which happens once a year, about the autumnal equinox. In adopting such a measure government may perhaps have considered, how little benefit the morals of the people were likely to derive from being the frequent spectators of the momentary pain that is required to take away the existence of a fellow mortal. All other punishments, however, that do not affect the life of man, are made as public as possible, and branded with the greatest degree of notoriety. The beating with the bamboo, in their ideas, scarcely ranks under the name of punishment, being more properly considered as a gentle correction, to which no disgrace is attached, but the cangue or, as they term it, the *tcha*, a kind of walking pillory, is a heavy tablet of wood, to which they are fastened by the neck and hands, and which they are sometimes obliged to drag about for weeks and months; this is a terrible punishment, and well calculated to deter others from the commission of those crimes of which it is the consequence, and the nature of which is always inscribed in large characters upon it.

The order that is kept in their jails is said to be excellent, and the debtor and the felon are always confined in separate places; as indeed one should suppose every where to be the case, for, as Sir George Staunton has observed, "To associate[379] guilt with imprudence, and confound wickedness with misfortune, is impolitic, immoral, and cruel[27]."

The abominable practice of extorting confession by the application of the torture is the worst part of the criminal laws of China; but they pretend to say this mode is seldom recurred to, unless in cases where the guilt of the accused has been made to appear by strong circumstantial evidence. It is however a common punishment to squeeze the fingers in cases of misdemeanour, and is particularly practised as a punishment of those females who purchase licences for breaking through the rules of chastity.

By the laws relating to property, women in China, as in ancient Rome, are excluded from inheriting, where there are children, and from disposing of property; but where there are no male children a man may leave, by will, the whole of his property to the widow. The reason they assign for women not inheriting is, that a woman can make no offering to deceased relations in the hall of ancestors; and it is deemed one of the first ideal blessings of life for a man to have some one to look up to, who will transmit his name to future ages, by performing, at certain fixed periods, the duties of this important ceremony. All their laws indeed respecting property, as I have already observed, are insufficient to give it that security and stability which alone can constitute the pleasure of accumulating wealth. The avarice of men in power may overlook those who are in moderate circumstances, but the affluent rarely [380] escape their rapacious grasp. In a word, although the laws are not so perfect as to procure for the subject general good, yet neither are they so defective as to reduce him to that state of general misery, which could only be terminated in a revolution. The executive administration is so faulty, that the man in office generally has it in his power to govern the laws, which makes the measure of good or evil depend greatly on his moral character.

Such are indeed the disposition and the habits of the people, that so long as the multitude can procure their bowl of rice and a few savory sauces, that cost only a mere trifle, there will be less danger of a revolt; and the government is so well convinced of this, that one of its first concerns is to lay up, in the public magazines erected in every part of the empire, a provision of grain, to serve as a supply for the poor in times of famine or scarcity. In this age of revolutions, a change, however, seems to be taking place in the minds of the people, which I shall presently notice.

The system of universal and implicit obedience towards superiors pervades every branch of the public service. The officers of the several departments of government, from the first to the ninth degree, acting upon the same broad basis of paternal authority, are invested with the power of inflicting the summary punishment of the bamboo, on all occasions where they may judge it proper, which, under the denomination of a fatherly correction, they administer without any previous trial, or form of inquiry. The slightest offence is punishable in this manner, at the will or the caprice of the lowest ma[381]gistrate. Such a summary proceeding of the powerful against the weak naturally creates in the latter a dread and distrust of the former; and the common people, accordingly, regard the approach of a man in office, just as schoolboys observe the motions of a severe master; but the fatherly kindness of the Emperor is recognised even in punishment; the culprit may claim the exemption of every fifth blow as the Emperor's *coup-de-grace*; but in all probability he gains little by such remission, as the deficiency in number may easily be made up in weight.

This practical method of evincing a fatherly affection is not confined to the multitude alone, but is extended to every rank and description of persons, ceasing only at the foot of the throne. Each officer of state, from the ninth degree upwards to the fourth, can, at any time, administer a gentle correction to his inferior; and the Emperor orders the bamboo to his ministers, and to the other four classes, whenever he may think it necessary for the good of their morals. It is well known that the late *Kien Long* caused two of his sons to be bambooed long after they had arrived at the age of maturity, one of which, I believe, is the present reigning Emperor.

In travelling through the country, a day seldom escaped without our witnessing the application of the *Pan-tsé* or bamboo, and generally in such a manner that it might be called by any other name except a *gentle* correction. A Chinese suffering under this punishment cries out in the most piteous manner; a Tartar bears it in silence. A Chinese, after receiving a certain number of strokes, falls down on his knees, as a matter[382] of course, before him who ordered the punishment, thanking him, in the most humble manner, for the fatherly kindness he has testified towards his son, in thus putting him in mind of his errors; a Tartar grumbles, and disputes the point as to the right that a Chinese may have to flog him; or he turns away in sullen silence.

Ridiculous as it may appear to a foreigner, in observing an officer of state stretching himself along the ground for the purpose of being flogged by order of another who happens to rank one degree above him; yet it is impossible, at the same time, to suppress a glow of indignation, in witnessing so mean and obsequious a degradation of the human mind, which can bring itself, under any circumstances, patiently to submit to a vile corporal punishment, administered by the hand of a slave, or by a common soldier; and when this is done, to undergo the still more vile and humiliating act of kissing the rod that corrects him. But the policy of the government has taken good care to remove any scruples that might arise on this score. Where paternal regard was the sole motive, such a chastisement could not possibly be followed with dishonour or disgrace. It was a wonderful point gained by the government, to subject every individual, the Emperor only excepted, to the same corporal correction; but it must have required great address, and men's minds must have been completely subdued, or completely convinced, before such a system of universal obedience could have been accomplished, the consequence of which, it was obvious, could be no other than universal servility. It could not fail to establish a most effectual check against the complaints of the[383] multitude, by shewing them that the same man, who had the power of punishing them, was equally liable to be corrected in his turn, and in the same manner, by another. The punishment of the bamboo must, I suspect, be one of the most ancient institutions of China. Indeed we can scarcely conceive it ever to have been introduced into a society already civilized; but rather to have been coeval with the origin of that society.

A similar kind of personal chastisement for light offences, or misconduct, was inflicted in Russia on persons of all ranks, but with this difference, that the correction was private and by order of the Sovereign alone. The Czar Peter, indeed, generally bestowed a drubbing on his courtiers with his own hand; who, instead of being dishonoured or disgraced by such a castigation, were supposed, from that very circumstance, to be his particular favourites, and to stand high in his confidence. The great Mentzikoff is said to have frequently left his closet with a black eye or a bloody nose; and seemed to derive increasing importance from the unequivocal marks of his master's friendship. Even at the present day, or till very lately, little disgrace was attached to the punishment of the *knout*, which was a private flagellation by order of the court; but this abominable practice either is altogether discontinued, or in its last stage of existence. Such arbitrary proceedings could not long remain in force among an enlightened people.

These two great empires, the greatest indeed that exist in the world, dividing between them nearly a fifth part of the whole habitable globe, each about a tenth, exhibit a singular dif[384]ference with regard to political circumstances. One century ago Russia was but just emerging from a state of barbarism, and in a century hence, in all human probability, she will make a conspicuous figure among European nations, both in arts and arms. Two thousand years ago China was civilized to the same degree, or nearly so, that she is at present. The governments were both arbitrary, and the people were slaves. The natural genius of the Russian, cramped perhaps in some degree by his frozen climate, is less susceptible of improvement than that of the Chinese. Whence then, it may be asked, proceeds the very great difference in the progressive improvement of the two nations? principally, I should suppose, from the two following reasons. Russia invites and encourages foreigners to instruct her subjects in arts, sciences, and manufactures. China, from a spirit of pride and self-importance, as well as from jealousy, rejects and expels them. The language of Russia is easily acquired, and her subjects as easily learn those of other countries, whilst that of China is so difficult, or their method of learning it so defective, as to require the study of half the life of man to fit him for any of the ordinary employments of the state, and they have no knowledge of any language but their own. The one is in a state of youthful vigour, advancing daily in strength and knowledge; the other is worn out with old age and disease, and under its present state of existence is not likely to advance in any kind of improvement.

To the principle of universal obedience the Chinese government has added another, which is well calculated to satisfy[385] the public mind: the first honours and the highest offices are open to the very lowest of the people. It admits of no hereditary nobility; at least none with exclusive privileges. As a mark of the Sovereign's favour a distinction will sometimes descend in a family, but, as it confers no power nor privilege nor emolument, it soon wears out. All dignities may be considered as merely personal; the princes of the blood, even, sink gradually into the common mass, unless their talents and their application be sufficient to qualify them for office, independent of which there can be neither rank nor honours, and very little if any distinction, not even in the imperial family, beyond the third generation. On public days the Emperor, at a single glance, can distinguish the rank of each of the many thousand courtiers that are assembled on such occasions by their dress of ceremony. The civilians have a bird, and the military a tyger, embroidered on the breast and back of their upper robe; and their several ranks are pointed out by different coloured globes, mounted on a pivot on the top of the cap or bonnet. The Emperor has also two orders of distinction, which are conferred by him alone, as marks of particular favour; the order of the yellow vest and of the peacock's feather.

The influence that, in nations of Europe, is derived from birth, fortune, and character, is of no weight in the Chinese government. The most learned, and I have already explained how far the term extends, provided he be not of notorious bad character, is sure to be employed; though under the present Tartar government, the Chinese complain that they never arrive at the highest rank till they are advanced in years. Learning[386] alone, by the strict maxims of state, leads to office, and office to distinction. Property, without learning, has little weight, and confers no distinction, except in some corrupt provincial governments, where the external marks of office are sold, as in Canton. Hence property is not so much an object of the laws in China as elsewhere, and consequently has not the same security. In the governments of Europe, property seldom fails to command influence and to force dependence: in China, the man of property is afraid to own it, and all the enjoyments it procures him are stolen.

Sometimes, indeed, the highest appointments in the state are conferred, as it happens elsewhere, by some favourable accident, or by the caprice of the monarch. A striking instance of this kind was displayed in the person of *Ho-tchung-tang*, the last prime minister of the late *Kien-long*. This man, a Tartar, happened to be placed on guard in the palace, where his youth and comely countenance struck the Emperor so forcibly in passing, that he sent for him to the presence; and finding him equally agreeable in his conversation and manners, he raised him rapidly, but gradually, from the situation of a common soldier, to the highest station in the empire. Such sudden changes, from a state of nothingness to the summit of power, have frequently been observed to be attended with consequences no less fatal to the man so elevated, than pernicious to the public: and thus it happened to this favourite minister. During the life of his old master, over whom, in his later years, he is said to have possessed an unbounded influence, he availed himself of the means that offered, by every species of fraud and ex[383]tortion, by tyranny and oppression, to amass such immense wealth in gold, silver, pearls, and immoveable property, that his acquisitions were generally allowed to have exceeded those of any single individual, that the history of the country had made known. His pride and haughty demeanour had rendered him so obnoxious to the royal family that, at the time we were in Pekin, it was generally supposed, he had made up his mind to die with the old Emperor, for which event he had always at hand a dose of poison, not chusing to stand the severe investigation which he was well aware the succeeding prince would direct to be made into his ministerial conduct. It seems, however, when that event actually happened, the love of life, and the hope of escaping, prevailed on him to change his purpose and to stand the hazard of a trial. Of the crimes and enormities laid to his charge he was found, or rather he was said to have pleaded, guilty. The vast wealth he had extorted from others was confiscated to the crown, and he was condemned to suffer an ignominious death[28].[388]

But *Ho-tchung-tang*, if guilty of inordinate ambition, or acts of injustice, is far from being the only instance of such conduct in men thus raised from humble situations. The officers[389] of government in general, though intended by the constitution as a kind of barrier between the prince and the people, are the greatest oppressors of the latter, who have seldom any means of redress, or of conveying their complaints to the Imperial ear. There is no middle class of men in China: men whose property and ideas of independence give them weight in the part of the country where they reside; and whose influence and interest are considered as not below the notice of the government. In fact, there are no other than the governors and the governed. If a man, by trade, or industry in his profession, has accumulated riches, he can enjoy them only in private. He dares not, by having a grander house, or finer clothes, to let his neighbour perceive that he is richer than himself, lest he should betray him to the commanding officer of the district, who would find no difficulty in bringing him within the pale of the sumptuary laws, and in laying his property under confiscation.

Sometimes, indeed, the extortions that the officers practise upon the people, as in the case of *Ho-tchung-tang*, meet the hand of justice. Other magistrates keep a steady eye upon their proceedings, and, in proper time, transmit the necessary information to court. Spies also are detached from court into the[390] provinces, under the name of inspectors. Jealous of each other, they let no opportunity slip of making unfavourable reports to their superiors. Notwithstanding which, with all the precautions taken by government in favour of the subject, the latter finds himself most dreadfully oppressed. It is true, for very slight offences preferred against men in office, the court directs a public reprimand in the official Gazette; for those of a more serious nature, degradation from rank; and every officer so degraded is under the necessity of proclaiming his own disgrace in all his public orders; not only to put him in mind of his past conduct, but likewise to shew the people how watchful the eye of government is over the actions of its servants. The last stage of public degradation, which amounts to a sentence of infamy, is an order to superintend the preparation of the Emperor's tomb, which implies that the person so sentenced is more fit to be employed among the dead than the living. *Tchang-ta-gin*, the late viceroy of Canton, was condemned to this degrading service[29].

The viceroy of a province can remain in that office no longer than three years, lest he might obtain an undue influence. No servant of the crown can form a family alliance in the place where he commands, nor obtain an office of importance in the city or town wherein he was born. Yet with these, and other precautions, there is still little security for the subject. He has no voice whatsoever in the government, either directly or by [391]representation; and the only satisfaction he possibly can receive for injuries done to him, and that is merely of a negative kind, is the degradation or the removal of the man in power, who had been his oppressor, and who perhaps may be replaced by another equally bad.

The ingenious Mr. Pauw has observed, that China is entirely governed by the whip and the bamboo. To these he might have added the yearly calendar and the Pekin Gazette, both of which, as engines in the hands of government, contribute very materially to assist its operations. By the circulation of the first is kept alive the observance of certain superstitions which it is, apparently, the study of government to encourage. The second is a vehicle for conveying into every corner of the empire the virtues and the fatherly kindness of the reigning sovereign, shewn by punishing the officers of his government, not only for what they have done amiss, but for what they may have omitted to do. Thus, if a famine has desolated any of the provinces, the principal officers are degraded for not having taken the proper precautions against it. This paper, in the shape of a small pamphlet, is published every second day. The missionaries have pretended that immediate death would be the consequence of inserting a falsehood in the Imperial Gazette. Yet it is famous for describing battles that were never fought, and for announcing victories that were never gained. The truth of this observation appears from several proclamations of *Kaung-shee*, *Tchien Long*, and the present Emperor, warning the generals on distant stations from making false re[392]ports, and from killing thousands and ten thousands of the enemy, sometimes even when no engagement had taken place[30]. The reverend gentlemen only mean to say, that the editor would be punished if he ventured to insert any thing not sent to him officially by the government.

The press in China is as free as in England, and the profession of printing open to every one, which is a singular circumstance, and perhaps the only instance of the kind, in a despotic government. It has usually been supposed that, in free countries only where every person is equally under the protection, and equally liable to the penalties, of the law, the liberty of the press could be cherished; and that it was a thing next to impossible, that power, founded on error and supported by oppression, could long be maintained where the press was free. It was the press that in Europe effected the ruin of priestly power, by dispelling the clouds that had long obscured the rays of truth; and by opening a free access to the doctrines of that religion which, of all others, is best calculated for the promotion of individual happiness and public virtue[31].

In China the liberty of the press seems to excite no apprehensions[393] in the government. The summary mode of punishing any breach of good morals, without the formality of a trial, makes a positive prohibition against printing unnecessary, being itself sufficient to restrain the licentiousness of the press. The printer, the vender, and the reader of any libellous publication, are all equally liable to be flogged with the bamboo. Few, I suppose, would be hardy enough to print reflexions on the conduct of government, or its principal officers, as such publications would be attended with certain ruin. Yet, notwithstanding all the dangers to which the printing profession is liable, daily papers are published in the capital, circulating, something like our own, private anecdotes, domestic occurrences, public notices of sales, and the wonderful virtues of quack medicines. We were told that, in one of these papers, the Portuguese missionary mentioned in Mr. Grammont's letter got a paragraph inserted, purporting the great neglect of the English in having brought no presents for the princes of the blood, nor for the Emperor's ministers. This false and malicious paragraph was said to be followed by another, insinuating that those for the Emperor were common articles of little value. Another pretended to give a catalogue of them, and included an elephant about the size of a rat, giants, dwarfs, wishing pillows, and such like nonsense. These, however, and other publications,[394] were industriously kept from our sight. Under the generous idea of being the Emperor's guests, we were not allowed to purchase any thing. He alone was to supply our wants, but his officers took the liberty of judging what these wants should consist in.

It is a singular phenomenon in the history of nations, how the government of an empire, of such vast magnitude as that of China, should have preserved its stability without any material change, for more than two thousand years; for, dropping their pretensions to an extravagant antiquity, for which however they have some grounds, there can be no doubt they were pretty much in the same state, regulated by the same laws, and under the same form of government as they now are, four hundred years before the birth of Christ, about which time their renowned philosopher flourished, whose works are still held in the highest reputation. They contain indeed all the maxims on which their government is still grounded, and all the rules by which the different stations of life take their moral conduct; and the monarchy is supposed to have been established two thousand years before his time.

If the test of a good government be made to depend on the length of its continuance, unshaken and unchanged by revolutions, China may certainly be allowed to rank the first among civilized nations. But, whether good or bad, it has possessed the art of moulding the multitude to its own shape in a manner unprecedented in the annals of the world. Various accidents, improved by policy, seem to have led to its durability. Among[395] these the natural barriers of the country, excluding any foreign enemy, are not to be reckoned as the least favourable; whilst the extreme caution of the government in admitting strangers kept the world in ignorance, for many ages, of the existence even of the most extensive, powerful, and populous empire among men. Secluded thus from all intercourse with the rest of the world, it had time and leizure to mould its own subjects into the shape it wished them to retain; and the event has sufficiently proved its knowledge in this respect.

A number of fortunate circumstances, seldom combined in the same country, have contributed to the preservation of internal tranquillity in China. The language is of a nature well calculated to keep the mass of the people in a state of ignorance. They are neither prohibited from embracing any religion of which they may make a choice, nor coerced to contribute towards the support of one they do not approve. The pains that have been taken to inculcate sober habits, to destroy mutual confidence, and render every man reserved and suspicious of his neighbour, could not fail to put an end to social intercourse. No meetings were held, even for convivial purposes, beyond the family circle, and these only at the festival of new year. Those kind of turbulent assemblies, where real or imagined grievances are discussed with all the rancour and violence that malicious insinuations against government, added to the effects of intoxicating draughts, too frequently inspire, never happen among the Chinese. Contented in having no voice in the government, it has never occurred to them that they have any[396] rights[32]: and they certainly enjoy none but what are liable to be invaded and trampled on, whenever the sovereign, or any of his representatives, from interest, malice, or caprice, think fit to exercise the power that is within their grasp. The doctrine of employing resistence against oppression, applied to the people and the government, is so contrary to every sentiment of the former, that the latter has little to fear on that score.

132

Partial insurrections occasionally happen, but they are generally owing to the extreme poverty of the people which, in seasons of scarcity and famine, compels them to take by violence the means of subsisting life, which otherwise they could not obtain. To this cause may be referred the origin of almost all the commotions recorded in their history, through some of which, when the calamity became general, the regular succession has been interrupted, and even changed. We were told, however, by our Chinese attendants, that certain mysterious societies did exist in some of the provinces, whose chief object was to overturn the Tartar government; that they held secret [393]meetings, in which they gave vent to their complaints against Tartar preponderancy, revived the memory of ancient glory, brooded over present injuries, and meditated revenge. If even this be the case, the present state of society is little favourable to their views. Nor indeed would a revolution be a desirable event for the Chinese themselves. It could not fail of being attended with the most horrible consequences. The Tartar soldiers would be tired with slaying, and millions that escaped the sword must necessarily perish by famine, on the least interruption of the usual pursuits of agriculture; for they have no other country to look to for supplies, and they raise no surplus quantity in their own.

In order to prevent as much as possible a scarcity of grain, and in conformity to their opinion, that the true source of national wealth and prosperity consists in agriculture, the Chinese government has in all ages bestowed the first honours on every improvement in this branch of industry. The husbandman is considered as an honourable, as well as useful, member of society; he ranks next to men of letters, or officers of state, of whom indeed he is frequently the progenitor. The soldier in China cultivates the ground. The priests also are agriculturists, whenever their convents are endowed with land. The Emperor is considered as the sole proprietary of the soil, but the tenant is never turned out of possession as long as he continues to pay his rent, which is calculated at about one-tenth of what his farm is supposed capable of yielding; and though the holder of lands can only be considered as a tenant at will, yet it is his own fault if he should be dispossessed. So accustomed are the Chinese[398] to consider an estate as their own, while they continue to pay the rent, that a Portuguese in Macao had nearly lost his life for endeavouring to raise the rent upon his Chinese tenants. If any one happens to hold more than his family can conveniently cultivate, he lets it out to another on condition of receiving half the produce, out of which he pays the whole of the Emperor's taxes. A great part of the poorer peasantry cultivate lands on these terms.

There are, in fact, no immense estates grasping nearly the whole of a district; no monopolizing farmers, nor dealers in grain. Every one can bring his produce to a free and open market. No fisheries are let out to farm. Every subject is equally entitled to the free and uninterrupted enjoyment of the sea, of the coasts, and the estuaries; of the lakes and rivers. There are no manor lords with exclusive privileges; no lands set apart for feeding beasts or birds for the profit or pleasure of particular persons; every one may kill game on his own grounds, and on the public commons. Yet with all these seeming advantages, there are rarely three successive years without a famine in one province or another.

As in the Roman Empire examples were not wanting of the first characters in the state glorying to put their hands to the plough, to render the earth fertile, and to engage in the natural employment of man; as,

In ancient times the sacred plough employ'd,
The kings and awful fathers,

So, in China, the Emperor at the vernal equinox, after[399] a solemn offering to the God of Heaven and Earth, goes through the ceremony of holding the plough, an example in which he is followed by the viceroys and governors and great officers in every part of the empire. This ceremony, though, in all probability, the remains of a religious institution, is well calculated to give encouragement to the labouring peasantry, whose profession, thus honourably patronized, cannot fail to be pursued with more energy and cheerfulness than where it receives no such marks of distinction. Here merchants, tradesmen, and mechanics, are considered far beneath the husbandman. So far from obtaining the honours attendant on commerce in the ancient city of Tyre, "whose merchants were princes, whose traffickers were the honourable of the earth"—or the ancient immunities granted in Alfred's reign, by which an English merchant, who had made three foreign voyages by sea, was raised to the rank of nobility, the man who, in China, engages in foreign trade is considered as little better than a vagabond. The home trade only is supposed to be necessary, and deserving the protection of government. It allows all goods and manufactures, the produce of the country, to be interchanged between the several provinces, on payment only of a small transit duty to the state, and certain tolls on the canals and rivers, applied chiefly to the repairs of flood-gates, bridges, and embankments. This trade, being carried on entirely by barter, employs such a multitude of craft of one description or other, as to baffle all attempts at a calculation. I firmly believe, that all the floating vessels in the world besides, taken collectively, would not be equal either in number or tonnage to those of China.[400]

Foreign trade is barely tolerated. So very indifferent the court of Pekin affects to be on this subject, that it has been hinted, on some occasions, and indeed serious apprehensions have been entertained in Europe, that they were half disposed to shut the port of Canton against foreigners. The treatment, indeed, which strangers meet with at this place, from the inferior officers of government, is of itself sufficient to exclude them, and such as could only be tolerated in consideration of the importance of the trade, and especially in the supply of tea; an article which, from being about a century ago a luxury, is now become, particularly in Great Britain, one of the first necessities of life.

The taxes raised for the support of government are far from being exorbitant or burthensome to the subject. They consist in the tenth of the produce of the land paid usually in kind, in a duty on salt, on foreign imports, and a few smaller taxes, that do not materially affect the bulk of the people. The total amount of taxes and assessments which each individual pays to the state, taken on an average, does not exceed four shillings a year.

With such advantages, unknown in most other countries, and such great encouragement given to agriculture, one would be led to suppose that the condition of the poor must be less exposed to hardships here than elsewhere. Yet in years of scarcity many thousands perish from absolute want of food. And such years so frequently occur in one province or another, either from unfavourable seasons of drought or inundations, the ill effects of both of which might probably be counteracted by proper[401] management, or by an honest application of the sums of money voted for the purpose out of the public revenue, that government has seldom been able to lay up in store a sufficient quantity of grain to meet the necessities of the people in seasons of general calamity; and they have no other relief to depend on but this precarious supply, seldom administered with alacrity, on account of the number of hands it has to pass through. This leads them to commit outrages against their wealthier neighbours. There are few public charities; and it is not a common custom to ask alms. I did not observe a single beggar from one extremity of China to the other, except in the streets of Canton. Nor are there any poor-laws griping the industrious husbandman and labourer, to feed the lazy, and to feast those who have the care of them; no paupers of any description, supported from funds that have been levied on the public. The children, if living and, if not, the next of kin, must take care of their aged relations; and the parents dispose of their children in what manner they may think best for the family interest. As several generations live together, they are subsisted at a much cheaper rate than if each had a separate household. In cases of real distress the government is supposed to act the parent; and its good intentions in this respect cannot be called in question; whenever it appears that any of its officers, through neglect or malice, have withheld grain from the poor, they are punished with singular severity, sometimes even with death.

Another great advantage enjoyed by the Chinese subject is, that the amount of his taxes is ascertained. He is never re[402]quired to contribute, by any new assessment, to make up a given sum for the extraordinary expences of the state, except in cases of rebellion, when an additional tax is sometimes imposed on the neighbouring provinces. But in general the executive government must adapt its wants to the ordinary supplies, instead of calling on the people for extraordinary contributions. The amount of the revenues of this great empire has been differently stated. As the principal branch, the land-tax, is paid in kind, it is indeed scarcely possible to estimate the receipt of it accurately, as it will greatly depend on the state of the crop. An Emperor who aims at popularity never fails to remit this tax or rent, in such districts as have suffered by drought or inundation. *Chou-ta-gin* gave to Lord Macartney, from the Imperial rent-roll, a rough sketch of the sums raised in each province, making them to amount in the whole to about sixty-six millions sterling; which is not more than twice the revenue of the state in Great Britain, exclusive of the poor's-rate and other parochial taxes, in 1803, and which gives, as I before observed, if reduced to a capitation, the sum of about four shillings for each individual, whilst that of Great Britain, by an analogous computation, would amount to about fifteen times that sum. I should suppose, however, that a shilling in China, generally speaking, will go as far as three in Great Britain.

From the produce of the taxes the civil and military establishments, and all the incidental and extraordinary expences, are first paid on the spot where they are incurred, out of the provincial magazines, and the remainder is remitted to the Imperial treasury in Pekin to meet the expences of the court, the [103] establishment of the Emperor, his palaces, temples, gardens, women, and princes of the blood. The confiscations, presents, tributes, and other articles, may be reckoned as his privy purse. The surplus revenue remitted to Pekin, in the year 1792, was stated to be about 36,000,000 ounces of silver, or 12,000,000l. sterling. It is a general opinion among the Chinese part of his subjects, that vast sums of the surplus revenue and such as arise from confiscations are annually sent to Moukden, the capital of Mantchoo Tartary; but this should appear to be an erroneous opinion founded on prejudice. Notwithstanding the enormous wealth of *Ho-tchung-tang*, that filled the Imperial coffers, the present Emperor found it necessary the same year to accept an offering, as it was called, of 500,000 ounces of silver, or 166,666l. sterling, from the salt merchants of Canton, and sums of money and articles of merchandize from other quarters, to enable him to quell a rebellion that was raging in one of the western provinces. He even sent down to Canton a quantity of pearls, agates, serpentines, and other stones of little value, in the hope of raising a temporary supply from the sale of them to foreign merchants. The Emperor of China, therefore, has not so much wealth at his disposal as has usually been imagined. He even accepts of patriotic gifts from individuals, consisting of pieces of porcelain, silks, fans, tea, and such-like trifling articles, which afterwards serve as presents to foreign embassadors, and each gift is pompously proclaimed in the Pekin gazette.

The chief officers in the civil departments of government, independent of the ministers and the different boards in Pekin, [404] according to the statement of *Tchou-ta-gin*, with their salaries and allowances reduced into silver, will be seen from the following table, which, with that of the military establishment, is published in the appendix to the authentic account of the embassy by Sir George Staunton; and as they differ very little from the court calendar published in 1801, and as I have occasion to make a few remarks on them, as well as on that of the population, which will be given in a subsequent chapter, I have not hesitated to introduce them into the present work.

Quality.	Number.	Salaries in ounces of silver.	Total.
Viceroys over one or more provinces	11	20,000	220,000
Governors of provinces	15	16,000	240,000
Collectors of revenue	19	9,000	171,000

135

Presidents of criminal tribunals	1 8	6 ,000	10 8,000
Governors of more than one city of the first order	8 5	3 ,000	25 8,000
Governors of one city only of the first order	1 84	2 ,000	36 8,000
Governors of a city of the second order	1 49	1 ,000	14 9,000
Governors of a city of the third order	1 305	8 00	1, 044,000
Presidents of literature and examinations	1 7 }	3 ,000	40 2,000
Inspectors general	1 17 }		
otal oz.			2,9 60,000

The inferior officers acting immediately under the orders of these, and amounting to many thousands, together with the salaries and expences of the different boards in the capital, all of which are paid out of the public treasury, must require a sum at least equal to the above; so that on a moderate calculation, the ordinary expences of the civil establishment will amount to the sum of 5,920,000 ounces, or 1,973,333*l.* sterling.

Some idea may be formed of the numerous appointments, and the frequent changes in administration, from the circumstance of the Court Calendar, or red book, being published every three months making four tolerable large volumes, or sixteen volumes every year.

The fatherly attention, the wise precautions, and the extreme jealousy of the government, have not been considered as alone sufficient for the internal and external protection of the empire, without the assistance of an immense standing army. This army, in the midst of a profound peace, was stated by *Van-ta-gin* to consist of eighteen hundred thousand men, one million of which were said to be infantry, and eight hundred thousand cavalry. As this government, however, is supposed to be much given to exaggeration in all matters relating to the aggrandisement of the country, and to deal liberally in hyperboles, wherever numbers are concerned, the authenticity of the above statement of their military force may perhaps be called in question. The sum of money, that would be required to keep in pay and furnish the extraordinaries of so immense an army, is so immoderate that the revenues would appear to be unable to bear it. If the pay and the appointments of each soldier, infantry and cavalry one with another, be supposed to amount to a shilling a day, the sum required for the pay alone would amount to 33,000,000*l.* sterling a year!

To come nearer the truth, let us take the calculation drawn up by Lord Macartney from the information of *Van-ta-gin.*[406]

Rank	Number	Salaries, oz.	Total
Tau-ton,	18	4000	72,000
Tsung-ping	62	2400	148,800
Foo-tsung	121	1400	157,300
Tchoo-tsung	165	800	132,000
Tchoo-tze	373	600	223,800
Too-tze	425	400	170,000
Sciou-foo	825	320	264,000
Tsien-tsung	1680	160	268,800
Pa-tsung	3622	130	420,370
Commissaries of provisions of first rank	44	320	14,080
Commissaries of provisions of second rank	330	160	52,800
		Total	1,974,450

1,000,000 infantry, at two ounces of silver each *per* month, provisions included	24,000,000
800,000 cavalry, at four ounces each, provisions and forage included	38,400,000
800,000 horses, cost at twenty ounces each, 16,000,000 oz. the annual wear and tear at 10 _per cent._ will be	1,600,000
Uniforms for 1,800,000 men once a year, at four ounces	7,200,000
Yearly wear and tear of arms, accoutrements, and contingencies, at one ounce *per* man	1,800,000

		T otal ounces	74,974,4 50

And as no allowance is made in the above estimate for the expence of artillery, tents, war equipage, nor for vessels of force on the different rivers and canals, the building and keeping in repair the military posts, the flags, ceremonial dresses, boats, waggons, musical bands, all of which are included in the extraordinaries of the army, these may probably be equal to the ordinaries; thus the whole military establishment would require the sum of 149,948,900 ounces, or 49,982,933*l.* sterling.[407]

The disposal of the revenues will then stand as follows:

Total amount of the revenue	-		*£.* 66,000,000
Civil establishment-	*£.* 1,973,333		
Militar y ditto-	49,98 2,933		
		———— ————	51,95 6,266
		———	
Surplus, being for the Emperor's establishment			*£.* 14,043,734

which accords pretty nearly with the sum said to be remitted to Pekin in the year 1792.

It will appear then that if the revenues be admitted as accurate, and I see no just reason for supposing the contrary, they are more than sufficient to meet the expences of so apparently an enormous establishment. If, however, the King of Prussia, the Monarch of a small indistinguishable speck on the globe, when put in comparison with the empire of China, can keep up an army of one hundred and eighty or two hundred thousand men, I can perceive nothing either extravagant or extraordinary in supposing that a Sovereign whose dominions are eight times the extent of those of France, before her late usurpations, should have ten times as great a force as that of the King of Prussia. It may perhaps be asked in what manner are they employed, seeing the nation is so little engaged in foreign war? The employments for which the military are used differ materially from those among European nations. Except a great part of the Tartar cavalry, who are stationed on the northern frontier and in the conquered provinces of Tartary, and the Tartar infantry, who are distributed as guards for the different cities of the empire, the rest of the army is[408] parcelled out in the smaller towns, villages, and hamlets; where they act as jailors, constables, thief-takers, assistants to magistrates, subordinate collectors of the taxes, guards to the granaries; and are employed in a variety of different ways under the civil magistracy and police. Besides these, an immense multitude are stationed as guards at the military posts along the public roads, canals, and rivers. These posts are small square buildings, like so many little castles, each having on its summit a watch-tower and a flag; and they are placed at the distance of three or four miles asunder. At one of these posts there are never fewer than six men. They not only prevent robberies and disputes on the roads and canals, but convey the public dispatches to and from the capital. An express sent from post to post travels between the capital and Canton in twelve days, which is upwards of one hundred miles a day. There is no other post nor mode of conveying letters for the convenience of the public.

A great part then of the Chinese army can only be considered as a kind of militia, which never has been, and in all human probability never will be, embodied, as a part of the community not living entirely on the labour of the rest, but contributing something to the common stock. Every soldier stationed on the different guards has his portion of land assigned to him, which he cultivates for his family, and pays his quota of the produce to the state. Such a provision, encouraged by public opinion, induces the soldier to marry, and the married men are never removed from their stations.[409]

It will not be expected that men thus circumstanced should exhibit a very military appearance under arms. In some places, where they were drawn out in compliment to the Embassador, when the weather happened to be a little warm, they were employed in the exercise of their fans, instead of their matchlocks; others we found drawn up in a single line, and resting very composedly on their knees to receive the Embassador, in which posture they remained till their commanding officer passed the word to rise. Whenever we happened to take them by surprize, there was the greatest scramble to get their holyday dresses out of the guard-house, which, when put on, had more the appearance of being intended for the stage than the field of battle. Their quilted petticoats, sattin boots, and their fans, had a mixture of clumsiness and effeminacy that ill accorded with the military character.

The different kinds of troops that compose the Chinese army consist of

Tartar cavalry, whose only weapon is the sabre; and a few who carry bows.

Tartar infantry, bowmen; having also large sabres.

Chinese infantry, carrying the same weapons.

Chinese matchlocks.

Chinese Tygers of war, bearing large round shields of basket-work, and long ill-made swords. On the shields of the last are painted monstrous faces of some imaginary animal, intended to frighten the enemy, or, like another gorgon, to petrify their beholders.

The military dress varies in almost every province. Sometimes[410] they wore blue jackets edged with red, or brown with yellow; some had long pantaloons; some breeches, with stockings of cotton cloth; others petticoats and boots. The bowmen had long loose gowns of blue cotton, stuffed with a kind of felt or wadding, studded all over with brass knobs, and bound round the middle with a girdle, from which the sabre was appended behind, hanging with the point forwards, and on the right, not the left, side as in Europe. On the head they wore a helmet of leather, or gilt pasteboard, with flaps on each side that covered the cheeks and fell upon the shoulder. The upper part was exactly like an inverted funnel, with a long pipe terminating in a kind of spear, on which was bound a tuft of long hair dyed of a scarlet colour.

The greatest number we saw at any one place might be from two to three thousand, which were drawn up in a single line along the bank of a river; and as they stood with an interval between each equal to the width of a man, they formed a very considerable line in length. Every fifth man had a small triangular flag, and every tenth a large one; the staffs that supported them were fixed to the jacket behind the shoulders. Some of the flags were green, edged with red; others blue, edged with yellow. I never saw the Chinese troops drawn out in any other way than a single line in front; not even two deep.

The Tartar cavalry appear to be remarkably swift, and to charge with great impetuosity; but the horses are so small and are broken into so quick and short a stroke that the eye is deceived. Their real speed, in fact, is very moderate. Their[411] saddles are remarkably soft, and raised so high both before and behind, that the rider cannot easily be thrown out of his seat. The stirrups are so short that the knee is almost as high as the chin. They have very little artillery, and that little is as wretched as it well can be. I suspect it is borrowed from the Portugueze, as the matchlock most unquestionably has been.

When our fellow-traveller *Van-ta-gin* was asked the reason of their pretending to give a preference to the clumsy matchlocks over the firelocks now in use among European troops, he replied, it had been found, after a severe engagement in Thibet, that the matchlocks had done much more execution than the firelocks. It is difficult to combat prejudices; but it was not very difficult to convince *Van* that the *men* might probably have been quite as much in fault as the *musquets*, and that the superior steadiness of the fire from the matchlocks might possibly be owing to their being fixed, by an iron fork, into the ground. The missionaries have assigned a very absurd reason for firelocks not being used in China; they say the dampness of the air is apt to make the flint miss fire. With equal propriety might these gentlemen have asserted that flints would not emit fire in Italy. Their want of good iron and steel to manufacture locks, or the bad quality of their gunpowder, might perhaps be offered as better reasons; and as the best of all their want of courage and coolness to make use of them with that steadiness which is required to produce the effects of which they are capable. Their favourite instrument is the bow, which, like all other missile weapons, requires less courage to|112| manage, than those which bring man to oppose himself in close contest with man.

Although the Tartars have found it expedient to continue the Chinese army on the old footing, it may naturally be supposed they would endeavour to secure themselves by all possible means in the possession of this vast empire, and that they would use every exertion to recruit the army with their own countrymen, in preference to the Chinese. Every Tartar male child is accordingly enrolled. This precaution was necessary, as their whole army, at the time of the conquest, is said not to have exceeded eighty thousand men. At this time, in fact, a weak administration had suffered the empire to be torn asunder by convulsions. Every department, both civil and military, was under the control of eunuchs. Six thousand of these creatures are said to have been turned adrift by the Tartars on taking possession of the palace in Pekin.

The conduct of the Mantchoo Tartars, whose race is now on the throne, was a master-piece of policy little to be expected in a tribe of people that had been considered but as half civilized. They entered the Chinese dominions as auxiliaries against two rebel chiefs, but soon perceived they might become the principals. Having placed their leader on the vacant throne, instead of setting up for conquerors, they melted at once into the mass of the conquered. They adopted the dress, the manners, and the opinions of the people. In all the civil departments of the state they appointed the ablest Chinese, and all vacancies were filled with Chinese in preference to|113| Tartars. They learned the Chinese language; married into Chinese families; encouraged Chinese superstitions; and, in short, omitted no step that could tend to incorporate them as one nation. Their great object was to strengthen the army with their own countrymen, whilst the Chinese were so satisfied with the change, that they almost doubted whether a change had really taken place.

The uninterrupted succession of four Emperors, all of whom were endowed with excellent understandings, uncommon vigour of mind, and decision of character, has hitherto obviated the danger of such an enormous disproportion between the governors and the governed. The wisdom, prudence, and energy of these Emperors have not only maintained the family on the throne, the fifth of which now fills it, but have enlarged the dominions to an extent of which history furnishes no parallel. The present Emperor, *Kia-king*, is said to possess the learning and prudence of his father, and the firmness of *Kaung-shee*; but it is probable he will have a more difficult task in governing the empire than either of his predecessors. In proportion as the Tartar power has increased, they have become less felicitous to conciliate the Chinese. All the heads of departments are now Tartars. The ministers are all Tartars; and most of the offices of high trust and power are filled by Tartars. And although the ancient language of the country is still preserved as the court language, yet it is more than probable that Tartar pride, encreasing with its growing power, will ere long be induced to adopt its own.|114|

The Emperor *Kaung-shee* indeed took uncommon pains to improve the Mantchoo language, and to form it into a systematic *Thesaurus* or dictionary; and *Tchien-Lung* directed that the children of all such parents as were one a Tartar, the other a Chinese, should be taught the Mantchoo language; and that they might pass their examinations for office in that language. I could observe, that the young men of the royal family at *Yuen-min-yuen* spoke with great contempt of the Chinese. One of them, perceiving that I was desirous of acquiring some knowledge of the Chinese written character, took great pains to convince me that the

Tartar language was much superior to it; and he not only offered to furnish me with the alphabet and some books, but with his instructions also, if I would give up the Chinese, which, he observed, was not to be acquired in the course of a man's whole life. I could not forbear remarking, how very much these young princes enjoyed a jest levelled against the Chinese. An ill-natured remark, for instance, on the cramped feet and the hobbling gait of a Chinese woman met with their hearty approbation; but they were equally displeased on hearing the clumsy shoes worn by the Tartar ladies compared to the broad flat-bottomed junks of the Chinese.

Although the ancient institutes and laws, the established forms of office, the pageantry of administration, were all retained, and the dress, the manners, and external deportment of the vanquished were assumed by the victors, yet the native character remained distinct; and now, in the higher departments of office especially, it bursts through all disguise. The conscious[415] superiority of the one checks and overawes the other. "Most of our books," observes Lord Macartney, "confound the two people together, and talk of them as if they made only one nation under the general name of China; but whatever might be concluded from any outward appearances, the real distinction is never forgotten by the sovereign who, though he pretends to be perfectly impartial, conducts himself at bottom by a systematic nationality, and never for a moment loses sight of the cradle of his power. The science of government in the *Eastern* world, is understood by those who govern very differently from what it is in the *Western*. When the succession of a contested kingdom in Europe is once ascertained, whether by violence or compromise, the nation returns to its pristine regularity and composure: it matters little whether a Bourbon or an Austrian fills the throne of Naples or of Spain, because the sovereign, whoever he be, then becomes to all intents and purposes, a Spaniard or Neapolitan, and his descendants continue so with accelerated velocity. George the First and George the Second ceased to be foreigners from the moment our sceptre was fixed in their hands; and His present Majesty is as much an Englishman as King Alfred or King Edgar, and governs his people not by Teutonic, but by English laws.

"The policy of Asia is totally opposite. There the prince regards the place of his nativity as an accident of mere indifference. If the parent root be good, he thinks it will flourish in every soil, and perhaps acquire fresh vigour from transplantation. It is not locality, but his own cast and family;[416] it is not the country where he drew his breath, but the stock from which he sprung; it is not the scenery of the theatre, but the spirit of the drama, that engages his attention and occupies his thoughts. A series of two hundred years, in the succession of eight or ten monarchs, did not change the Mogul into a Hindoo, nor has a century and a half made *Tchien-Lung* a Chinese. He remains, at this hour, in all his maxims of policy, as true a Tartar as any of his ancestors."

Whether this most ancient empire among men will long continue in its stability and integrity, can only be matter of conjecture, but certain it is, the Chinese are greatly dissatisfied, and not without reason, at the imperious tone now openly assumed by the Tartars; and though they are obliged to cringe and submit, in order to rise to any distinction in the state, yet they unanimously load them with

"Curses, not loud, but deep, mouth-honour, breath[33]."

Whenever the dismemberment or dislocation of this great machine[417] shall take place, either by a rebellion or revolution, it must be at the expence of many millions of lives. For, as is well observed by Lord Macartney, "A sudden transition from slavery to freedom, from dependence to authority, can seldom be borne with moderation or discretion. Every change in the state of man ought to be gentle and gradual, otherwise it is commonly dangerous to himself, and intolerable to others. A due preparation may be as necessary for liberty, as for inoculation of the small-pox, which, like liberty, is future health but, without due preparation, is almost certain destruction. Thus then the Chinese, if not led to emancipation by degrees, but let loose on a burst of enthusiasm, would probably fall into all the excesses of folly, suffer all the paroxysms of madness, and be found as unfit for the enjoyment of rational freedom, as the French and the negroes."

CHAP. VIII.

Conjectures on the Origin of the Chinese.—Their Religious Sects,—Tenets,—and Ceremonies.

Embassy departs from Pekin, and is lodged in a Temple.—Colony from Egypt not necessary to be supposed, in order to account for Egyptian Mythology in China.—Opinions concerning Chinese Origin.—Observations on the Heights of Tartary.—Probably the Resting-place of the Ark of Noah.—Ancients ignorant of the Chinese.—Seres.—First known Intercourse of Foreigners with China.—Jews.—Budhists.—Nestorians.—Mahomedans.—Roman Catholics.—Quarrels of the Jesuits and Dominicans.—Religion of Confucius.—Attached to the Prediction of future Events.—Notions entertained by him of a future State.—Of the Deity.—Doctrine not unlike that of the Stoics.—Ceremonies in Honour of his Memory led to Idolatry.—Misrepresentations of the Missionaries with regard to the Religion of the Chinese.—The Tao-tze or Sons of Immortals.—Their Beverage of Life.—The Disciples of Fo or Budhists.—Comparison of some of the Hindu, Greek, Egyptian, and Chinese Deities.—The Lotos or Nelumbium.—Story of Osiris and Isis, and the Isia compared with the Imperial Ceremony of Ploughing.—Women visit the Temples.—Practical Part of Chinese Religion.—Funeral Obsequies.—Feast of Lanterns.—Obeisance to the Emperor performed in Temples leads to Idolatry.—Primitive Religion lost or corrupted.—Summary of Chinese Religion.

THE suspicious and watchful conduct of the Chinese government[418] towards strangers was ill suited to the free and independent spirit of Britons. Confined within the limits of their hotel, the populous capital of China was to them little better[419] than a desert. It was, therefore, less painful to be obliged to quit a place which they could consider in no other light than as an honourable prison, and to take leave of a people, whose general character seemed to be strongly marked with pride, meanness, and ignorance. After having passed some time in a nation, where every petty officer is a tyrant, and every man a slave, how doubly precious do the blessings of that true liberty appear, which our happy constitution affords to every one the means of enjoying at home; where property is secured from violence, and where the life of the meanest subject is equally protected with that of the prince. Let those visionary men, who amuse themselves in building Utopian governments, and those who, from real or fancied injury or neglect, feel the chagrin of disappointment, visit other countries, and experience how justice is administered in other nations; they will then be taught to confess that real liberty exists only in Great Britain—in that happy island where, to use the expression of an eminent writer on the laws of nations[34], "an enlightened piety in the people is the firmest support of lawful authority; and in the sovereign's breast, it is the pledge of the people's safety, and excites their confidence."

Impressed with such sentiments, on the evening of the 7th of October I rode through the streets of Pekin, for the last time, in company with Mr. Maxwell. We were quite alone, not a single Chinese servant, nor soldier, nor officer to conduct us; yet we had no difficulty in finding our way. We passed [420] through the broad streets of this capital from one extremity to the other without the least molestation, or, indeed, the least notice. We could not forbear remarking the extraordinary contrast, that the two greatest cities in the world exhibited at this hour of the day. In the public streets of Pekin, after five or six o'clock in the evening, scarcely a human creature is seen to move, but they abound with dogs and swine. All its inhabitants, having finished the business of the day, are now retired to their respective homes to eat their rice and, agreeably with the custom of their great Emperor, which to them is a law, to lie down with the setting sun; at which time in London, the crowd is so great, from Hyde Park corner to Mile End, as to interrupt each other. In Pekin, from the moment the day begins to dawn, the buzz and the bustle of the populace is like that of a swarm of bees; whilst, on the contrary, the streets of London at an early hour in the morning are nearly deserted. At eight in the evening, even in summer, the gates of Pekin are shut, and the keys sent to the governor, after which they cannot be opened on any consideration.

The Embassador and the rest of the suite, with the soldiers, servants and musicians had, several hours before us, set out in a sort of procession, in which an officer of government on horseback took the lead, with the letter of the Emperor of China to the King of England slung across his shoulders, in a wooden case covered with yellow silk. At a late hour in the night, we joined the rest of the party in the suburbs of *Tong-tchoo-foo*, where we were once more lodged among the gods of the nation, in a temple that was consecrated to the patronizing deity of the city.[421] There are no inns in any part of this vast empire; or, to speak more correctly (for there are resting-places), no inhabited and furnished houses where, in consideration of paying a certain sum of money, a traveller may purchase the refreshments of comfortable rest, and of allaying the calls of hunger. The state of society admits of no such accommodation, and much less such as, in many countries, proceeds from a spirit of disinterested hospitality; on the contrary, in this country, they invariably shut their doors against a stranger. What they call inns are mean hovels, consisting of bare walls where, perhaps, a traveller may procure his cup of tea for a piece of copper money, and permission to pass the night; but this is the extent of the comforts which such places hold out. The practice indeed of travelling by land is so rare, except occasionally in those parts of the country which admit not the convenience of inland navigations, or at such times when these are frozen up, that the profits which might arise from the entertainment of passengers could not support a house of decent accommodation. The officers of state invariably make life of the conveniences which the temples offer, as being superior to any other which the country affords; and the priests, well knowing how vain it would be to resist, or remonstrate, patiently submit, and resign the temporary use of their apartments without a murmur.

In most countries of the civilized world, the buildings appropriated for religious worship and the repositories of their gods, are generally held sacred. In the monasteries of those parts of Europe, where inns are not to be found, the apartments of the monks are sometimes resorted to by travellers, but in China the [422] very *sanctum sanctorum* is invaded. Every corner is indiscriminately occupied by men in power, if they should require it. Sometimes, also, the whole building is made a common place of resort for vagrants and idlers, where gamblers mix with gods, and priests with pick-pockets. In justice, however, it must be observed, that the priests of the two popular religions which predominate in the country shew no inclination to encourage, by joining in, the vicious practices of the rabble; but having no pay nor emolument from government, and being rather tolerated than supported, they are obliged to submit to and to overlook abuses of this nature, and even to allow the profane practices of the rabble in the very hours of their devotion. Yet there is a decency of behaviour, a sort of pride and dignity in the deportment of a Chinese priest, that readily distinguish him from the vulgar. The calumnies, which some of the Roman Catholic missionaries have so industriously circulated against them, seem to have no foundation in truth. The near resemblance of their dress and holy rites to those of their own faith was so mortifying a circumstance, that none of the missionaries I conversed with could speak with temper of the priests of China. I could not even prevail on our interpreter of the *propaganda fide*, who still manifested a predilection for the customs of his country in every other respect, to step into the temple where the altar was placed; nor could he be induced, by any persuasion, to give or to ask an explanation of their mysterious doctrines.

There is no subject, perhaps, on which a traveller ought to speak with less confidence, than on the religious opinions of [423] the people he may chance to visit, in countries out of Europe, especially when those opinions are grounded on a very remote antiquity. The allegorical allusions in which they might originally have been involved, the various changes they may since have undergone, the ceremonies and types under which they are still exhibited, in their modern dress, render them so wholly unintelligible that, although they may have been founded in truth and reason, they now appear absurd and ridiculous; equally inexplicable by the people themselves who profess them, as by those who are utter strangers. The various modes, indeed, under which the Creator and Ruler of the Universe is recognised by various nations, all tending to one point, but setting out in very different directions, can only be understood and reconciled by a thorough knowledge of the language, the history, and the habits of the people; of their origin and connections with other nations; and, even after such knowledge has been obtained, it is no easy task to separate fable from metaphor, and truth from fiction. For these reasons, the religion of China appears to be fully as obscure and inexplicable as that of almost any other of the oriental nations. The language of the country, added to the jealousy of the government in admitting foreigners, have thrown almost insuperable obstacles in the way of clearing up this intricate subject; and those few, who only have had opportunities of overcoming these difficulties, were unfortunately men of that class, whose opinions were so warped by the prejudices imbibed with the tenets of their own religion, that the accounts given by them are not always to be depended upon. As

I have already observed, they[424] cannot bring themselves to speak or to write of the priests of China with any degree of temper or moderation.

It would be presumptuous in me to suppose, for a moment, that I am qualified to remove the veil of darkness that covers the popular religion of China. But as, in the practice of this religion, it is impossible not to discover a common origin with the systems of other nations in ancient times, it may not be improper to introduce a few remarks on the subject, and to enquire if history will enable us to point out, in what manner they might have received or communicated the superstitions and metaphysical ideas that seem to prevail among them. The obvious coincidence between some parts of the mythological doctrines of the ancient Egyptians and Greeks, with those of China, induced the learned Monsieur de Guignes and many of the Jesuits to infer, that a colony from Egypt, at some remote period, had passed into China. This however does not appear probable. The Chinese are not a mixed but a distinct race of men; and their countenance has nothing of the ancient Egyptian in it. Nor indeed is it necessary to suppose any such connection, in order to explain the vestiges of Egyptian mythology that may appear in their temples. We are informed by history that when Alexander marched into India, about three centuries before the birth of Christ, many learned Greeks accompanied him on this memorable expedition; and we are further informed that, two centuries after this period when the persecutions and cruelties of Ptolemy Physcon expelled great numbers of learned and pious Greeks and Egyptians from the city of Alexandria, they travelled eastward in search[425] of an asylum among the Persians and the Indians; so that there is nothing extraordinary in meeting with Greek and Egyptian superstitions among nations of the East; even where no vestige of their language remains. For it may be observed that, whenever colonies emigrate from their own country and settle among strangers, they are much more apt to lose their native language, than their religious dogmas and superstitious notions. Necessity indeed may compel them to adopt the language of the new country into which they have emigrated, but any compulsive measures to draw them to another religion serve only to strengthen them in their own. The French refugees at the Cape of Good Hope totally lost their language in less than seventy years; and, singular as it may appear, I met with a deserter from one of the Scotch regiments, on the borders of the Kaffer country, who had so far forgot his language, in the course of about three years, that he was not able to make himself intelligible by it. Many languages, we know, have totally been lost, and others so changed as scarcely to preserve any traces of their original form[35].

Mr. Bailly, with some other learned and ingenious men,[426] was of opinion, that many fragments of the old and absurd fables of China are discoverable in the ancient history of the Hindus, from the birth of *Fo-shee*, the founder of the empire (*Fo-hi*, as the French write the word,) until the introduction of Budha, or Fo. Like the Hindus, it is true, they have always shewn a remarkable predilection for the number *nine*. Confucius calls it the most perfect of numbers. But the Scythians, or Tartars, have also considered this as a sacred number. It is true, likewise, they resemble some of the Indian nations, in the observance of solstitial and equinoxial sacrifices; in making offerings to the manes of their ancestors; in the dread of leaving no offspring behind them, to pay the customary obsequies to their memory; in observing eight cardinal or principal points of the world; in the division of the Zodiac, and in a variety of other coincidences, which the learned Mr. Bryant accounts for by supposing the Egyptians, Greeks, Romans, and Indians, to be derived from one common stock, and that some of these people carried their religion and their learning into China. No proof however is adduced, either by him or others, of such a communication; and an assertion directly the contrary might have been made with equal plausibility.[427]

That the Chinese do not owe their origin to the same stock, their physical character is of itself a sufficient proof. The small eye, rounded at the extremity next the nose, instead of being angular, as is the case in that of Europeans, its oblique instead of horizontal position, and the flat and broad root of the nose, are features or characters entirely distinct from the Hindu, the Greek, or the Roman; and belong more properly to the natives of that vast extent of country, which was known to the ancients by the name of Scythia, and, in modern times, by that of Tartary. There is scarcely in nature two of the human species that differ more widely than a Chinese and a Hindu, setting aside the difference of colour, which however modern enquiries have determined to have little or no relation to climate, but rather to some original formation of the different species. The Mantchoo, and indeed all the other Tartar tribes bordering upon China, are scarcely distinguishable from the Chinese. The same colour, except in a few instances as I have elsewhere observed, the same eyes, and general turn of the countenance prevail, on the continent of Asia, from the tropic of Cancer to the Frozen Ocean[36]. The peninsula of Malacca, and the vast multitude of islands spread over the eastern seas, and inhabited by the Malays, as well as those of Japan and Lieou-kieou, have clearly been peopled from the same common stock. The first race of people to the northward of Hindostan, that possess [428] the Tartar countenance, so different from that of the Hindus, are the inhabitants of Bootan. "The *Booteeas*," says Captain Turner, "have invariably black hair, which it is their fashion to cut short to the head. The eye is a very remarkable feature of the face; small, black, with long pointed corners[37], as though stretched and extended by artificial means. Their eye-lashes are so thin as to be scarcely perceptible, and the eye-brow is but slightly shaded. Below the eyes is the broadest part of the face, which is rather flat, and narrows from the cheek-bones to the chin; a character of countenance appearing first to take its rise among the Tartar tribes, but is by far more strongly marked in the Chinese."

The heights of Tartary, bulging out beyond the general surface of the globe, have been considered, indeed, by many as the cradle of the human species, or still more emphatically, and perhaps more properly, as *the foundery of the human race*. This opinion did not arise solely from the vast multitudes of people corresponding with the Tartar character, that are spread over every part of the eastern world, and who in countless swarms once overran all Europe, but was grounded on a supposition, that the whole surface of the globe, or the greater part of it, has at one time been submerged in water, and that Tartary was the last to be covered, and the first that was uncovered; and the place from whence, of course, a new set of creatures were forged as in a workshop, from some remnant of the old stock, to be the germs of future nations.

[429]

Almost every part of the earth, indeed, affords the most unequivocal indications that such has actually been the case, not only in the several marine productions that have been discovered in high mountains, at a distance from any sea, and equally deep under the surface of the earth; but more especially in the formation of the mountains themselves, the very highest of which, except those of granite, consisting frequently of tabular masses piled on each other in such regular and horizontal strata, that their shape and appearance cannot be otherwise accounted for, or explained by any known principle in nature, except by supposing them at one time to have existed in a state of fluidity, by the agency of fire or of water, a point which seems to be not quite decided between the Volcanists and the Neptunists. The heights of Tartary are unquestionably the highest land in the *old* world. In America they may, perhaps, be exceeded. *Gerbillon*, who was a tolerable good mathematician and furnished with instruments, assures us, that the mountain *Pe-tcha*, very inferior to many in Tartary, is nine Chinese *lees*, or about fifteen thousand feet, above the level of the plains of China. This mountain, as well as all the others in the same country, is composed of sand stone, and rests upon plains of sand, mixed with rock salt and saltpetre. The *Sha-moo*, or immense desert of sand, which stretches along the north-west frontier of China and divides it from western Tartary, is not less elevated than the *Pe-tcha*, and is said to resemble the bed of the ocean. Some of the mountains starting out of this *sea of sand*, which its name implies, cannot be less than twenty thousand feet above the level of the eastern ocean. [430]

The formation of the earth affords a wide field for speculation; and, accordingly, many ingenious theories have been conceived to explain the various appearances which its surface exhibits. The best modern naturalists seem, however, to agree, that water has been one of the principal agents to produce these effects. The great Linnæus, whose penetrating mind pervaded the whole empire of nature, after many and laborious enquiries, acquiesced in the truth of the sacred writings, that the whole globe of the earth was, at some period of time, submerged in water, and covered with the vast ocean, until in the lapse of time one little island appeared in this immense sea, which island must have been of course the highest mountain upon the surface of the earth. In support of his hypothesis, he adduces a number of facts, many of which have fallen within his own observation, of the progressive retreat of the sea, the diminution of springs and rivers, and the necessary increment of land. Among the most remarkable of these are the observations made by the inhabitants of Northern Bothnia upon the rocks on the sea coast, from whence it appeared that, in the course of a century, the sea had subsided more than four feet; so that six thousand years ago, supposing the rate of retiring to have been the same, the sea was higher than at present by two hundred and forty feet. Such great and sensible depression of the water of the sea must, however, have been only local, otherwise, as I have elsewhere observed, the Red Sea and the Mediterranean would have joined within the period of history. The sea, it is true, in some parts of the world, gains upon the land, and in others the land upon the sea, but these effects arise from a different cause to that which is supposed to produce a ge[431]neral retreat. It is true, also, that in the neighbourhood of mountains and great rivers, very material changes have taken place in the course of a few ages. The fragments of the former, worn away by the alternate action of the sun and rains, are borne down by the torrents of the latter, and deposited in the eddies formed by the two banks of the rivers where they join the sea, producing thus alluvious land as, for example, the Delta of Egypt, which has gradually been deposited out of the soil of Abyssinia and Upper Egypt; the plains of the northern parts of China, which have been formed out of the mountains of Tartary; and those of India from the Thebetian mountains, and the other high lands to the northward and westward of the peninsula. As, however, a much greater proportion of the fragments borne down by rivers must be deposited in the bosom of the deep than on its shores, the sea by this constant and effective operation ought rather to advance than to retreat. We may therefore, perhaps, conclude that, whatever the changes may have been which the surface of the earth has undergone, with regard to the proportion and the portion of land and water, the appearances we now behold in various parts of the globe can only be explained by supposing some temporary and preternatural cause, or else by assuming an incalculable period of time for their production.

But to return from this digression to the more immediate subject of the present section. It is sufficiently remarkable, and no inconsiderable proof of the truth of the Sacred Writings, that almost every nation has some traditionary account of a deluge, some making it universal, and others local: presuming,[432] however, the former to be correct, which is not only justified by the testimony of the author of the Pentateuch, but by natural appearances, it might perhaps be shewn, with no great deviation from the generally received opinion, that, instead of Persia being the hive in which was preserved a remnant of the ancient world for the continuation of the species, those who have supposed Tartary to be the cradle, from whence the present race of men issued, have adopted the more plausible conjecture. If it be borne in mind that, in every part of the Bible history, the expressions are accommodated to the understandings of those for whom they were intended, rather than strictly conformable to facts, and more consonant to appearances than realities, it may be supposed, without any offence to the most rigid believer, that by the mount Ararat was not strictly meant the identical mountain of that name, which has been recognised in Armenia, but rather the highest mountain on the face of the globe; for, if this were not the case, the Mosaic account would be contradictory in itself, as we are told that, "all the high hills that were under the whole Heaven were covered." This concession being allowed, we may suppose that the ark, instead of resting in Armenia, first struck ground in that part of Tartary which is now inhabited by the Eleuths, as being the most elevated tract of country in the old world. From these heights large rivers flow towards every quarter of the horizon. It is here that the sources of the Selenga are found, descending to the northward into the lake Baikal, and from thence by the Enesei and the Lena into the Frozen Ocean: of the Amour, which empties its waters to the eastward into the gulph of Tartary: of the two great rivers of China flowing to the southward, and[433] of numberless lakes and rivers discharging their waters to the westward, some burying themselves in deserts of sand, and others working their way to the great lake of Aral and the Caspian sea.

From such a situation, admitting the earth to have been peopled in succession, the two great rivers which took the southerly direction and crossed the fertile and extensive plains of China, were fully as likely to direct the few survivors of the deluge to this country, as that they should follow any of the other streams; and probably more so, as these led to a warmer and more comfortable climate, where fewer wants were felt and those few more easily supplied. Considered in this point of view, the opinion of the Jesuits will not appear so ill founded, which supposes that Noah, separating from his rebellious family, travelled with a part of his offspring into the east, and founded the Chinese monarchy; and that he is the same person as the *Foo-shee*[38] of their history. The words of scripture *from the east*, an ingenious commentator has observed, ought more properly to be translated, *at the beginning*. At all events, the fact I conclude to be irresistible, that the Tartars and the Chinese have one common origin, and the question then is simply this, whether the fertile plains of China were abandoned for the bleak and barren heights of Tartary, or that the wandering and half-famished [434]Scythians descended into regions whose temperature and productions were more congenial to the nature of man.

If, however, we allow China to have been among the first nations formed after the flood, it does not appear to have kept pace in learning and in arts with the Chaldeans, the Assyrians, or the Egyptians. Before the time of Confucius, its progress in civilization seems to have been very slow. He was the first person who digested any thing like a history of the kings of Loo; for, in his time, the country was divided among a number of petty princes, who lived at the head of their families, much in the same manner as formerly the chiefs of the clans in the Highlands of Scotland; or, perhaps, more properly speaking, like the German princes, whose petty states are so many parts of one great empire. It is now about two thousand years since the several monarchies were consolidated in one undivided and absolute empire. There are several reasons for supposing that, before this period, China made no great figure among the polished nations of the world, although it produced a Confucius, some of whose works demonstrate a vigorous and an enlightened mind. From the commentaries of this philosopher on one of their classical books[39], it would appear that a regular succession of Emperors could be traced near two thousand years back from his time, or more than four thousand years from the present period. The duration of the dynasties, with their several Emperors, which he enumerates, and the detail of occurrences in each reign, make the truth of the history sufficiently plausible, though the chronology, from their total ignorance of astro[435]nomy, must necessarily be defective. It is still an extraordinary circumstance, that none of the ancient classical authors should have had the least knowledge of such a nation. Homer neither mentions them nor makes any allusion to such a people; and Herodotus seems to have been equally ignorant of their existence; and yet, according to the best chronologists, Herodotus and Confucius must have been contemporaries. It may fairly be concluded then, that the early Greeks had no knowledge of the Chinese. Even more than a century after the father of history flourished, when the Persian empire was overthrown by Alexander, it does not appear that the Chinese were known to this nation; which in all probability would have been the case, notwithstanding their aversion to any intercourse with foreigners, had they constituted, at that time, a large and powerful empire; perhaps, indeed, the ignorance of the Persians might arise from the intervention of the civilized nations of India, whose numbers might have made it prudent in the former to direct their arms constantly towards the west rather than to the east.

It has been an opinion pretty generally adopted, that the people known to the ancients by the name of *Seres* were the same as the Chinese, partly on account of their eastern situation, and partly because the principal silk manufactures were supposed to be brought from thence, which gave the Romans occasion name the country *Sericum*. The Romans, however, received the trifling quantity of silk made use of by them from Persia, and not from China, nor from the country of the Seres. Nor is it probable, that the latter should be the Chinese, who are said to have sent an embassy to Augustus, in order to court[436] the friendship of the Romans, it being so very contrary to their fundamental laws, which not only prohibit any intercourse with strangers, but allow not any of the natives to leave the country. The fact, indeed, of this embassy rests solely upon the authority of Lucius A. Florus, who wrote his history, if it may so be called, nearly a century after the death of Augustus: and, as none of the historians contemporary with that Emperor, take any notice of such an event, it is more than probable that no such embassy was sent to Rome[40].

The first people that we know to have travelled into China[137] was a colony of Jews who, according to the records kept by their descendants, and which I understood from some of the missionaries are corroborated as to the time by Chinese history, first settled there shortly after the expedition of Alexander had opened a communication with India. Nor is it at all improbable that this adventurous and industrious people were the first to carry with them, into their new country, the silk worm and the mode of rearing it, either from Persia, or some of the neighbouring countries. The Emperor *Kaung-shee*, in his observations on natural history, takes notice that the Chinese are greatly mistaken when they say that silk was an exclusive product of China, for that the upper regions of India have a native worm of a larger growth, and which spins a stronger silk than any in China. Although indeed ancient authors are silent as to the article of silk, there are grounds for supposing it was not unknown in Tangut and Kitai. Several expressions in the Bible warrant the opinion that silk was used in the time of Solomon, and the *vestes perlucidæ ac fluidæ Medis* of Justin seem to convey a description of silken robes. This mode of the first introduction of silk into China is offered as mere conjecture, for which I have no other authority in support of, than what is here mentioned, with[458] the circumstance of the Jews being settled chiefly in the silk provinces, and of their being at this time in considerable numbers near *Hang-tchoo-foo*, where they carry on the principal trade in this article, and have acquired the reputation of fabricating the best stuffs of this material that are made in China; nor do I know in what other way they could recommend themselves to the Chinese, so far as to have obtained the protection of this jealous government, and to be allowed to intermarry with the women of the country. It is true they have practised no underhand attempts to seduce the natives from their paternal religion, and to persuade them to embrace their own; and although they are not very famous for the cultivation of the sciences, yet they might have rendered themselves extremely useful in suggesting improvements in many of the arts and manufactures. Many of them, indeed, forsake the religion of their forefathers, and arrive at high employments in the state. Few among them, I understand, except the Rabbis, have any knowledge of the Hebrew language, and they have long been so intermixed with the Chinese, that the priests at the present day are said to find some difficulty in keeping up their congregations. So different are the effects produced by suffering, instead of persecuting, religious opinions.

One of the missionaries has given an account of his visit to a synagogue of Jews in China. He found the priests most rigorously attached to their old law: nor had they the least knowledge of any other Jesus having appeared in the world, except the son of Sirach, of whom, he says, their history makes mention. If this be really the fact, their ancestors could not have[439] been any part of the ten tribes that were carried into captivity, but may rather be supposed to have been among the followers of Alexander's army, which agrees with their own account of the time they first settled in China. They possessed a copy of the Pentateuch and some other fragments of the Sacred Writings, which they had brought along with them from the westward, but the missionary's information is very imperfect, as he was ignorant of the Hebrew language[441].

Although a very great similarity is observable between many of the ancient Jewish rites and ceremonies and those in use among the Chinese, yet there seems to be no reason for supposing that the latter received any part of their religion from the [440]ancestors of those Jews that are still in the country. This, however, is not the case with regard to the priests of Budha, who, according to the Chinese records, came by the invitation of one of their Emperors from some part of India, near Thibet, about the sixtieth year of the Christian era. These priests succeeded so well in introducing the worship of Budha, that it continues to this day to be one of the popular religions of the country; and that no traces of the original name should remain is the less surprising, as they could not possibly pronounce either the B or the D; beside, they make it an invariable rule, as I have already observed, not to adopt any foreign names.

In some part of the seventh century, a few Christians of the Nestorian sect passed from India into China where, for a time, they were tolerated by the government. But, having most probably presumed upon its indulgence, and endeavoured to seduce the people from the established religions of the country, they were exposed to dreadful persecutions, and were at length entirely extirpated, after numberless instances of their suffering martyrdom for the opinions they had undertaken to propagate to the "utmost corners of the earth." When Gengis-Khan invaded China, in the beginning of the thirteenth century, a number of

Christians of the Greek church followed his army into this country; and they met with such great encouragement from the Tartars, that when Kublai-Khan succeeded to the government and built the city of Pekin, he gave them a grant of ground within the walls of the city for the purpose of building a church, in order to retain in the empire men of so much learning and of abilities so much superior to those of the[441] Chinese; who, however, on their part, have affected, in their history, to consider the Monguls as the greatest barbarians, for turning their horses into the apartments of the palaces, while they themselves were contented to pitch their tents in the courts or quadrangular spaces surrounded by the buildings. Father Le Compte, in his memoirs of China, says, but I know not on what authority, that at the taking of the city of Nankin the Tartars put all the Chinese women in sacks, without regard to age or rank, and sold them to the highest bidder; and that such as, in thus "buying the pig in the poke," happened to purchase an old, ugly, or deformed bargain, made no ceremony in throwing it into the river. If Father Le Compte was not the inventor of this, among many other of his pleasant stories, it certainly tells as little in favour of the Chinese, who must have been the purchasers, as of the Tartars; but we will charitably suppose the thing never happened. It seems, however, that the overthrow of the Chinese empire by the Mongul Tartars, was an event not to be regretted by the nation at large. By means of the learned and scientific men, who accompanied the expedition from Balk and Samarcand, astronomy was improved, their calendar was corrected, instruments for making celestial observations were introduced, and the direct communication between the two extremities of the empire was opened, by converting the streams of rivers into an artificial bed, forming an inland navigation, not to be paralleled in any other part of the world.

It was about this period when the celebrated Venetian traveller Marco Polo visited the Tartar Khan, then sitting on the[412] throne of China; and who, on his return, gave the first accounts of this extraordinary empire; which appeared indeed so wonderful that they were generally considered as his own inventions. His relations of the magnificent and splendid palaces of the Emperor, of his immense wealth, of the extent of his empire, and the vast multitudes of people, were held to be so many fabrications; and as, in speaking of these subjects, he seldom made use of a lower term than millions, his countrymen bestowed upon him the epithet of *Signor Marco Millione*—Mr. Mark Million. They had no hesitation, however, in giving credit to the only incredible part of his narrative, where he relates a few miracles that were performed, in the course of his journey through Persia, by some Nestorean Christians. Young Marco is said to have accompanied three missionaries of the Dominican order, sent from Venice to the capital of China, at the express desire of Kublai-Khan; but, whether they met with little encouragement in the object of their mission, on account of being preceded by the Christians of the Greek church, or their zeal at that time was less ardent than in later days, is not stated; but it seems they did not remain long in the East, returning very soon to their native country much enriched by their travels.

During the continuance of the Tartar government, which was not quite a century, great numbers of Mahomedans likewise found their way from Arabia to China. These people had long, indeed, been in the habit of carrying on a commercial intercourse with the Chinese; which, however, as at the present day, extended no further than the sea-ports on the southern[443] coast. They now found no difficulty in getting access to the capital, where they rendered themselves particularly useful in adjusting the chronology of the nation, and making the necessary calculations for the yearly calendar. Having acquired the language and adopted the dress and manners of the people, by degrees they turned their thoughts to the extending of their religious principles, and bringing the whole country to embrace the doctrine of their great prophet. For this end, they bought and educated at their own expence such children of poor people as were likely to be exposed in times of famine; and they employed persons to pick up, in the streets of the capital, any infants that should be thrown out in the course of the night, and who were not too much weakened or otherwise injured to be recovered.

About the middle of the sixteenth century, several Roman Catholic missionaries, of the order of Jesus, penetrated into the East; and the indefatigable zeal of one of these, Francis Xavier, carried him as far as *San-Shian*, a small island on the coast of China, where he died in the year 1552, in consequence of the uncommon fatigues he had undergone. His brother missionaries have calculated that he travelled, on foot, not less than one hundred thousand English miles, a great part of which was over mountains and desarts and forests and burning sands. Since a more easy communication with India and China has been effected by the way of the Cape of Good Hope, numbers of missionaries of the Catholic religion have volunteered their services into those countries; and although the sole object of their mission is the propagation of the Christian faith, they find it[444] necessary, in order to forward that object, to make themselves useful to the government. In China, they are occasionally employed as astronomers, mathematicians, mechanics, and interpreters. "It must have appeared a singular spectacle," observes Sir George Staunton, "to every class of beholders, to see men actuated by motives different from those of most human actions, quitting for ever their country and their connexions, to devote themselves for life to the purposes of changing the tenets of a people they had never seen; and in pursuing that object to run every risk, suffer every persecution, and sacrifice every comfort; insinuating themselves, by address, by talent, by perseverance, by humility, by application to studies foreign from their original education, or by the cultivation of arts to which they had not been bred, into notice and protection; overcoming the prejudices of being strangers in a country where most strangers were prohibited, and where it was a crime to have *abandoned the tombs of their ancestors*, and gaining, at length, establishments necessary for the propagation of their faith, without turning their influence to any personal advantage."

Most of those, however, who were established in Pekin, to the spiritual consolation of having laboured in the vineyard of the gospel not altogether in vain (for they do sometimes gain a proselyte) add the substantial satisfaction of not having neglected their worldly concerns. Besides the emoluments arising from their several communities, they have shops and houses in the capital, which they rent to Chinese. They have also their country villas and estates, where they cultivate the vine and[445] other fruits, and make their own wine. The revenues of the two Portuguese seminaries are stated to amount to twelve thousand ounces of silver, or four thousand pounds a year. The mission *de propaganda fide* is poor. The French Jesuits were once rich; but their property was dissipated on the dissolution of their society. The French *missions étrangères* drew on their superiors at Paris before the revolution, but since that event are reduced to a most deplorable situation. And it seemed to me, from what I could perceive at *Yuen-min-yuen*, that they were not much disposed to assist one another. Each nation had its separate interest, and they were not willing to lose any opportunity of calumniating their fellow-labourers. The French and Italians were the most moderate and liberal; the Portuguese the most inveterate. The missionaries of this nation appeared to be inspired with a jealousy and hatred, more than theological, against the rest. It is said indeed that their rich possessions, and the high situations they unworthily hold in the board of mathematics, render them jealous of all other Europeans; and they use every means of excluding them from the country.

From the frequent dissensions, indeed, among the different orders, and their perpetual broils, originated the persecutions which they and their proselytes suffered in China. The most violent of these disputes was carried on between the Jesuits and the Dominicans. The Jesuits endeavoured to assimilate their doctrines and their opinions to those of the Chinese, at least as far as they conscientiously could venture to do, in conformity to the nature of their mission; by which means, together with their apparently disinterested conduct, they soon collected[446] a numerous set of followers, half Christians and half Pagans. Unluckily for the cause of Christianity, a different sect of the same religion, but with principles more austere and of course less tolerant of others that deviated from their own, speedily followed the Jesuits into the East. The Dominicans, meeting with some of the half-christianized converts, soon gave them to understand that nothing less than eternal damnation would be the lot of all such as did not forsake their ancient superstitious and idolatrous practices; and especially that of sacrificing to their deceased relations in the Hall of Ancestors. The Franciscans having joined the Dominicans they represented to the Pope the abominable practices of the Jesuits, who had persuaded the Chinese they were come among them for the sole purpose of restoring their ancient religion to its original purity, as delivered by their Great Philosopher Confucius. The Pope, upon this, sent over a bull, interdicting all the missionaries in China from admitting any extraneous ceremonies or idolatrous worship, to be blended with those of Holy Catholic Church.

The Jesuits, however, by their superior talents, having made themselves useful at court, and obtained the notice and protection of *Caung-shee* the ruling monarch, and the greatest perhaps that ever filled the throne of China, treated this bull with contempt, and continued to make converts in their own way. They even obtained from the Emperor a sum of money and a grant of land, towards building a church in Pekin. And they further managed their affairs so well as to procure, from the succeeding Pope, a dispensation in favour of their mode of proceeding to convert the Chinese to Christianity. The Domini[147]cans and Franciscans, piqued beyond measure at the success of the Jesuits, represented them to the Pope, in the strongest terms, as the greatest enemies to the Christian faith. The Jesuits, in their turn, transmitted to Rome a manifesto, signed by the Emperor himself, attesting that the ceremonies of homage to the dead, retained by the Chinese Christians, were not of a religious but a civil nature, agreeable to the long established laws of the empire, which could not, on any consideration, be dispensed with. In short, their disputes and quarrels ran so high, and proceeded to such lengths; and Bulls and Embassadors were sent from Rome, with such imperious and threatening commands for the Chinese Christians to desist from all ceremonies that were not warranted by the Catholic church, that the Emperor began to think it was high time to interpose his authority, and to interdict the Christian religion from being preached at all in his dominions. And his son and successor *Yung-chin* commenced his reign with violent persecutions against the missionaries. He ordered many of them immediately out of the empire; others were thrown into prison[142], where they lingered [148]out a miserable life; and some were put to death by the bow-string. Those few, who were found necessary to assist in the astronomical part of the calendar, he allowed to remain in the capital.

Notwithstanding the persecutions that, in every reign, have been violently carried on against them by the officers of government in the several provinces, numbers of new missionaries have continued, from time to time, to steal into the country. At Macao we found two young missionaries, who had been waiting there a long time, in vain, for an opportunity of getting privately into the country. They accused the Portuguese of throwing every obstacle in their way, while pretending to afford them assistance; but, on application to the British Embassador, he found no difficulty in procuring them leave to proceed to the capital; and as one of these gentlemen had been a pupil of the celebrated La Lande, his services may probably supersede those of the right reverend bishop who at present directs the astronomical part of the important national almanack.

From the short view that has here been taken of the different people who, at various times, have gained admission into China, and some of them for no other purpose than that of[149] disseminating their religious tenets, it may be concluded, that the primitive worship of the country has experienced many changes and innovations, especially since the mass of the people, from the nature of the language, the maxims of the government, and other circumstances, have always been kept in a state of profound ignorance. Jews, Christians, Indians, and Mahomedans, have severally met with encouragement. The Jesuits had but one obstacle to overcome, the law that directed offerings to be made to deceased relations, and by giving way to this, which they were inclined to do had they not been thwarted by the more rigorous Dominicans, they might have converted the whole nation and Christianity would have become, in all probability, the prevailing religion, instead of that introduced from India. The paraphernalia and almost all the mummeries of the Romish church, the bells, the beads, the altars, the images, the candles, the dress, and the sanctimonious deportment of the priests in the hours of devotion, their chaunting and their incense, were already made familiar to the people in every temple of *Fo.* But, as Lord Macartney has observed, "the prohibition or restriction of sensual gratifications in a despotic country, where there are so few others, is difficult to be relished. Confession is repugnant to the close and suspicious character of the nation, and penance would but aggravate the misery of him whose inheritance is his labour, and poverty his punishment. Against it also is the state of society in China, which excludes women from their proper share of influence and importance. A religion which requires that women should at stated times communicate to priests, in private, their thoughts and actions, must be parti[450]cularly disgusting to a Chinese husband, who had not himself been suffered to see his wife till the day of his marriage; and who but seldom allows her afterwards to see even her near relations of another sex. A religion like that of Mahomet can only be extended by violence and terror; for the natural stubbornness of men does not readily give way to novel impressions; but the mild spirit of the gospel is alone to be infused through the means of gentleness, persuasion, and imperceptible perseverance. These are the proper instruments of conversion, and peculiarly belong to the fair sex, whose eloquence, on such occasions, gives charms to devotion and ornaments to truth. The earliest stages of Christianity received no small support from female agency and example; and for what shew of religion still appears in *our* churches, we are surely not a little indebted to the piety and attendance of women." Nothing, in fact, more tended to alarm the Chinese than the imprudent practice of the Romish missionaries of seducing the Chinese women to their churches whom, as they avow in their correspondence, they sometimes coaxed out of their jewels and money; adding, by way of justification, that it was to promote the service of God.

The primitive religion of China or, at least, those opinions, rites, and ceremonies that prevailed in the time of Confucius, (and before that period all seems to be fable and uncertainty) may be pretty nearly ascertained from the writings that are ascribed to that philosopher. He maintains in his physics, that "out of nothing there cannot possibly be produced any thing;—that material bodies must have existed from all eter[151]nity;—that the *cause* (*lee, reason*) or principle of things, must have had a co-existence with the things themselves;—that, therefore, this cause is also eternal, infinite, indestructible, without limits, omnipotent and omnipresent;—that the central point of influence (*strength*) from whence this cause principally acts, is the blue firmament (*tien*) from whence its emanations spread over the whole universe;—that it is, therefore, the supreme duty of the prince, in the name of his subjects, to present offerings to *tien*, and particularly at the equinoxes, the one for obtaining a propitious seed-time, and the other a plentiful harvest."

These offerings to the Deity, it may be observed, were always placed on a large stone, or heap of stones, erected on the summit of a high mountain, on the supposition, probably, that their influence would be so much the greater, in proportion as they should approach the seat and fountain of creative power; like the ancient Persians who, according to Herodotus, considered the whole circle of the Heavens to be the great ruling power of the universe, to which they also sacrificed on high mountains. Thus Tacitus, in speaking of the practice of worshipping the gods on high mountains, observes, that the nearer mortals can approach the heavens, the more distinctly will their prayers be heard; and on the same principle, Seneca says, that the people always strove for the seat next to the image of the deity in the temples, that their prayers might be the better heard. Thus also Noah, after quitting the ark, built an altar on the mountain where it rested, and made a burnt-offering, whose smoke ascending to heaven was pleasing to the Lord.[152] And Abraham was commanded to offer his only son Isaac on a mountain in the land of Moria; and Balak carried Balaam to the top of Mount Pisgah to offer a sacrifice there, and to curse Israel. Thus, indeed, all nations in their infancy adopted the natural idea of paying adoration to Heaven from high places.

The large stones, or the heaps of stones, that have been appropriated for religious uses at different times, in almost every part of the world, might have been introduced, as Lord Kames supposes, from the custom among savage nations to mark with a great stone the place where their worthies were interred: that such worthies being at length deified, in the superstitious notions of their votaries, the stones that were dedicated to their memory became essential in every act of religious worship performed in honour of their new deities. The very particular homage, that for time immemorial has been paid to the memory of the dead by the Chinese, renders the above explanation extremely probable as to the origin of their altar of four stones which in their language are called *Tan*, and which in former times were erected on most of their high mountains; and it is singular enough that, at the present day, the *tan* should be represented, upon many of the altars erected in their temples, by four loose stones placed on the four corners of the altar, as the horns were in the corners of the Jewish altars. When population increased, and the people were spread wide over the empire, the inconvenience of ascending any particular mountain must necessarily be felt, and the *tan* was then transferred to places that were better suited for general accommodation. The same idea indeed is still retained in our[453] churches, the *altar* and *high place* being synonimous words. In the city of Pekin, which stands on a sandy plain, the *tien-tan*, or altar of Heaven; the *tee-tan* or altar of earth; and the *sien-nong-tan* or altar of ancient agriculturists, are erected upon artificial mounts within the walls of the palace; and here the Emperor continues, to this day, to sacrifice at appointed times, exclusively, as the son of Heaven, and the only being on earth worthy to intercede for his people. The same doctrine prevailed in the time of Confucius, who observes, that the distance between the all-creative power, or cause of all things, and the people is so immeasurably great, that the king or ruler, as high priest, can alone offer such a sacrifice; and that this power is best satisfied when man performs the moral duties of life; the principal of which he makes to consist in filial piety, and unlimited obedience to the will of the prince.

His religious notions and morals do him great credit, but his metaphysics are so obscure as not to be intelligible which, however, may partly be owing to the nature of the language. In his writings appears a strong predilection for a kind of fortune-telling, or predicting events by the mystical lines of *Fo-shee*. By the help of these lines, and the prevailing element at the commencement of the reign of a prince, he pretended to foretel the events that would take place and the length of its continuance; but, at the same time, he was cautious enough to wrap them up in such ambiguous and mysterious expressions that, like most prophecies of the kind, they might admit of a variety of interpretations. This manner of expounding the lines of Fo-shee by Confucius, the supposed system of binary[454] arithmetic by Leibnitz, laid the foundation of consulting future destiny, at this day universally sought after by the Chinese[43].

Predestination in all ages, and in all nations, has formed one of the leading features of religion; and, in consideration perhaps of popular opinion, has been foisted into the articles of the Christian faith, though unwarranted by any passage in the holy scriptures. It is a doctrine little calculated for the promotion of good morals, and still less so for conveying spiritual consolation. The Chinese, however, confine the influence of lots to the events of this life. It would perhaps be doing injustice to the understanding of Confucius to suppose, that he really believed in the doctrine of fatality. Being prime minister of one of the kings of China, it was necessary for him to act the politician as [455]well as the philosopher; and he could not fail to know, that the superstitions of the people were among the best supports of the government. He might have been aware of the folly and absurdity of such a doctrine, and yet found it prudent to enforce the observance of it; just as the Greeks thought proper to continue their *Lots*. These, instead of sticks, as used by the Chinese, were three stones that, according to some, were first discovered and presented to Pallas by the nymphs, the daughters of Jupiter, who rejected an offering that rather belonged to Apollo, and threw them away;—an excellent moral, observes Doctor Tytler, the learned translator of the hymns and epigrams of Callimachus, shewing that those persons who are guided by Pallas, or Wisdom, will improve the present time, without being too anxious to pry into futurity. The Greek poet, however, like the Chinese philosopher, ascribed to the possessor of the Lots, the talent of reading future destiny.

"By him the sure events of Lots are given;
By him the prophet speaks the will of Heaven."TYTLER.

The Romans had also their lots to determine future events, which were a kind of wooden dice, and their priests examined the marks and interpreted the signification of the throw. And the ancient Germans, according to Tacitus, made use of little sticks, notched at the ends which, like the Chinese, they threw three times in case they did not approve of the first throw. Herodotus traces the custom of predicting future events to the ancient Egyptians, and seems to think the Greeks had it from them. But is not the desire of prying into futu[456]rity to be ascribed rather to a weakness in human nature, than as a custom borrowed by one nation from another? Are we entirely free from it in modern Europe? However humiliating the reflection may be, yet it is certainly true, that men of the strongest minds and soundest judgments have sometimes, towards the close of an useful life, devoted their time to the exposition of old prophecies without meaning, or applicable only to events that were already in train to be accomplished when the prediction was made. Among many others, the great *Napier*, the inventor of logarithms, might be produced as an instance of this remark. From the Apocalypse of Saint John he predicted the day of judgment; but his calculations in this instance not being founded on *data* equally solid with those on which he constructed his tables, he unfortunately survived the day he had named to blush at his own weakness.

Other parts of the doctrine of Confucius were well calculated to keep alive the superstitious notions that still prevail among the multitude. He taught them to believe that the human body was composed of two principles, the one light, invisible, and ascending; the other gross, palpable, and descending; that the separation of these two principles cause the death of man; that at this awful period the light and spiritual part of the human body ascends into the air, whilst the gross and corporeal matter sinks into the earth. The word *death*, in fact, never enters into the philosophy of Confucius; nor, indeed, on common occasions is it employed by the Chinese at the present day. When a person departs this life, the common expression is, *he has returned to his family.* And although the body re[457]solves itself in the course of time into its primitive elements, and becomes a part of the universe; yet, he contended, the spirits of such as had performed their duty in life were permitted to visit their ancient habitations, or such places as might be appointed for receiving the homage of their descendants, on whom they had the power of conferring benefactions. On this ground it became the indispensable duty of every good man to observe a strict obedience of the performance of sacred rites in the temple consecrated to the memory of ancestors. He maintained that all such as neglected this great branch of moral duty would be punished for their neglect, after death, by their spiritual part being deprived of the privilege of visiting the hall of ancestors; and, consequently, of the pleasure arising from the homage bestowed by their descendants. Such a system could not fail to establish a belief in good and evil genii, and of tutelar spirits presiding over families, towns, cities, houses, mountains, and other particular places. It afterwards required no great stretch of the imagination to give to these "airy nothings a local habitation and a name."

It does not appear, however, that either Confucius or any of his disciples attached the least idea of a *personal being* to the deity; nor does it seem ever to have entered into their minds to represent the *great first cause* under any image or personification. They considered the sun, moon, stars and the elements, with the azure firmament, as the creative and productive powers, the immediate agents of the Deity and inseparably connected with him, and they offered adoration to these agents, united in one word *tien* (Heaven). It cannot be supposed, after what[458] has already been observed in the sixth chapter, that I should lay any stress on the similarity of words in different languages, or on the analogy of their signification, in order to prove a common origin; but if the conjecture of the learned Bos be right, that Θεος may be derived from Θεειν to move forward, in allusion to the motion of the heavenly bodies which the ancient Greeks, as well as the Persians, worshipped, *tien* certainly comes very near the Greek both in sound and signification; nearer it could not come in sound, as the Chinese by no effort could pronounce the Θ *th*. The word *tien* not only signifies *heaven*, but a revolution of the heavenly bodies, and is in common use both in writing and conversation for *day*, as *ye, ul, san tien*, one, two, three days.

The Confucionists, like the Stoics, seem to have considered the whole universe as one animated system, made up of one material substance and one spirit, of which every living thing was an emanation, and to which, when separated by death from the material part it had animated, every living thing again returned. In a word, their conceptions of the Deity might be summed up in those two beautiful and expressive lines of Pope,

"All are but parts of one stupendous whole,
Whose body nature is, and God the soul."

But that which is most surprizing is, that the enthusiastic followers of Confucius have never erected any statue to his memory, nor paid him divine honours as erroneously has been supposed. In every city is a public building, a kind of college,[459] wherein examinations are held for degrees of office, and this building is called the house of Confucius. Here, on certain appointed days, the men of letters assemble to pay respect to the memory of their esteemed philosopher. In the great hall appropriated for this ceremony a plain tablet is erected, on which is painted an inscription, in gilt characters, to this effect: "O *Cong-foo-tse*, our revered master, let thy spiritual part descend and be pleased with this our respect which we now humbly offer to thee!" Fruit and wine, flowers, perfumes and other articles are then placed before the tablet, during which are also burning various kinds of scented gums, frankincense, tapers of sandal wood and gilt paper. This ceremony, which in every respect is the same to that which he taught as an observance towards the manes of departed relations, they are persuaded is agreeable to the invisible spirits of those to whom it is offered, who delight in hovering over the grateful odour of flowers, of fruit, and the smoke of incense. Thus, in like manner, did the Romans on their birth-days offer flowers and fruit and wine, and burn incense to invisible spirits, whom they called the *genii*,

"Funde merum genio."

"Fill a glass to Genius."

But the priests, who, in all ages and in most nations, have been crafty enough to turn to their own account the credulity and superstitions of the people, having once established as a religious duty the offering of sweet-smelling herbs and other perfumes, found little difficulty in persuading the multitude, that [460] that the tutelar spirits could eat as well as smell, and that sacrifices and meat-offerings would be acceptable to the gods. The priests of China lost no time in introducing sacrifices, even of living creatures, and offerings of corn and rice and wine and precious metals upon their altars, not however to that extent which was practised in the temples of Greece and Rome, whose gods were the most mercenary of all nations, being rarely induced to grant a favour without a fee. Nor in modern days have the monks and priests of the Catholic faith been backward in this respect particularly in sanctioning the doctrine of *composition for sins*, for the absolution of which the rate was not even fixed in proportion to the magnitude; and what is still more astonishing, this impious practice of bargaining with the Almighty has survived the dark ages, and exists to a certain degree at this moment.

The moral and religious opinions of Confucius were, in fact, too sublime and too metaphysical to preserve their purity among a people so unprepared, as his countrymen were, to receive and cherish them. The attention of the multitude would seem, indeed, in all nations to require being fixed on something gross and material. How difficult was it for the priest and the leader of the Jews, to restrain their people from practices of idolatry. In the short absence even of Moses on Mount Sinai, they made for themselves a molten calf of gold as an object of divine worship, in imitation, probably, of what they had beheld in the temples of Egypt. The invisible god made little impression on their gross and untutored understandings. Nor was Numa more successful than Moses or Confucius, in his attempt to esta [461] blish among the people the worship of an ideal or mental object of adoration. Thus also it happened with the Chinese. The sublime conceptions of their great philosopher, too refined indeed for untutored human nature, they could not comprehend. They required some visible object on which they might fix their attention. It was not enough merely to imagine that the spirits of men, who had done their duty in this life, were permitted to haunt the places where their bodies were interred, or where their surviving friends should assemble to do them honour: it was necessary to give them a form and substance. In the same manner was the purity of the Christian religion contaminated by the multitude of images that were invented in the monkish ages, when every city, town, and church, and even individuals, provided they could pay for them, had their particular patron, or tutelar saint.

Like the temples of Confucius, those of the ancient Egyptians are supposed to have been entirely free from statues; and Herodotus seems to be of opinion, that Hesiod and Homer were the first who introduced the genealogy of the gods among the Greeks; imposed names upon each, assigned their functions and their honours, and clothed them in their several forms. And we learn from Silius Italicus, that the ancient temple of Hercules at Gades had no visible type of the Deity.

"Sed nulla effigies, simulacrave nota deorum,
Majestate locum, et sacro implevere timore."

"No statues of the gods appear within,
Nor images; but rev'rend horror round,

And gloom majestic guard the sacred ground."

TYTLER'S MS.

The missionaries in their writings have endeavoured to impress[462] the world with an idea that the Chinese, and particularly the Confucionists, are atheists; that they disbelieve in a future state of existence; and that they are the victims of a senseless superstition. Nothing can be more unjust than such an accusation. Could *Caung-shee* be an atheist, when he inscribed with his own hands the Jesuit church in Pekin,

"To the only true principle of all things," &c.

And can a people be justly accused of a disbelief in a state of future existence, when the whole nation, of what sect soever, presents its offerings at stated seasons to the *spirits* of its departed ancestors? Does the ejaculation, "Let thy spiritual part descend and be pleased with this our respect which we now humbly offer to thee!" convey any such supposition? And of all others, the missionaries ought to have been the last to accuse the Chinese of senseless superstitions. Surely it is not more repugnant to reason, nor less consonant with human feelings, to offer grateful gifts to the manes of deceased parents and friends, than to fall down before the Virgin Mary and the thousand saints whom caprice or cabal have foisted into their calendar, and of whose history and actions even their votaries are totally ignorant? Chinese superstition, in this respect is, to say the worst of it, an amiable weakness. If the supposition be allowed that beings who have departed this life may possess an influence over remaining mortals, it is surely more natural to address those whose care and kindness had already been felt, than those of whom we have no further knowledge than the name. There is perhaps no stronger incentive to virtuous[163] actions, nor a more effectual check against vicious pursuits, than the idea that the departed spirit of a beloved parent may continue to watch over and direct our conduct. The Chinese, at all events, are not illiberal in their superstitions: they made not the least difficulty in allowing the corpse of one of our artists, who died at *Tong-tchoo*, though a Christian and consequently in their opinion a heretic, to be deposited in the midst of their public burying ground. With as little reason does an angry missionary complain of the dresses and ceremonies of their priests, as they certainly borrowed nothing from the Catholics, who, on their part, are much indebted to the heathen Greeks for a great part of the paraphernalia of their own religion. "There is no country," says he, "where the devil has so successfully counterfeited the true worship of the holy church. These priests of the infernal spirit wear long loose gowns, exactly resembling those of some of the fathers of the church; they live in temples like so many monasteries, and they chaunt in the same manner as with us."

Another religion, much better calculated to gain popularity, sprung up about the time of, or very shortly after, the death of Confucius. A man of the name of *Lao-Kung*, having travelled into Thibet, became in part acquainted with the worship of the priests of Lama, which he thought would suit his countrymen, and might also be the means of raising his own reputation. He accordingly established a sect, under the name of *Tao-tze*, or "Sons of Immortals." He maintained, like Epicurus, that to live at his ease and to make himself happy were the chief concerns of man: that, to seize the present moment,[464] regardless of the past and of that to come, was the business of life,

"Carpe diem, quàm minimum credula postero."

"——Swift the fleeting pleasure seize,
Nor trust to-morrow's doubtful light."

But as ills would come, and disease and death seemed to be the common lot of mankind, the beverage of immortal life was a glorious idea to hold out to mortal man. In fact, immortality was one of the attributes of the *Delai Lama*, who is supposed never to die; the soul of the reigning Lama passing immediately into the person of his successor. This doctrine, a branch of the Metempsycosis, was converted by *Lao-Kung* into the art of producing a renovation of the faculties in the same body, by the means of certain preparations taken from the three kingdoms of nature. The infatuated people flew with avidity to the fountain of life. Princes even sought after the draughts that should render them immortal, but which, in fact, brought on premature death. Numerous instances are said to be on record, wherein the eunuchs have prevailed on the sovereign to swallow the immortal liquor which seldom failed to dispatch him. Father Trigault, who was in Pekin when the Tartars took possession of it, speaking of the propensity of the upper classes for the beverage of life, observes, "Even in this city, there are few of the magistrates or eunuchs or others in office free from this insanity; and as there are plenty who wish to learn the secret, there is no want of professors." This seems to be the only species of alchemy to which the Jesuits have said the Chinese are addicted. The preparation of the [465] liquor of life is their philosopher's stone; and, in all probability, is composed of opium and other drugs which, by encreasing the stimulus, gives a momentary exhilaration to the spirits; and the succeeding languor requiring another and another draught till at length, the excitability being entirely exhausted, the patient "puts on immortality."

How much soever we may find ourselves disposed to censure the absurdity of the Chinese beverage of life, we are not a great way behind them in this respect, or the *Perkinses*, the *Solomons*, the *Velnos*, and the *Brodums*, with an innumerable host of quacks, whose indecent advertisements disgrace our daily prints, would not derive their subsistence, much less rise to affluence, by the credulity of Englishmen; for many of these pests of society are foreigners, too contemptible in their own country to meet with encouragement. What conclusion would a Chinese be apt to draw of our national character, if he had only a smattering of our language, just sufficient to enable him to read these daily effusions that are forced upon public notice[44]? And what must he think of the reveries of Condorcet, and of his English disciples, whose monstrous doctrines (under the abused name of philosophy) would persuade him that sleep was a disease! That

"Sleep, that knits up the ravell'd sleave of care,
The death of each day's life, fore labour's bath,
Balm of hurt minds, great nature's second course,
Chief nourisher in life's feast"——

[466]

was a bodily infirmity, which the *perfectibility of the human mind* (so happily commenced by the French subversion) would completely eradicate! Let us not altogether condemn the ignorant, perhaps designing, priests of *Tao-tse*, and the still more ignorant multitude, when the strong and enlightened mind of a *Descartes* could amuse itself with the fanciful hope of being able to discover the secret of prolonging the life of man far beyond the usual limits which seem to be assigned to the human species.

Consistent with the principle of "taking no thought for the morrow," the priests of *Lao-Kung* devoted themselves to a state of celibacy, as being more free from cares than the incumbrances which necessarily attend a family connexion; and the better to accomplish this end, they associated in convents. Here they deal out to their votaries the decrees of the oracle agreeably to the rules prescribed by Confucius; and they practice also a number of incantations, magic, invocations of spirits, and other mystical rites that are probably as little understood by themselves as by the gazing multitude. In performing these magic tricks they march in procession round the altar, on which the sacred flame is supposed to be kept perpetually burning, being a composition of wax and tallow mixed up with sandal wood shavings and other perfumes; they chaunt in unison a kind of recitative, and they bow their heads obsequiously every time they pass before the front of the altar. The great *Gong* is struck at intervals, accompanied by tinkling sounds emitted by gently striking small metal plates suspended in a frame as in the plate of musical instruments. Their temples are crowded with large and monstrous figures, some made of wood, some of stone, and others of baked clay daubed over [467] with paint and varnish, and sometimes gilt. To such figures however they do not seem to pay any kind of homage. They are intended merely to represent the good and evil genii under the various passions to which human nature is liable. The good genii, or pleasing affections, are placed on one side of the temple, and their opposites on the other. Thus the personifications of mirth and melancholy, love and hatred, pleasure and pain, are contrasted together. The conditions of men are also represented, and their figures opposed to one another. In this light at least they appeared to us; though the priest at *Tong-tchoo* informed us they were intended to pourtray the different characters of the monks that had belonged to the monastery. In some temples also are met with the statues of such Emperors or ministers of state as had shewn themselves favourable to any particular convent. If, for instance, a great man should occupy the apartments of a temple and at his departure leave a considerable sum of money, the priests, out of gratitude, would place his image in a niche of the temple. In looking into one of these edifices a stranger would be apt to conclude that they were Polytheists, which I do not understand to be the case. Like the saints of the Catholics the great *Fo*, of whom I shall presently speak, with *Poo-sa*, *Shing-moo*, and many others, are considered only in the light of agents and intercessors, or as emanations of one creating, destroying, and renovating power, whose good providence has divided itself into a number of attributes for the better government of the universe[45].

Next to this religion of the immortals, was introduced another[468] of nearly the same growth which, from being patronized by the court, soon became no less popular than the former. The priests of *Fo*, coming by invitation from India, imported with them a great portion of the Hindu mythology, which some learned men have supposed to be the origin from whence the Polytheism of Egypt and Greece had its source; and others the direct contrary. Be that as it may, the affinity seems to be too strong not to ascribe them to a common parent; and the representations and the histories of many of the gods of these nations were imported, in all probability, with the religion of *Fo*, from India into China. This will better appear by comparing a few as they are observed in the different nations.

The *Budha* of the Hindus was the son of *Ma ya*, and one of his epithets is *Amita*: the *Fo* of China was the son of *Mo-ya*, and one of his epithets is *Om-e-to*; and, in Japan, whose natives are of Chinese origin, the same god *Fo* is worshipped under the name of *Amida*. I could neither collect from any of the Chinese what the literal meaning was of *Om-e-to*, nor could I decypher the characters under which it is written, but it appeared to be used as a common ejaculation on most occasions, just as we Europeans are too apt to make a familiar and impious use of the name of God. Perhaps it might not seem inconsistent in considering it to be derived from the Hindu mystic word *Om*.[469]

Since the accession of the Tartar princes to the throne of China, the court religion, or at least the Tartar part of the court, which before adhered to the tenets of Confucius, has been that of *Fo* or *Budha*. The priests are numerous, mostly dressed in yellow gowns, live in a state of celibacy in large convents or temples, which the Chinese call *Poo-ta-la*, evidently derived from *Budha-laya*, or habitation of *Budha*, this name being adopted by the Tartars, which the Chinese have been under the necessity of following as nearly as their organs of speech would admit. They wear a sort of chapelet round their necks, consisting of a number of beads. In some of their ceremonies they march, like the *Tao-tses*, in procession round the altar, counting their beads, repeating at every bead *Om-e-to-fo*, and respectfully bowing the head. The whole string being finished, they chalk up a mark, registering in this manner the number of their ejaculations to *Fo*. This counting of their beads was one of the ceremonies that very much exasperated the missionaries.

The *Ganesa* of the Hindus, the *Janus* of the Romans, and the *Men-shin*, or guardian spirit of the door of the Chinese, are obviously one and the same deity. Sometimes he is painted with a club in one hand, and a key in the other, representing the protector of the house. On almost every door in China, where the inhabitants profess the religion of *Fo*, is drawn the figure of *Men-shin*, or otherwise the two characters of this word, agreeing exactly with what Sir William Jones has observed of the new town of Gayá in Hindostan, "that every new built house, agreeably to an immemorial usage of the Hindus, has the name of *Ganésa* superscribed on its door: and[470] in the old town his image is placed over the gates of the temples."

The *Vishnu* of the Hindus, riding on an eagle, and sometimes attended by an eagle, has been considered as the *Jupiter* of the Greeks; and the *Lui-shin* of the Chinese, or spirit of thunder, is figured under a man with the beak and talons of an eagle, sometimes surrounded with kettle drums, carrying in one hand a batoon and in the other a flame of fire. The *Osiris* of the Egyptians, from whence the Greeks had their *Jupiter*, comes still nearer to the *Lui-shin* of the Chinese. When represented as the emblem of the sun, he was drawn under the figure of a man with an eagle's beak, carrying in his hand a batoon on which was painted an eye. The ingenious and fertile imagination of the Greeks separated the emblem from the god, and made the bird of prey the attendant of the divinity, which the Egyptians and the Chinese united under one symbol. It is a curious coincidence of opinion, if it be not founded on fact, that the Chinese should assign the same reason for giving an eagle's face to their *Lui-shin*, that Pliny has for the consecration of that bird to *Jupiter*, namely, that no instance was ever known of an eagle being destroyed by lightning. The Chinese have also an observation with regard to this bird, which has been made by other nations, and which is, that the eagle, in a thunder storm, always mounts above the clouds.

The *Varuna* of the Hindus, riding on a fish, the *Neptune* of the Greeks, and the Chinese *Hai-vang*, or king of the sea,[471] reposing on the waves, with a fish in his hand, are unquestionably one and the same personage.

The giant *Briareus*, with his hundred hands, is truly in China of a most stupendous and colossal stature, being commonly from fifty to sixty feet in height, and sometimes as tall as eighty feet. But the largest of all their deities is a woman of the family of *Poo-sa*[46], apparently a personification of nature. This goddess is modelled in a variety of ways; sometimes she is to be found with four heads, and forty or fifty arms, the heads looking towards the four cardinal points of the compass, and each arm holding some natural product of the earth subservient to the use of man. Sometimes each arm produces several smaller arms, and on the head stands a pyramidal groupe of smaller heads. Van Braam mentions his having seen a statue of this goddess that was ninety feet high, having four heads and forty-four arms. It is no uncommon thing to meet with temples in ruins, in the midst of which these monstrous gods and goddesses are seen entire, exposed to the elements. It seems the inferior temples are generally upheld by the voluntary gifts of the people; and that, whenever any unusual calamity befals a town or village, such as severe famine, epidemic disease, inundations, or the like, whose dire effects cease not [472] on repeated applications to the protecting saint, by way of punishing the gods, they literally pull down the temple over their heads, and leave them sitting in the open air. The grotesque and barbarous manner of representing the manifold powers of nature, or the goddess of nature, by a plurality of heads and hands in one idol, is by no means favourable to the supposition of a refined or superior understanding in the people who adopt them into their religious worship. It can be considered only as a very short step beyond the conceptions of savages, who have no other idea than that of supplying by number, or a repetition of the same thing, what may be wanting in power. The same figure, with numerous arms, appears in the Hindu temples that are excavated out of solid granite mountains, the most ancient and among the most wonderful monuments of art and persevering labour that have hitherto been discovered on the face of the globe, the fountain perhaps from whence the arts, the sciences, and the religious mysteries of the Egyptians and the Greeks derived their origin.

But the most common of all the female deities in China is the *Shing-moo*, or holy mother, or rather the mother of *perfect intelligence*[47]. This lady is the exact counterpart of the Indian *Ganga* or goddess of the river, the *Isis* of the Egyptians, and the *Ceres* of the Greeks. Nothing shocked the missionaries so much on their first arrival in China as the image of this lady, in whom they discovered, or thought they discovered, the most striking resemblance to the Virgin Mary. They found her ge[473]nerally shut up with great care in a recess at the back part of the altar, and veiled with a silken screen to hide her from common observation; sometimes with a child in her hand, at other times on her knee, and a glory round her head. On hearing the story of the *Shing-moo* they were confirmed in this opinion. They were told that she conceived and bore a son while yet a virgin, by eating the flower of the *Lien-wha* (the *Nelumbium*) which she found lying upon her clothes on the bank of a river where she was bathing: that, when the time of her gestation was expired, she went to the place where she had picked up the flower and was there delivered of a boy; that the infant was found and educated by a poor fisherman; and, in process of time, became a great man and performed miracles. Such is her story, as told by the Chinese priests. When the image of this goddess is standing, she generally holds a flower of the Nelumbium in her hand; and when sitting, she is usually placed upon the large peltate leaf of the same plant.

The Egyptian Lotos, not that esculent plant from the use of which the *Lotophagi* had their name, but another of a very different genus consecrated to religious purposes, is said[48] to have been ascertained from a statue of *Osiris*, preserved in the Barberini palace at Rome, to be that species of water lilly which grows in abundance in most parts of the eastern world, and which was known to botanists under the name of *Nymphæa Nelumbo*; but I understand it is now considered as a new *genus*, distinguished under a modification of its former specific name, by that of *Nelumbium*. This plant, however, is no longer to be found in [174] Egypt. The two species that grow, at present, on the banks and canals of the Nile are totally different, which furnishes a very strong presumption that, although a sacred plant and cultivated in the country, it might nevertheless be of foreign growth. In China, few temples are without some representation of the Nelumbium; sometimes the *Shing-moo* is painted as standing upon its leaves in the midst of a lake. In one temple I observed the intelligent mother sitting upon the broad peltate leaf of this plant, which had been hewn out of the living rock. Sometimes she holds in her hand a cornucopia filled with the ears of rice, of millet, and of the capsule or seed-vessel of the Nelumbium, these being articles of food which fall to the share of the poorest peasant. This very beautiful water lilly grows spontaneously in almost every lake and morass, from the middle of Tartary to the province of Canton; a curious circumstance, when we consider the very great difficulty with which it can be preserved, even by artificial means, in climates of Europe, whose temperature are less warm and less cold than many of those where, in China, it grows in a state of nature, and with the greatest degree of luxuriance. On the heights of Tartary it is found in an uncultivated state where, in winter, the thermometer frequently stands at, and generally far below, the freezing point. But here the roots strike at the bottom of very deep waters only, a circumstance from which we may perhaps conclude, that the plant may rather require uniformity of temperature, than any extraordinary degree either one way or other. Not only the seed of the Nelumbium, which is a kind of nut nearly as large as an acorn, but the long roots, jointed like [175] canes, furnish articles of food for the table. In the capital, during the whole summer season, the latter are sliced and laid on ice, and in this state serve as part of the desert; the taste differs very little from that of a good juicy turnip, with a slight degree of astringency.

There is something so very striking and remarkable in this plant, that it is not surprizing the Egyptians and the Indians, fond of drawing allusions from natural objects, should have considered it as emblematic of creative power. The leaves of the succeeding plant are found involved in the middle of the seed, perfect, and of a beautiful green. When the sun goes down, the large leaves that spread themselves over the surface of the water close like an umbrella, and the returning sun gradually unfolds them. Now, as these nations considered water to be the primary element, and the first medium on which creative influence began to act, a plant of such singularity, luxuriance, utility and beauty, could not fail to be regarded by them as a proper symbol for representing that creative power, and was accordingly consecrated by the former to *Osiris* and to *Isis*, the emblems of the sun and moon, and by the latter to *Ganga*, the river goddess, and to the sun. The coincidence of ideas between those two nations, in this respect, may be drawn from that beautiful Hindu hymn, addressed to Surya or the sun, and translated by Sir William Jones—

"Lord of the Lotos, father, friend and king,
O Sun! thy powers I sing."—&c.[49]

Whether the Chinese, like the Hindus, entertained the same[476] notions of creative power, or its influence upon water as the primary element, I could not learn. No information as to the ground-work of their religion is to be looked for from the priests of the present day, who are generally very ignorant; but I suspect the dedication of the Lotos to sacred uses to be much older than the introduction of Hindu mythology by the priests of Budha. They even ascribe the fable of eating the flower to the mother of their first Emperor *Foo-shee*; and the Lotos and the lady are equally respected by all the sects in China; and even by the Mantchoo Tartars, whose history commences with the identical story of a young virgin conceiving and bearing a son, who was to be the progenitor of a race of conquerors, by eating the flower of a water lilly. If, indeed, any dependence is to be placed on the following well known inscription found on an ancient monument of Osiris, Egyptian rites may be supposed to have made their way into the east and probably into China, or, on the other hand, those of the east adopted by the Egyptians, at a period of very remote antiquity. "Saturn, the youngest of all the gods, was my father. I am Osiris, who conducted a large and numerous army as far as the deserts of India, and travelled over the greatest part of the world, &c. &c."

It may not, perhaps, be thought improbable (I offer it, however, merely as conjecture) that the story of *Osiris* and *Isis*[477] was known in China at a very early period of the history of this country. *Osiris*, king of Egypt, and husband of *Isis*, was worshipped under the form of an ox, from his having paid particular attention to the pursuits of agriculture, and from employing this animal in the tillage of the ground.

"Primus aratra manu solerti fecit Osiris."
Osiris first constructed ploughs with dext'rous skill.

Historians say, that *Isis*, on the murder of her husband, enjoined the priests of Egypt, by a solemn oath, to establish a form of worship in which divine honours should be paid to their deceased prince; that they should select what kind of animal they pleased to represent the person and the divinity of *Osiris*, and that they should inter it with solemn funeral honours when dead. In consideration of this apotheosis, she allotted a portion of land to each sacerdotal body. The priests were obliged to make a vow of chastity; their heads were shaven and they went barefooted. Divine honours were likewise conferred on *Isis* after her death, and she was worshipped under the form of a cow.

Now, although the festival in China, at which the Emperor holds the plough in the commencement of the spring, be considered at this day as nothing more than a political institution, and continued as an example to the lower orders of people, an incitement for them to pursue the labours of agriculture as the most important employment in the state;— yet, as this condescension of the sovereign militates so strongly against all their maxims of government, which place an immense distance be[478]tween him and the first of his people, it may not, perhaps, be much amiss in supposing it to have originated in some religious opinion. Indeed he still continues to prepare himself for the solemn occasion, by devoting three days entirely to pious ceremonies and rigid devotion. On the day appointed by the tribunal of mathematics, a *cow* is sacrificed in the *Tee-tan*, or temple dedicated to the earth; and on the same day, in some of the provinces, the figure of a cow of baked clay, of an immense size, is carried in procession by a number of the peasantry, followed by the principal officers of government and the other inhabitants. The horns and the hoofs are gilded and ornamented with silken ribbons. The prostrations being made and the offerings placed on the altar, the earthen cow is broken in pieces and distributed among the people. In like manner the body of *Osiris*, worshipped afterwards under the form of an ox, was distributed by *Isis* among the priests; and the *Isia*[50] were long celebrated in Egypt in the same manner as the festival of holding the plough is at this day observed in China, both being intended, no doubt, to commemorate the persons [479]who had rendered the most solid advantages to the state, by the encouragement they had held out for the cultivation of the ground.

The disputes, quarrels, persecutions and massacres, that have happened at various times among the different sects of Christianity in Europe, have not been much less violent, nor productive of less dreadful consequences, between the sect of immortals and that of Fo, in China, whenever the court, or rather the intriguing eunuchs, seemed to favour the opinions of one sect in preference to those of the other. Persecutions never failed to begin whenever either party was fortunate enough to gain over to its side the chief of the eunuchs, who had always sufficient influence with the reigning monarch to prevail upon him to espouse the same cause. They were, however, wars of priests alone in which the people remained neutral, or took no active part. Whole monasteries have been levelled with the ground, and thousands of priests put to death on both sides. Since, however, the accession of the present Tartar dynasty, they have met with no particular marks of favour or distinction; and, on that account, are apparently reconciled to each other; indeed, they are scarcely distinguishable either by their temples or by their dress. The prediction of future events being best suited to the minds of the multitude, and most sought after, the oracle of fate may be consulted in any temple, whether of *Fo* or of *Tao-tze*. The government interferes not in religious opinions, and it gives no support to any particular sect, except that of the Lama, whose priests are paid and maintained as a part of the[180] Imperial establishment.

The Tartar officers of state are likewise attached to the faith of the Lama, without the absurdities that have been mixed with it by the immortals.

However strictly the women may be kept at home by the customs of the country, they are nevertheless permitted, on certain occasions, to consult their destiny at the altar, without being exposed to the censure of vulgarity or impropriety. Barren wives are even encouraged to visit the temples, not so much for the purpose of knowing their destiny, as under a firm belief that, by rubbing the bellies of certain little copper gods, they shall conceive and bear children. But, the women in general who, from habit, feel little inclination to stir abroad, except on very pressing occasions, encourage a set of fortune-tellers, mountebanks and jugglers, who thus pick up a livelihood by travelling the country and telling fortunes from house to house. They are known by a wretched squalling flute on which they play, and are beckoned to call where their art is required. By being made acquainted with the day and hour of a person's birth, they pretend to *cast his nativity*, which is called *Swan-ming*, or the art of discovering events by means of numbers. A Chinese, even in the higher ranks, has no great idea of a man's learning, if he be ignorant of the *Swan-ming*. I was very frequently applied to at *Yuen-min-yuen*, by persons in office, to know if I could tell them their fortune; and it was difficult to persuade them I had any knowledge of the astronomical instruments intended for the Emperor, after professing my ignorance in *casting a nativity*.[48.1]

The priests of both sects are supposed to be no less attentive in keeping up a perpetual fire burning upon the altars than the Roman Vestals were in this respect; but no expiation nor punishment being considered necessary, as in the latter case, they cannot boast that "flames unextinguish'd on their altars shine." They are, in fact, frequently extinguished by carelessness or accident. No virgins attend this holy flame, but the charge of it is committed generally to young boys under training for the priesthood. Like the Greeks and the Romans, the Chinese have also their penates or household gods, which are not represented under any particular personification, but generally by a tablet bearing a short inscription and a taper burning before it. Every ship, however small, has its tablet and its taper; and within the compass-box or binnacle a taper is continually kept burning.

In every city, town and village, sometimes in the midst of woods, in the mountains and most lonely places, are small temples, the doors of which are continually left open for the admittance of such as may be desirous of consulting their destiny. The practical part of Chinese religion may, in fact, be said to consist in predestination. A priest is not at all necessary for unravelling the book of fate. If any one be about to undertake a journey, or to purchase a wife, or to build a house, or, above all, to bury a deceased relation, and any doubt should arise in his mind as to the fortunate result of such undertaking, he repairs to the nearest temple; and, if he should not be able to read himself, he takes a friend by the hand who can. On the altar of every temple is placed a wooden cup, filled with a[48.2] number of small sticks, marked at the extremities with certain characters. Taking the cup in his hands he shakes it till one of the sticks falls upon the ground and, having examined the character upon it, he looks for the corresponding mark in a book which is generally appended to the wall of the temple. The lot, in this manner, is cast several times, and if one lucky flick in three should happen to turn up, he is willing to consider the omen as favourable; and, if the event should answer the expectation he has been led to form from the book of fate, he considers it as a duty to return to the temple and to burn a sheet or two of painted paper, or of paper covered with tin foil, and to deposit a few pieces of copper money on the altar, in token of gratitude for the favour he has received[52]. In this manner is consumed the greatest part of the tin that is carried[18.3] to China by the trading companies of Europe. I have already observed that they have no communion of worship to offer up, in a public manner, their prayers or thanksgivings.

Formerly it was the custom to bury slaves with emperors and princes and sometimes also their concubines alive; but this cruel practice has given way, in modern times, to the more harmless one of burning representations of their domestics in tin foil, cut into the shape of human beings, and of placing their statues in wood or stone upon their graves; this seems to be the remains of a Scythian or Tartar custom, which, according to Herodotus, was commonly observed at the funerals of their sovereigns, when their horses, their slaves, and their concubines were impaled alive and placed in order round the tyrant's tomb. The last

162

remains of a relation are interred with all the honours that the family can afford. I never passed between the capital and *Yuen-min-yuen* without observing numbers of funeral processions. Those of great officers of state would sometimes extend for nearly half a mile. The train was usually arranged in the following order. In front marched a priest uncovered, next a group of musicians with flutes, trumpets, and cymbals; after these the male relations of the deceased in long white frocks and behind them the chief mourner, supported by two friends, whose exertions to prevent him from tearing his cheeks and hair appeared to be truly ridiculous. Then followed the coffin, covered by a magnificent canopy and borne generally by four men, sometimes by eight. After the canopy the female relations proceeded in chairs, or more generally in the[484] little covered carts, wearing white frocks like the men, their hair dishevelled, and broad white fillets bound across their foreheads. On approaching a bridge or a temple the procession always halted while the priest burned little images of tin foil, or let off a few crackers, upon which the noisy *gong* and the rest of the band made a flourish.

The famous feast of lanterns, when the whole empire is lighted up from one extremity to the other, in every possible way that fancy can suggest, is an ancient religious usage of which, at the present day, they can give no plausible account. It is just possible that, among other Egyptian ceremonies, this may be one derived from a common origin with an annual illumination of the same kind mentioned by Herodotus; which was generally observed, from the cataracts of the Nile to the borders of the Mediterranean, by hanging lamps of different kinds to the sides of the houses. On this day the Chinese not only illuminate their houses, but they also exercise their ingenuity in making transparencies in the shape of different animals, with which they run through the streets by night. The effect when perfectly dark is whimsical enough. Birds, beasts, fishes, and other animals are seen darting through the air, and contending with each other; some with squibs in their mouths, breathing fire, and others with crackers in their tails: some sending out sky-rockets, others rising into pyramids of party-coloured fire, and others bursting like a mine with violent explosions. But the most ingenious are those that, Proteus-like, change their shape from time to time, and under every form exhibit a different display of fire-works.[485]

I have observed, at the beginning of this chapter, that the temples are occasionally appropriated to the use of state-officers, embassadors and other public characters, when travelling through the country, there being no other houses affording accommodations equally suitable. On quitting the temple it is generally thought necessary to perform an act of reverence bordering on devotion, not however to the Deity, but to the name of the Emperor inscribed on the altar. This custom, together with that of depositing rice and other grain, tea and oil at certain seasons, especially on the day of his nativity, although perhaps, in the first instance, a token only of respect and gratitude, and in the other an acknowledgment of his being the sole proprietary of the soil, are nevertheless acts that tend, from the sanctity of the place where they are performed, to the encouragement of idolatry. By thus associating the offerings made to the Deity and to the Monarch, the vulgar become apt to magnify the power of the latter and to raise it on a level with that of the former. A Chinese in speaking of a propitious event occurring, either in his own or any other country, generally attributes it to the joint Will of Heaven and the Emperor of China.

The conversion of the temples into lodging-houses is attended with some temporal advantages to the priests, by the donations that are generally made on such occasions. Most of them being supported entirely by voluntary contributions and trifling legacies that may be left by pious persons, they are thankful for the smallest gifts: for as there is little or no connection between the church and the state, they derive no pay, nor[486] emolument, nor preferment from the latter. The Emperor pays his own priests, which are those of all his Tartar subjects; the Chinese Confucionists, or men of learning, and the state officers contribute to the maintenance of theirs, whether of *Fo* or *Tao-tze*, and the mass of the people, from the prevailing propensity of enquiring into futurity, afford the means of support to many thousands, I might perhaps say millions of priests, by the offerings carried to the altars whenever they find it necessary to consult the book of fate, which is done on most of the common occurrences in life.

From the short view I have here taken of the different sects, I think it may justly be concluded that the primitive religion of China no longer exists, or exists only in a corrupted state; that there is at present no national nor scarcely a state religion: and that the articles of faith are as various as the modes of worship; in all of which the people appear to be rather actuated by the dread of evil in this life, than by the fear of punishment in another: that the duties they perform are more with a view to appease an angry deity and to avert impending calamities, than from any hope of obtaining a positive good: that they rather consult or enquire of their gods what may happen, than petition them to accomplish or avert it; for a Chinese can scarcely be said to pray; he is grateful when the event proves favourable to his wishes; petulant and peevish with his gods when adverse.

Little as the priests, or the numerous noviciates that are found in all the principal temples, are employed in the duties| 187 | of their office, or in worldly concerns, they are not less uncleanly in their persons and their apartments than those are whose time is taken up in providing for the necessities of life. The room, in which some of us *should* have slept, was so full of scorpions and scolopendras, and they crept in such numbers into our beds, that we were fairly driven out and obliged to swing our cots in the open air between two trees. Here we were not much less annoyed by myriads of musquitoes and the unceasing noise of the chirping cicadas, which continued without intermission until the still more noisy *gong*announced the break of day, and summoned the holy men to their morning devotions.

CHAP. IX.

Journey from Tong-choo-foo to the Province of Canton—Face of the Country, and its Productions.—Buildings and other Public Works.—Condition of the People—State of Agriculture.—Population.

Attentions paid to the Embassy—Observations on the Climate and Plains of Pe-tche-lee—Plants of—Diet and Condition of the People.—Burying-place—Observation on Chinese Cities—Trackers of the Yachts—Entrance of the Grand Canal.—The Fishing Corvorant—Approach to the Yellow River—Ceremony of crossing this River.—Observations on Canals and Roads—Improvements of the Country in advancing to the Southward—Beauty of, near Sau-choo-foo—Bridge of ninety-one Arches—Country near Hang-choo-foo.—City of—Appearance of the Country near the Po-yang Lake.—Observations in Proceeding through Kiang-see.—The Camellia Sesanqua—Retrospective View of the Climate and Produce, Diet and Condition of the People, of Pe-tche-lee—Some Observations on the Capital of China—Province of Shan-tung—Of Kiang-nan.—Observations of the State of Agriculture in China—Rice Mills—Province of Tche-kiang.—Of Kiang-see.—Population of China compared with that of England—Erroneous Opinions entertained on this Subject.—Comparative Population of a City in China and in England—Famines accounted for.—Means of Prevention.—Causes of Populousness of China.

ON the 8th of October we embarked, for the second time, on| 188| the Pei-ho in yachts, however, that were very different from those on which we had ascended the river, being much smaller but broader in proportion to their length, and so shallow and| 489| flat-bottomed, that they required little depth of water; yet we found them sufficiently commodious. Of the necessity of such a change in the accommodation yachts, on account of the low state of the river, we were speedily convinced, which, previous to our embarkation, had been by some attributed to a different cause. It was supposed that the men in office throughout the country, piqued at the refusal of the Embassador to submit to their degrading ceremony, would not fail to retaliate the affront by depriving us of every little comfort and convenience, and by otherwise rendering the long journey before us extremely unpleasant. The character of the people at large justified such a conclusion; and, I believe, every individual had laid his account of meeting with difficulties and disagreeable occurrences on the journey to Canton. In justice, however, to those who had the superintendence of the embassy, and particularly to the two most worthy characters *Van* and *Chou*, who were more immediately connected with its concerns, it is but fair to observe that no attention was wanting, nor expense spared, to render our situation as easy and comfortable as possible. Supplies of every kind were sent on board in the greatest profusion and with the most scrupulous punctuality. And as a singular proof of attention shewn to us in the commencement of this journey, our conductors, having observed that we used milk with our tea, had purchased two fine cows in full milk, which were put on board a yacht prepared for their reception, for a supply of that article. And, it was observed, that whenever the chief officers of the provinces, through which the embassy was to pass, prepared an entertainment in honour of the occasion, they had[490] given themselves all possible trouble to render it more acceptable, by endeavouring to serve it up, as they thought, in the English style. In some of those feasts we had hogs roasted whole, that could not have weighed less than fifty pounds; quarters of mutton, geese, ducks, and fowls roasted or boiled whole, a mode of cookery altogether different to the practice of the country, which is chiefly confined to that of stewing small morsels of meat with greens or rice. The awkward manner in which they were prepared, being generally burnt and glazed over with oil, was entitled to and found an ample excuse in the desire thus testified of pleasing.

From the time that we first embarked in August at the mouth of the Pey-ho, or White River, until our return, we experienced only a single shower of rain. It is observed, indeed, that during the autumnal months the northern provinces enjoy a cloudless sky; an advantage of which they avail themselves in thrashing out the different kinds of grain in the field, thus saving the labour of bearing it into barns or piling it into stacks. It is either thrashed out on clay floors with flails, similar to our own, beat out of the ear against the edge of a plank, or trodden by oxen or buffalos. The grain that we had noticed just striking into the ear, on ascending the river, was now generally reaped. It consisted principally of the different species of millet, as before observed, and a small proportion of *polygonum fagopyrum* or buck-wheat. A species of *Dolichos* or bean, that had been sown between the drills of the Holcus, or tall millet, was now in flower.[491]

The range of Fahrenheit's thermometer in the province of *Pe-tche-lee*, during the month of August, was from 80° to 88° in the middle of the day, and during the night it remained generally about 60° to 64°. In September, the medium temperature at two o'clock was about 76°; and in October about 68°; but in the latter month, it decreased in the night sometimes to 44°.

In the neighbourhood of the *Pei-ho* a light sandy soil chiefly prevails, with a mixture of argillaceous earth and slimy matter, interspersed with shining particles of mica: but not a stone of any magnitude, nor pebbles, nor even gravel occur in the whole extent of country through which this river is navigable. The surface, indeed, is so flat and uniform, that the tide, which rises only nine or ten feet in the gulph of *Pe-tche-lee*, flows to the distance of thirty miles beyond *Tien-sing*, or one hundred and ten miles from the mouth of the river; and it frequently submerges the whole country, notwithstanding the great pains bestowed by the inhabitants in raising and keeping in order artificial banks. Such inundations, although frequently the causes of great fertility, are sometimes productive of general calamity, especially if they happen at a season when the crop is too far advanced. These plains exhibit the appearance of a more than ordinary incroachment of the land upon the sea. The general level of the face of the country, at high water, is not more elevated than two feet above the surface of the river, of which not only the bed, but also the substratum of the enclosing banks, are composed entirely of fine sand similar to that on the shore of the sea. The deepest part of the[492] wide gulph of *Pe-tche-lee* exceeds not twelve fathoms, and the prodigious number of small sandy islands, just appearing above the surface, are said to have been created within the records of history. A great portion of the enormous mass of mud that is perpetually wafted down the Yellow River, and which was found by experiment to exceed two million solid feet in an hour, is borne by a strong current from the Yellow Sea into the gulph of *Pe-tche-lee*, where the stillness of the water allows it to subside. In the map of Marco Polo, which was most probably copied by him from one in the possession of Gengis-khan, or some of the learned men about his court, *Tien-sing* is placed upon the sea coast; and a branch of the Yellow River, after traversing the provinces *Kiang-nan*, *Shan-tung*, and part of *Pe-tche-lee*, in the direction nearly of the present canal, discharges itself into the gulph near the *Pei-ho*. Were this branch of the river actually turned, the rapidity with which the gulph of *Pe-tche-lee* is filling up is the less surprising, as the only stream to keep its waters in motion at present is the *Pei-ho*. It has been calculated that, by the simple turning of the great river that falls from Winandermere-lake, the estuary of Morecombe Bay, which it now crosses, would, in the natural course of events, be converted in a few years into a green meadow. If the abovementioned chart be correct, it would prove also that the Mongul Tartars did actually first bring the grand navigation of China to the state in which it now appears.

This uniform plain of China afforded little interest to the traveller. Few trees appeared, except now and then a clump of firs surrounding a temple, or the plantations contiguous to[493] the dwelling of some officer of government. In such situations were also large elms, willows, and a species of ash unknown in Europe. There were no hedge-rows. Property here is divided only by narrow ditches, serving at the same time for drains, or by ridges of unploughed ground, as in the common fields of England, which answer the purpose of foot-paths. These ridges were generally well covered with that family of running trefoil, known by the name of *Melilotos*, intermixed with a species of *Poa* or meadow grass, *Avena* or wild oats, and *Briza* or quaking grass. In the ditches, beside the common reed the *Arundo phragmites*, were growing two species of *Cyperus*, and a *Scirpus* or club-rush. None of the artificial grasses, usually so called, are cultivated by the Chinese. It is not an object with them to fodder their cows for the sake of obtaining a greater quantity of milk, this nutritive article of food being very sparingly used either in its raw state or in any preparation; and they are either ignorant of the processes of converting it into butter and cheese, or, for certain reasons, prefer to employ the little they make use of in its original state. Horses are rarely kept for luxury or for labour; and the few animals employed in agriculture, which are mostly asses, mules, or buffalos, subsist in the winter season on chaff and straw; and their chief support in the summer is derived from the strong grasses that grow in the ditches and the common reed, with which, in this part of the country, large tracts of swampy ground are covered.

On approaching *Tien-sing*, we observed several large fields cultivated with a vegetable called by the Chinese the *Pe-tsai*, or white herb, apparently a species of *Brassica* or cole; though[494] insipid in its taste, being not unlike that of the cos-lettuce, it is held in preference to all other vegetables; and the capital is most abundantly supplied with it in the summer season fresh from the gardens in its vicinity and, in the winter, salted and prepared somewhat in the same manner as the *Sour-Krout* of the Germans. We observed also in the gardens, carrots, turnips, black radishes, a species of asparagus, the *Solanum Melongena*, a species of *physalis* or winter-cherry, water-melons and musk-melons, pumpkins and cucumbers. Onions and garlic were common vegetables planted near every peasant's house. The *Trapa* or water-caltrops grew in the ditches, the nuts of which, with the seeds and the roots of the Nelumbium, generally furnished out our desert; to which, indeed, sometimes were added tolerably good peaches, dry spongy apples not unlike quinces in appearance, and pears of an immense size but of a harsh and austere taste.

However unfavourable the country might be for an extended cultivation, which did not appear to be the case, the proximity to the capital would have led one to expect a corresponding population. Nothing of the kind appeared; the vast numbers we had observed in ascending the river were drawn from the distance of many miles out of mere curiosity; the inhabitants only of the vicinity now shewed themselves; and we were rather surprized at the fewness of these, as well as at the very ruinous and miserable condition of almost all the cottages. These mean huts were built, some of half-burnt bricks and others of clay, and they were thatched with the straw of grain or with reeds. Some were enclosed within walls of mud, or with a kind of[495] course matting made of reeds, or the stalks of the *holcus sorghum*, which enclosure generally contained the families of two or three generations, the cattle, pigs, poultry, and all the living creatures belonging to the establishment. The Chinese have a common saying, that "although there be poverty without Pekin, there is plenty within its walls." The appearance, indeed, of all the peasantry in this province was marked with every indication of poverty; nor was the condition much better of those who were employed about the vessels which carried the Embassador and his train. With the greatest thankfulness they received the offals of our allowance; and the tea-leaves, which we had used, were sought after by them with avidity and boiled up for their beverage. A little boiled rice, or millet, with a few vegetables, commonly the *Pe-tsai*, and onions fried in oil, constituted their principal meals, of which they made only two regular ones in the day, one about ten o'clock in the morning, and the other at four or five in the afternoon. They generally however had the frying-pan on the fire at three or four o'clock in the morning. The wine or liquor, which we received in large jars, and which was so miserably bad as not to be used, afforded a great treat to the poor people, whose circumstances seldom allowed them to taste it. This liquor is brewed from a mixture of rice and millet, and from its quickly turning sour seems to have little strength, and to have undergone a very imperfect degree of fermentation. Their *hot wine* is seldom used except by the upper class of people who, not satisfied with the strong empyreumatic flavour communicated in the distillation, drink it boiling hot in the midst of summer.[196]

At *Tien-sing* our principal conductor *Sun-ta-gin* had prepared for us a sumptuous entertainment, consisting of excellent mutton, pork, venison, and poultry of all kinds, a great variety of confectionary, of fruits then in season, peaches, plumbs, grapes, chesnuts, walnuts, and water-caltrops. We very soon found indeed that we were treated with more studied attention, with a more marked distinction, and with less constraint, than when we ascended the river. Our dignified conductor made no difficulty in allowing us to walk on shore as much as we pleased; but recommended us not to quit the banks of the river for fear of retarding the yachts or of being left behind. He hinted to us, at the same time, that the officers *Van* and *Chou* would be responsible at court for any accident that might happen to us, so long as we were under the protection of the Emperor.

In passing *Tien-sing* we found considerable difficulty in getting our fleet through the immense crowds of shipping of every description that were collected there to remain for the winter; among which were about five hundred of the Emperor's revenue vessels with grain for the capital. The *Eu-ho*, or precious river, called also the *Yun-leang-ho*, or river upon which grain is transported, falling from the westward, forms, at the head of this city, a confluence with the *Pei-ho*. Our barges were at least four hours in getting through the multitude of vessels that were moored, for their winter-quarters, in this small river; which, however, is rendered important by its communication with the grand artificial canal.[497]

Having passed the fleet of shipping and the suburbs, a plain extending beyond the reach of sight opened out on the left of the river, upon which were observed many thousands of small sandy tumuli, of a conical form, resembling those hillocks which in myriads are thrown up on the continent of Africa by the *Termites*, or white ants. In several parts of this plain were small buildings, in the form of dwelling-houses, but not exceeding four or five feet in height; in other places were circular, semicircular, and square enclosures of stonework, and here and there were interspersed small pillars of stone or brick and other erections of every variety of form. This was the first common burying-ground that we had observed, except a very small one at *Tong-tchoo*; and the tumuli and the different erections marked out the mansions of the dead. In many parts of this extensive enclosure we met with massy coffins lying upon the surface, some new, others newly painted, but none in a mouldering state. It was explained to us, by our interpreter, that some of these coffins had been deposited there, until the proper advice should be obtained from the priest or the oracle consulted, or from casting lots, as to the most propitious place of interment, and the most favourable day for performing the obsequies; some were placed there till the pecuniary circumstances of the surviving relatives would enable them to bestow a suitable interment, and others were left to dry and moulder, to a certain degree, in order to be burnt and the ashes collected and put into stone jaw or other receptacles[53]. On no occasion [198] do the Chinese bury their dead within the precincts of a city or town, much less within the walls of their temples; but always deposit them at a proper distance from the dwellings of the living, in which respect they have more discretion than the Europeans; who not only allow the interment of dead bodies in the midst of their populous cities, but have thrust them also into places of public worship, where crowded congregations are constantly exposed to the nauseous effluvia, and perhaps infection, arising from putrid carcases. Yet so tenacious are the people of the privilege of interment within the walls of the church, in some countries of Europe, that any attempt to discontinue the imprudent custom would be attended with some degree of danger, as happened to the late Grand Duke of Tuscany who, having built a commodious and spacious cemetery without the city of Florence, to which it was intended to remove the coffins out of the vaults of the church, had nearly raised a rebellion among his subjects. In *Render*'s tour through Germany, an instance is given of the fatal effects of burying in churches, the relation of which makes one shudder with horror.

The bank of the river, being one of the enclosing fences to the burying-ground, was ornamented with beautiful weeping willows which, with a few solitary cypresses interspersed among[499] the tombs, were the only trees that appeared in this part of the country.

In a corner of the cemetery was a temple, built after the usual plan, with an altar in the center; and a number of deities moulded in clay were ranged on each side on stone pedestals. We observed no priests; but an elderly lady was very busily employed in throwing the sticks of fate, in order to obtain a lucky number in which, however, she failed. During the operation of shaking the cup, her countenance betrayed a greater degree of eagerness and anxiety than usually appears on the face of a Chinese; and she left the temple in a peevish and muttering tone, sufficiently expressive of the greatness of her disappointment which, it seemed, was no less than a refusal, on the part of the oracle, to hold out the hope of her being blessed with a second husband. Till this circumstance had been explained to us by the keeper of the temple, it was concluded that the old lady had been muttering imprecations against us for disturbing her in the midst of her devotions.

After two days' sail from *Tien-sing* we arrived at a city of the third order[54] called *Tchien-shien*. The surface of the interjacent country had continued the same uniform plain, without a pebble in the soil: the extent of cultivation by no means extraordinary; and the few scattered villages of mean houses indicated [500]no great degree of population; the dwellings that floated on the water were numerous and crowded with inhabitants. We observed several plots of young wheat rising in drills a few inches above the ground. Buck-wheat was in full flower and several plantations of the cotton plant, *gossypium herbaceum*, were in pod, some of them perfectly ripe. Fahrenheit's thermometer on the 14th, 15th, and 16th of this month stood at 52° and 53° in the morning, and about 70° in the middle of the day.

On the 17th, beside a great number of towns, villages and military posts, which are regularly placed at intervals of about three miles, we passed two cities of the third order, one of which, from the length of its walls, appeared to be of very considerable importance. No true idea, however, can be formed of the population and magnitude of a Chinese city by the extent of its enclosing walls. Few are without large patches of unoccupied ground within them which, in many instances, far exceeds the quantity of land that is built upon. Even in that part of the capital called the Chinese city, several hundred acres are under cultivation. The Imperial city, containing the palace and buildings for the officers of state, the eunuchs and artificers, occupies very nearly a square mile, more than two-thirds of which is a kind of park and pleasure grounds; and under the north wall of the Tartar city there is a pond or swamp covered almost with the Nelumbium, which appeared to be fully twice the dimensions of Lincoln's-Inn-Fields, or four times their space, namely near fifty acres. Such spaces of unoccupied ground might perhaps have been reserved for the use of the inhabitants in case of siege, as the means of supply[501]ing a few vegetables of the pungent kind, as onions and garlic, for the besieged, which are the more necessary for a people who use so small a portion of animal food, and little or no milk. Thus the cities of Babylon and Nineveh, which were so frequently exposed to the calamities of war and siege, had gardens and corn-lands within their walls.

On the 18th we passed two cities and a great number of towns and villages. The face of the country still level and entirely open; not a hedge-row appearing on any side and very few trees. Almost all the vessels that we met in the course of the day were laden with sacks of cotton wool. This being the night of full moon, we were allowed to enjoy very little rest. The observance of the usual ceremonies, which consist of firing their small petards, beating at intervals the noisy gong, harsh squalling music and fire-works, required that our vessels should remain stationary, and these nocturnal orgies ceased only with the appearance of the sun. There was, however, another cause of detention at this place. In sailing against the stream of the *Eu-ho*, it was necessary the barges should be tracked by men and these men were to be pressed or forced into this laborious service from the villages bordering upon the river. The usual way of doing this was to send out the soldiers or attendants of the officers before the vessels, in the dusk of the evening, to take the poor wretches by surprize in their beds. But the ceremony of the full moon, by retarding their usual hour of retiring to rest, had put them on their guard; and, on the approach of the emissaries of government, all that were liable to be pressed into this service had[502] absconded, so that, in addition to the noise of the gongs and the trumpets and crackers, our ears were frequently assailed by the cries and lamentations of persons under the punishment of the bamboo or the whip, for claiming their exemption from joining the yachts and acting as trackers. When the groupe that had been collected for this purpose was brought together in the morning, it was impossible not to regard it with an eye of pity. Most of them consisted of infirm and decrepit old men, and the rest were such lank, sickly-looking, ill-clothed creatures, that the whole groupe appeared to be much fitter for an hospital than for performing any kind of labour. Our companions pretended to say that every farmer, who rented lands upon the public rivers or canals, was obliged, by the tenure on which he held his lease, to furnish such a number of men to track the vessels in the service of government whenever it might be required; but that, on the present being an extraordinary occasion, they had resolved to pay them, as they called it, in a handsome manner, which was at the rate of something less than seven-pence a day, without any allowance for returning to their homes; a price for labour which bore no sort of proportion to that of the necessaries of life; and it was even doubtful if this pittance was ever paid to them.

Having cleared the fleet of shipping that was assembled at this place, a favourable breeze relieved our invalids and rendered their slender exertions unnecessary for the greater part of the day, in the course of which we entered the province of *Shan-tung*. In this province nothing worthy of notice occurred until the 22d, when we quitted the *Eu-ho* and turning towards[503] the south entered the grand canal, out of which we observed a gentle current flowing into the river. At this point of junction the pagoda of *Lin-tsin*, an octagonal pyramid, was erected, perhaps as a monument of this great and useful undertaking, which, however, in its present state, apparently had not stood many ages. In the hope of finding within it some inscription, that might point out its designation, we mounted with some difficulty upon the first of its nine stages or roofs (for the little door on a level with the ground was walled up with bricks) but it contained only the bare walls, not even a stair-case remained nor any possible means of ascending to the top, and the lower part was choaked up with rubbish. These pagodas (or as the Chinese name them *Ta*) that so frequently occur in the country, seem to be intended only as embellishments to particular grounds, or objects to terminate villas or prospects. Sometimes, it is true, they appear as appendages to temples, but are never appropriated for the purposes of sacred worship. Whatever their intention might have been, it would seem the rage of building them no longer exists, not one of a late erection having appeared in the whole country, and more than two-thirds of those we saw being in ruins.

At the junction of the canal with the *Eu-ho* there was no lock nor flood-gate; the gentle current of the former was interrupted only from place to place, by loose planks let down in grooves cut in stone piers. These dams seldom occasioned the difference of a foot in the level of the water; and at each was a guard-house with double the usual number of soldiers stationed, to assist in drawing up or letting down the planks,[504] as occasion might require. The canal, which at the commencement was from sixty to one hundred feet in width, was contracted at such places by the stone piers of the flood-gates to about thirty feet.

Towards the evening of the 23d, as we approached the city *Tong-tchang-foo*, we were much amused with a military manœuvre, which was evidently intended to astonish us. Under the walls of this city about three hundred soldiers were drawn out in a line, which, however, the darkness of the night had rendered invisible. But just as we were coming to anchor, each soldier, at the sound of the gong, produced from under his cloak a splendid lantern with which he went through a regular manual exercise. The following morning we observed, for the first time, a few hillocks breaking the line of the horizon to the eastward. The country appeared to be in a tolerable state of cultivation; but the mode of tillage exhibited no extraordinary degree of skill or of labour. Villages of considerable extent were erected along the banks of the canal, at intervals of about three miles from each other; and, in the gardens contiguous to these, grew in abundance the tobacco plant whose leaves were small, hairy, and viscous, and the flowers of which were of a greenish yellow passing into a faint rose colour at the edges of the petals. We observed also small patches of hemp. A greater use is made of the seeds and leaflets of this plant, as a substitute for or to mix with tobacco, than of its fibres for cloth, a purpose to which it is as rarely converted by the Chinese as by the Hindoos, being little esteemed for those valuable uses to which, since its introduction into Eu[505]rope, it has been applied. The number of lateral branches, which in a warm climate each stem throws out close above the surface of the ground, breaks the length of fibre and renders it unfit for those purposes for which, in the northern regions of Europe, its tall branchless stem is so well adapted. The sow thistle, a plant that occurs in almost every part of the world, was nothing different here from its usual habit in Europe. We observed also a species of *Chenopodium* and of *Artemisia* or wormwood; abundance of the *Pe-tsai*, and other common culinary vegetables. In the small flower gardens, without which we scarcely observed a single cottage, were balsams, several kinds of beautiful asters, holy-hocks, two species of *Malva*, an *Amaranthus*, and the showy and handsome shrub the *Nerium Oleander*.

Having passed on the 26th October the walls of the city *Tsie-ning*, where a multitude of small craft were lying at anchor, we came to an extensive lake of the same name, navigated by a great number of sailing boats. From the east side of this lake the canal was separated only by an immense mound of earth. To the westward the whole country, beyond the reach of sight, was one continued swamp or morass, upon which were interspersed pools or ponds of water abounding with the Nelumbium, at this time in full flower. The morass being several feet below the surface of the water in the canal afforded the means of regulating the quantity; and, accordingly, at certain distances, we observed stone arches turned in the earthen embankment to let off the superfluous water that might be occasioned by the swelling of the feeding rivers. About this place[506] also, it was remarked, that the bed of the canal was carried in a line so nearly horizontal, that the water had a gentle current either to the northward or the southward, according as these sluices were kept shut or thrown open; this line being ascertained, perhaps, rather by the surface of the lake than by the assistance of instruments; for it was sufficiently remarkable, that no opportunity had been omitted in carrying this great work along the side, or through the middle, of lakes or other pools of water wherever it could be done.

The nature of the country admitted of such management for three days' journey, or about eighty miles from *Tsie-ning*. The whole of this extensive plain consisted in lakes or swampy ground half covered with water. On the former were constantly seen moving about vessels with sails and boats of every description, conveying an animated picture of activity, industry, and commerce. Almost all the lakes were studded with islands and these were covered with villages, that were chiefly inhabited by fishermen. Here, for the first time, we observed the *Leu-tzé* or fishing corvorant, the *Pelicanus Sinensis*, diving after the finny tribe and seemingly no less anxious than its master to take them. This bird is so like another species of the pelican, called the *Carbo* or common corvorant which in England, as naturalists inform us, was formerly trained for fishing, that it has usually been considered the same, but from several specimens brought home with us it appears to be a different species. The usual practice is to take ten or twelve of these birds, in the morning when fasting, upon a raft of bamboo poles lashed together, and to let one or two at most at a time dive for fish,[507] which are taken from them the moment they bring them to the surface. These birds, not much larger than the common duck, will seize and gripe fast fishes that are not less than their own weight. When the proprietor judges the first pair to be pretty well fatigued, they are suffered to feed by way of encouragement on some of the fish they have taken, and a second pair are dispatched upon the water. The fish we observed them to take was a species of perch. In the course of three days' navigation, we saw several thousand boats and rafts employed in this kind of fishing.

Except on the water and the islands, the whole of the swampy country might be said to be uninhabited and totally void of any kind of cultivation. Sometimes, indeed, a few miserable mud huts appeared on the small hillocks that here and there raised their heads out of the dreary waste of morass; but the chief inhabitants were cranes, herons, guillemots and a vast variety of other kinds of birds that frequent the waters and swamps. Here too are great numbers of that singular and beautiful bird, the *Anas Galericulata*, usually known by the name of the *Mandarin duck* which, like the gold and silver fishes, is caught and reared as an article of sale to the opulent and curious. The great extent of water had a sensible effect on the temperature of the air, especially in the mornings and evenings, when Fahrenheit's thermometer was sometimes below 40°.

Having passed the lakes and swamps, we entered suddenly, on the 31st, upon a most delightful part of the country, crowded with temples and villages and towns and cities, near all of[508] which, and on every part of the canal, were vast numbers of the revenue vessels, collecting the surplus taxes paid in kind, in order to transport them to the capital. Wheat and cotton appeared to be the two principal articles of culture. The surface of the country was now broken into hill and dale, every inch appeared to be under tillage, except the summit of the knolls, which were generally crowned with forest trees, and few of the detached houses or temples were without extensive gardens and orchards. Apples, pears, plums, peaches, apricots and pomgranates, were the common kinds of fruit, and the culinary vegetables were the same as those of *Pe-tche-lee*. The canal at this place is, perhaps, the grandest inland navigation in the whole world, being nearly a thousand feet in width and bordered on each side by stone quays, built with massy blocks of grey marble mixed with others of granite; and this immense aqueduct, although forced up several feet above the surface of the country by embankments thrown up by the labour of man, flowed with a current of three miles an hour nearly towards the Yellow River, to which we perceived we were fast approaching, by the bustle and activity both on shore and on the numberless canals that branched out in every direction from the main trunk; on whose banks, for several miles on either side, one continued town extended to the point of junction with this large river, celebrated in every period of the Chinese history. A village was particularly pointed out by the bargemen, whose name was derived from a miracle, which is most sacredly believed by the Chinese. Tradition says, that the famous astronomer *Heu* was carried up to Heaven in his[509] house, which stood at this place, leaving behind him an old faithful servant who, being thus deprived of his master and his habitation, was reduced to beggary; but happening by accident to throw a little prepared rice into the ground, it immediately grew and produced grain without chaff for his sustenance; from whence the place is called *Sen-mee, rice growing ready dressed*, to this day.

Before our barges launched into the stream of the Yellow River, which rolled in a very rapid torrent, certain ceremonies were conceived to be indispensably necessary. In the practical part of religion (which indeed may be considered as nearly the whole) a Chinese is not less solicitous to avert a possible evil, than to procure an eventual good; and of all evils personal danger is most apprehended. It was therefore deemed expedient, that an oblation should be made in every vessel of the fleet to the genius of the river. The animals that were sacrificed, on this occasion, were different in different yachts, but they generally consisted of a fowl or a pig, two animals that were very common in Grecian sacrifices. The blood, with the feathers and the hair, was daubed upon the principal parts of the vessel. On the forecastle of some were placed cups of wine, oil and salt; in others, tea, flour and salt; and in others, oil, rice and salt. The last article appears to be thought by the Chinese, as well as by the Hebrews, a necessary accompaniment to every sacrifice. "Every oblation of thy meat-offering shalt thou season with salt: neither shalt thou suffer the salt of the Covenant of thy God to be lacking from thy *meat*-offering." As, however, the high priest and his friends[510] were to feast on those parts of the meat-offering, which were considered as unworthy the acceptance of heaven, which parts, by the way, were always the best of the victim, one might, perhaps, assign a reason for the strong injunction of offering salt, this being a scarce article in many countries of the East and the best preservative of meat against putrefaction[55].

The cups, the slaughtered animal and several made-dishes remained on the forecastle, the Captain standing over them on one side and a man with a gong in his hand on the other. On approaching the rapid part of the stream, at the signal given by the gong, the Captain took up the cups one by one, in order that, like the Greeks of old, he might "perform the rites and pour the ruddy wine," which he did by throwing their contents over the bow of the vessel into the river. The libation performed, a quantity of crackers and squibs and gilt tin foil were burnt, with uplifted hands, whilst the deep-sounding gong was incessantly struck with increasing violence as the vessels were swept along with the current. The victim and the other dishes were then removed for the use of the Captain and crew, and the ceremony

171

ended by three genuflexions and as many prostrations. The Emperor is never satisfied with less than nine.

[511]

Our fleet consisted of about thirty sail, and from each vessel there proceeded, on its launching into the stream, such a din of gongs and crackers and such volumes of smoke from the burnt offerings, that the deity of the river must have been in a very surly humour if he was not pleased with such a multitude of oblations. The safe arrival, on the opposite bank, of the whole squadron was a proof of his having accepted the homage, and accordingly he was again addressed in a volley of crackers as a token of thanks for his propitious and friendly aid.

The width of the river at this place was full three quarters of a mile; and the stream, where strongest, ran with the rapidity of seven or eight miles an hour; and the water was as thick and muddy as if the heaviest torrents of rain had just descended, whereas, in fact, there had not fallen a shower for many months.

The length of that part of the canal which lies between the *Eu-ho* and the Yellow River, and which we had now sailed over, is about two hundred English miles. The natural slope of the country being from North to South, the projectors of this work seem to have fixed upon the middle point, or nearly so, between these two rivers for the commencement of their operations: so that from this middle point to the northward, or rising part of the country, they have been under the necessity, in order to preserve their level, of cutting down to the depth of thirty, forty, and even to seventy feet, below the surface; whilst from the same point to the southward, or descending part of the country, they have been obliged to force up the [512] water between immense banks of earth and stone, far above the level of the flat surface; consisting almost entirely of lakes, swamps, and morass. The quantity of human labour that must have been employed, in amassing together the different materials that compose this immense aqueduct, could not have been supplied, in any reasonable length of time, except in a country where millions could be set to work at the nod of a despot. The greatest works in China have always been, and still continue to be, performed by the accumulation of manual labour, without the assistance of machinery, except on very particular occasions, where some mechanical power may be absolutely necessary to be brought in aid of human strength. Thus, where canals are carried over surfaces that are too hilly and uneven to admit of one continued level, they descend from place to place, as it were by steps, at each of which is an inclined plane; the height from the upper canal to the lower being generally from six to ten feet; and the angle of the plane from forty-five to fifty degrees. All vessels navigating such canals must be hoisted up these planes by the assistance of upright capstans, without which it would scarcely be possible to get those of large demensions, together with their cargo, out of one canal into the other; and they are gently lowered in the same manner. This awkward contrivance may, perhaps, less imply the ignorance of locks or other methods practised elsewhere, than the unwillingness of the government to suffer any innovation that might be the means of depriving many thousands of obtaining that scanty subsistence, which they now derive from their attendance at these capstans. However slightly such a notion may be held in Europe, there can be no doubt that a general intro [513] duction of machinery into China, for the purpose of facilitating and expediting labour would, in the present state of the country, be attended with the most pernicious and distressing consequences; were it only for this simple reason that, despising, as they affect to do, all foreign commerce, the demand for the products of machinery, however much they might be reduced in price, would not be encreased, whilst that of manual labour would considerably be diminished.

Sensible as the Chinese seem to be of the advantages derived from an easy communication between the different parts of the empire, by means of canals, it is the more surprizing what the motives could have been that, till this moment, have restrained them from facilitating an intercourse by means of good roads, in such parts of the country as have no inland navigations. In this respect they fall short of most civilized nations. Except near the capital, and in some few places where the junction of the grand canal with navigable rivers is interrupted by mountainous ground, there is scarcely a road in the whole country that can be ranked beyond a foot-path. Hence it happens that in the northern provinces, during winter, it is impossible to travel with any degree of ease, convenience, or safety; all the canals to the northward of the Yellow River, which runs from 34° to 35° latitude being frozen up. It is equally surprizing that their ingenuity has not extended itself to the invention of sledges or some sort of carriages suitable for travelling on ice,[511] which other nations have converted into the best of roads[56].

The continuation of the Grand Canal, from the Yellow River to the *Yang-tse-kiang*, was constructed upon the same[515] principles as that part between the Yellow River and the *Eu-ho*. The country being level and abounding with lakes and marshy grounds, it was carried upon a mound of earth kept together by retaining walls of stone the whole distance, which is about ninety miles, being in parts not less than twenty feet above the general level of the country; and the sheet of water it contained was two hundred feet in width, running sometimes at the rate of three miles an hour. Canals of communication supplied it from the westward; and the superfluous water was let off upon the low marshes. The tops of the walls of *Pao-yng-shien* were just on a level with the surface of the water in the canal, so that if the bank opposite to it were to burst, the whole city must inevitably be inundated. Very little cultivation appeared in this low marshy country, but abundance of towns and villages, the inhabitants of which subsisted by fishing. A prodigious extent of low country on each side of the Yellow River, perhaps not much less than the surface of all England, is liable to inundations. The Chinese say, the overflowing of this river has been more fatal to the country than war, pestilence, or famine. The Emperor *Kaung-shee*, in order to distress a rebel in the province of *Honan*, ordered a bank to be broken down behind a city he had got possession of; but the inundation was so great, that not only the rebel forces were destroyed, but almost half a million of people were completely swept away; and among these were several European missionaries. Vast sums of money were expended in confining this river within its banks. The same Emperor in his last will declares, that the sums of money issued annually from the Imperial treasury for the embankments to prevent inundations, were never less, during his whole reign,[516] than 3,000,000 ounces of silver, equivalent to one million sterling.

On approaching the *Yang-tse-kiang* the appearance of the country improved, just as it had done in the vicinity of the Yellow River. The town of *Sau-poo*, extending along the quay of the canal, consisted of houses that were generally two stories high, apparently well built, white-washed with lime and kept in neat and clean order. The inhabitants were also better cloathed than we had hitherto been accustomed to see them. The women were less shy in their advances; their complexions were much fairer and their features more soft and handsome than any we had yet observed in the northern provinces.

The walls and gates of *Yang-tchoo-foo* bore marks of great antiquity, being partly in ruins and almost entirely overgrown with moss and creeping plants. A thousand vessels, at least, of different descriptions were lying under its walls. Here we remained for the night; and the following morning, being the 5th of November, we launched into the grand and beautiful river called the *Yang-tse-kiang*, which at this place was about two miles in width; but the current was so gentle, that no oblation to the presiding deity was thought to be necessary. The numerous islands rising out of the river and covered with verdure, the multitude of ships of war, of burden and of pleasure, some gliding down the stream, others sailing against it; some moving by oars and others lying at anchor; the banks on either side covered with towns and houses, as far as the eye could reach, presented a prospect more varied and cheerful than any[517] that had hitherto occurred. Nor was the canal, on the opposite side, less lively; for two whole days we were continually passing among fleets of vessels of different constructions and dimensions, those belonging to the revenue department being the largest, each capable of carrying, at least, two hundred tons. Cities, towns and villages were continued along the banks without intermission: and vast numbers of stone bridges were thrown across the canal, some having one, some two, and others three arches. The face of the country was beautifully diversified with hill and dale and every part of it in the highest state of cultivation. The chief produce was that particular species of cotton, of a yellowish tinge, known in Europe by the name of nankin.

The suburbs of *Sou-tchoo-foo* employed us full three hours in passing before we reached the walls of the city, where a multitude of vessels were lying at anchor. The numerous inhabitants that appeared upon and without the walls of this extensive city, were better dressed and seemed to be more contented and cheerful, than we had yet observed them in any other place. For the most part they were cloathed in silk. The ladies were here dressed in petticoats and not in trowsers, as they had hitherto appeared to the northward. The general fashion of the head-dress was a black satin cap with a triangular peak, the point descending to the root of the nose, in the middle of which, or about the centre of the forehead, was a crystal button. The whole face and neck were washed with a preparation of white lead and the cheeks highly rouged; and two vermillion spots, like wafers, were particularly conspicuous, one on the centre of the under lip and the other on the chin. Their[518] feet were universally squeezed down to an unnatural size. Few females were seen among the immense crowds that the novelty of the sight had brought together, but great numbers had assembled in the houses and particularly on board the pleasure or passage yachts, with the intention of satisfying their curiosity. The superior style of dress and the appearance of the women in public at this place, so different from the general custom of the country, could only be explained to us by the writings of the Christian missionaries, who observe that the concubines of mandarins and men of property are chiefly procured from the cities of *Yang-tchoo* and of *Sou-tchoo*, where they are educated in the pleasing arts of singing, music and dancing and every other accomplishment suitable to women of superior rank, in order to render them the more agreeable and fascinating. That such women are generally purchased by persons engaged in the trade, in different parts of the country, and trained in these cities, where they are disposed of to the highest bidder, "*this being the principal branch of trade that is carried on in those two cities.*" How do these holy men reconcile so infamous a traffic among a people whom they have adorned with every virtue? a people whom they have rendered remarkable among nations for their filial piety! Is there on earth a crime more revolting against civilized nature, or more detestable to civilized society, than that of a parent selling his own child and consigning her, expressly and voluntarily, into a state of prostitution? Those unfortunate wretches who, in Europe, have by any accident reduced themselves to that degraded and deplorable condition of becoming subservient to the pleasures of a man, whom they probably detest, are generally the objects of[519] pity, however their conduct may be disapproved; but a parent, who should be the cause of reducing them to such a state, would be execrated; but the assertion is as absurd as ridiculous, and the writer must have been very credulous to suppose, that the *principal trade* of one of the largest cities in the world, whose population cannot be less than a million of souls, should consist in buying and selling ladies of pleasure. Buying females in the legal way is certainly the greatest branch of trade throughout China, as every woman there is bought and sold. These reverend gentlemen likewise inform us, with great indifference, that if a man be desirous of having a male child and his wife should happen to be barren, he will purchase one of these concubines for the sole purpose of getting an heir; and, when this is accomplished, he either provides her with a husband, or turns her adrift. Such are the moral virtues of the Chinese, compared with whom all other nations have been accounted barbarous[57].

To the west of *Sau-tchoo-foo* is a range of mountains higher than any we had yet seen, well covered with wood; and an extensive lake stretches along their base, famed in China for its picturesque beauties and for its fish. We would gladly have made a party of pleasure to this delightful spot, but innumerable objections, as usual, were started by our conductors, on the score of delay that such an excursion would occasion.

[520]

The two great products of this part of the country are rice and silk; the former of which, at this time, they were busily employed in reaping. Plantations of the mulberry tree were extended on both sides of the canal and into the country beyond the reach of sight. They appeared to be of two distinct species; the one, the common mulberry, *morus nigra*, and the other having much smaller leaves, smooth and heart-shaped, and bearing a white berry about the size of the field strawberry. The latter had more the habit of a shrub, but the branches of neither were suffered to run into strong wood, being frequently pruned in order that the trunk might annually throw out young scions, whose leaves were considered to be more tender than such as grew from old branches. Another reason was also assigned for this operation. A tree, when left to itself, throws out the greatest part of its leaves at once, in the spring of the year, but if the thick wood be cut out from time to time, new leaves will continue to push below the parts so cut off during the whole season; and, accordingly, the Chinese are particularly attentive to prune afresh in the autumn, in order to obtain a supply of young leaves in the after spring. The thermometer at this place, on the 9th of November at sun-rise, stood at 64°, and at noon in the shade at 70° degrees.

It was in this part of the canal where the bridge of ninety-one arches, mentioned in the sixth chapter, was thrown across the arm of a lake that joined the canal. I lament exceedingly that we passed this extraordinary fabric in the night. It happened to catch the attention of a Swiss servant who, as the yacht glided along, began to count the arches, but finding them increase in[521] number much beyond his expectation and, at the same time, in dimensions, he ran into the cabin calling out with great eagerness, "For God's sake, gentlemen, come upon deck, for here is a bridge such as I never saw before; it has no end." Mr. Maxwell and I hastened upon deck and, by the faint light, could sufficiently distinguish the arches of a bridge running parallel with the eastern bank of the canal, across the arm of a vast lake, with which the navigation thus communicated. From the highest point, or what appeared to us to be the central arch, I counted forty-five to the end; here they were very small, but the central arch I guessed to be about thirty feet high and forty wide; and the whole length of the bridge I calculated to be about half a mile. The construction of such a bridge, in such a situation, could obviously have been employed for no other purpose than that of opening a free communication with the lake; and, at the same time, of avoiding the labour and expence of accumulating materials sufficient for making a solid embankment.

After sailing a great part of the day through a forest of mulberry trees, planted with much regularity, we arrived on the 10th at the city of *Hang-tchoo-foo*, the capital of the province of *Tche-kiang*. Here that branch of the grand canal which communicates with the *Yang-tse-kiang* terminates in a large commodious bason, at this time crowded with shipping. From this bason a number of smaller canals, passing through arches turned in the walls and intersecting the city in every direction, are finally united in a lake beyond the western wall called the *See-hoo*. The natural and artificial beauties of this lake far[522] exceeded any thing we had hitherto had an opportunity of seeing in China. The mountains surrounding it were lofty and broken into a variety of forms that were highly picturesque; and the vallies were richly cloathed with trees of different kinds, among which three species were remarkably striking, not only by their intrinsic beauty, but also by the contrast they formed with themselves and the rest of the trees of the forest. These were the *Laurus Camphora* or camphor tree, the *Croton sebiferum* or tallow tree, and the *Thuia Orientalis* or arbor vitæ. The bright shining green foliage of the first, mingled with the purple leaves of the second, and overtopped by the tall and stately *tree of life*, of the deepest green, produced a pleasing effect to the eye; and the landscape was rendered still more interesting to the mind, by the very singular and diversified appearance of several repositories of the dead, upon the sloping sides of the inferior hills. Here, as well as elsewhere, the sombre and upright cypress was destined to be the melancholy companion of the tombs. Higher still among the woods, avenues had been opened to admit of rows of small blue houses, supported on white colonnades which, on examination, were also found to be mansions of the dead. Naked coffins of extraordinary thickness were every where lying upon the surface of the ground.

The lake that extended from the walls of the city to the feet of the mountains, and threw its numerous arms into the wooded vallies, was the seat of pleasure, as well as of profit, to the inhabitants of *Hang-tchoo-foo*. These amusements, however, of floating upon barges in the lake are principally confined to one[523] sex. Few women, except those of loose character, join in the parties of men. How miserable or, at best, how little interest can be raised in that state of society where no social intercourse of the sexes exists; where sentiment, nice feeling and the sport and play of the softer passions are totally unknown, and where reason and philosophy are at so low an ebb! In more enlightened countries, when age may have weakened the ardour of joining in the sprightly female circle, or inclination lead to more serious conversations, numberless resources are still left to exercise the faculties of the mind, and society may always be had for such as can relish

"The feast of reason and the flow of soul."

But in China the tenor of their conversation must be always nearly the same, turning chiefly on the affairs of the neighbourhood, the injustice of the magistrates, the tricks and stratagems of the crafty merchant, or of the low mechanic. In entertainments given by those who can afford to drink wine, it is seldom served round as in other countries, but a number of puerile contrivances are practised to determine which of the party is to drink, as in the case I have already noticed of *the game of the fingers*. Thus, a nosegay is passed round from hand to hand, whilst a man in an adjoining room beats a drum or the gong, and he who happens to hold the nosegay when the instrument ceases must drink a cup of wine. Many other methods still more childish are resorted to, in order to pass the time and to give a zest to their wine; but the usual resource here, as well as elsewhere, against the tediousness of time, is gaming. An attachment to this vice accompanies the lowest[521] Chinese wherever he goes. It is said that in one of our eastern colonies, where Chinese are encouraged to settle, they pay to the government the annual sum of ten thousand dollars for a licence to keep gaming tables and sell opium.

Our route being necessarily delayed for two days at this place, on account of an intervening neck of land over which all the baggage was to be transported, I prevailed upon our good natured companion *Van-ta-gin* to make a party to the lake *See-hoo*, to which he readily assented; and this was the only excursion that we had in the course of the whole journey. We had a splendid yacht and another made fast to it to serve as a kitchen; the dinner began the instant we went on board and ceased only when we stepped a-shore. It consisted of at least a hundred dishes in succession, among which were excellent eels, fresh caught in the lake and dressed in a variety of ways; yet the water was clear as crystal. Vast numbers of barges were sailing to and fro, all gaily decorated with paint and gilding and streaming colours; the parties within them apparently all in pursuit of pleasure. The margins of the lake were studded with light aereal buildings, among which one of more solidity and of greater extent than the rest was said to belong to the Emperor. The grounds were enclosed with brick walls and mostly planted with vegetables and fruit trees; but in some there appeared to be collections of such shrubs and flowers as are most esteemed in the country. Among the fruits we got at this place was the *Jambo* or rose apple; and, for the first time, fresh from the tree, but not yet perfectly ripe, two species of oranges, the common China and the small one usually called the Man[523]darin orange; pomgranates, bananas very indifferent and melons equally bad; apricots far from being equal to those of our own country; a large plumb, resembling the egg plumb, also indifferent, and peaches that might have been much improved by judicious culture; apples and pears that in England we should have no hesitation in pronouncing execrably bad; and a species of fruit unknown to all of us which the Chinese called *Zee-tsé*, of a sweet sickly taste when ripe, otherwise most insufferably astringent. Some of the gentlemen thought they saw hazel nuts among the shruberry, but it is more than probable they were mistaken. A few bad grapes were sometimes brought to us, but the party who went from hence to *Chu-san* met with abundance of this fruit, and of very good quality, growing upon standards erected in the several canals and forming a shade under which the barges could pass.

Among the most conspicuous of the shrubs, on the borders of the lake *See-hoo*, was the *Hibiscus mutabilis*, the *Hibiscus Syriacus*, the *Syringa Vulgaris* or common lilac, and the paper mulberry; we observed also a species of *Mimosa*, a *Crotularia, Cratægus, Rosa, Rhamnus, Sambucus, Juniper* and the cotton plant. Of flowers we particularly noticed a large purple-coloured double poppy which, with the *Nelumbium* that grew here in all the ponds and a species of *pæonia*, appear most frequently on the large sheets of painted paper used for covering the walls of their apartments. A great variety of beautiful balsams were also in flower, a species of *Amaranthus*, a *Xeranthemum* and *Gnaphalium*. I mention only such plants as caught the eye in passing, for our Chinese companions, who had a much better appetite[526] for the eels of the lake and other goods things they had taken care to provide than for botany, had no notion of being detained by a bush or a flower.

The next day Lieutenant Colonel, now General, Benson, Doctor Gillan, and myself, accompanied by a military officer and his orderly, rode over the neck of land to look at the yachts that were preparing for our future journey. As it was rather late before we returned, I proposed that we should pass through the city as I had done the day before with our conductor *Van*, which would save us half the distance. The officer perceiving our intention endeavoured to draw us off to the right, but finding us persevere he whispered the orderly, who immediately pushed forward towards the gate. Aware that the intention of this measure was to shut the gate against us, we spurred our horses and followed him, upon which the officer and his orderly set up such a hue and cry that the whole suburbs were presently in a state of commotion. The gates were instantly shut and surrounded by a crowd. Within all was confusion. Message after message was dispatched to the Governor, the gongs were beat and the guards were drawn out in every part of the city. I assured them there was nothing to fear; that we were only three, and had no other design but to pass to our yachts. During this time our *mandarin of war*, in presence of the whole populace, was down on his knees in the dirt, first before one and then another, intreating us to give up the point; so mean and despicable have the maxims of the government made these people. At length our friends *Van* and *Chou*, with the interpreter and a numerous train of soldiers and attendants, made[527] their appearance, and pretended to enjoy the joke of three Englishmen having caused so much alarm to one of their strongest cities, which at that time had a garrison of three thousand men within its walls. On expressing our surprise at such unnecessary precaution, *Van* observed, that our conductor did not know us so well as he did, and, as he was responsible for our safe return, he would rather have travelled us all night through the country than brought us among the crowd in the streets. When the new viceroy of Canton (who travelled with us from hence) heard of this affair, and understood from our conductors that the English found great pleasure in walking and looking about them (a pleasure of which a Chinese can form no idea) he immediately gave orders that the gentlemen in the train of the Embassador should walk whenever they pleased without any molestation.

In the city of *Hang-tchoo-foo*, being particularly famed for its silk-trade, we were not surprized to meet with extensive shops and warehouses; in point of size and the stock contained within them they might be said to vie with the best in London. In some of these were not fewer than ten or twelve persons serving behind the counter; but in passing through the whole city not a single woman was visible, either within doors or without. The crowd of people, composed of the other sex, appeared to be little inferior to that in the great streets of Pekin. Here, though mostly narrow they had in other respects much the advantage of those in the capital, being paved with broad flagstones, resembling the Merceria of Venice or courts of the Strand; Cranburn-Alley is rather too wide for a Chinese street,[528] but those of this city were equally well paved. They appeared to be kept extremely neat and clean. In every shop were exposed to view silks of different manufactures, dyed cottons and nankins, a great variety of English broad-cloths, chiefly however blue and scarlet, used for winter cloaks, for chair covers and for carpets; and also a quantity of peltry intended for the northern markets. The rest of the houses, in the public streets through which we passed, consisted of butchers and bakers' shops, fishmongers, dealers in rice and other grain, ivory-cutters, dealers in laquered ware, tea-houses, cook-shops, and coffin makers; the last of which is a trade of no small note in China. The population of the city alone, I should suppose, from its extent and appearance, to be not much inferior to that of Pekin; and the number of inhabitants in the suburbs, with those that constantly resided upon the water, were perhaps nearly equal to those within the walls.

Here our conductor *Sun-ta-gin* took his leave, after having introduced to the Embassador the new Viceroy of Canton, who was now to accompany the Embassy to the seat of his government. His manners appeared to be no less amiable than those of the Minister. He had travelled post from Pekin and, with many assurances on the part of the Emperor of the highest satisfaction he had derived from the embassy, he brought an additional present from him to His Majesty, consisting of gold tissued silks, purses taken from his own person and the *Card of Happiness*. This is an ornamented piece of paper, neatly folded up and having in the centre the character *foo* or happiness inscribed by the Emperor's own hand, and is considered[529] as the strongest mark a sovereign of China can give to another prince of his friendship and affection. Another card was given to the Embassador of a similar import, as a testimony of his approbation of the conduct of the embassy, which was further confirmed by a present of silks, tea, fans and other trinkets to every individual of it.

A few miles beyond the city we again took shipping on the river *Tcheng-tang-chiang*, which might properly be called an estuary, the tide rising and falling six or seven feet at the place of embarkation, which was not very distant from the Yellow Sea. After seven days of tedious navigation, if dragging by main strength over a pebbly bottom on which the boats were constantly aground and against a rapid stream, could be so called, we came to its source near the city of *Tchang-san-shien*. But its banks were not deficient in beautiful views and picturesque scenery. The general surface of the country was mountainous and romantic, but well cultivated in all such places as would admit the labours of the husbandman. One city only occurred in the course of seven days; but we passed numerous villages, situated in the valleys and the glens between the ridges of mountains; and fishermen's huts were constantly in view. There was here no want of trees, among which the most common were the tallow-tree and the camphor, cedars, firs and the tall and majestic arbor vitæ. Groves of oranges, citrons and lemons were abundantly interspersed in the little vales that sloped down to the brink of the river; and few of the huts were without a small garden and plantation of tobacco. The larger plains were planted with the sugar-cane. We had thus[530] far passed through the country without having seen a single plant of the tea-shrub, but here we found it used as a common plant for hedge-rows to divide the gardens and fruit groves, but not particularly cultivated for its leaves.

At the city of *Tchang-san-shien* we had again a neck of land to cross, in order to join the barges that were prepared on another river falling towards the westward, by which a connexion was formed with the usual route from Pekin to Canton, from whence we had deviated at the *Yang-tse-kiang* river, on account of some of the suite being intended to join the Hindostan in the harbour of *Tchu-san*. We were the less sorry for this deviation, as it gave us an opportunity of seeing a part of the country over which there is no general communication with the grand route. In passing this neck of land, on a very fine causeway, judiciously led through the defiles of the mountains, we first observed the terrace system of agriculture, so frequently mentioned in the writings of the missionaries. The Chinese seem to entertain a particular aversion against sowing or planting on sloping ground and, accordingly, when such occurs, they level it into a number of terraces one rising above the other, which they support by stone walls, if the earth should not be thought sufficiently strong for the purpose. The great conveniency of leading the water from the uppermost to the lowest terrace, without losing any of its nutritive effects by a rapid course, seems to have suggested this mode of preparing the ground. In a hot and dry country, vegetation becomes languid without the command of water; and I observed that on the uppermost terrace there was invariably a tank or reservoir to collect the[531] waters falling from the upper parts of the hills. The expense of labour, that had evidently been employed on such terraces, was so great as to make any suitable return to the husbandman apparently impossible; and still less so in other places where the hills were completely dug away to the skeleton rocks, and the soil carried upon the marshy ground at their feet.

With all this industry it might be concluded, from the general appearance of the people, that they merely gained a subsistence. It was with the utmost difficulty that the officers of government could procure, in the whole city which we last departed from, a sufficient number of chairs for themselves and those gentlemen of the embassy who preferred to be thus carried, and horses for the rest. For the soldiers, indeed, that composed his Excellency's guard, they had prepared a sort of open bamboo chair, fixed between two poles and meant to be carried shoulder-height. But the soldiers, squeezed into these little chairs and elevated in the air, with their feathers and their firelocks, soon perceived that they cut such ridiculous figures and that the soon wretches who carried them were in so miserable a condition, both with regard to their clothing and their habit of body, that, ashamed to be thus dragged along, they presently dismounted and insisted, in their turn, upon carrying the Chinese. Our conductors affected to consider this as a good joke, but others were evidently nettled at it, supposing it might have been meant as a kind of oblique reflection on the indifferent accommodations that had been provided at this place for the Embassador and his retinue; which were[532] however the best that it was possible for them to procure by any exertions.

Having finished this land journey, of about twenty-four miles, in the course of the day, we lodged at *Eu-shan-shien*, a small city of mean appearance and the following day embarked on flat-bottomed barges, remarkably long and narrow, on the river *Long shia-tong*, but two complete days of heavy rain obliged us to remain quietly at anchor.

On the 24th of November we dropped down the river, which by the rains was swelled to an enormous size and in some places had overflowed its banks, though in general high and rocky composed of a deep brown-coloured freestone. Several rice mills were so completely inundated, that their thatched roofs were but just visible above the surface of the water; others were entirely washed away; and the wrecks of them scattered upon the banks of the river. A vessel of our squadron was upset upon the roof of one of these mills.

During two days' sail the surface of the country was hilly and well wooded with camphors, firs, and tallow-trees; but as we approached the *Po-yang* lake, a small inland sea, it began to assume the uniform appearance of an extended marsh, without any visible signs of cultivation: here and there a few small huts, standing on the brink of pools of water, with twice the number of small boats floating or drawn up on shore, sufficiently indicated the occupation of the inhabitants. In this part of the [533] country we had an opportunity of seeing the various means practised by the Chinese to catch fish: rafts and other floating vessels with the fishing corvorant: boats with moveable planks turning on hinges, and painted so as to deceive fishes on moonlight nights and entice them to leap out of the water upon the planks; nets set in every form; and wicker baskets made exactly in the same manner as those used in Europe. Large gourds and blocks of wood were floating on the water, in order to familiarize the various kinds of water-fowl to such objects, which gave the Chinese an opportunity, by sticking their heads into gourds or earthen pots and keeping their bodies under water, to approach the birds in a gentle manner sufficiently near to take them by the legs and draw them quietly under the water; a method which is said to be practised by the natives of South America.

The nearer we approached the great lake *Po-yang*, the more dreary was the appearance of the country; and for the distance of ten miles around it, or at least on the south and west sides, was a wild waste of reeds and rank grasses, such as the *Scirpus*, *Cyperus*, and bulrushes, interrupted only by stagnant pools of water. Not a human dwelling of any description was to be seen. This place may justly be considered as the sink of China, into which rivers fall from every point of the compass. It is scarcely possible for the imagination to form to itself an idea of a more desolate region than that which surrounds the Po-yang lake. The temperature was so reduced, by the circumambient waters, that on the 27th November, with drizzling showers, the thermometer was down to 48° in the forenoon. We sailed near four whole days over the same kind of country and came, [534] towards the evening of the last, to the city of *Nan-tchang-foo*, the capital of *Kiang-see*, where we observed from four to five hundred of the revenue vessels lying at anchor. We waited at this place a few hours to take in the necessary provisions and to receive a present of silk, tea, and some other trifles from the viceroy. We were told of a famous temple in the neighbourhood of the city, but we had no curiosity to go out of the way to see it, which was dedicated to the man who, as we have already observed, made his *apotheosis* comfortably in his own house; that there was a well belonging to this temple full of large snakes, whom the priests venerate and to whom they admonish the people to make sacrifices, as being children of the dragons which, if not constantly appeased by oblations to these their offspring, would destroy the whole world. Thus, in all countries where votaries of superstition are to be found, will knaves be met with to take advantage of their weakness. The priests of this temple are said to have made one observation, which is perhaps no superstition, that when these water snakes appear on the surface, rains and inundations are sure to follow. I took advantage, however, of the short delay, to go on board one of the revenue vessels and to measure the capacity of its hold. It was in length 115 feet, breadth 15 feet, and depth 6 feet; the sides streight and the width nearly the same fore and aft; so that the burden might fairly be estimated at 250 tons. Independent, therefore, of the innumerable small craft, there were lying before this city 100,000 tons of shipping.

The city of *Nan-tchang-foo* is situated upon the left bank of the river *Kan-kiang-ho* falling from the southward into the [535] *Po-yang* lake. It was here about five hundred yards in width, against the stream of which we made a rapid progress with a brisk breeze. For the first sixty miles the country was flat and uncultivated, except in places where we observed a few fields of rice. But there was no want of population. Towns and villages were constantly in sight, as were also manufactories of earthen ware, bricks and tiles. The farther we advanced up the river, the more populous was the country, the more varied and agreeable the surface, and the more extended the cultivation. The banks were skirted with large trees, that cast a cool and comfortable shade on the walks beneath. Of these, some were willows, others camphors, but by far the greatest number were the *Yang-tchoo*, a large spreading tree that threw its branches down to the ground where, like the *Ficus Indicus*, of which indeed it was a variety, they took root and became stems.

At the city *Kei-shui-shien*, which like most cities in China offered little worthy of remark, the river divided into two branches; and at *Kin-gan-foo*, a city of the first order, which we passed the same night, by the river contracting suddenly the current became stronger and of course our progress slower. To track the barges it was necessary again to press a number of men; here, however, it may be observed, they undertook the service with more willingness than to the northward. The river meandered through a mountainous and barren country, rich only in picturesque beauty which, though pleasing to the eye of the artist and the connoisseur, has less charms for the philosopher, who finds more real beauties to exist in a soil, [536] however tame and uniform, that can be rendered subservient to the uses of man.

On the 3d of November we approached that part of the river which, on account of the numerous ship-wrecks that have happened there, is held in no small degree of dread by the Chinese. They call it the *Shee-pa-tan*, or the eighteen cataracts: which are torrents formed by ledges of rock running across the bed of the river. They have not, however, any thing very terrific in them, not one being half so dangerous as the fall at London bridge about half-tide. But the Chinese have no great dexterity in the management of their vessels. They are so easily alarmed, that they frequently miscarry through timidity, when a little recollection and resolution would have secured them success. The mountains between which the river was hemmed in were covered with forests of the larch fir; the glens and vallies abounded with the bamboo, of which we here observed two species, one the same that is common in other parts of the East, and the second much smaller in its growth, seldom exceeding the height of ten feet; and the fibres of its small stem are more hard and solid than those of the other species. The Chinese use it in the finer parts of such household furniture and other articles as are constructed of bamboo. From the margins of the river to the feet of the forests the lower parts of the mountains were covered with coppice, among which the most common shrub bore a close resemblance to the tea plant, and accordingly the Chinese called it the *Tcha-wha*, or flower of tea. It was the *Camellia Sesanqua* of Thunberg, to which they had given the same name (not being very nice in specific distinc [537] tions), as to the *Camellia Japonica* of Linnæus. From the nut of the former not unlike to, though somewhat smaller than, the chesnut, a very pleasant oil is expressed and used for similar purposes to the Florence oil in Europe.

This intricate part of the river, where innumerable pointed rocks occurred, some above, some even with, and others just below the surface of the water, required two long days' sail with a fair breeze; and the falls became more rapid and dangerous the farther we advanced. At the fifteenth cataract we perceived two or three vessels lying against the rocks with their flat-bottoms uppermost; a terrible sight for our bargemen who, like the countryman in the fable, instead of applying the shoulder to the wheel, began to implore the assistance of the river god by sounding the gong, in order to rouse his attention and by regaling his olfactory nerves with the smoke of sandal-wood matches; so that had we been dropping down the stream, instead of going against it, there was every reason to apprehend that our barge would have shared a similar fate; for it received many a gentle rub against the rocks.

The appearance of the country in the neighbourhood of the cataracts was extremely beautiful. The transparency of the stream, the bold rocks finely fringed with wood, and the varied forms of the mountains called to mind those delightful streams that are discharged from the lakes of the northern counties of England. Like these too, the *Kan-kiang-ho* abounded with fish, not however with the delicious trout but one of much less flavour, a species of perch. Great numbers of rafts were[538] floating on the river with the fishing corvorant, and we observed that he seldom dived without success. For the whole distance of three days' journey, the hilly country bordering on the river produced very little but the *Camellia Sesanqua*, which appeared to be every where of spontaneous growth.

We halted on the 6th of December, late in the evening, before the city of *Kan-tchoo-foo*, which is remarkable for nothing that I could learn except for the great quantity of varnish trees the *Rhus vernix* I suppose, that are cultivated in the neighbourhood. In the course of the journey we had picked up two varieties of the tea plant, taken out of the ground and potted by our own gardener; and which, being in good growing order, were intended to be sent to Bengal as soon as occasion might serve after our arrival at Canton. Knowing we should be hurried away, as usual, in the morning and wishing to procure a few young plants of the varnish tree, I prevailed on our good friend *Van-ta-gin* to dispatch some person for that purpose, to add to those of the tea plant and the *Camellia Sensanqua. Van* made application to the men in office at this place, with the best intention of serving us, but these gentry, either conceiving that their compliance might be treason to the state, or else, in the true spirit of the nation, determined to play a trick upon the strangers, certainly procured the plants and sent them on board in pots, just as we were departing the next morning. In a short time they all began to droop, the leaves withered and, on examination, it was found that not a single plant among them had the least portion of a root, being nothing more than small branches of trees which, from the nature[539] of the wood, were not likely nor indeed ever intended to strike root.

From *Kan-tchoo-foo* the face of the country became more uniform and suitable for the labours of agriculture; and, accordingly, we found a very small portion of it unoccupied. Wheat about six inches above ground and extensive plantations of the sugar cane fit for cutting, were the chief articles under cultivation: and the farther we advanced to the southward, the more abundant and extended were those of the latter. The canes were remarkably juicy and their joints from six to nine inches in length. To express the juice from them and convert it into a consistent mass, temporary mills were erected in different places among the plantations. The process was very simple. A pair of cylinders, sometimes of stone but more generally of hard wood, placed vertically, were put in motion by oxen or buffalos and from the foot of these the expressed juice was conveyed, by a tube carried under the floor, into a boiler that was sunk in the ground at the end of the apartment; where it was boiled to a proper degree of consistence the expressed canes serving as fuel. Though unacquainted with the process of refining sugar, the natural tendency that the syrup possesses of forming itself into crystals in cooling had suggested to them the means of obtaining very fine and pure sugar-candy which, in the market of Canton, is sold in a pulverized state as white as the best refined sugar. The coarse syrup, usually called treacle or molasses, and the dregs, are not employed, as in the West India islands, in the distillation of rum, but are sometimes thrown into the still with fermented rice, in order to procure a[540] better kind of *Seau-tchoo* or *burnt*wine; the chief use, however, of the molasses is to preserve fruits and other vegetable productions; and particularly the roots of ginger, a conserve of which the Chinese are remarkably fond.

The bed of the river having, in the lapse of ages, settled to the depth of twenty, thirty, or even forty feet below the general level of the country, it became necessary to employ some artificial means of obtaining the water for the purpose, of irrigation. The contrivance made use of to raise it to the height of the banks was simple and ingenious; and from hence it was conveyed in small channels to every part of the cane plantations. Of the useful machine employed for this purposes consisting of a bamboo wheel which I understand has been adopted in America, a view and section may be seen among the plates accompanying Sir George Staunton's authentic account of the embassy. I shall therefore content myself with observing in this place, that the axis excepted, it is entirely constructed of bamboo, without the assistance of a single nail or piece of iron; that the expence of making it is a mere trifle; that in its operations it requires no attendance, and that it will lift, to the height of forty feet, one hundred and fifty tons of water in the course of twenty-four hours[58]. Every plantation near this part of the river had its wheel and some of them two; [511]and the water raised by them was sometimes conveyed at once into the plots of canes and some times into reservoirs, out of which it was afterwards pumped, as occasion might require, by the chain-pump and carried to those places where it might be wanted along small channels coated with clay.

The women of this province were more robust than ordinary and well suited, by their strength and muscular powers, to endure the hard labour and drudgery of the field, which seemed to be their chief employment. This sort of labour, however, might be the cause, rather than the consequence, of their extraordinary strength and masculine form. The habitual use of hard labour, to which the women are here brought up, fits them best to become the wives of the peasantry in the neighbouring provinces; and accordingly, when a Chinese farmer is desirous of purchasing a working wife he makes his offers in *Kiang-see*. It was here that we saw a woman yoked literally by traces to a plough, whilst the husband or master had the lighter task of holding it by one hand and drilling in the seed with the other. The exertion of labour together with the constant exposure to the weather, in a climate situated under the twenty-fifth to the twenty-ninth parallel of latitude, have contributed to render more coarse and forbidding the features of the fair sex of *Kiang-see*, in the formation of which, indeed, Nature had not been too bountiful. Like the women of the Malay nation, with whom they most probably are derived from one common stock, they fixed their strong black hair close to the head by two metal skewers. Their dress, in other respects, was the same as that of the men, and like these they wore straw sandals on their feet.[512] Thus far, by avoiding the pain attendant on fashionable feet, and enjoying the free use of their limbs, they might be said to have the advantage of the city ladies. It was, indeed, observed that even such as were not employed in the labours of the field, but kept constantly at home for domestic purposes, were, in this province, equally exempted from the barbarous fashion of cramping the feet.

On the 9th we again entered a narrow defile and here with difficulty the vessels were forced along against a strong current; and over the pebbly bottom, against which they were constantly striking. At *Nan-gan-foo*, where we arrived in the evening, the river ceases to be navigable. Indeed the whole of the three last days' navigation might, with propriety, in England be called only a trout stream; upon which no nation on earth, except the Chinese, would have conceived the idea of floating any kind of craft; they have however adapted, in an admirable manner, the form and construction of their vessels to the nature and depth of the navigation; towards the upper part of the present river they drew only, when moderately laden, about six inches of water. They were from fifty to seventy feet in length, narrow and flat-bottomed, a little curved, so that they took the ground only in the middle point. Yet, in several places, the water was so shallow that they could not be dragged over until a channel had been made, by removing the stones and gravel with iron rakes. The length of this river, from its source at *Nan-gan-foo* to the *Po-yang* lake, is nearly three hundred English miles. The banks in the low part of the province of *Kiang-see* consisted of a deep soil of black earth,[543] supported on clay of a dark red or brown colour; denoting the presence of iron. The mountains were chiefly of red sand-stone; and the soil of the hills, producing the *Camellia*, was a brown loam mixed with particles of mica.

We had now before us another land-journey, over the steep and lofty mountain of *Me-lin*, whose summit is the boundary between the two provinces of *Kiang-see* and *Quan-tung*; on the south side of which commences the river *Pei-kiang-ho* that flows by the port of Canton; and whose mouth is familiarly known in Europe by the name of the *Bocca Tigris*. The ascent of this mountain, which some undertook on horseback and others in chairs, was made by a well-paved road, carried in a zig-zag manner over the very highest point, where a pass was cut to a considerable depth through a granite rock; a work that had evidently not been accomplished with any moderate degree of labour or expence. In the middle of the pass was a military post, much stronger than ordinary, and it was defended or, more correctly speaking, it was supplied with two old pieces of cannon, that had been cast, in all probability, near two hundred years ago, perhaps by the Jesuits who first taught them an art which they seem already to have forgotten or neglected.

The view from the summit towards the southward, over the province of Canton, was as rich and enchanting as that on the opposite side was dreary and barren. In descending the gradual slope of about twelve miles, before the mountain had blended with the general surface of the country, there was a constant[544] succession of dwellings; so that this whole distance might almost be considered as one continued street. Half of the buildings consisted, however, of places of convenience to which passengers might retire to obey the calls of nature, and the doors, or rather the openings into such erections, were always invitingly fronting the street. To each single dwelling, whether alone or joined with others, was annexed a fabric of this description. Each was constructed upon a large terrace cistern, lined with such materials that no absorption could take place; and straw and other dry rubbish are thrown in by the owners, from time to time, to prevent evaporation. In one of the streets of Canton is a row of buildings of this kind which, in so warm a climate, is a dreadful nuisance; but the consideration of preserving that kind of manure, which by the Chinese is considered as superior for forcing vegetation to all others, has got the better of both decency and prudence.

All the passengers we met upon this road were laden with jars of oil expressed from the Camellia. In the course of eighteen miles, which is about the distance from the summit of *Me-lin* to the city of *Nan-sheun-foo*, we passed at least a thousand persons on their way to *Nan-gan-foo*, each bearing ten or twelve gallons of oil and among these were a number of women.

Having now traversed five of the provinces of China, that are considered among the most populous and productive in the empire, a general sketch may be drawn, by taking a retrospective view, of the state of agriculture and the condition of [545] the people; of their habitations, dress, diet and means of subsistence; and some conclusion drawn as to the population of the country.

W. Alexander del. *T. Medland sculp.*
A Village and Cottages

W. Alexander del. *T. Medland sculp.*
Dwelling of a Mandarin or Officer of State

Pub. May 2, 1804, by Mess. *Cadell, & Davies, Strand, London.*

It was a remark too singular to escape notice that, except in the neighbourhood of the *Po-yang* lake, the peasantry of the province in which the capital stands were more miserable, their houses more mean and wretched, and their lands in a worse state of cultivation, than in any other part of the route—a remark which also agrees with the accounts given by the Dutch embassy of that part of *Pe-tche-lee*, on the south-west side of the capital, through which they passed. Four mud walls covered over with a thatch of reeds, or the straw of millet, or the stems of holcus, compose their habitations; and they are most commonly surrounded with clay walls, or with a fence made of the strong stems of the *Holcus Sorghum*. A partition of matting divides the hovel into two apartments; each of which has a small opening in the wall to admit the air and light; but one door generally serves as an entrance, the closure of which is frequently nothing more than a strong mat. A blue cotton jacket and a pair of trowsers, a straw hat and shoes of the same material, constitute the dress of the majority of the people. Matting of reeds or bamboo, a cylindrical pillow of wood covered with leather, a kind of rug or felt blanket made of the hairy wool of the broad-tailed sheep, not spun and woven but beat together as in the process for making hats, and sometimes a mattress stuffed with wool, hair, or straw, constitute their bedding. Two or three jars, a few basons of earthen-ware of the coarsest kind, a large iron pot, a frying-pan and a portable[546] stove, are the chief articles of furniture. Chairs and tables are not necessary; both men and women sit on their heels; and in this posture they surround the great iron pot, with each a bason in his hands, when they take their meals. The poverty of their food was sufficiently indicated by their meagre appearance. It consists chiefly of boiled rice, millet, or other grain, with the addition of onions or garlic, and mixed sometimes with a few other vegetables that, by way of relish, are fried in rancid oil, extracted from a variety of plants, such as the *Seffamum, Brassica orientalis, Cytisus Cadjan*, a species of *Dolichos*, and, among others, from the same species of *Ricinus* or *Palma-Christi*, from which the Castor is drawn, and used only in Europe as a powerful purgative. Its drastic qualities may probably be diminished by applying less pressure in extracting the oil, or by habit, or by using it fresh, as it does not appear that the Chinese suffer any inconvenience in its application to culinary purposes. As well as I could understand, the seeds were first bruised and then boiled in water, and the oil that floated on the surface was skimmed off. Our Florence oil they affected not to admire having, as they said, no taste. The Chinese, like the inhabitants of the South of Europe, seem to attach a higher value on oils, in proportion as age has given to them a higher degree of rancidity.

Fish of any kind, in this part of the country, is a great rarity; few are caught in the rivers of *Pe-tche-lee*. We met with none in the whole province, except at *Tien-sing* and in the capital, whose market, no doubt, like that of London, draws to its center the choice products of a very extensive circuit. Salt and dried fish, it is true, are brought from the southward as articles of commerce, but the poor peasantry cannot afford to purchase them for general use. They obtain them only sometimes by bartering millet or vegetables in exchange. A morsel of pork to relish their rice is almost the only kind of meat that the poor can afford to taste. They have little milk and neither butter, nor cheese, nor bread; articles of nourishment to which, with potatoes, the peasantry of Europe owe their chief support. Boiled rice, indeed, and not bread, is considered as an article of the first necessity, the staff of life in China. Hence the monosyllable *fan*, which signifies boiled rice, enters into every compound that implies eating; thus *tche-fan*, the name of a meal in general, is to eat rice; breakfast is called the *tsao-fan* or morning rice, and supper the *ouan-fan* or evening rice. Their principal and indeed their best beverage is bad tea, boiled over and over again as long as any bitter remains in the leaves, taken without milk or sugar, or any other ingredient except, in cold weather, a little ginger. In this weak state the only purpose it seems to answer is that of carrying down the sediment of muddy water that abounds in all the flat provinces of China, which the leaves of tea (as I fancy those of any other plant would) are found to do. These poor creatures, however, are instructed by popular opinion to ascribe to it many extraordinary qualities[59].

It would require a more familiar acquaintance with the people and a longer residence among them, than was allowed to us, to explain the true reason of such real poverty among the peasantry in the vicinity of the capital. Perhaps, indeed, it may be owing, in a great degree, to the proximity of the court, which in all countries has the effect of drawing together a crowd of people to consume the products of the soil, without contributing any portion of labour towards their production. The encouragement that is here given to idleness and dissipation is but too apt to entice the young peasantry in the neighbourhood from their houses, and thus rob the country of its best hands. The soil, likewise, near the capital is barren and sandy, producing few supplies beyond the wants of the several tenants; and all other necessaries of life not raised by them must be purchased extravagantly dear. It is, indeed, surprizing how this immense city, said to contain three millions of inhabitants, is contrived to be supplied at any rate, considering the very sterile and unproductive state of the country for many miles around it. It might not, however, be a matter of less astonishment to a Chinese, nor less difficult for him to conceive, in what manner our own capital receives its daily supplies, especially after he had observed that there is not a single road, by which London can be approached, that is not carried over vast tracts of uncultivated commons and waste grounds.

The vallies of Tartary furnish beeves and broad-tailed sheep for Pekin, and grain is brought by water from every part of the country, of which the government takes the precaution to lay up in store a sufficient quantity for a twelvemonth's consumption. Of animal food, pork is mostly consumed. Few peasants are without their breed of hogs; these animals, indeed, are likewise kept in large cities, where they become public nuisances. Bad beef in Pekin sells for about six-pence the pound; mutton and pork eight-pence; lean fowls and ducks from two to three shillings; eggs are generally about one penny each; small loaves of bread that are boiled in steam, without yeast or leaven, are about four-pence a pound; rice sells usually at three-halfpence or two-pence the pound; wheat flour at two-pence halfpenny or three-pence; fine tea from twelve to thirty shillings a pound; that of the former price, at least such as was procured clandestinely for us, not drinkable, and the latter not near so good as that of about six shillings in London[60]. There are, indeed, plenty of tea-houses in and near the capital, where the labouring people may purchase their cup of tea for two small copper coin (not quite a farthing) but it is miserably bad. A tolerable horse and a man-slave are usually about the same price, being from fifteen to twenty ounces of silver. The article of dress worn by the common people is not[550] very expensive. The peasantry are invariably clad in cotton; and this article is the produce of most of the provinces. The complete dress of a peasant is about fifteen shillings; of a common tradesman three pounds; an officer of government's common dress ten pounds; of ceremony about thirty pounds; and if enriched with embroidery and gold and silver tissue, between two and three hundred pounds: a pair of black satin boots twenty shillings; and a cap or bonnet about the same sum. The price of labour, however, and particularly in Pekin, bears no sort of proportion to the price of provisions. A mechanic in this city thinks himself well paid if he gets a shilling a-day. A common weaver, joiner, or other tradesman earns a bare subsistence for his family; and the best servants may be hired for an ounce of silver a-month. Many are glad to give their services in exchange for their subsistence, without any consideration in hard money. Tobacco being an indispensable article for all ranks of every age and sex bears of course a high price in the capital. It is singular enough, that this plant should have found its way into every part of the world, among savage as well as civilized nations, even into the deserts of Africa, where it was found in constant use among the Booshuanas, a people, till very lately, totally unknown; and it is equally singular, that an herb of so disagreeable a taste should, by habit, obtain an ascendency so far over the appetite, as not easily to be relinquished.

The climate of the northern provinces is unfavourable to the poor peasantry. The summers are so warm that they go[551] nearly naked and the winters so severe that, what with their poor and scanty fare, their want of fuel, clothing, and even shelter, thousands are said to perish from cold and hunger. In such a condition the ties of nature sometimes yield to self-preservation, and children are sold to save both the parent and offspring from perishing for want; and infants become a prey to hopeless indigence. We have seen in the notes taken by the gentleman in the Dutch embassy, how low the temperature is at Pekin in the winter months; and they have no coals nearer than the mountains of Tartary, which are all brought on the backs of dromedaries; of course, they are extravagantly dear. In fact, they are scarcely ever burned pure, but are crumbled to dust and mixed up with earth, in which state they give out a very strong heat, but no flame, and are suitable enough for their small close stoves.

Although it is a principle of the Chinese government to admit of no distinctions among its subjects, except those that learning and office confer; and although the most rigid sumptuary laws have been imposed to check that tendency to shew and splendor, which wealth is apt to assume; and to bring as much as possible on a level, at least in outward appearance, all conditions of men; yet, with regard to diet, there is a wider difference perhaps between the rich and the poor of China, than in any other country. That wealth which, if permitted, would be expended in flattering the vanity of its possessors, is now applied in the purchase of dainties to pamper the appetite. Their famous *Gin-sing*, a name signifying *the life of man*(the *Panax quinquefolium* of Linnæus) on account of its supposed invigo[552]rating and aphrodisiac qualities was, for a length of time, weighed against gold. The sinewy parts of stags and other animals, with the fins of sharks, as productive of the same effects, are purchased by the wealthy at enormous prices: and the nests that are constructed by small swallows on the coasts of Cochin-China, Cambodia, and other parts of the East, are dearer even than some kinds of *Gin-sing*. Most of the plants that grow on the sea-shore are supposed to possess an invigorating quality, and are, therefore, in constant use as pickles or preserves, or simply dried and cut into soups in the place of other vegetables. The leaves of one of these, apparently a species of that genus of sea-weed called by botanists *fucus*, after being gathered, are steeped in fresh water and hung up to dry. A small quantity of this weed boiled in water gives to it the consistence of a jelly, and when mixed with a little sugar, the juice of an orange, or other fruit, and set by to cool, I know of no jelly more agreeable or refreshing. The leaf is about six inches long, narrow and pointed, deeply serrated, and the margins ciliated; the middle part smooth, semi-transparent, and of a leathery consistence. The Chinese call it *Chin-chou*.

185

The great officers of state make use of these and various other gelatinous viands for the purpose of acquiring, as they suppose, a proper degree of corpulency[61], which is considered[553] by them as respectable and imposing upon the multitude; of a great portion of whom it may be observed, as Falstaff said of his company, "No eye hath seen such scare-crows." It would be rare to find, among the commonalty of China, one to compare with a porter-drinking citizen or a jolly-looking farmer of England. They are indeed naturally of a slender habit of body and a sickly appearance, few having the blush of health upon their cheeks. The tables of these are covered with a vast variety of dishes, consisting mostly of stews of fish, fowl and meat, separately and jointly, with proper proportions of vegetables and sauces of different kinds. Their beverage consists of tea and whiskey. In sipping this ardent spirit, made almost boiling hot, eating pastry and fruits, and smoking the pipe, they spend the greatest part of the day, beginning from the moment they rise and continuing till they go to bed. In hot weather they sleep in the middle of the day, attended by two servants, one to fan away the flies and the other to keep them cool.

The province of *Pe-tche-lee* embraces an extent of climate from 38° to 40½° of north latitude. The temperature is very[554] various. In summer Fahrenheit's thermometer is generally above 80° during the day, sometimes exceeding 90°; and, in the middle of winter, it remains for many days together below the freezing point, descending occasionally to zero or 0. But it generally enjoys a clear pure atmosphere throughout the whole year.

In the practical part of agriculture, in this province, we observed little to attract attention or to commend. The farmer gets no more than one crop off the ground in a season, and this is generally one of the species of millets already mentioned, or holcus, or wheat; but they sometimes plant a *Dolichos* or bean between the rows of wheat, which ripens after the latter is cut down. They have no winter crops, the hard frosty weather usually setting in towards the end of November and continuing till the end of March. The three different modes of sowing grain, by drilling, dibbling, and broadcast, are all in use but chiefly the first, as being the most expeditious and the crop most easy to be kept free from weeds; the last is rarely practised on account of the great waste of seed; and dibbling is used only in small patches of ground near the houses when they aim at neatness. The soil, being in general loose and sandy and free from stones, is worked without much difficulty, but it seemed to require a good deal of manure; and this necessary article from the paucity of domestic animals is extremely scarce. Very few sheep or cattle were observed, yet there was an abundance of land that did not seem for many years to have felt the ploughshare.[555]

The draught cattle most generally in use are oxen, mules, and asses. Horses are scarce and of a small miserable breed, incapable of much work; a remark, indeed, which will apply to every province of the empire; though those of Tartary, which composed the Emperor's stud, according to the Embassador's description, were not wanting in point of size, beauty, or spirit. No pains, however, are bestowed to effect, nor do they seem to be sensible of the advantages to be derived from, an improvement in the breed of cattle. Nor indeed is any care taken of the bad breed which they already possess. It would be supposed that, where a regular establishment of cavalry is kept up to an amount that seems almost incredible, some attention would be paid to the nature and condition of their horses. This, however, is not the case. A Scotch poney, wild from the mountains, which has never felt the teeth of a currycomb and whose tail and mane are clotted together with dirt, is in fit condition to join a regiment of Tartar cavalry. Those kept by men in office are equally neglected. The Chinese have no idea that this noble animal requires any attention beyond that of giving him his food; and of this, in general, he receives a very scanty portion.

That part of the province of *Shan-tung* through which we travelled exhibited a greater variety of culture than *Pe-tche-lee*; but the surface of the northern parts especially was equally uniform. The soil, consisting generally of mud and slime brought apparently by the inundations of rivers, contained not a single pebble. The season was too late to form any estimate of the crops produced upon the immense plains of *Shan-tung*;[556] but the young crops of wheat, standing at this time (the middle of October) a few inches above the ground, looked extremely well. Little waste ground occurred, except the footpaths and the channels which served as division marks of property. Some attempts indeed were here made at the division of grounds by hedge-rows, but with little success; the plant they had adopted, the *Palma-Christi*, was ill-suited for such a purpose. As we advanced to the southward, in this province, the proportion of wheat under cultivation diminished, and its place was employed by plantations of cotton, whose pods were now ripe and bursting. The plant was low and poor in growth, but the branches were laden with pods. Like the wheat it was planted or dibbled in rows. The cotton produced the second year was said to be considered as equally good with that of the first, but being found to degenerate the third year, it was then rooted out[557] and the ground prepared for fresh seed[62].

The southern parts of *Shan-tung* are composed of mountains and swamps. Here, lakes of various magnitudes occur and large tracts of country similar to those which are known to us by the name of peat-moss. In such places the population could not be expected to be excessive; and, accordingly, we met with few inhabitants, except those who subsisted their families by fishing. So great were the numbers engaged in this employment, who lived entirely in floating vessels, that we judged[558] the waters to be fully as populous as the land. No rent is exacted by the government, nor toll, nor tythe, nor licence-money for permission to catch fish; nor is there any sort of impediment against the free use of any lake, river or canal whatsoever. The gifts that nature has bestowed are cautiously usurped by any power, even in this despotic government, for individual use or profit; but are suffered to remain the free property of all who may chuse by their labour to derive advantage from them. But even this free and unrestrained use is barely sufficient to procure for them the necessaries, much less any of the comforts, of life. The condition of the peasantry, in the northern parts of this province, was much more desirable. Their clothing was decent; their countenances cheerful, indicating plenty; and their dwellings were built of bricks or wood, appearing more solid and comfortable than those of the province in which the capital is situated. But the poor fishermen carried about with them unequivocal marks of their poverty. Their pale meagre looks are ascribed to the frequent, and almost exclusive, use of fish; which is supposed to give them a scrophulous habit of body. Their endeavours, however, are not wanting to correct any acid or unwholesome humours that this sort of diet may produce, by the abundant use of onions and garlic, which they cultivate even upon the waters. Having no houses on shore, nor stationary abode, but moving about in their vessels upon the extensive lakes and rivers, they have no inducement to cultivate patches of ground, which the pursuits of their profession might require them to leave for the profit of another; they prefer, therefore, to plant their onions on rafts of bamboo, well interwoven with reeds and strong grass and[559] covered with earth; and these floating gardens are towed after their boats.

The women assist in dragging the net and other operations of taking fish; but the younger part of the family are sometimes employed in breeding ducks. These stupid birds here acquire an astonishing degree of docility. In a single vessel are sometimes many hundreds which, like the cattle of the Kaffers in southern Africa, on the signal of a whistle leap into the water, or upon the banks to feed, and another whistle brings them back. Like the ancient Egyptians, they use artificial means of hatching eggs, by burying them in sand at the bottom of wooden boxes, and placing them on plates of iron kept moderately warm by small furnaces underneath. Thus the old birds which, provided they hatched their eggs themselves, would only produce one brood, or at most two, in the course of the year, continue to lay eggs almost every month. Hogs are also kept in many of the fishing craft. In fact, ducks and hogs affording the most savory meat, most abounding in fat and, it may be added, best able to subsist themselves, are esteemed above all other animals. The ducks being split open, salted, and dried in the sun, are exchanged for rice or other grain. In this state we found them an excellent relish; and, at our request, they were plentifully supplied during the whole progress through the country.

The province of *Shan-tung* extends in latitude from thirty-four and a half to thirty-eight degrees. The mean temperature, from the 19th of October to the 29th of the same month,[560] was about fifty-two degrees at sun-rise, to seventy degrees at noon. A constant clear and cloudless sky.

The numerous canals and rivers, that in every direction intersect the province of *Kiang-nan*, and by which it is capable of being flooded to any extent in the dryest seasons, render it one of the most valuable and fertile districts in the whole empire. Every part of it, also, having a free communication with the Yellow Sea by the two great rivers, the *Whang-*

ho and the *Yang-tse-kiang*, it has always been considered as the central point for the home trade; and, at one time, its chief city Nankin was the capital of the empire. That beautiful and durable cotton of the same name is here produced and sent to the port of Canton; from whence it is shipped off to the different parts of the world. The Chinese rarely wear it in its natural colour, except as an article of mourning; but export it chiefly, taking in return vast quantifies of unmanufactured white cotton from Bengal and Bombay, finding they can purchase this foreign wool at a much cheaper rate than that at which the nankin sells. For mourning dresses and a few other purposes white cotton is made use of, but in general it is dyed black or blue: among some of our presents were also pieces of a beautiful scarlet. Near most of the plantations of cotton we observed patches of indigo; a plant which grows freely in all the middle and southern provinces. The dye of this shrub being no article of commerce in China is seldom, if ever, prepared in a dry state, but is generally employed to communicate its colouring matter from the leaves, to avoid the labour and the loss that would be required to reduce it to a solid substance.[561] We observed that, in the cotton countries, almost every cottage had its garden of indigo. As in ancient times, in our own country, when every cottager brewed his own beer; kept his own cow for milk and butter; bred his own sheep, the wool of which being spun into yarn by his own family was manufactured into cloth by the parish weaver; and when every peasant raised the materials for his own web of hempen cloth; so it still appears to be the case in China. Here there are no great farmers nor monopolists of grain; nor can any individual nor body of men, by any possibility, either glut the market, or withhold the produce of the ground, as may best suit their purpose. Each peasant is supposed, by his industry, to have the means of subsistence within himself; though it often happens that these means, from adverse circumstances which hereafter will be noticed, fail of producing the desired effect.

In the province of *Kiang-nan* each grows his own cotton; his wife and children spin it into thread and it is woven into a web in his own house, sometimes by his own family, but more frequently by others hired for the purpose. A few bamboos constitute the whole machinery required for this operation. Money he has none; but his produce he can easily barter for any little article of necessity or luxury. The superfluities of life, which those in office may have occasion to purchase, are paid for in bars of silver without any impression, but bearing value for weight, like the Roman *as* or the Hebrew *shekel*. The only coin in circulation is the *tchen*, a piece of some inferior metal mixed with a small proportion of copper, of the value of the thousandth part of an ounce of silver; with this small piece of money the[562] little and constantly demanded necessaries of life are purchased, such as could not conveniently be obtained by way of barter. Silver is rarely lent out at interest, except between mercantile men in large cities. The legal interest is twelve per cent. but it is commonly extended to eighteen, sometimes even to thirty-six. To avoid the punishment of usury, what is given above twelve per cent. is in the shape of a *bonus*. "Usury, in China," observes Lord Macartney, "like gaming elsewhere, is a dishonourable mode of getting money; but by a sort of compact between necessity and avarice, between affluence and distress, the prosecution of a Jew or a sharper is considered by us as not very honourable even in the sufferers."

The greater the distance from the capital, the better was the apparent condition of the people. The Viceroy, when he received his Excellency on the entry of the embassy into this province, happened to cast his eye upon the half-starved and half-naked trackers of the boats; and being either ashamed of their miserable appearance, or feeling compassion for their situation, he ordered every man immediately a suit of new cloaths. In the morning, when our force was mustered, we were not a little surprized to see the great alteration that had taken place in the appearance of our trackers: every man had a blue cotton jacket edged with red, a pair of new white trowsers, and a smart hat with a high crown and feather. The natural fertility of the country, its central situation commanding a brisk trade, the abundance of its fisheries on the large rivers and lakes were incentives to industry, for the vast population that seemed to be equally distributed over every part of the province.[563]

Rice being the staple of China was abundantly cultivated, in all such places as afforded the greatest command of water. The usual average produce of corn-lands is reckoned to be from ten to fifteen for one; and of rice, from twenty-five to thirty; commonly about thirty. Those corn-lands that will admit of easy irrigation are usually turned over with the plough immediately after the grain is cut; which, in the middle provinces, is ready for the sickle early in June, about the same time that the young rice fields stand at the height of eight or ten inches. These being now thinned, the young plants are transplanted into the prepared wheat lands, which are then immediately flooded. Upon such a crop they reckon from fifteen to twenty for one. Instead of rice one of the millets is sometimes sown as an after-crop, this requiring very little water, or the *Cadjan*, a species of *Dolichos* or small bean, for oil, requiring still less. Or, it is a common practice, after taking off a crop of cotton and indigo, in the month of October, to sow wheat, in order to have the land again clear in the month of May or June. Such a succession of crops, without ever suffering the land to lie fallow, should seem to require a large quantity of manure. In fact, they spare no pains in procuring composts and manures; but they also accomplish much without these materials, by working the soil almost incessantly and mixing it with extraneous matters as, for instance, marle with light and sandy soils, or if this is not to be had, stiff clay; and on clayey grounds they carry sand and gravel. They also drag the rivers and canals and pools of water for slime and mud; and they preserve, with great care, all kinds of urine, in which it[56] is an universal practice to steep the seeds previous to their being sown. If turnip-seeds be steeped in lime and urine, the plant is said not to be attacked by the insect. Near all the houses are large earthen jars sunk in the ground, for collecting and preserving these and other materials that are convertible, by putrefactive fermentation, into manure. Old men and children may be seen near all the villages with small rakes and baskets, collecting every kind of dirt, or offals, that come in their way. Their eagerness to pick up whatever may be used as manure led to some ridiculous scenes. Whenever our barges halted and the soldiers and servants found it necessary to step on shore, they were always pursued to their place of retirement by these collectors of food for vegetables. It may literally be said in this country, that nothing is suffered to be lost. The profession of shaving is followed by vast numbers in China. As the whole head is shaved, except a small lock behind, few, if any, are able to operate upon themselves. And as hair is considered an excellent manure, every barber carries with him a small bag to collect the spoils of his razor.

The common plough of the country is a simple machine and much inferior to the very worst of ours. We saw one drill plough in *Shan-tung* different from all the rest. It consisted of two parallel poles of wood, shod at the lower extremities with iron to open the furrows; these poles were placed on wheels: a small hopper was attached to each pole to drop the seed into the furrows, which were covered with earth by a transverse piece of wood fixed behind, that just swept the surface of the ground.[565]

The machine usually employed for clearing rice from the husk, in the large way, is exactly the same as that now used in Egypt for the same purpose, only that the latter is put in motion by oxen and the former commonly by water. This machine consists of a long horizontal axis of wood, with cogs or projecting pieces of wood or iron fixed upon it, at certain intervals, and it is turned by a water-wheel. At right angles to this axis are fixed as many horizontal levers as there are circular rows of cogs; these levers act on pivots, that are fastened into a low brick wall built parallel to the axis, and at the distance of about two feet from it. At the further extremity of each lever, and perpendicular to it, is fixed a hollow pestle, directly over a large mortar of stone or iron sunk into the ground; the other extremity extending beyond the wall, being pressed upon by the cogs of the axis in its revolution, elevates the pestle, which by its own gravity falls into the mortar. An axis of this kind sometimes gives motion to fifteen or twenty levers. This machine[63], as well as the plough, still in use in modern Egypt, which is also the same as the Chinese plough, have been considered by a member of the French Institute to be the same instruments as those employed in that country two thousand years ago; and judging from the maxims of the Chinese government, and the character of the people, an antiquity equally great may be assigned to them in the latter country. The bamboo wheel for raising water, or something approaching very near to it, either with buckets appended to the circumference, or with fellies hollowed out so as to scoop up water, was also in [566]use among the ancient Egyptians; and, as I have before observed, continue to be so among the Syrians; from these they are supposed to have passed into Persia, where they are also still employed, and from whence they have derived, in Europe, the name of Persian wheels. The chain-pump of China, common in the hands of every farmer, was likewise an instrument of husbandry in Egypt.

A very erroneous opinion seems to have been entertained in Europe, with regard to the skill of the Chinese in agriculture. Industrious they certainly are, in an eminent degree, but their labour does not always appear to be bestowed with judgment. The instruments, in the first place, they make use of are incapable of performing the operations of husbandry to the greatest advantage. In the deepest and best soils, their plough seldom cuts to the depth of four inches, so that they sow from year to year upon the same soil, without being able to turn up new earth, and to bury the worn-out mould to refresh itself. Supposing them, however, to be supplied with ploughs of the best construction, we can scarcely conceive that their mules and asses and old women, would be equal to the task of drawing them.

The advantage that large farms in England possess over small ones consists principally in the means they afford the tenant of keeping better teams than can possibly be done on the latter, and consequently of making a better *tilth* for the reception of seed. The opulent farmer, on the same quantity of ground, will invariably raise more produce than the cottager can pretend|56 | to do. In China nine-tenths of the peasantry may be considered as cottagers, and having few cattle (millions I might add none at all) it can scarcely be expected that the whole country should be in the best possible state of cultivation. As horticulturists they may perhaps be allowed a considerable share of merit; but, on the great scale of agriculture, they are certainly not to be mentioned with many European nations. They have no knowledge of the modes of improvement practised in the various breeds of cattle; no instruments for breaking up and preparing waste lands; no system for draining and reclaiming swamps and morasses; though that part of the country over which the grand communication is effected between the two extremities of the empire, abounds with lands of this nature, where population is excessive and where the multitudes of shipping that pass and repass create a never failing demand for grain and other vegetable products. For want of this knowledge, a very considerable portion of the richest land, perhaps, in the whole empire, is suffered to remain a barren and unprofitable waste. If an idea may be formed from what we saw in the course of our journey, and from the accounts that have been given of the other provinces, I should conclude, that one-fourth part of the whole country nearly consists of lakes and low, sour, swampy grounds, which are totally uncultivated: and which, among other reasons hereafter to be mentioned, may serve to explain the frequent famines that occur in a more satisfactory way, than by supposing, with the Jesuits, that they are owing to the circumstance of the nations bordering upon them to the westward being savage and growing no corn. Their ignorance of draining, or their dread of inundations, to which|568| the low countries of China, in their present state, are subject, may perhaps have driven them, in certain situations, to the necessity of levelling the sides of mountains into a succession of terraces; a mode of cultivation frequently taken notice of by the missionaries as unexampled in Europe and peculiar to the Chinese; whereas it is common in many parts of Europe. The mountains of the *Pays de Vaud*, between *Lausanne* and *Vevay*, are cultivated in this manner to their summits with vines. "This would have been impracticable," says Doctor Moore, "on account of the steepness, had not the proprietors built strong stone walls at proper intervals, one above the other, which support the soil, and form little terraces from the bottom to the top of the mountains." But this method of terracing the hills is not to be considered, by any means, as a common practice in China. In our direct route it occurred only twice, and then on so small a scale as hardly to deserve notice. The whole territorial right being vested in the sovereign, the waste lands of course belong to the crown; but any person, by giving notice to the proper magistrate, may obtain a property therein, so long as he continues to pay such portion of the estimated produce as is required to be collected into the public magazines.

When I said that the Chinese might claim a considerable share of merit as horticulturists, I meant to confine the observation to their skill and industry of raising the greatest possible quantity of vegetables from a given piece of ground. Of the modes practised in Europe of improving the quality of fruit, they seem to have no just notion. Their oranges are naturally good and|569| require no artificial means of improvement, but the

European fruits, as apples, pears, plums, peaches and apricots are of indifferent quality. They have a common method of propagating several kinds of fruit-trees, which of late years has been practised with success in Bengal. The method is simply this: they strip a ring of bark, about an inch in width, from a bearing branch, surround the place with a ball of fat earth or loam bound fast to the branch with a piece of matting; over this they suspend a pot or horn with water having a small hole in the bottom just sufficient to let the water drop, in order to keep the earth constantly moist; the branch throws new roots into the earth just above the place where the ring was stripped off; the operation is performed in the spring, and the branch is sawn off and put into the ground at the fall of the leaf; the following year it bears fruit. They have no method of forcing vegetables by artificial heat, or by excluding the cold air and admitting, at the same time, the rays of the sun through glass. Their chief merit consists in preparing the soil, working it incessantly, and keeping it free of weeds.

Upon the whole, if I might venture to offer an opinion with respect to the merit of the Chinese as agriculturists, I should not hesitate to say that, let as much ground be given to one of their peasants as he and his family can work with the spade, and he will turn that piece of ground to more advantage, and produce from it more sustenance for the use of man, than any European whatsoever would be able to do; but, let fifty or one hundred acres of the best land in China be given to a farmer, at a mean rent, so far from making out of it the value of three rents, on|570| which our farmers usually calculate, he would scarcely be able to support his family, after paying the expence of labour that would be required to work the farm.

In fact there are no great farms in China. The inhabitants enjoy every advantage which may be supposed to arise from the lands being pretty equally divided among them, an advantage of which the effects might probably answer the expectations of those who lean towards such a system, were they not counteracted by circumstances that are not less prejudicial, perhaps, to the benefit of the public, than monopolizing farmers are by such persons supposed to be in our own country. One of the circumstances I allude to is the common practice, in almost every part of the country, of assembling together in towns and villages, between which very frequently the intermediate space of ground has not a single habitation upon it; and the reason assigned for this custom is the dread of the bands of robbers that infest the weak and unprotected parts of the country. The consequence of such a system is, that although the lands adjoining the villages be kept in the highest state of cultivation, yet those at a distance are suffered to remain almost useless; for having no beasts of burden, it would be an endless task of human labour to bear the manure that would be required, for several miles, upon the ground, and its produce from thence back again to the village. That such robbers do exist who, in formidable gangs, plunder the peasantry, is very certain: *She-fo-pao* was watching his grain to prevent its being stolen, when he had the misfortune of shooting his relation, who had also gone out for the same purpose. They are sometimes indeed so numerous, as|571| to threaten their most populous cities. The frequency of such robberies and the alarm they occasion to the inhabitants are neither favourable to the high notions that have been entertained of the Chinese government, nor of the morals of the people. Another, and perhaps the chief, disadvantage arising from landed property being pretty equally divided, will be noticed in speaking of the population and the frequent famines.

The province of *Kiang-nan* extends from about 31° to 34½° of northern latitude; and the mean temperature, according to Fahrenheit's thermometer, from the 30th of October to the 9th of November, was 54° at sun-rise and 66° at noon; the sky uniformly clear.

The province of *Tche-kiang* abounds in lakes and is intersected with rivers and canals like *Kiang-nan*; but the produce, except that of a little rice, is very different, consisting principally of silk. For feeding the worms that afford this article, all the fertile and beautiful vallies between the mountains, as well as the plains, are covered with plantations of the mulberry-tree. The small houses, in which the worms are reared, are placed generally in the centre of each plantation; in order that they may be removed as far as possible from any kind of noise; experience having taught them, that a sudden shout, or the bark of a dog, is destructive of the young worms. A whole brood has sometimes perished by a thunder storm. The greatest attention is, therefore, necessary; and, accordingly, they are watched night and

191

day. In fine weather, the young worms are exposed to the sun, upon a kind of thin open gauze stretched[572] in wooden frames; and at night they are replaced in the plantation houses. The trees are pruned from time to time, in order to cause a greater quantity and a constant succession of young leaves. The inhabitants of this province, especially in the cities, are almost universally clothed in silks; this rule among the Chinese of consuming, as much as possible, the products of their own country, and receiving as little as they can avoid from foreign nations, extends even to the provinces; a practice arising out of the little respect that, in China, as in ancient Rome, is paid to those concerned in trade and merchandize.

Besides silk *Tche-kiang* produces camphor, tallow from the *Croton*, a considerable quantity of tea, oranges, and almost all the fruits that are peculiar to the country. Every part of the province appeared to be in the highest state of cultivation and the population to be immense. Both the raw and manufactured silks, nankins and other cotton cloths, were sold at such low prices in the capital of this province, that it is difficult to conceive how the growers or the manufacturers contrived to gain a livelihood by their labour. But of all others, I am the most astonished at the small returns that must necessarily be made to the cultivators of the tea plant. The preparations of some of the finer kinds of this article are said to require that every leaf should be rolled singly by the hand; particularly such as are exported to the European markets. Besides this, there are many processes, such as steeping, drying, turning, and packing, after it has been plucked off the shrub leaf by leaf. Yet the first cost in the tea provinces cannot be more than from four-[573]pence to two shillings a pound, when it is considered that the ordinary teas stand the East India Company in no more than eight-pence a pound; and the very best only two shillings and eight-pence[64]. Nothing can more clearly point out the patient and unremitting labour of the Chinese, than the preparation of this plant for the market. It is a curious circumstance that a body of merchants in England should furnish employment, as might easily be made appear, to more than a million subjects of a nation that affects to despise merchants, and throws every obstacle in the way of commercial intercourse.

The mean temperature of *Tche-kiang*, in the middle of November, was from fifty-six degrees at sun-rise, to sixty-two degrees at noon. The extent from North to South is between the parallels of twenty-eight and thirty-four and a half degrees of northern latitude.

The northern part of *Kiang-see* contains the great *Po-yang* lake, and those extensive swamps and morasses that surround it, and which, as I have already observed, may be considered as the sink of China. The middle and southern parts are mountainous. The chief produce is sugar and oil from the *Camellia Sesanqua*. In this province are the principal manufactories of porcelain, whose qualities, as I have in a former chapter ob[57]served, depend more on the care bestowed in the preparation and in the selection of the materials, than in any secret art possessed by them. There are also, in this province, large manufactories of coarse earthen ware, of tiles, and bricks.

The extent of *Kiang-see* is from twenty-eight to thirty degrees, and the temperature, in November, was the same as that of the neighbouring province of *Tche-kiang*.

I have now to mention a subject on which much has already been written by various authors, but without the success of having carried conviction into the minds of their readers, that the things which they offered as facts were either true or possible; I allude to the populousness of this extensive empire. That none of the statements hitherto published are strictly true, I am free to admit, but that the highest degree of populousness that has yet been assigned may be possible, and even probable, I am equally ready to contend. At the same time, I acknowledge that, prepared as we were, from all that we had seen and heard and read on the subject, for something very extraordinary; yet when the following statement was delivered, at the request of the Embassador, by *Chou-ta-gin*, as the abstract of a census that had been taken the preceding year, the amount appeared so enormous as to surpass credibility. But as we had always found this officer a plain, unaffected, and honest man, who on no occasion had attempted to deceive or impose on us, we could not consistently consider it in any other light than as a document drawn up from authentic materials; its inaccuracy, however,[576] was obvious at a single glance, from the several sums being given in round millions. I have added to the table the extent of the provinces, the number of people on a square mile, and the value of the surplus taxes remitted to Pekin in the year 1792, as mentioned in the seventh chapter.

Provinces.	Population.	Square Miles.	No. on each square Mile.	Surplus taxes remitted to Pekin.
				oz. silver.
Pe-tche-lee	38,000,000	58,949	44	3,036,000
Kiang-nan	32,000,000	92,961	44	8,210,000
Kiang-see	19,000,000	72,176	63	2,120,000
Tche-kiang	21,000,000	39,150	36	3,810,000
Fo-kien	15,000,000	53,480	80	1,277,000
{ Hou-pee	14,000,000 }			{ 1,310,000
Houquang { Hou-nan	13,000,000 }	144,770	87	{ 1,345,000
Honan	25,000,000	65,104	84	3,213,000
Shan-tung	24,000,000	65,104	68	3,600,000
Shan-see	27,000,000	55,268	88	3,722,000
Shen- see } one	18,000,000 }			{ 1,700,000
Kan- soo } province	12,000,000 }	154,008	95	{ 340,000
Se-tchuen	27,000,000	166,800	62	670,000
Quan-tung	21,000,000	79,456	64	1,340,000
Quang-see	10,000,000	78,250	28	500,000

Yu-nan	8,000,000	107,969	7 4	210,000
Koei-tchoo	9,000,000	64,554	1 40	145,000
Totals	313,000,000	1,297,999[65]	—	36,548,000

Considering then the whole surface of the Chinese dominions[576] within the great wall to contain 1,297,999 square miles, or 830,719,360 English acres, and the population to amount to 333,000,000, every square mile will be found to contain two hundred and fifty-six persons, and every individual might possess two acres and a half of land. Great Britain is supposed to average about one hundred and twenty persons on one square mile, and that to each inhabitant there might be assigned a portion of five acres, or to each family five-and-twenty acres. The population of China, therefore, is to that of Great Britain as 256 to 120, or in a proportion somewhat greater than two to one; and the quantity of land that each individual in Great Britain might possess is just twice as much as could be allowed to each individual of China. We have only then to enquire if Britain, under the same circumstances as China, be capable of supporting twice its present population, or which is the same thing, if twelve and an half acres of land be sufficient for the maintenance of a family of five persons? Two acres of choice land sown with wheat, under good tillage, may be reckoned to average, after deducting the seed, 60 bushels or 3600 pounds, which every baker knows would yield 5400 pounds of bread, or three pounds a day to every member of the family for the whole year. Half an acre is a great allowance for a kitchen-garden and potatoe bed. There would still remain ten acres, which must be very bad land if, besides paying the rent and taxes, it did not keep three or four cows; and an industrious and managing family would find no difficulty in rearing as many pigs and as much poultry as would be necessary for home consumption,[577] and for the purchase of clothing and other indispensable necessaries. If then the country was pretty equally partitioned out in this manner; if the land was applied solely to produce food for man; if no horses nor superfluous animals were kept for pleasure, and few only for labour; if the country was not drained of its best hands in foreign trade and in large manufactories; if the carriage of goods for exchanging with other goods was performed by canals and rivers and lakes, all abounding with fish; if the catching of these fish gave employment to a very considerable portion of the inhabitants; if the bulk of the people were satisfied to abstain almost wholly from animal food, except such as is most easily procured, that of pigs and ducks and fish; if only a very small part of the grain raised was employed in the distilleries, but was used as the staff of life for man; and if this grain was of such a nature as to yield twice, and even three times, the produce that wheat will give on the same space of ground; if, moreover, the climate was so favourable as to allow two such crops every year—if, under all these circumstances, twelve and a half acres of land would not support a family of five persons; the fault could only be ascribed to idleness or bad management.

Let us then, for a moment, consider that these or similar advantages operate in China; that every product of the ground is appropriated solely for the food and clothing of man; that a single acre of land, sown with rice, will yield a sufficient quantity for the consumption of five people for a whole year, allowing to each person two pounds a-day, provided the returns of his crop are from twenty to twenty-five for one, which are considered as extremely moderate, being frequently more than[578] twice this quantity; that in the southern provinces two crops of rice are produced in the year, one acre of which I am well assured, with proper culture, will afford a supply of that grain even for ten persons, and that an acre of cotton will clothe two or three hundred persons, we may justly infer that, instead of twelve acres to each family, half that quantity would appear to be more than necessary; and safely conclude, that there is no want of land to support the assumed population of three hundred and thirty-three millions. This being the case, the population is not yet arrived at a level with the means which the country affords of subsistence.

There is, perhaps, no country where the condition of the peasantry may more justly be compared with those of China than Ireland. This island, according to the latest survey, contains about 17,000,000 English acres, 730,000 houses and 3,500,000 souls; so that, as in Great Britain, each individual averages very nearly five acres and every family five-and-twenty. An Irish cottager holds seldom more than an Irish acre of land, or one and three-quarters English nearly, in cultivation, with a cow's grass, for which he pays a rent from two to five pounds. Those on Lord Macartney's estate at Lissanore have their acre, which they cultivate in divisions with oats, potatoes, kale, and a little flax; with this they have besides the full pasturage of a cow all the year upon a large waste, not overstocked, and a comfortable cabin to inhabit, for which each pays the rent of three pounds. The cottager works perhaps three days in the week, at nine-pence a-day; if, instead of which, he had a second acre to cultivate, he would derive more benefit from its[579] produce than from the product of his three days' labour *per* week; that is to say, provided he would expend the same labour in its tillage. Thus then, supposing only half of Ireland in a state of cultivation and the other half pasturage, it would support a population more than three times that which it now contains; and as a century ago it had no more than a million of people, so within the present century, under favourable circumstances, it may increase to ten millions. And it is not unworthy of remark, that this great increase of population in Ireland has taken place since the introduction of the potatoe, which gives a never-failing crop.

I am aware that such is not the common opinion which prevails in this country, neither with regard to Ireland nor China; on the contrary, the latter is generally supposed to be overstocked with people; that the land is insufficient for their maintenance, and that the cities stand so thick one after the other, especially along the grand navigation between Pekin and Canton, that they almost occupy the whole surface. I should not, however, have expected to meet with an observation to this effect from the very learned commentator on the *voyage of Nearchus*, founded on no better authority than the crude notes of one *Æneas Anderson*, a livery servant of Lord Macartney, vamped up by a London bookseller as a speculation that could not fail, so greatly excited was public curiosity at the return of the Embassy. I would not be thought to disparage the authority on account of its being that of a livery servant; on the contrary, the notes of the meanest and dullest person, on a country so little travelled over, would be deserving attention before they came into the[580] hands of a *book-dresser*; but what dependence can be placed on the information of an author who states as a fact, that he saw tea and rice growing on the banks of the *Pei-ho*, between the thirty-ninth and fortieth parallels of latitude, two articles of the culture of which, in the whole province of *Pe-tche-lee*, they know no more than we do in England; and who ignorantly and impertinently talks of the shocking ideas the Chinese entertained of English cruelty, on seeing one of the guard receive a few lashes, when, not only the common soldiers, but the officers of this nation are flogged most severely with the bamboo on every slight occasion. If Doctor Vincent, from reading this book, was really persuaded that the cities of China were so large and so numerous, that they left not ground enough to subsist the inhabitants, I could wish to recall his attention for a few moments to this subject, as opinions sanctioned by such high authority, whether right or wrong, are sure, in some degree, to bias the public mind. We have seen that if China be allowed to contain three hundred and thirty-three millions of people, the proportion of its population is only just double that of Great Britain. Now if London and Liverpool and Birmingham and Glasgow, and all the cities, towns, villages, gentlemen's villas, farm-houses and cottages in this island were doubled, I see no great inconvenience likely to arise from such duplication. The unproductive land, in the shape of gentlemen's parks and pleasure grounds, would, I presume, be much more than sufficient to counterbalance the quantity occupied by the new erections; and the wastes and commons would perhaps be more than enough to allow even a second duplication. But the population of an English city is not to be compared with, or considered as similar to, the[581] populousness of a Chinese city, as will be obvious by considering the two capitals of these two empires. Pekin, according to a measurement supposed to be taken with great accuracy, occupies a space of about fourteen square miles. London, with its suburbs, when reduced to a square, is said to comprehend about nine square miles. The houses of Pekin rarely exceed a single story; those of London are seldom less than four; yet both the Chinese and the missionaries who are settled in this capital agree that Pekin contains three millions of people; while London is barely allowed to have one million. The reason of this difference is, that most of the cross streets of a Chinese city are very narrow, and the alleys branching from them so confined, that a person may place one hand on one side and the other on the other side as he walks along[66]; that the houses in general are very small, and that each house contains six, eight, or ten persons, sometimes twice the number. If, therefore, fourteen square miles of buildings in China contain three millions of inhabitants, and nine square miles of buildings in England one million, the population of a city in China will be to that of a city in England as twenty-seven to fourteen, or very nearly as two to one; and the former, with a proportion of inhabitants double to that of the latter, will only have the same proportion of buildings; so that there is no necessity of their being so closely crowded together, or of their occupying so great a portion of land, as to interfere with the quantity necessary for the subsistence of the people.[582]

I have been thus particular, in order to set in its true light a subject that has been much agitated and generally disbelieved. The sum total of three hundred and thirty-three millions is so enormous, that in its aggregate form it astonishes the mind and staggers credibility; yet we find no difficulty in conceiving that a single square mile in China may contain two hundred and fifty-six persons, especially when we call to our recollection the United Provinces of Holland, which have been calculated to contain two hundred and seventy inhabitants on a square mile. And the United Provinces have enjoyed few of the advantages favourable to population, of which China, for ages past, has been in the uninterrupted possession.

The materials for the statement given by Father Amiot of the population of China appear to have been collected with care. The number of souls in 1760, according to this statement

as	w	196,8 37,977
n 1761	I	198,2 14,553
		——— ———
nnual increase	A	1,376 ,576

This statement must however be incorrect, from the circumstance of some millions of people being excluded who have no fixed habitation, but are constantly changing their position on the inland navigations of the empire, as well as all the islanders of the Archipelago of *Chu-san* and of Formosa. Without, however, taking these into consideration, and by supposing the number of souls in 1761, to amount to 198,214,553, there ought to have been, in the year 1793, by allowing a progres[583]sive increase, according to a moderate calculation in political arithmetic, at least 280,000,000 souls.

Whether this great empire, the first in rank both in extent and population, may or may not actually contain 333 millions of souls, is a point that Europeans are not likely ever to ascertain. That it is capable of subsisting this and a much greater population has, I think, been sufficiently proved. I know it is a common argument with those who are not willing to admit the fact, that although cities and towns and shipping may be crowded together in an astonishing manner, on and near the grand route between the capital and Canton, yet that the interior parts of the country are almost deserted. By some of our party going to *Chu-san*, we had occasion to see parts of the country remote from the common road, and such parts happened to be by far the most populous in the whole journey. But independent of the small portion of country seen by us, the western provinces, which are most distant from the grand navigation, are considered as the granaries of the empire; and the cultivation of much grain, where few cattle and less machinery are used, necessarily implies a corresponding population. Thus we see from the above table, that the surplus produce of the land remitted to Pekin from the provinces of

		Oz . silver.
Honan	remote from the grand navigation, were	3,213,000
Shan-see		3,722,000
Shen-see		2,040,000
		Whilst those of
Pe-tche-lee	on the grand navigation, were	3,036,000
Shan-tung		3,600,000
Tche-kiang		3,810,000

chiefly in rice, wheat, and millet. There are no grounds therefore[584] for supposing that the interior parts of China are deserts.

There are others again who are persuaded of the population being so enormous, that the country is wholly inadequate to supply the means of subsistence; and that famines are absolutely necessary to keep down the former to the level of the latter. The loose and general way in which the accounts of the missionaries are drawn up certainly leave such an impression; but as I have endeavoured to shew that such is far from being the case, it may be expected I should also attempt to explain the frequency of those disastrous famines which occasionally commit such terrible havock in this country. I am of opinion then, that three principal reasons may be assigned for them. First, the equal division of the land: Secondly, the mode of cultivation: and Thirdly, the nature of the products.

If, in the first place, every man has it in his option to rent as much land as will support his family with food and clothing, he will have no occasion to go to market for the first necessities; and such being generally the case in China, those first necessities find no market, except in the large cities. When the peasant has brought under tillage of grain as much land as may be sufficient for the consumption of his own family, and the necessary surplus for the landlord, he looks no further; and all his neighbours having done the same, the first necessities are, in fact, unsaleable articles, except in so far as regards the demands of large cities, which are by no means so close upon[585] one another as has been imagined. A surplus of grain is likewise less calculated to exchange for superfluities or luxuries than many other articles of produce. This being the case, if, by any accident, a failure of the crops should be general in a province, it has no relief to expect from the neighbouring provinces, nor any supplies from foreign countries. In China there are no great farmers who store their grain to throw into the market in seasons of scarcity. In such seasons the only resource is that of the government opening its magazines, and restoring to the people that portion of their crop which it had demanded from them as the price of its protection. And this being originally only a tenth part, out of which the monthly subsistence of every officer and soldier had already been deduced, the remainder is seldom adequate to the wants of the people. Insurrection and rebellion ensue, and those who may escape the devouring scourge of famine, in all probability, fall by the sword. In such seasons a whole province is sometimes half depopulated; wretched parents are reduced, by imperious want, to sell or destroy their offspring, and children to put an end, by violence, to the sufferings of their aged and infirm parents. Thus, the equal division of land, so favourable to population in seasons of plenty, is just the reverse when the calamity of a famine falls upon the people.

In the second place, a scarcity may be owing to the mode of cultivation. When I mention that two-thirds of the small quantity of land under tillage is cultivated with the spade or the hoe, or otherwise by manual labour, without the aid of draught[586]-cattle or skilful machinery, it will readily be conceived how very small a portion each family will be likely to employ every year; certainly not one-third part of his average allowance.

The third cause of famines may be owing to the nature of the products, particularly to that of rice. This grain, the staff of life in China, though it yields abundant returns in favourable seasons, is more liable to fail than most others. A drought in its early stages withers it on the ground; and an inundation, when nearly ripe, is equally destructive. The birds and the locusts, more numerous in this country than an European can well conceive, infest it more than any other kind of grain. In the northern provinces, where wheat, millet and pulse are cultivated, famines more rarely happen; and I am persuaded that if potatoes and Guinea corn (*Zea-Mays*) were once adopted as the common vegetable food of the people, those direful famines that produce such general misery would entirely cease, and the encrease of population be as rapid as that of Ireland. This root in the northern provinces, and this grain in the middle and southern ones, would never fail them. An acre of potatoes would yield more food than an acre of rice, and twice the nourishment. Rice is the poorest of all grain, if we may judge from the slender and delicate forms of all the people who use it as the chief article of their sustenance; and potatoes are just the contrary[67].

As Dr. Adam Smith observes, "The chairmen, porters, and [587] coal-heavers in London, and those unfortunate women who live by prostitution, the strongest men and the most beautiful women perhaps in the British dominions, are said to be, the greater part of them, from the lowest rank of the people in Ireland, who are generally fed with this root; no food can afford a more decisive proof of its nourishing quality, or of its being peculiarly suitable to the health of the human constitution." The Guinea corn requires little or no attention after the seed is dropped into the ground; and its leaves and juicy stems are not more nourishing for cattle than its prolific heads are for the sustenance of man.

Various causes have contributed to the populousness of China. Since the Tartar conquest it may be said to have enjoyed a profound peace; for in the different wars and skirmishes that have taken place with the neighbouring nations on the side of India, and with the Russians on the confines of Siberia, a few Tartar soldiers only have been employed. The Chinese army is parcelled out as guards for the towns, cities, and villages; and stationed at the numberless posts on the roads and canals. Being seldom relieved from the several guards, they all marry and have families. A certain portion of land is allotted for their use, which they have sufficient time to cultivate. As the nation has little foreign commerce there are few seamen; such as belong to the inland navigations are mostly married. Although there be no direct penalty levied against such as remain batchelors, as was the case among the Romans[588] when they wished to repair the desolation that their civil wars had occasioned, yet public opinion considers celibacy as disgraceful, and a sort of infamy is attached to a man who continues unmarried beyond a certain time of life. And although in China the public law be not established of the *Jus trium liberorum*, by which every Roman citizen having three children was entitled to certain privileges and immunities, yet every male child may be provided for, and receive a stipend from the moment of his birth, by his name being enrolled on the military list. By the equal division of the country into small farms, every peasant has the means of bringing up his family, if drought and inundation do not frustrate his labour; and the pursuits of agriculture are more favourable to health, and consequently to population, than mechanical employments in crowded cities, and large manufactories, where those who are doomed to toil are more liable to become the victims of disease and debauchery, than such as are exposed to the free and open air, and to active and wholesome labour. In China there are few of such manufacturing cities. No great capitals are here employed in any one branch of the arts. In general each labours for himself in his own profession. From the general poverty that prevails among the lower orders of people, the vice of drunkenness is little practised among them. The multitude, from necessity, are temperate in their diet to the last degree. The climate is moderate and, except in the northern provinces where the cold is severe, remarkably uniform, not liable to those sudden and great changes in temperature, which the human constitution is less able to resist, than

198

the[589] extremes of heat or cold when steady and invariable, and from which the inconveniences are perhaps nowhere so severely felt as on our own island. Except the small-pox and contagious diseases that occasionally break out in their confined and crowded cities, they are liable to few epidemical disorders. The still and inanimate kind of life which is led by the women, at the same time that it is supposed to render them prolific, preserves them from accidents that might cause untimely births. Every woman suckles and nurses her own child.

The operation of these and other favourable causes that might be assigned, in a country that has existed under the same form of government, and preserved the same laws and customs for so many ages, must necessarily have created an excess of population unknown in most other parts of the world, where the ravages of war, several times repeated in the course of a century, or internal commotions, or pestilential disease, or the effects of overgrown wealth, sometimes sweep away one half of a nation within the usual period allotted to the life of man.

"What a grand and curious spectacle," as Sir George Staunton observes, "is here exhibited to the mind of so large a proportion of the whole human race, connected together in one great system of polity, submitting quietly and through so considerable an extent of country to one great sovereign; and[590] uniform in their laws, their manners, and their language; but differing essentially in each of these respects from every other portion of mankind; and neither desirous of communicating with, nor forming any designs against, the rest of the world." How strong an instance does China afford of the truth of the observation, that men are more easily governed by opinion than by power.

CHAP. X.
Journey through the Province of Canton.—Situation
of Foreigners trading to this Port.—Conclusion.

*Visible change in the Character of the People.—Rugged Mountains.—Collieries.—Temple in a Cavern.—Stone Quarries—Various Plants for Use and Ornament.—Arrive at Canton—Expence of the Embassy to the Chinese Government.—To the British Nation—Nature and Inconveniences of the Trade to Canton—The Armenian and his Pearl.—Impression of the Officers of Government instanced.—Principal Cause of them is the Ignorance of the Language.—Case of Chinese trading to London.—A Chinese killed by a Seaman of His Majesty's Ship Madras.—Delinquent saved from an ignominious Death, by a proper Mode of Communication with the Government—*CONCLUSION.

WE had no sooner passed the summit of the high mountain[591] *Me-lin*, and entered the province of *Quan-tung*, or Canton, than a very sensible difference was perceived in the conduct of the inhabitants. Hitherto the Embassy had met with the greatest respect and civility from all classes of the natives, but now even the peasantry ran out of their houses, as we passed, and bawled after us *Queitze-fan-quei*, which, in their language, are opprobrious and contemptuous expressions, signifying *foreign devils, imps,* epithets that are bestowed by the enlightened Chinese on[592] all foreigners. It was obvious, that the haughty and insolent manner in which all Europeans residing at, or trading to, the port of Canton are treated, had extended itself to the northern frontier of the province, but it had not crossed the mountain *Me-lin*; the natives of *Kiang-see* being a quiet, civil, and inoffensive people. In *Quan-tung* the farther we advanced, the more rude and insolent they became. A timely rebuke, however, given to the governor of *Nau-sheun-foo* by *Van-ta-gin*, for applying the above mentioned opprobrious epithets to the British Embassy, had a good effect on the Canton officers, who were now to be our conductors through their province.

This contempt of foreigners is not confined to the upper ranks, or men in office, but pervades the very lowest class who, whilst they make no scruple of entering into the service of foreign merchants residing in the country, and accepting the most menial employments under them, performing the duties of their several offices with diligence, punctuality, and fidelity, affect, at the same time, to despise their employers, and to consider them as placed, in the scale of human beings, many degrees below them. Having one day observed my Chinese servant busily employed in drying a quantity of tea-leaves, that had already been used for breakfast, and of which he had collected several pounds, I inquired what he meant to do with them: he replied, to mix them with other tea and sell them. "And is that the way," said I, "in which you cheat your own countrymen?" "No," replied he, "my own countrymen are too wise to be so easily cheated, but your's are stupid enough to let serve you such like tricks; and indeed," continued he,[593] with the greatest *sang froid* imaginable, "anything you get from us is quite good enough for you." Affecting to be angry with him, he said, "he meant for the *second sort* of Englishmen," which is a distinction they give to the Americans[68].

The city of *Nan-sheun-foo* was pleasantly situated on the high bank of the river *Pei-kiang-ho*. The houses appeared to be very old, the streets narrow, large tracts of ground within the walls unbuilt, others covered with ruins. While the barges were preparing to receive on board the baggage, we took up our lodgings in the public temple, that was dedicated to the memory of Confucius, being, at the same time, the college where the students are examined for their different degrees. It consisted of a long dark room, divided by two rows of red pillars into a middle and two side aisles, without furniture, paintings, statues, or ornaments of any kind, except a few paper lanterns suspended between the pillars; the floor was of earth, and entirely broken up: to us it had more the appearance of a large passage or gang-way to some manufactory, as a brewhouse or iron foundery, than of the hall of Confucius. On each side, and at the farther extremity, were several small apartments, in which we contrived to pass the night.

The barges in which we now embarked were very small, owning to the shallowness of the river. The officers, assembled [594] here from different parts of the country, detained us a whole day in order to have an opportunity of laying their several complaints before our physician, at the recommendation of *Van-ta-gin*, who had felt the good effects of his practice. Here, for once, we had an instance of Chinese pride giving way to self-interest, and usurped superiority condescending to ask advice of barbarians. We sailed for two days in our little barges, through one of the most wild, mountainous, and barren tracts of country that I ever beheld, abounding more in the sublime and horrible, than in the picturesque or the beautiful. The lofty summits of the mountains seemed to touch each other across the river and, at a distance, it appeared as if we had to sail through an arched cavern. The massy fragments that had fallen down from time to time, and impeded the navigation, were indications that the passage was not altogether free from danger. Five remarkable points of sand-stone rock, rising in succession above each other with perpendicular faces, seemed as if they had been hewn out of one solid mountain: they were called *ou-ma-too*, or the five horses' heads. The mountains at a distance on each side of the river were covered with pines, the nearer hills with coppice wood, in which the Camellia prevailed; and in the little glens were clusters of fishermen's huts, surrounded by small plantations of tobacco.

Within the defile of these wild mountains, we observed several extensive collieries, which were advantageously worked by driving levels from the river into their sides. The coals brought out of the horizontal *adits* were immediately lowered from a pier into vessels that were ready to receive and trans[595]port them to the potteries of this province, and of *Kiang-see*. Coal is little used in its raw state, but is first charred in large pits that are dug in the ground. Coal dust, mixed with earth, and formed into square blocks, is frequently used to heat their little stoves, on which they boil their rice.

At the city of *Tchao-tchoo-foo*, where we arrived on the 13th, we exchanged our flat-bottomed boats for large and commodious yachts, the river being here much increased by the confluence of another stream. The boats before this city were mostly managed by young girls, whose dress consisted of a neat white jacket and petticoat and a gipsey straw hat. Having for so great a length of time scarcely ever set our eyes upon a female, except the heads of some at a distance, peeping from behind the mud walls that surround the houses, or labouring in the grounds of *Kiang-see*, the ferry girls, though in reality very plain and coarse-featured, were considered as the most beautiful objects that had occurred in the whole journey. To the occupation of ferrying passengers over the river it seemed they added another, not quite so honourable, for which, however, they had not only the consent and approbation of their parents, but also the sanction of the government, or perhaps, to speak more correctly, of the governing magistrates, given in consideration of their receiving a portion of the wages of prostitution.

In this mountainous district a few fishermen's huts and those of the colliers were the only habitations that occurred; but the defect of population was abundantly supplied by the[596] number of wooden dwellings that were floating on the river. Small huts, to the number of thirty or forty, were sometimes erected upon a single floating raft of fir baulks, lashed together by the ends and the sides. On these rafts the people carry on their trade or occupation, particularly such as work in wood.

Our conductors directed the yachts to halt before a detached rock, rising with a perpendicular front from the margin of the river to the height of seven hundred feet. In this front we observed a cavern, before which was a terrace that had been cut out of the rock, accessible by a flight of steps from the river. Proceeding from the terrace into the cavity of the rock, we ascended another flight of stairs, also cut out of solid stone, which led into a very spacious apartment. In the centre of this apartment sat the goddess *Poo-sa* upon a kind of altar, constituting a part of the rock, and hewn into the shape of the *Lien-wha* or Nelumbium. A small opening, next the river, admitted a "dim religious light," suitable to the solemnity of the place, which we were told was a temple consecrated to *Poo-sa*, and a monastery for the residence of a few superannuated priests. On the smooth sides of the apartment was inscribed a multitude of Chinese verses, some cut into the rock, and others painted upon it. The lodgings of the priests were small caves branching out of the large temple. A third flight of steps led from this to a second story, which was also lighted by a small aperture in front, that was nearly choaked up by an immense mass of stalectite that had been formed, and was still increasing, by the constant oozing of water holding in solution calcareous matter, and suspended from a projection of the upper part[597] of the rock. But the light was sufficient to discover a gigantic image with a Saracen face, who "grinn'd horrible a ghastly smile." On his head was a sort of crown; in one hand he held a naked scymeter, and a firebrand in the other; but the history of this colossal divinity seemed to be imperfectly known, even to the votaries of *Poo-sa* themselves. He had in all probability been a warrior in his day, the Theseus or the Hercules of China. The cave of the Cumæan Sibyl could not be better suited for dealing out the mysterious decrees of fate to the superstitious multitude, than that of the *Quan-gin-shan*, from whence the oracle of future destiny, in like manner,

"Horrendas canit ambages, antroque remugit,
Obscuris vera involvens."

"The wond'rous truths, involv'd in riddles, gave,
And furious bellow'd round the gloomy cave."

Lord Macartney observed that this singular temple brought to his recollection a Franciscan monastery he had seen in Portugal, near Cape Roxent, usually called the *Cork Convent*, "which is an excavation of considerable extent under a hill, divided into a great number of cells, and fitted up with a church, sacristy, refectory, and every requisite apartment for the accommodation of the miserable Cordeliers who burrow in it. The inside is entirely lined with cork: the walls, the roofs, the floors, are covered with cork; the tables, seats, chairs, beds, couches, the furniture of the chapel, the crucifixes, and every other implement, are all made of cork. The place was certainly dismal and comfortless to a great degree, but it wanted the gigantic form, the grim features, the terrific[598] aspect which distinguish the temple of *Poo-sa*, in the rock of *Quan-gin-shan*." Dismal as this gloomy den appeared to be, where a few miserable beings had voluntarily chained themselves to a rock, to be gnawed by the vultures of superstition and fanaticism, it is still less so than an apartment of the Franciscan convent in Madeira, the walls of which are entirely covered with human skulls, and the bones of legs and arms, placed alternately in horizontal rows. A dirty lamp suspended from the ceiling, and constantly attended by an old bald-headed friar of the order, to keep the feeble light just glimmering in the socket, serves to shew indistinctly to strangers this disgusting *memento mori*. It would be difficult to determine which of the three were the most useless members of society, the monks of *Poo-sa*, the monks of the Cork convent, or the monks of Golgotha.

In several places among the wild and romantic mountains through which we were carried on this river, we noticed quarries of great extent, out of which huge stones had been cut for sepulchral monuments, for the arches of bridges, for architraves, for paving the streets, and for various other uses. To obtain these large masses, the saw is applied at the upper surface, and they work down vertically to the length required. Each stone is shaped and fashioned to the size that may be wanted, before it is removed from the parent rock, by which much difficulty is avoided and less power required in conveying it to its destination. Rude misshapen blocks, requiring additional labour for their removal, are never detached from the rock in such a state. In this respect they are more provident than the[599] late Empress of Russia who, at an immense expense and with the aid of complicated machinery, caused a block of stone to be brought to her capital, to serve as a pedestal for the statue of the Czar Peter, where it was found expedient to reduce it to two-thirds of its original dimensions.

Between the city of Canton and the first pagoda on the bank of the river, there is a continued series of similar quarries, which appear not to have been worked for many years. The regular and formal manner in which the stones have been cut away, exhibiting lengthened streets of houses with quadrangular chambers, in the sides of which are square holes at equal distances, as if intended for the reception of beams; the smoothness and perfect perpendicularity of the sides, and the number of detached pillars that are scattered over the plain, would justify a similar mistake to that of Mr. Addison's Doctor of one of the German universities, whom he found at Chateau d'Un in France, carefully measuring the free-stone quarries at that place, which he had conceived to be the venerable remains of vast subterranean palaces of great antiquity.

Almost all the mountains that occurred in our passage through China were of primæval granite, some few of sand-stone, and the inferior hills were generally of lime-stone, or coarse grey marble. Except the Ladrone islands on the south, and some of the *Chusan* islands on the east, we observed no appearances in the whole country of volcanic productions. The high mountains, indeed, that form great continental chains are seldom, if ever, of volcanic formation. The presence of a[600] vast volume of water seems to be indispensably necessary to carry on this operation of nature and, accordingly, we find that volcanic mountains are generally close to the sea coast, or entirely insulated. Thus, although a great part of the islands on the coast of China are volcanic, we met with no trace of subterranean heat, either in volcanic products or thermal springs, on the whole continent. Yet earthquakes are said to have been frequently felt in all the provinces, but slight and of short duration.

About seven miles to the southward of the temple in the rock, the mountains abruptly ceased, and we entered on a wide extended plain which, to the southward and on each side, was terminated only by the horizon. This sudden transition from barrenness to fertility, from the sublime to the beautiful, from irregularity to uniformity, could not fail to please, as all strong contrasts usually do. The country was now in a high state of tillage; the chief products were rice, sugar-canes, and tobacco; and the river was so much augmented by the tributary streams of the mountains, which we had just left behind, that it was nearly half a mile in width. Canals branched from its two banks in every direction. At the city of *San-shwee shien*, we observed the current of the river receding, being driven back by the flux of the tide.

On the 10th, we halted before a village which was just within sight of the suburbs of Canton. Here the Embassador was met by the Commissioners of the East India Company, whom the Chinese had allowed to proceed thus far from the factory,[601] and to which place the servants of the Company are occasionally permitted to make their parties of pleasure. In the neighbourhood of this village are extensive gardens for the supply of the city with vegetables. In some we observed nurseries for propagating the rare, the beautiful, the curious, or the useful plants of the country; which are sent to Canton for sale. On this account we were not sorry to be obliged to spend the remainder of the day at this place. Among the choice plants we noticed the large *Peonia* before mentioned, white, red, and variegated; the elegant *Limodorum Tankervilliæ*, and that singular plant the *Epidendrum flos aeris* so called from its vegetating without the assistance of earth or water; the *Hybiscus mutabilis*, the *Abelmoschus*, and other species of this genus; the double variegated *Camellia Japonica*; the great holly-hock; the scarlet *amaranthus* and another species of the same genus, and a very elegant *Celosia* or cock's comb; the *Nerium Oleander*, sometimes called the Ceylon rose, and the *Yu-lan*, a species of magnolia, the flowers of which appear before the leaves burst from the buds. Of the scented plants the *plumeria* and a double flowering jasmine were the most esteemed. We observed also in pots the *Ocymum* or sweet Basil, *Cloranthus inconspicuous*, called *Chu-lan*, whose leaves are sometimes mixed with those of tea to give them a peculiar flavour; the *Olea fragrans*, or sweet scented olive, said also to be used for the same purpose; a species of myrtle; the much esteemed *Rosa Sinica*; the *Tuberose*; the strong scented *Gardenia florida*, improperly called the Cape Jasmine; the China pink and several others, to enumerate which would exceed the limits of this work.[602]

Of fruits we noticed a variety of figs, and three species of mulberries; peaches and almonds; the *Annona* or custard-apple; the *Eugenia Jambos*, or rose-apple; the much-esteemed *Lee-tchee* or *Sapindus-edulis*; and the *Kœlreuteria*, another species of the same genus; the *Averhoa Carambola*, an excellent fruit for tarts; and the *Ou-long-shoo*, the *Sterculia platanifolia*. Besides these were abundance of oranges and bananas.

As vegetables for the table, was a great variety of beans and calavances, among which was the *Dolichos Soja* or soy plant, and the *polystachios*, with its large clusters of beautiful scarlet flowers; the *Cytisus Cadjan*, whole seed yields the famous bean-milk, which it is the custom of the Emperor to offer to Embassadors on their presentation; large mild radishes, onions, garlic, *Capsicum* or Cayenne-pepper; *convolvulus batatas*, or sweet potatoes; two species of tobacco; *Amomum*, or ginger, in great quantities, the root of which they preserve in syrup; *Sinapis*, or mustard, and the *Brassica orientalis*, from which an oil is expressed for the table.

Of plants that were useful in the arts, we observed the *Rhus vernix*, or varnish-tree, and two other species of the same genus; *Curcuma*, or turmeric; *Carthamus* used as a dye, and the *polygonum Chinense* for the same purpose; the *Rhapis flabelliformis*, the dried leaves of which are used for fans among the common people, and particularly by those who live in vessels; *Corchorus* whose bark, in India, is used as flax; but not, I believe, to any extent in China, the white nettle being here preferred.[603] The only medicinal plants were the *Rheum palmatum*, *Artemisia*, and the *Smilax* or China root.

To make our *entré* into Canton the more splendid, a number of superb barges were sent to meet us, carrying flags and streamers and umbrellas and other insignia of office; and in some were bands of music. About the middle of the day we arrived before the factories, which constitute a line of buildings in the European style, extending along the left bank of the river, where the Embassador was received by the *Song-too*, or Viceroy, the Governor, the *Ho-poo*, or collector of the customs, and all the principal officers of the government. From hence we were conducted to the opposite side of the river, where a temporary building of poles and mats had been prepared for the occasion; within which was a screen of yellow silk bearing the name of the Emperor in gilt characters. Before this screen the Viceroy and other officers performed the usual prostrations, in token of gratitude to his imperial Majesty, for his having vouchsafed us a prosperous journey.

It is but doing justice to the Chinese government and to the individuals in its employ who had any concern in the affairs of the embassy, to observe, that as far as regarded ourselves, their conduct was uniformly marked by liberality, attention, and an earnest desire to please. Nor is there any vanity in saying that, after observing us closely in the course of a long journey and daily intercourse, the officers of government gradually dismissed the prejudices imbibed against us, as foreigners, from their earliest youth. Gained by our frank and open manners, and by little attentions, they seemed to fly with pleasure to our society as a[604] relief from the tedious formalities they were obliged to assume in their official capacity. *Van* and *Chou* constantly passed the evenings in some of our yachts. It is impossible to speak of those two worthy men in terms equal to their desert. Kind, condescending, unremitting in their attentions, they never betrayed one moment of ill-humour from the time we entered China till they took their final leave at Canton. These two men were capable of real attachments. They insisted on accompanying the Embassador on board the Lion, where they took their last farewell. At parting they burst into tears and shewed the strongest marks of sensibility and concern. Their feelings quite overcame them, and they left the Lion sorrowful and dejected. Early the following morning they sent on board twenty baskets of fruit and vegetables, as a farewell token of their remembrance. We had the satisfaction to hear, that immediately on their arrival at Pekin they both were promoted. *Chou* is at present in a high situation at court, but *Van*, the cheerful good-humoured *Van*, has paid the debt of nature, having fallen honourably in the service of his country. On the conduct of *Lee*, our Chinese interpreter, any praise that I could bestow would be far inadequate to his merit. Fully sensible of his perilous situation, he never at any one time shrank from his duty. At Macao he took an affectionate leave of his English friends, with whom, though placed in one of the remotest provinces of the empire, he still contrives to correspond. The Embassador, Lord Macartney, has had several letters from him; the last of which is of so late a date as March 1802; so that his sensibility has not been diminished either by time or distance.[605]

It is the custom of China to consider all Embassadors as guests of the Emperor, from the moment they enter any part of his dominions, until they are again entirely out of them. The inconvenience of this custom was severely felt by us, as it prevented us from purchasing, in an open manner, many trifling articles that would have been acceptable. The very considerable expence, incurred by the court on this account, may be one reason for prescribing the limited time of forty days for all embassadors to remain at the capital. To meet the expences of the present Embassy, *Van-ta-gin* assured me, that they were furnished with an order to draw on the public treasuries of the different provinces through which we had to pass, to the amount of five thousand ounces of silver a-day, or about one thousand six hundred pounds sterling: and that fifteen hundred ounces a-day had been issued out of the treasury at Pekin for the support of the Embassy during its continuance there. Supposing then these data to be correct, and I see no reason for calling their authenticity in question, we may form an estimate of the whole expence of this Embassy to the Chinese government.

		Oz.
From the 6th of August (the day we entered the Pei-ho) to the 21st (when we arrived in Pekin) inclusive	16 days,	80,000
From the 22d August to the 6th October (in Pekin and in Gehol)	46 days,	69,000
From the 7th October to the 19th December (when we arrived at Canton)	74 days,	370,000
Total ounces of silver		519,000

Or one hundred and seventy-three thousand pounds sterling;[606] three Chinese ounces being equal to one pound sterling.

It is hardly possible that this enormous sum of money could have been expended on account of the Embassy, though I have no doubt of its having been issued out of the Imperial treasury for that purpose. One of the missionaries informed me, in Pekin, that the Gazette of that capital contained an article stating the liberality of the Emperor towards the English Embassador, in his having directed no less a sum than fifteen hundred ounces of silver to be applied for the daily expences of the Embassy, while stationary in the capital and at Gehol. The same gentleman made an observation, that the great officers of government, as well as those who had the good luck to be appointed to manage the concerns of a foreign embassy, considered it as one of the best wind-falls in the Emperor's gift, the difference between the allowances and the actual expenditure being equivalent to a little fortune.

Van-ta-gin, indeed, explained to us, that although the Imperial warrant was signed for those sums, yet that having a number of offices to pass through, in all of which it diminished a little, the whole of it was not actually expended on the Embassy. He gave to the Embassador an excellent illustration of the manner in which the Imperial bounty was sometimes applied. An inundation had swept away, the preceding winter, a whole village in the province of *Shan-tung*, so suddenly, that the inhabitants could save nothing but their lives. The Emperor having once lodged at the place immediately ordered[607] 100,000 ounces of silver for their relief, out of which the first officer of the treasury took 20,000, the second 10,000, the third 5,000, and so on, till at last there remained only 20,000 for the poor sufferers. So that the boasted morality of China is pretty much the same, when reduced to practice, as that of other countries.

The real expence, however, of the British Embassy, could not have been a trifle, when we consider what a vast multitude of men, horses, and vessels were constantly employed on the occasion. *Van-ta-gin* assured me, that there were seldom fewer than one thousand men, and frequently many more, employed one way or other in its service; and I am persuaded he did not intend to exaggerate. In the first place, from the mouth of the *Pei-ho* to *Tong-tchoo*, we had forty-one yachts or barges, each on an average, including boatmen, trackers, and soldiers, having on board fifteen men; this gives six hundred and fifteen men to the boats only. Caterers running about the country to collect provisions, boatmen to bring them to the several barges, the conducting officers, and their numerous retinue, are not included in this estimate. From *Tong-tchoo* near three thousand men were employed to carry the presents and baggage, first to *Hung-ya-yuen*, beyond Pekin, and then back again to the capital, which took them three days. In our return from *Tong-tchoo* to *Hang-tchoo-foo*, we had a fleet of thirty-vessels, with ten men at least and, for the greatest part of the journey, twenty additional trackers to each vessel; this gives nine hundred people for the yachts alone.[608]

From *Hang-tchoo-foo* to *Eu-shan-shien* and from *Hang-tchoo-foo* to *Chu-san*, there might probably be employed about forty vessels, with twelve men to each, or four hundred and eighty in the whole. And, besides the people employed by the officers of government to purchase provisions, numbers were stationed in different parts of the rivers to contract the stream, by raking together the pebbles where, otherwise, the water would have been too shallow for the boats to pass; and others to attend at all the fluices on the canals to assist the vessels in getting through the same.

From *Tchang-shan-shien* to *Eu-shan-shien*, overland, we had about forty horses, and three or four hundred men to carry the baggage.

From the *Po-yang* lake to Canton, we had generally about twenty-six vessels with twenty men to each, including boatmen, soldiers, and trackers, which gives five hundred and twenty men for these alone.

The Embassy consisted of near one hundred persons, but as for the several officers and their numerous retinue of guards, attendants, and runners, I have not the least idea to what their numbers might amount; all of whom, being on extraordinary service, were supported at the public expence.

The whole expence of the Embassy to this country, including the presents, did not exceed eighty thousand pounds; an inconsiderable sum for such a nation as Great Britain on such an occasion, and[609] not more than a fourth part of what has been generally imagined.

Although the British factory was in every sense more comfortable than the most splendid palace that the country afforded, yet it was so repugnant to the principles of the government for an Embassador to take up his abode in the same dwelling with merchants, that it was thought expedient to indulge their notions in this respect, and to accept a large house in the midst of a garden, on the opposite side of the river, which was fitted up and furnished with beds in the European manner, with glazed sash windows, and with fire grates suitable for burning coals. On our arrival here we found a company of comedians hard at work, in the middle of a piece, which it seemed had begun at sun-rise; but their squalling and their shrill and harsh music were so dreadful, that they were prevailed upon, with difficulty, to break off during dinner, which was served up in a viranda directly opposite the theatre.

Next morning, however, about sun-rise, they set to work afresh, but at the particular request of the Embassador, in which he was joined by the whole suite, they were discharged, to the no small astonishment of our Chinese conductors, who concluded, from this circumstance, that the English had very little taste for elegant amusements. Players, it seems, are here hired by the day and the more incessantly they labour, the more they are applauded. They are always ready to begin any one piece out of a list of twenty or thirty, that is presented for the principal visitor to make his choice.

The nature of the trade carried on by foreign nations at the port of Canton is so well known, that it would be superfluous[610] for me to dwell on that subject. The complaints of all nations against the extortions practised there have been loudly and frequently heard in Europe, but the steps that have hitherto been taken have proved unavailing. The common answer is, "Why do you come here? We take in exchange your articles of produce and manufacture, which we really have no occasion for, and give you in return our precious tea, which nature has denied to your country, and yet you are not satisfied. Why do you so often visit a country whose customs you dislike? We do not invite you to come among us, but when you do come, and behave well, we treat you accordingly. Respect then our hospitality, but don't pretend to regulate or reform it." Such is the language held to Europeans by all the petty officers of government with whom they have to deal.

With such sentiments one cannot be surprized that foreign merchants should be received with indifference, if not handled with rudeness, and that the fair trader should be liable to extortions. This is still more likely to happen from the complete monopoly of all foreign trade being consigned to a limited number of merchants, seldom, I believe, exceeding eight, who are sanctioned by government. The cargoes of tin, lead, cotton, opium, and large sums of Spanish dollars, sent to Canton from Europe, India, and America, all pass through the hands of these Hong merchants, who also furnish the return cargoes. As the capital employed is far beyond any thing of the kind we can conceive in Europe by so few individuals, their profits must be proportionally great, or they could not be able to bear the[611] expence of the numerous and magnificent presents which they are expected to make to the superior officers of government at Canton, who, in their turn, find it expedient to divide these with the Emperor and his ministers in the capital. The various toys, automatons, moving and musical figures from Coxe's museum, the mathematical and astronomical instruments, clocks, watches, machinery, jewellery, all made in London, and now in the different palaces of the Emperor of China, are said to be valued at no less a sum than two millions sterling, all presents from Canton. The principal officers of this government are invariably sent down from Pekin; they arrive poor and, in the course of three years, return with immense riches. How much of the enormous wealth of *Ho-tchung-tang* came from the same quarter it is difficult to say, but the great influence he possessed over the Emperor, and his intimacy with the viceroy of Canton, who was superseded in 1793, leave no doubt, that a very considerable part of it was drawn from this port. The large pearl, which forms one of the charges preferred against him, was a present from Canton, of which I have been told a curious history by a gentleman who was on the spot at the time it happened. An Armenian merchant brought this pearl to Canton, in the expectation of making his fortune. Its size and beauty soon became known and attracted the attention of the officers and the merchants, who paid their daily visits to the Armenian, offering him prices far inadequate to its value. At length, however, after minute and repeated examinations, a price was agreed upon and a deposit made, but the Armenian[612] was to keep possession of the pearl till the remaining part of the purchase-money should be ready; and in order to obviate any possibility of trick, the box in which it was kept was sealed with the purchaser's seal. Several days elapsed without his hearing any thing further from the Chinese; and, at length, the time approached when all foreign merchants are ordered down to Macao. The Armenian, in vain, endeavoured to find out the people who had purchased his pearl, but he contented himself with the reflection that, although he had been disappointed in the main object of his journey, he still had his property, and that the deposit was more than sufficient to defray his expences. On reaching his home, he had no longer any scruple in breaking open the seal; but his mortification may easily be supposed, on discovering that his real pearl had been exchanged for an artificial one, so very like as not to be detected but by the most critical examination. The daily visits of these people, it seems, were for no other purpose than to enable them to forge an accurate imitation, which they had dexterously substituted for the real one, when they proposed the cunning expedient of sealing the box in which it was inclosed. The Armenians, however, were determined not to be outdone by the Chinese. A noted character, of the name of *Baboom*, equally well known in Bengal and Madras as in Canton, just before his failure in about half a million sterling, deposited a valuable casket of pearls, as he represented them, in the hands of one of the *Hong* merchants, as a pledge for a large sum of money, which, when opened, instead of pearls was found to be *a casket of peas.*[613]

It has always been considered that a foreigner has little chance of obtaining justice at Canton. The import and export duties, which by the law of the country ought to be levied *ad valorem*, are arbitrarily fixed according to the fancy of the collector. And although the court is at all times ready to punish, by confiscation of their property, such as have been guilty of corruption and oppression, yet by accepting their presents, it seems to lend them its encouragement. Besides, the distance from Canton to the metropolis is so great, the temptations so strong, and the chances of impunity so much in their favour, that to be honest, when power and opportunity lend their aid to roguery, is a virtue not within the pale of Chinese morality. A striking instance of their peculation appeared in a circumstance that was connected with the British Embassy. In consideration of the Hindostan having carried presents for the Emperor, an order was issued from Court that she should be exempt from duties at any of the ports where she might take in a cargo. It happened that the Hong merchants had already paid the Hindostan's duties with those of the other ships, of which her particular share was 30,000 ounces of silver. The *Hoo-poo* or collector was therefore requested to return this sum agreeably to the order from court, but he refunded only into Mr. Browne's hands 14,000 dollars, which can be reckoned as little more than 11,000 ounces, observing, that so much was the exact amount of the Emperor's duties. As in this instance of a public nature the collector could not be supposed to act without circumspection, we may conclude how very small a proportion of the duties, extorted from foreigners trading to Canton, finds its way into the Imperial treasury.[611]

Thus the taxes, which, if we may judge of them from those paid by their own countrymen, are extremely moderate, by the abuses of the administration become serious grievances to the foreign merchant who, however, has never hitherto employed the only probable mean of obtaining redress—that of making himself acquainted with the language of the country, so as to be able to remonstrate to the high officers of state, against the oppressions and impositions of those who act in inferior capacities; for, however rapacious and corrupt the first in authority may be, his timid nature would shrink immediately from a bold, clamorous, and able complainant, who possessed the means of making his delinquency notorious. This observation has been verified by a recent occurrence. A fraudulent suppression of a bankruptcy, for which the government stood responsible, and by which the interests of the East India Company, as well as of several individuals in India and Canton, would materially have suffered, was completely frustrated by the simple circumstance of Mr. Drummond, the chief of the factory, rushing into the city of Canton, and repeating aloud a few words which he had got by heart whilst, at the same time, he held up a written memorial; the consequence of which was, that the memorial was immediately carried to the viceroy, and the grievance complained of therein redressed. It would have been in vain to convey it through any of the inferior officers or the Hong merchants, as they were all interested in keeping it from the knowledge of government.

The supposed difficulty of acquiring the Chinese language has hitherto intimidated the residents in Canton from making[615] the attempt. Satisfied in transacting the Company's concerns through the medium of a jargon of broken English, which all the Hong merchants and even the inferior tradesmen and mechanics find it worth their while to acquire, they have totally neglected the language, as well as every other branch of information respecting the most interesting and extraordinary empire on the face of the globe. The attainment in fact of four or five thousand characters, which are sufficient to write clearly and copiously on any subject, is much less difficult than usually has been imagined, but it would require great attention and unremitting perseverance, such perhaps as few are willing to bestow, who are placed in situations which enable them to calculate, almost to a certainly, on realizing a fixed sum in a given number of years. The climate may also be adverse to intense application, but if the foundation was laid in England, much of the difficulty would thus be obviated. The French, aware of the solid advantages that result from the knowledge of languages, are at this moment holding out every encouragement to the study of Chinese literature; obviously not without design. They know that the Chinese character is understood from the Gulph of Siam to the Tartarian Sea, and over a very considerable part of the great Eastern Archipelago; that the Cochin Chinese, with whom they have already firmly rooted themselves, use no other writing than the pure Chinese character, which is also the case with the Japanese. It is to be hoped therefore that the British nation will not neglect the means of being able to meet the French, if necessary, even on this ground. The method of accomplishing this desirable object appears to be extremely simple. If the Directors of the[616] East India Company were to make it a rule that no writer should be appointed to China until he had made himself acquainted with five hundred or a thousand characters of the language[69], I will be bold to say that, where the number sent out is so few (the establishment not exceeding twenty) and the emoluments so very liberal, there would be as little danger as at present, by such a regulation, of the appointments being made out of their own families. The noble Marquis at the head of their affairs in India has established an institution, which seems to bid fair for producing a mutual benefit to the parent state and the native Indians. The exertions of Sir William Jones and a few others had, indeed, long before this, been productive of the happiest effects; and great numbers, both on the civil and military establishments of the Company, made themselves acquainted, in a certain degree, with the different languages spoken in the country. In fact, it became a matter of necessity, in order to remove prejudices imbibed against us and to meet those of the natives. The Portuguese and the Dutch adopted a different policy; and, like our residents at Canton, communicated only with the natives in a jargon of their own languages. Mr. Thunberg tells a story of a Dutch gentleman, who had resided as chief of their factory in Japan for fourteen years, during which period he had been four times in the capacity of Embassador to the court, [617] yet, on being asked the name of the Emperor of Japan, freely avowed that it had never occurred to him to ask it. In fact, his grand object was the accumulation of so many millions of florins in a given time; in the pursuit of which he had completely lost sight of the Emperor of Japan and his millions of subjects.

If then, by neglecting to study the language of the Chinese, we are silly enough to place ourselves and concerns so completely in their power, we are highly deserving of the extortions and impositions so loudly complained of. If the trade of London was exclusively vested in the hands of *eight merchants*, and if the foreigners who visited its port could neither speak nor write one single word of the language of England, but communicated solely on every subject with those eight merchants, through a broken jargon somewhat resembling the languages of the several foreigners, it might fairly be questioned, without any disparagement to the merchants of London, if those foreigners would have less reason of complaint than the Europeans have who now trade to China? Even as things are, would a Chinese arriving in England find no subject of complaint, no grievances nor vexations at the custom-house, which, for want of knowing our language, he might be apt to consider as extortions and impositions? Two years ago two Chinese missionaries landed in England, in their way to the college *de propaganda Fide* at Naples. Each had a small bundle of clothes under his arm and, according to the custom of their country, a fan in his hand. Being observed by one of those voracious sharks who, under the pretext of preventing[618] frauds on the revenue, plunder unprotected foreigners and convert the booty to their own advantage, the poor fellows were stripped by him of the little property they carried in their hands, and were not, without difficulty, allowed to escape with the clothes on their backs. Can we blame these people for representing us as a barbarous, unfeeling, and inhospitable nation, however undeserving we may be of such a character?

Our case at Canton is pretty nearly the same as that of the two Chinese missionaries. Every petty officer of the government knows he can practise impositions on our trade with impunity, because we have not the means of bringing his villainy to the knowledge of his superiors. For, how great soever may be the propensity of the Chinese people to fraud and extortion, I have little doubt of the justice and moderation of the Chinese government, when the case is properly represented. A recent circumstance may be mentioned in support of this opinion. In the year 1801, a sailor on board his Majesty's ship the Madras fired upon and mortally wounded a Chinese who was passing in a boat. A discussion, as usual, took place with the Chinese government; but it was conducted in a very different manner from what had hitherto been usual on similar occasions. Instead of entering into any explanation or defence through the medium of the Hong merchants, who tremble at the lowest officer of government, a memorial was addressed to the Viceroy, drawn up in a proper and becoming manner by the present Sir George Staunton, the only Englishman in the Company's service who was skilled in the Chinese language.[619] Several conversations were also held on the subject with the officers of justice, from which the Hong merchants were excluded. Captain Dilkes setting up a plea of recrimination on the ground of some Chinese having cut his cable with an intent to steal it, the government assented to have the matter tried in the supreme court of justice in the city of Canton. By the law of China, if the wounded person survive forty days, the sentence of death is commuted for that of banishment into the wilds of Tartary; yet so favourably did the court incline to the side of the accused in this instance, that although the time was not expired, and there was little hope of the wounded man recovering, they allowed Captain Dilkes to take the seaman into his own custody, requiring only that he should leave in court a written promise to produce him in case the wounded should not survive the time prescribed by law. The man lingered near fifty days and then died, upon which a message was sent by the court, intimating to the Captain, that the court saw no impropriety, in this instance, in leaving it to him to punish the delinquent according to the laws of his own country; thus, for the first time, assenting to set aside a positive law in favour of foreigners. By this proper mode of interference an English subject was saved from an unjust and ignominious death, which would otherwise inevitably have happened, as on all former occasions of a similar kind, had the affair been left in the hands of men whose interest it is to represent us as barbarians, and who, however well they might be disposed, have not the courage to plead our cause. Hitherto the Chinese have invariably made a point of executing immediately, and without a regular trial, any foreigner who should[620] kill a Chinese, or some substitute in the place of the actual criminal, as I have already instanced in the seventh chapter. One of the most intelligent of the East India Company's servants at Canton, speaking on this subject, in answer to certain queries proposed to him about the time of the Embassy, remarks, "I cannot help observing, that the situation of the Company's servants and the trade in general is, in this respect, very dangerous and disgraceful. It is such that it will be impossible for them to extricate themselves from the cruel dilemma a very probable accident may place them in, I will not say with *honour*, but without *infamy*, or exposing the whole trade to ruin." Yet we have just now seen, on the recurrence of such an accident, that by the circumstance of a direct and immediate communication with the government, the affair was terminated, not only without disgrace or infamy, but in a that was honourable to both parties.

CONCLUSION.

I have now gone over most of the points relative to[621] which I have been able to recollect the remarks and observations which arose in my mind during my attendance on this memorable Embassy. The comparisons I have made were given with a view of assisting the reader to form in his own mind some idea what rank the Chinese may be considered to hold, when measured by the scale of European nations; but this part is very defective. To have made it complete would require more time and more reading, than at present I could command. The consideration of other objects, those of a political nature, which are of the most serious importance to our interests in China, is more particularly the province of those in a different sphere, and would, therefore, be improper for me to anticipate or prejudge, by any conjectures of my own. It belongs to other persons, and perhaps to other times[70]; but it is to be hoped that the information, reflections, and opinions of the Embassador himself, may one day be fully communicated to the public, when the present objections to it shall cease, and the moment arrive (which is probably not very distant) that will enable us to act upon the ideas of that nobleman's capacious and enlightened mind, and to prove to the world that the late Embassy, by shewing the character and dignity of the British na[622]tion in a new and splendid light, to a court and people in a great measure ignorant of them before, however misrepresented by the jealousy and envy of rivals, or impeded by the counteraction of enemies, has laid an excellent foundation for great future advantages, and done honour to the wisdom and foresight of the statesman[71] who planned the measure, and directed its execution.

INDEX.

214

216

THE END.

Printed by A. Strahan,
Printers-Street.

FOOTNOTES

[1]Monsieur (I beg his pardon) *Citoyen* Charpentier Cossigny.

[2]This expression alludes to the ancient opinion that China was surrounded by the sea, and that the rest of the world was made up of islands. Yet though they now possess a tolerable notion of geography, such is their inveterate adherence to ancient opinion, that they prefer retaining the most absurd errors, rather than change one single sentiment or expression that Confucius has written.

[3]The expence occasioned to the court of China by the British embassy, will be stated in a subsequent chapter.

[4]In the very next page (202) he however corrects himself, by observing that *either* the Chinese or Malays navigated as far as Madagascar.

[5]If any argument were wanting to prove the originality of the magnetic needle as used in China, the circumstance of their having ingrafted upon it their most ancient and favourite mythology, their cycles, constellations, elements, and, in short, an abstract of all their astronomical or astrological science, is quite sufficient to settle that point. Those who are acquainted with the Chinese character will not readily admit that their long established superstitions should be found incorporated on an instrument of barbarian invention.

[6]Plin. lib. xvii. cap. 3.

[7]I should not have taken notice of this odious vice, had not the truth of its existence in China been doubted by some, and attributed by others to a wrong cause. Professing to describe the people as I found them, I must endeavour to draw a faithful picture, neither attempting to palliate their vices, nor to exaggerate their virtues.

[8]Adam's Roman Antiquities.

[9]Mr. Torreen.

[10]Linn. Systema Naturæ.

[11]See *Gibbon*, under Emperor Justinian; and *Menagiana*, in which is given the translation of a very extraordinary passage from *Procopius*.

[12]T. Calpurnius.

[13]Duke of Buckingham. See the notes on this character in Shakespear's Henry VIII. Act. i, Scene 2.

[14]For the curiosity of those who may be inclined to speculate in etymological comparisons between the Chinese and other languages, I here subjoin a short list of words in the former, expressing some of the most striking objects in the creation, a few subjects of natural history, and of such articles as from their general use are familiar to most nations, these being of all others the most likely to have retained their primitive names. The orthography I have used is that of the English language.

The Earth	*tee*
The Air	*kee*
Fire	*ho*
Water	*swee*
The Sea	*hai*
A River	*ho*
A Lake	*tang*
A Mountain	*shan*
A Wilderness	*ye-tee*
The Sun	*jee-to*
The Moon	*yué*
The Stars	*sing*
The Clouds	*yun*
Rain	*yeu*
Hail	*swee-tan*

Snow		*swé*
Ice		*ping*
Thunder		*luie*
Lightning		*shan-tien*
The Wind		*fung*
The Day	*n*	*jee* or *tie*
The Night	*shang*	*ye* or *van*
The Sky or Heaven		*tien*
The East		*tung*
The West		*see*
The North		*pee*
The South		*nan*
Man		*jin*
Woman		*foo-jin*
A Quadruped		*shoo*
A Bird		*kin*
A Fish		*eu*
An Insect		*tchong*
A Plant		*tsau*
A Tree		*shoo*
A Fruit		*ko-ste*
A Flower		*wha*
A Stone		*shee*

Gold	*tchin*
Silver	*in tse*
Copper	*tung*
Lead	*yuen*
Iron	*tié*
The Head	*too*
The Hand	*shoo*
The Heart	*sin*
The Leg	*koo*
The Foot	*tchiau*
The Face	*mien*
The Eyes	*yen-shing*
The Ears	*cul-to*
The Hair	*too fa*
An ox	*nieu*
A Camel	*loo-too*
A Horse	*ma*
An Ass	*loo-tse*
A Dog	*kioon*
A Frog	*tchoo*
A Sheep	*yang*
A Goat, or mountain Sheep	*shan-yang*
A Cat	*miau*

A Stag	*shan loo*
A Pidgeon	*koo-tse*
Poultry	*kee*
An Egg	*kee-tan*
A Goose	*goo*
Oil	*yeo*
Rice	*mee*
Milk	*nai*
Vinegar	*tsoo*
Tobacco	*yen*
Salt	*yen*
Silk	*tsoo*
Cotton	*mien-wha*
Flax Plant	*ma*
Hemp	*ma*
Wool (Sheep's Hair)	*yangmau*
Coals	*tan*
Sugar	*tang*
Cheese, they have none but thick Milk	*nai-ping*, or iced milk
A House	*shia*
A Temple	*miau*
A Bed	*tchuang*
A Door	*men*

A Table	*tai*
A Chair	*ye-tzé*
A Knife	*tau*
A Pitcher	*ping*
A Plough	*lee*
An Anchor	*mau*
A Ship	*tchuan*
Money	*tsien*

I must observe, however, for the information of these philologists, that scarcely two provinces in China have the same oral language. The officers and their attendants who came with us from the capital could converse only with the boatmen of the southern provinces, through the medium of an interpreter. The character of the language is universal, but the name or sound of the character is arbitrary. If a *convention of sounds* could have been settled like a convention of marks, one would suppose that a commercial intercourse would have effected it, at least in the numeral sounds, that must necessarily be interchanged from place to place and myriads of times repeated from one corner of the empire to the other. Let us compare then the numerals of Pekin with those of Canton, the two greatest cities in China.

	Pekin.	Canton.
1.	Ye	yat
2.	ul	ye
3.	san	saam
4.	soo	see
5.	ou	um
6.	leu	lok
7.	tchee	tsat
8.	pas	pat
9.	tcheu	kow
10.	shee	shap
11.	shee-ye	shap-yat

225

12.	shee-ul	shap-ye
20.	ul-shee	ye-shap
30.	san-shee	saam-shap
31.	san-shee-ye	saam-shap-yat
32.	san-shee-ul	saam-shap-ye
100.	pe	paak
1000.	tsien	tseen
10,000.	van	man
100,000.	she-van	shap-man

If then, in this highly civilized empire, the oral language of the northern part differs so widely from the southern that, in numerous instances, by none of the etymological tricks[15] can they be brought to bear any kind of analogy; if the very word which in Pekin implies the number *one*, be used in Canton to express *two*, how very absurd and ludicrous must these learned and laboured dissertations appear, that would assign an oriental origin to all our modern languages?

[15]Such as the addition, deduction, mutation, and transposition of letters, or even syllables. Thus Mr. Webbe thinks that the derivation of the Greek γυνὴ *a woman*, from the Chinese *na-gin*, is self-evident.

[16]By Mr. Pauw.

[17]That the Chinese method, however, is defective, may be inferred from the circumstance of the present Sir George Staunton having not only acquired, in little more than twelve months, and at the age of twelve years, such a number of words and phraseology as to make himself understood, and to understand others on common topics of conversation, but he also learned to write the characters with such facility and accuracy, that all the diplomatic papers of the Embassy addressed to the Chinese government were copied by him (the Chinese themselves being afraid to let papers of so unusual a style appear in their own hand-writing) in so neat and expeditious a manner as to occasion great astonishment. It may be observed, however, that few youths of his age possess the talents, the attention, and the general information with which he was endowed.

[18]The invention, in Europe, is usually attributed to one Schwartz, a German Monk, about the year 1354, which, however, is very doubtful, as there is every reason to believe that cannon was made use of at the battle of Cressy, which happened in the year 1346. And Mariana, in his account of the siege of Algeziras by the Spaniards, in the year 1342, or 1343, as quoted by Bishop Watson, observes, "that the Moors very much annoyed the Christians with their iron shot;" and he further adds, that "this is the first mention made in history of the use of gunpowder and ball." It is therefore extremely probable, that the first introduction of gunpowder into Europe was by some Mahomedans from the eastward, and that Schwartz

was not the inventor, although he might perhaps have been the first publisher of the discovery.

[19]I am aware that those laboured pieces, of Italian make, of ivory cut into landscapes, with houses, trees, and figures, sometimes so small as to be comprehended within the compass of a ring, may be quoted against me; but the work of a solitary and secluded monk to beguile the weary hours, is not to be brought in competition with that of a common Chinese artist, by which he earns his livelihood.

[20]Mr. Dutens.

[21]A bridge with ninety-one arches will be noticed in a subsequent chapter.

[22]Sir William Jones.

[23]It is called the *Ta-tchin Leu-Lee*, the laws and institutes under the dynasty *Ta-tchin*, which is the name assumed by the present family on the throne.

[24]Various accidents having happened at different times to Chinese subjects in the port of Canton, which have generally led to disagreeable discussions with the Chinese government, the supercargoes of the East India Company thought proper, on a late occasion of a person being wounded by a shot from a British ship of war, to make application for an extract from the criminal code of laws relating to homicide, in order to have the same translated into English, and made public. This extract consisted of the following articles:

1. A man who kills another on the supposition of theft, shall be strangled, according to the law of homicide committed in an affray.

2. A man who fires at another with a musquet, and kills him thereby, shall be beheaded, as in cases of wilful murder. If the sufferer be wounded, but not mortally, the offender shall be sent into exile.

3. A man who puts to death a criminal who had been apprehended, and made no resistance, shall be strangled, according to the law against homicide committed in an affray.

4. A man who falsely accuses an innocent person of theft (in cases of greatest criminality) is guilty of a capital offence; in all other cases the offenders, whether principals or accessaries, shall be sent into exile.

5. A man who wounds another unintentionally shall be tried according to the law respecting blows given in an affray, and the punishment rendered more or less severe, according to the degree of injury sustained.

6. A man who, intoxicated with liquor, commits outrages against the laws, shall be exiled to a desert country, there to remain in a state of servitude.

In this clear and decisive manner are punishments awarded for every class of crimes committed in society; and it was communicated to the English factory from the viceroy, that on no consideration was it left in the breast of the judge to extenuate or to exaggerate the sentence, whatever might be the rank, character, or station of the delinquent.

[25]The following law case, which is literally translated, from a volume of reports of trials, published in the present reign of *Kia-King*, and with which I have been favoured by a friend (who was himself the translator), will serve to shew the mode of proceeding in criminal matters of the provincial courts of judicature. The circumstances of the transaction appear to have been enquired into fairly and impartially, and no pains spared to ascertain the exact degree of criminality. Being given to me about the time when the trial took place of Smith, for the murder of the supposed *Hammersmith ghost*, I was forcibly struck with the remarkable coincidence of the two cases, and with the almost identical defence set up by the Chinese and the English prisoners, and on that account it excited more interest than perhaps it might otherwise be considered to be entitled to.

Translation of an Extract from a Collection of Chinese Law Reports, being the Trial, Appeal, and Sentence upon an Indictment for Homicide by Gun firing.

At a criminal court held in the province of Fo-kien, upon an indictment for shooting, and mortally wounding a relation; setting forth, that *She-fo-pao*, native of the city of *Fo-ngan-sien*, did fire a gun, and by mischance, wound *Vang-yung-man*, so that he died thereof.

The case was originally reported, as follows, by *Vu-se-Kung*, sub-viceroy of the province of Fo-kien:

The accused *She-fo-pao*, and the deceased *Vang-yung-man*, were of different families, but connected by marriage, were well known to each other, and there had always been a good understanding between them.

In the course of the first moon, of the 25th year of *Kien-long, She-fo-pao* cultivated a farm on the brow of a hill belonging to *Chin-se-kien*, and which lay in the vicinity of certain lands cultivated by *Vang-yung-man* and *Vang-ky-hao*, inasmuch as that the fields of *Vang-yung-man* lay on the left of those of *She-fo-pao*, which were in the center, and those of *Vang-ky-hao* on the right side of the declivity of the hill. It occurred that on the 7th day of the 9th moon of the same year, *She-fo-pao* observing the corn in his fields to be nearly ripe, was apprehensive that thieves might find an opportunity of stealing the grain; and being aware, at the same time, of the danger which existed on those hills from wolves and tygers, armed himself with a musquet, and went that night alone to the spot, in order to watch the corn, and seated himself in a convenient place on the side of the hill. It happened that *Vang-ky-hao* went that day to the house of *Vang-yung-man*, in order that they might go together to keep watch over the corn in their respective fields. However *Vang-yung-tong* the elder brother of *Vang-yung-man*, conceiving it to be yet early, detained them to drink tea, and smoke tobacco until the second watch[26] of the night, when they parted from him, and proceeded on their expedition, provided with large sticks for defence.

Vang-ky-hao having occasion to stop for a short time upon the road, the other *Vang-yung-man* went on before, until he reached the boundary of the fields watched by *She-fo-pao*.

She-fo-pao, on hearing a rustling noise among the corn, and perceiving the shadow of a person through the obscurity of the night, immediately hailed him, but the wind blowing very fresh, he did not hear any reply. *She-fo-pao* then took alarm, on the suspicion that the sound proceeded from thieves, or else from wild beasts, and lighting the match-lock, which he held in his hand, fired it off, in order to repel the invaders whoever they might be.

Vang-yung-man was wounded by the shot in the head, cheeks, neck, and shoulder, and instantly fell to the ground. *Vang-ky-hao* hearing the explosion, hastened forward, and called aloud to enquire who had fired the gun. The other heard the voice, and going to the place from whence it proceeded, then learned whom he had wounded by the mischance. The wounds of *Vang-yung-man* being mortal, he expired after a very short interval of time had elapsed.

She-fo-pao, being repeatedly examined by the magistrate, acknowledged the fact without reserve, and, upon the strictest investigation and enquiry being entered upon, deposed, That it was really during the obscurity of the night that he had ascended the hill, in order to watch the corn, and on hearing a noise proceed from a quarter of the field that was extremely dark, and in which the shadow of some person was discernable, he had called out, but received no answer:—That the suspicion then arose in his mind, that they were either thieves or wild beasts, and alarmed him for the security of his person, being then entirely alone, he therefore fired the gun to repel the danger, and wounded *Vang-yung-man* by mischance, so that he afterwards died.

That he, the deponent, was not actuated by any other motive or intention on this occasion, nor desirous of causing the death of an individual. The relations of the deceased being then examined, give a corresponding evidence, and raised no doubts in other respects to the truth of the above deposition. In consideration, therefore, hereof it appears that, although *She-fo-pao* is guilty of homicide by gun-firing, yet, since he was upon the watch over the fields, in the darkness of the night, and perceived the shadow of a man, whom he hailed, and from whom he received no answer, and had in consequence apprehended the approach of thieves or wild beasts, to prevent which, he fired the gun that occasioned the wounds whereof the man is now dead—It follows, that there did not exist any premeditated intention of murder.—The act of which *She-fo-pao* stands convicted may be, therefore, ranked under the article of homicide committed in an affray, and the sentence accordingly is, to be strangled upon the next ensuing general execution or gaol delivery.

The above report being transmitted to the supreme criminal tribunal at Pekin,—They rejoin,

That, on investigation of the laws we find it ordained, that homicide by gun-firing shall receive a sentence conformable to the law against intentional murder; and that the law against intentional murder gives a sentence of decapitation on the next ensuing public execution, or gaol delivery. It is likewise found to be ordained by law, that whoever shall unwarily draw a bow, and shoot an arrow towards fields or tenements, so that any person unperceived therein shall be wounded, and die therefrom, the offender shall receive a hundred blows with the bamboo, and be banished to the distance of three thousands lys (near a thousand miles).

In the case now before us, *She-fo-pao*, being armed with a musquet, goes to watch the corn, hears a noise in the fields, and calls aloud, but, receiving no answer, suspects it to proceed from thieves or wild beasts, and fires the gun, by which *Vang-yung-man* was wounded, and is now dead. But in the deposition given in by the defendant, the declaration that he saw the shadow of some person does not accord with the suspicion afterwards expressed, that the noise arose from wild beasts. If, in truth, he distinguished traces of a man, at the time of his calling out, notwithstanding that the violence of the wind prevented his hearing the reply, *She-fo-pao* had ocular proof of the reality of the person from the shadow he had seen. Continuing our investigation, we have further to notice, that when *She-fo-pao* took his station in order to guard the middle ground, *Vang-yung-man* was engaged in watching his fields in a similar manner, and would have occasion to go near the limits of the middle ground in his way to his own farm, and which could not be far removed from the path leading to the middle ground; on which account it behoved *She-fo-pao* to hail the person repeatedly, previous to the firing of the gun, whose effect would be instantaneous, and occasion the death of the unknown person from whom the sound proceeded.

She-fo-pao not having repeatedly hailed the person from whom the noise had arisen to disturb him, and proceeding to the last extremity upon the first impulse or alarm, are grounds for suspecting that there exists a fallacy and disguise in the testimony given in this affair, in which case, a sentence conformable to the law against homicide, committed in an affray, would afford a punishment unequal and inadequate to the possible aggravation of the offence.

On the other hand, it would appear, in confirmation of his statement, that these fields were, according to the custom of the neighbouring villages, understood to be guarded at that time in a the manner aforesaid, and that circumstance proving true, the accident that followed might still be considered solely as the effect of apprehension of wild beasts by night, inducing the accused to fire towards fields or tenements, so as to wound a man mortally by the mischance.

Should a strict examination admit of this interpretation of the offence, the sentence may be awarded according to the law, immediately applicable to the subject, and not in conformity with the law against homicide committed in an affray. As the life or death of the offender rests on the preference to be shewn towards either of those expositions of the case, it is resolved to hold any immediate decision as premature, and we issue our directions to the said sub-viceroy to revise the prior decision; and, with the assistance of a renewed investigation, finally to determine and report to us the sentence which he may conceive most agreeable to the spirit of our laws.

After a second investigation, and reconsideration of the affair, the sub-viceroy sent in the following report to the supreme tribunal: Pursuant to the order for revisal issued by the supreme criminal tribunal, *She-fo-pao* has been again examined at the bar, and deposes, That on hearing a noise in the corn fields, he conceived it to proceed from thieves, and called out in consequence, but, receiving no answer, and finding the noise gradually to approach him, he then suspected it to have arisen from a wolf or tyger; and, in the alarm thus excited for his personal safety, had fired the gun, by which *Vang-yung-man* had been mortally wounded; That, since the event happened in the second watch of the night, after the moon had set, and while clouds obscured the faint light of the stars, it was really a moment of impenetrable darkness; and that it was only at the distance of a few paces that he distinguished the approach of the sound that had alarmed him, but, in fact, had never seen any shadow or traces whatsoever; That he had perceived any traces or shadow of that description, he would not have ceased to call out, though he had failed to receive an answer the first time, nor would he have had the temerity to fire the gun, and render himself guilty of murder.

That, on the preceding examination, the severity and rigour of the enquiry regarding the grounds upon which he suspected the approach of thieves, so as to induce him to fire, had overcome him with fear, being a countryman unused to similar proceedings, and produced the apparent incongruity in his deposition, but that the true meaning and intent was to express his absolute uncertainty whether the alarm arose from thieves or wild beasts and nothing farther, and that from such deposition he had never intentionally swerved in the course of the investigation.

According, therefore, to the amendment suggested by the supreme tribunal, it appears indeed, that when the noise was first perceived in the fields, *She-fo-pao* had called out, and on being prevented by the wind from hearing a reply, had taken alarm as aforesaid.

And whereas it was likewise deposed by *She-fo-pao*, That the grain being ripe at that season, the stems were exceeding high and strong, so as to render it difficult to walk amongst them, it seems that *Vang-yung-man*, in walking through the corn, had produced a rustling noise very audible to *She-fo-pao*, who was sitting on the declivity of the hill, and in a direction in which the wind favoured the progress of the sound; but when the latter called out, the wind, on the contrary, prevented him from being heard, and consequently from receiving an answer; this mischance, therefore, gave rise to his suspicion of the approach of wild beasts, which appears to have been the sole and undisguised motive for firing the gun.

This statement of facts being narrowly investigated, in compliance with the supreme tribunal's order for revisal, may be confided in as accurate, and worthy of credit; the result, therefore, is that the offender during the darkness of the night, and under the apprehension of the approach of a wolf or tyger, had fired a musquet in a spot frequented by men, and had mortally wounded a man by the mischance, which corresponds with the law suggested in the order for revisal issued by the supreme tribunal; namely, that law against an offender who should unwarily draw a bow and shoot an arrow towards fields or tenements, so that any person unperceived therein should be wounded and die therefrom.

The prior decision, conformably to the law against homicide committed in an affray, subsequent investigation does not confirm; and *She-fo-pao* is, therefore, only punishable with banishment.

This second report being received by the supreme criminal tribunal, they declare that,

The sentence having been altered on a revision by the sub-viceroy, and rendered conformable to the law, which ordains that, whoever shall unwarily draw a bow and shoot an arrow towards fields or tenements, so that any person unperceived therein may be wounded, and die therefrom, the offender shall receive a hundred blows with the bamboo, and suffer banishment to the distance of 3000 lys.

We confirm the sentence of a hundred blows of the bamboo, and banishment to the distance of 3000 lys; and further prescribe, that ten ounces of silver (3*l.* 6*s.* 3*d.*) shall be paid by the offender to the relations of the deceased for the expences of burial.

The sentence, being thus pronounced on the 19th day of the 5th moon, of the 27th year of *Kien-Long*, received the Imperial sanction on the 21st day of the same moon, in the following words: Pursuant to sentence be this obeyed.

KHIN-TSE.

[26]Each watch is two hours, and the second watch begins at eleven o'clock.

[27]A debtor is released when it appears that the whole of his property has been given up for the use of his creditors.

[28]The circumstances attending the downfal of this minister are curious, and shew, in its true light, the despotic nature of the Chinese government, notwithstanding their salutary laws. The new Emperor, determined on his ruin, makes a public declaration wherein, after apologizing for not abstaining agreeably to the laws of the empire from all acts of innovation, for the space of three years after his father's death, he observes, that the crimes and excesses of *Ho-tchung-tang* are of so horrid a nature, as to preclude him from acting towards him with any pity or indulgence. He then exhibits about twenty articles of accusation against him, the principal of which are,

Contumacy towards his father (the late Emperor) by riding on horseback to the very door of the hall of audience at *Yuen-min-yuen*.

Audacity, under pretence of lameness, in causing himself to be carried to and from the palace through the door set apart for the Emperor.

Scandalous behaviour, in taking away the virgins of the palace, and appropriating them to his own use.

Pride and insolence, in countermanding his (the new Emperor's) order, for all the princes of Tartary to be summoned to Pekin, those who had not had the small-pox excepted, to assist at the funeral of his father, and by issuing a new one, in which *none* were excepted.

Bribery and partiality, in selling and giving away appointments of weight to persons totally unqualified to fill them.

Arrogance, in making use of the wood *Nan-moo* (cedar) in his house, which is destined exclusively for royal palaces; and in building a house and gardens in the style and manner of those belonging to the Emperor.

For having in his possession more than two hundred strings of pearls, and an immense quantity of jewels and precious stones, which his rank did not allow him to wear, and among which was a pearl of such wonderful magnitude, that the Emperor himself had no equal to it.

For having in gold and silver alone, which has been already discovered and confiscated, the amount, at least, of ten million taels (about 3,300,000*l.* sterling).

One article is singularly curious. For having been guilty of the deepest treachery in informing him (the new Emperor) of his father's intention to abdicate the government in his (the new Emperor's) favour, *one day* before his father made it public, thinking by such means to gain his favour and affection!

After enumerating the several articles of accusation, the Emperor states, that this minister being interrogated by a Tartar prince on several points, had confessed the whole to be true, and, therefore, without further evidence, he commands the presidents and members of the several courts in Pekin, the viceroys of provinces, and governors of cities, on these articles of accusation being laid before them, to pass a proper sentence on the said *Ho-tchung-tang*. According to the majority, he was condemned to be beheaded; but as a peculiar act of grace and benevolence on the part of the Emperor, this sentence was mitigated to that of his being allowed to be his own executioner. A silken cord being sent as an intimation of this mark of the Emperor's favour, he caused himself to be strangled by some of his attendants.

Who could escape when the Emperor of China is himself the accuser? It will readily occur, from the fate of *Ho-tchung-tang*, that there is not that line of independence drawn between the executive and juridical authority, which the ingenious author of the Spirit of Laws has clearly proved to be the grand foundation of a just, legal, and efficient security of the life and property of the subject. In fact, in all state crimes, the Emperor becomes both the accuser and the judge. In the case of *Ho-tchung-tang* he may likewise be said to have been the only evidence.

[29]Among the various customs of China, particularized in the accounts of the two Mahomedan travellers in the ninth century, this remarkable one is noticed, affording, with the rest, equally singular and peculiar to this nation, an proof of the authenticity of these two relations.

[30]The words of *Kaung-shee*'s proclamation, repeated by *Kia-king*, are: "At present when an army is sent on any military service, every report that is made of its operations, contains an account of a victory, of rebels dispersed at the first encounter, driven from their stations, killed, and wounded, to a great amount, or to the amount of some thousands, or, in short, that the rebels slain were innumerable."

Pekin Gazette, 31st July, 1800.

[31]When the art of printing was first introduced into England, and carried on in Westminster Abbey, a shrewd churchman is said to have observed to the Abbot of Westminster, "If you don't take care to destroy that machine, it will very soon destroy your trade." He saw at a single glance of the press, the downfal of priestly dominion in the general diffusion of knowledge that would be occasioned by it, and had the rest of the clergy been equally clear-sighted, it is probable the dark ages of superstition and ignorance had still continued, or at least had been greatly protracted.

[32]When the mischievous doctrines of *Tom Paine*, expounded in his "Rights of Man," were translated into various languages, and industriously attempted to be propagated among the eastern nations, by means of French emissaries; when one of those assiduous disturbers of the peace of mankind had actually succeeded in furnishing the Seiks with an abstract of this precious work in their own language, he next turned his attention to the vast empire of China, a glorious theatre for those zealous cosmopolites to play their parts in, if they could once contrive to suit their drama to the taste of the people. The experiment, however, failed of success. The golden opinions of *Tom Paine* could not be transfused into the Chinese language; and these unfortunate people understood no other but their own; so that three hundred and thirty-three millions were doomed to remain in ignorance and misery on account of their language being incapable of conveying the enlightened doctrines of *Tom Paine*.

[33]The last accounts, indeed, that have been received from China, are rather of an alarming nature. A very serious rebellion had broken out in the western provinces, which had extended to that of Canton, the object of which was the overthrow of the Tartar government. It was known for some years past, as I before observed, that certain secret societies were forming in the different provinces, who corresponded together by unknown signs, agreed upon by convention, but they were not considered to be of that extent as to cause any uneasiness to the government. It appears, however, that not fewer than forty thousand men had assembled in arms in the province of Canton, at the head of whom was a man of the family of the last Chinese Emperor, who had assumed the Imperial Yellow. These rebels, it seems, are considerably encouraged in their cause by a prophesy, which is current among the people, that the present Tartar dynasty shall be overturned in the year 1804. The existence of such a prophecy may be more dangerous to the Tartar government than the arms of the rebels, by assisting to bring about its own accomplishment.

[34]Vattel.

[35]This consideration on the transient nature of languages, and especially of those whose fleeting sounds have never been fixed by any graphic invention, makes it the more surprizing how Lord Kames, in his sketch on the origin and progress of American nations, after observing that no passage by land had been discovered between America and the old world, should have given it as his opinion, that an enquiry, much more decisive at to the former being peopled by the latter, might be pursued, by ascertaining whether the same language be spoken by the inhabitants on the two sides of the strait that divides the northern regions of America from Kamskatka. And that, after finding this not to be the case, he should conclude that the former could not have been peopled by the latter. Had not Lord Kames written upon a system of a separate and local creation, pre-established in his own mind, he would unquestionably have laid more stress upon a resemblance in their physical characters, in their superstitions and religious notions, than on similarity of language; which, among the many acquirements of the human species, or of human institution, is not the least liable to change by a change of situation, especially where no written character has been employed to fix it. His Lordship's conclusion is the more extraordinary, as he had already observed that the resemblance between them was perfect in every other respect.

[36]It is sufficiently remarkable, that the Emperor *Kaung-shee*, in giving, by public edict, some account to his subjects of the different nations of Asia and Europe, should make the following observation. "To the southward of the *Cossack* country a horde of *Hoo-tse* (Turks) is established, who are descended from the same stock with *Yuen-tay-tse*, formerly Emperors of China."

[37]The *exterior* angles are here meant which, in the Chinese also, are extended in the same or a greater proportion than the *interior* ones are rounded off.

[38]As a corroborating proof of the Chinese being of Scythic origin, it may be observed, that the adjunct character *Shee* (to the family name *Foo*) is composed of a *sheep*, *rice*, an *arrow*, and the conjunctive character *also*, from whence may be inferred that he united the occupations of *shepherd*, *agriculturist*, and *warrior*.

[39]The *Shoo-king*.

[40]Ptolemy, the Geographer, places Serica adjoining to Scythia, *extra Imaum*, corresponding with Cashgar, Tangut, and Kitai, countries famous for the cultivation of the

cotton plant. It would seem, indeed, from all the passages which occur in ancient authors concerning the Seres, that cotton was the substance alluded to, rather than silk, and that these people were not the present Chinese, but the Tartars of Kitai.

Quid nemora Æthiopum molli canentia lana?
Velleraque ut foliis depectant tenuia Seres?
Virg. Georg. ii. v. 120.

——*Primique nova Phaethonte retecti*
Seres lanigeris repetebant vellera lucis.
Sil. Ital. 1. 6. v. 3.

——*Quod molli tondent de stipite Seres*
Frondea lanigeræ carpentes vellera Silvæ.
Claudian.

Seres lanificio Sylvarum nobiles perfusam aquá depectentes frondium canitiem.
Plin. 1. 6. 17.

Horace makes the Seres expert in drawing the bow, a weapon in the use of which the Scythians were always famous.
Doctus Sagittas tendere Sericas
Arcu paterno?
Hor. lib. i. Od. 29. v. 9.

It certainly cannot be inferred that by the *Seres*, in any of the above quotations, was meant the same people as the present Chinese; on the contrary, the probability is that it did not allude to this nation, and that the ancients had not the least knowledge of its existence. It appears from another passage in Pliny, that the best iron in the world was in *Sericum*, and that the Seres exported it with their cloths and skins. The iron of the Chinese, as I have had occasion to observe, is remarkably bad, and all their articles of peltry are imported.

[41]All our enquiries, in passing the city of Hang-tchoo-foo, were fruitless with regard to these Israelites. We had hitherto entertained a hope of being able to procure, in the course of our journey, a copy of this ancient monument of the Jewish history, which the late Doctor Geddes considered as very desirable to compare with those already in Europe; but the hasty manner in which we travelled, and the repugnance shewn by our conducting officers, *Chou* and *Van* excepted, who had little power or influence in the provinces, to enter into any of our views that might appear to occasion delay, prevented the fulfilment of those hopes. It were much to be wished, that the reverend missionaries would so far lay aside their antipathy against opinions, not exactly coinciding with their own, and enter into such a correspondence with the Jews, as would obtain from them, which they are no doubt possessed of, an account of the progress made by the Chinese in civilization and arts, since their first settling in that country, and of other particulars noted down by them. The circumstance of their carrying with them their code of laws, and the history of their tribes, is a sufficient proof that they understood a written language which there can be no doubt, they would use the utmost caution not to lose. Such an account would be more authentic than the Chinese annals, the best of which abound in hyperbole, and contain facts so disguised in metaphor, that it is no easy matter to extract from them the simple truth. At all events, the comparison of the two histories would serve to verify each other.

[42]In the year 1785, Kien Long liberated, by a public edict, twelve missionaries out of prison, who, being detected in privately seducing the Chinese from the religion and customs of the country, had been condemned to perpetual imprisonment. This edict, of which I procured a copy in Pekin, does great honour to the humane and benevolent mind of the Emperor. After stating their crime, apprehension, and trial, he observes, "Had they made known their arrival to the officers of government, they might have proceeded to the capital and found protection. But as transgressors of the law, which forbids the entrance of

strangers, they have stolen into the country, and secretly endeavoured to multiply converts to their way of thinking, it became my duty to oppose a conduct so deceitful, and to put a stop to the progress of seduction. Justly as they were found to deserve the punishment to which they have been condemned, touched, nevertheless, with compassion for their imprudence, it was not without injury to my feelings that I ratified the sentence. But recollecting afterwards that they were strangers—strangers perhaps ignorant of the laws of my empire, my compassion increased for them, and humanity suffers on account of their long confinement. I will, therefore, and command that these twelve strangers be set at liberty."

[43]The government even grants licences to certain persons, under the abused name of astronomers, who pretend to predict events, and cast out evil spirits by a charm, consisting of some character written by them, according to the supposed prevailing planet. The national almanack, not less minute in its predictions than those of Francis Moore or Vincent Wing, or even Partridge, points out the changes of the weather in every month, with the lucky and unlucky days for undertaking most of the important concerns of life. And that the fallacy of these is not detected, may afford less matter for surprize, on recollection that, in the wise and enlightened countries of Europe, and among very intelligent people, the state of the weather is pretended to be predicted by the phases of the moon, that is to say, they will prognosticate a change of weather to happen at the new moon, or the first quarter, or the full, or the last quarter, or, at all events, three days before, or three days after one or other of these periods; so that the predictor has, at the least, eight and twenty days out of a lunar revolution, in favour of his prediction being right, and the whole lunation is only twenty-nine and a half. He has also another great advantage: the accidental coincidence of one single prophecy with the event, establishes his fame for ever, whilst his blunders are either overlooked, or considered only as those of the person, and not the defect of the science.

[44]And which, together with their pernicious practices and infamous pamphlets, addressed chiefly to youth of both sexes, it may be added, have done more mischief than "plague, pestilence, or famine." Among the numerous societies that have been formed for the amendment of public morals and the suppression of vice, it is surprizing that no plan has been thought of for the suppression of impudent quacks.

[45]Thus among the inscriptions written over the doors of Temples, some are dedicated

To the Holy Mother, Queen of Heaven; the Goddess of peace and power, descended from the island of MOUI-TAO, who stills the waves of the sea, allays storms, protects the empire.

Another has

The ancient temple of the goddess (Kin-wha) of the golden flower, through whose influence fields are green and fertile like a grove of trees, and benefits are diffused as the frothy wave of the sea, that shines like splendid pearls.

[46]Poo-sa comprehends a class of superintending deities inferior to those of Fo, who are consulted on trivial occasions, and the ordinary affairs of life. Of course the greater number of temples are called by the general name of Poo-sa miau, temple of Poo-sa. The name implies all-helping. The character poo signifies support, and sa has the character of plant for its root or key united to that of preservation; the plant-preserving, or plant-supporting deity; from whence it may perhaps be concluded, that Poo-sa is the offspring of the Holy Mother of whom I am about to speak.

[47]The character shing is compounded of ear, mouth, and ruler or king, intending perhaps to express the faculty of hearing all that ear has heard and mouth uttered.

[48]By Mr. Pauw.

[49]Captain Turner found the name of the Lotos inscribed over most of the temples in Bootan and Thibet, and Colonel Symes, in the account of his embassy to the kingdom of Ava, which with Pegu, Aracan, and Laos, now constitute the Birman empire, describes the people as Budhists or of the sect of Fo; indeed their customs and appearance, as well as their religion, seem to indicate a Chinese or Tartar origin.

[50]No festivals, perhaps, were so universally adopted and so far extended, as those in honour of Isis. They not only found their way into every part of the East, but from Greece they were also received by the Romans, and from these they passed into Gaul. It has even

been conjectured, that the modern name of Paris has its derivation from a temple that was dedicated to this goddess, ϖαρα ισιν, not very distant from this ancient capital of Gaul. The city arms are a ship, which *Isis* was depicted to hold in her hand, as the patroness of navigation. In fact, a statue of *Isis*[51] is said to have been preserved with great care in the church of Saint Germain until the beginning of the sixteenth century, when the zeal of a bigotted cardinal caused it to be demolished as an unsanctified relick of pagan superstition.

[51]Encyclopédie des Connoissances Humaines.

[52]The present Emperor shewed his gratitude for his prayers having been heard, by granting in a public edict an additional title to the temple in which they were offered.

IMPERIAL EDICT.

"*The gracious protecting temple of the king of the dragons,* on the mountain of *Yu-chun,* has on every occasion of drought proved favourable to our prayers offered up there for rain, as duly observed on our sacred registers. From the summer solstice of the present year, a great want of rain has been experienced, on which account we were induced, on the 17th of this moon, to offer up our prayers and sacrifices in person at the said temple. During the very same day, a fall of small rain or dew was observed, and, on the day following, the country was relieved by frequent and copious showers. This further proof of efficacy in granting our requests, augments our veneration and, in testimony whereof, we direct that the temple of the propitious divinity shall receive an additional title, and be styled on all future occasions,

"*The gracious in protecting, and efficacious in preserving, the temple of the king of the dragons.*

"*Be our will obeyed.*"

Pekin Gazette, 23rd day of 5th Moon, of 6th year of Kia-King.

[53]From a passage in the manuscript journal of a Chinese who accompanied the Dutch embassy it would appear, that the art of embalming the dead was once known and practiced in this country. He observes, that at *Ou tebé* there is a temple or pagoda inhabited by a number of priests, who shew the body of a very ancient bonze, prepared in such a manner, and filled with such ingredients, that it does not decay, but remains perfectly entire. He is dressed in his robes of ceremony, and in his hand he holds a machine which was invented by him for cleaning rice.

[54]For the convenience of collecting and distributing the taxes raised in kind, the districts, and cities within them, are divided into three classes, distinguished by the adjuncts *foo, tchoo, shien.* The *shien* is answerable to the *tchoo;* the *tchoo* to the *foo;* and the *foo* to the board of revenue in the capital.

[55]The *Far et mica salis* were parts of most of the Roman sacrifices, and salt, in particular, was held in such veneration, and in such general use, that when any one obtained a salary or pension, he was said to have got his *Salarium,* or something to procure his salt, in the same sense, as we say, to get one's bread, and a common expression in India, denoting service, is, *I eat the salt of such a one,* and the Dutch in speaking of a dependent say, *he owes his salt to such a one.* These coincidences of opinion, or custom, among remote nations, however difficult they may be to explain, are nevertheless extremely interesting and are on that account here noticed.

[56]I infer that such is not the practice in China, from the manner in which the Dutch Embassadors were conveyed to and from the capital in the middle of winter. The inconveniences they suffered on this occasion are such as can scarcely be conceived to have happened in a civilized country. The perusal of the manuscript journal I have elsewhere noticed conveyed to my mind the idea of a country dreary and desolate, and of a people indigent and distressed; without humanity, and without hospitality. They travelled in little bamboo chairs, carried by four men, who were generally so weak and tottering that they could not go through the day's journey, but were obliged, frequently, in the middle of the night, to halt in an open uninhabited part of the country, where not a hovel of any description was to be met with to shelter them from the inclemency of the weather. And it most commonly happened, that the lodgings appointed for their reception, at the different stages were in such a miserable condition, admitting on every side the wind, rain, or snow, that they generally preferred taking a little rest in their bamboo chairs. They were surprized to find so few cities, towns, or villages in their route, and not less surprized at the ruinous

235

condition in which these few appeared to be. Near the capital a whole city exhibited only a mass of ruins. In many places they found the country under water, and the mud hovels completely melted down. Sometimes they passed extensive wastes, where not a trace was visible of any kind of cultivation, nor a single dwelling occurred in the distance of eight or ten English miles. And it was not before they had crossed the Yellow River that they perceived the marks of wheel-carriages imprinted on the roads, which were so little travelled upon that they could with difficulty be traced. Here they met old men and young women travelling in wheelbarrows; and litters carried by asses, one being fixed between the poles before, and one behind. The rivers had no bridges over them; and such as were too deep to be forded, they were under the necessity of crossing on rafts of bamboo. In short, before they arrived at the capital, the fatigue and hardships they had undergone considerably impaired their health, and the condition of their clothing was such as to excite the compassion of the mandarines, who made them a present of twenty sheep-skin jackets, dressed with the wool upon them; which, like the Hottentots, they wore inwards. One of these gentlemen assured me, that having satisfied his curiosity, no earthly consideration should tempt him to undertake a second journey by land to the capital; for that he believed the whole world could not furnish a like picture of desolation and misery. What a contrast is here exhibited to the ease and convenience with which our journey was made! But the whole treatment of the Dutch embassy seems to have been proportioned to the degree of importance which the Chinese attached to the political condition of this nation.

[57]It may be observed of almost all the writings of the missionaries concerning China, that virtues of so trifling a nature as hardly to deserve the name, have met their unqualified praise, whilst enormous vices have either been palliated or passed over in silence.

[58]The water-wheels still used in Syria differ only from those of China, by having loose buckets suspended at the circumference, instead of fixed tubes. "The wheels of Hama," says Volney, "are thirty-two feet in diameter. Troughs are fastened to the circumference, and so disposed as to fall in the river, and when they reach the vertex of the wheel, discharge the water into a reservoir."

[59]The simple boiling of the water indeed contributes greatly to the quick deposition of earthy particles, which may have been one cause of the universal practice of drinking every thing warm in China. They were surprised to see our soldiers and servants drinking the water of the Pei-ho cold, and told them it was very bad for the stomach and bowels. This complaint, in fact, attacked almost all the inferior part of the embassy, which Doctor Gillan did not hesitate to ascribe to the great impurity of the water. But the Chinese argued the point with the Doctor with regard to taking it cold, asking him why all the fluids of the body were warm, if nature had intended us to drink water and other liquids in a cold state! They seemed to have forgotten that all the warm-blooded animals, except man, must necessarily drink cold water.

[60]As these teas however were purchased by Chinese, I have no doubt they reserved to themselves a very large profit on the commission, for it is scarcely possible that this article, the growth and produce of the middle provinces, should bear a price so far beyond what the very best sells for in London.

[61]An old Frenchman (*Cossigny*) but a disciple of the new school, has found out that the Chinese are in possession of a new science, the existence of which was not even suspected by the enlightened nations of Europe. As he has the merit of making this wonderful discovery, it is but fair to announce it in his own words: "Je pense que nous devrions prendre chez eux (les Chinois) les premiers elements de la*spermatologie*, science toute nouvelle pour l'Europe, science qui intéresse l'humanité en général, en lui procurant des jouissances qui l'attachent à son existence, en entretenant la santé et la vigeur, en réparant l'abus des excès, en contribuant à l'augmentation de la population. Il feroit digne de la sollicitude des gouvernemens de s'occuper des recherches qui pourroient donner des connoissances sur une science à peine soupçonnée des peuples éclairés de l'Europe." He then announces his knowledge in preparing "des petites pastilles qui sont aphrodisiaques et qui conviennent sur-tout aux veillards, et à ceux qui ont fait des excès:" and he concludes with the mortifying intelligence that he is not permitted to reveal the important secret, "qui intéresse l'humanité en general."

[62]In the tenth volume of a very extensive agricultural work, is detailed the whole process of cultivating the cotton from the seed to the web. The author observes, "The cotton in its raw state affords a light and pleasant lining for clothes; the seed yields an oil, which, being expressed from them, the remainder is serviceable as manure; the capsules or pods, being hard and woody, are used for firing, and the leaves afford nourishment to cattle, so that every part of the vegetable may be appropriated to some useful purpose.

"The soil most favourable to this plant is a white sand, with a small proportion of clay or loam. The plant affects an elevated open situation, and cannot endure low marshy grounds.

"After all the cotton pods are gathered, the remaining stems and branches should be cleared away without loss of time, and the ground carefully ploughed up, to expose a new surface to the air and renew the vigour of the soil.

"When the plough has passed through the ground three times, the earth should be raked level, that the wind may not raise or dry up any part of it.

"——When there is an abundance of manure, it may be laid on previous to the use of the plough, but if it be scarce, &c. it will be preferable to apply it to the soil at the time of sowing the seed.

"The manure should be old and well prepared, and among the best ingredients for the purpose, is the refuse of vegetable substances, from which an oil has been expressed.

"In the southern provinces the cotton plant will last for two or three years, but to the northward the seed must be sown annually."

The author then enumerates nine distinct varieties and their comparative qualities; after which he proceeds to the choice of seed, under which head he observes, that if the seed be steeped in water, in which *eels* have been boiled, the plant will resist the attack of insects. He then describes the three methods of broadcast, drilling, and dibbling, and gives a decided preference of the last, though it be the most laborious.

"The ground being well prepared, holes are to be made at the distance of a cubit from each other, and the lines a cubit apart. A little water is first to be poured in, and then four or five seeds, after which each hole is to be covered with a mixture of soil and manure, and firmly trodden down with the foot. In the other methods a roller is to be used."

The next process is weeding, loosening, and breaking fine the earth.—He then observes, "After the plants have attained some degree of strength and size, the most advanced and perfect plant should be selected and all the rest rooted out, for if two or more be suffered to rise together, they will increase in height without giving lateral shoots; the leaves will be large and luxuriant, but the pods will be few." He next proceeds to the pruning of the plants to make them bear copiously—gathering the pods—preparing and spinning the wool—weaving the cloth.—This abridged account I have given to shew, that they are not deficient in writings of this kind.

[63]See the plate facing page 37.

[64]The East India Company pays from thirteen to sixty tales per pecul for their teas; some tea of a higher price is purchased by individuals, but seldom or ever by the Company. A tale is six shillings and eight-pence, and a pecul is one hundred and thirty-three pounds and one third.

[65]The measurement annexed to each of the fifteen ancient provinces was taken from the maps that were constructed by a very laborious and, as far as we had an opportunity of comparing them with the country, a very accurate survey, which employed the Jesuits ten years. I do not pretend to say that the areas, as I have given them in the table, are mathematically correct, but the dimensions were taken with as much care as was deemed necessary for the purpose, from maps drawn on a large scale, of which a very beautiful manuscript copy is now in his Majesty's library at Buckingham-house, made by a Chinese, having all the names written in Chinese and Tartar characters.

[66]One of the streets in the suburbs of Canton is emphatically called *Squeeze-gut-alley*, which is so narrow that every gentleman in the Company's service does not find it quite convenient to pass.

[67]The great advantage of a potatoe crop, as I before observed, is the certainty of its success. Were a general failure of this root to take place, as sometimes happens to crops of

rice, Ireland, in its present state, would experience all the horrors that attend a famine in some of the provinces of China.

[68]In the Canton jargon, *second chop Englishmen*; and even this distinction the Americans, I understand, have nearly forfeited in the minds of the Chinese.

[69]There are several good manuscript Chinese dictionaries in England; one of which is under publication by Doctor Montucci; who, I understand from good authority, by many years of indefatigable application, had succeeded in writing the characters with great neatness and accuracy; and is well qualified in other respects for the undertaking, in which, it is to be hoped, he may meet with suitable encouragement.

[70]This was written at the close of the year 1803.

[71]The Lord Viscount Melville.

Printed in Great Britain
by Amazon.co.uk, Ltd.,
Marston Gate.